THE ROLE OF THE
FORENSIC PSYCHOLOGIST

THE ROLE OF THE
FORENSIC PSYCHOLOGIST

Edited by

GERALD COOKE, Ph.D.

Chief Forensic Psychologist
Regional Forensic Psychiatric Center
Norristown State Hospital
Norristown, Pennsylvania

With a Foreword by

THE HON. DAVID L. BAZELON

Senior Circuit Judge
District of Columbia Circuit Court of Appeals
Washington, D.C.

CHARLES C THOMAS • PUBLISHER
Springfield • Illinois • U.S.A.

Published and Distributed Throughout the World by
CHARLES C THOMAS • PUBLISHER

BANNERSTONE HOUSE
301-327 East Lawrence Avenue, Springfield, Illinois, U.S.A.

© *1980 by* CHARLES C THOMAS • PUBLISHER
ISBN 0-398-03905-4
Library of Congress Catalog Card Number: 79-711

Library of Congress Cataloging in Publication Data

Gerald Cooke

Main entry under title:

The Role of the Forensic Psychologist.

Bibliography: p.
Includes index.
1. Psychology, Forensic. I. Cooke, Gerald, 1943- [DNLM: 1. Forensic
psychiatry. 2. Criminal psychology. W740 R745]
RA1148.R64   614'.19   79-711
ISBN 0-398-03905-4

Printed in the United States of America

N-11

To Penny,
Cindy, and Chris

CONTRIBUTORS

JAMES T. BARBASH, Ph.D., Psychologist, Penn Foundation for Mental Health, formerly Director of Psychological Services, Pennsylvania Bureau of Corrections.

JAMES L. BECK, Research Analyst, United States Bureau of Prisons.

DONALD N. BERSOFF, Ph.D., J.D., University of Maryland School of Law and the Johns Hopkins University.

ROBERT BUCKHOUT, Ph.D., Associate Professor and Director, Center for Responsive Psychology, Brooklyn College.

JOSEPH B. CENTIFANTI, Philadelphia, Pennsylvania.

JOSEPH J. COCOZZA, Ph.D., Research Scientist, Special Projects Research Unit, New York State Department of Mental Hygiene.

GERALD COOKE, Ph.D., Chief Forensic Psychologist, Regional Forensic Psychiatric Center, Norristown State Hospital, Norristown, Pennsylvania.

MARGARET COOKE, Coordinator, Death Penalty Project, American Civil Liberties Union of Pennsylvania.

AMIRAM ELWORK, Ph.D., Assistant Professor of Psychology, University of Nebraska-Lincoln.

RAYMOND FOWLER, Ph.D., Professor and Chairman, Department of Psychology, University of Alabama.

MARTIN S. GREENBERG, Ph.D., Associate Professor, Department of Psychology, University of Pittsburgh.

JAN C. GROSSMAN, Ph.D., Chief Forensic Psychologist, Philadelphia State Hospital and Clinical Assistant Professor of Psychiatry, Hahnemann Medical College and Hospital of Philadelphia.

NEWTON L. P. JACKSON, Ph.D., Center for Forensic Psychiatry, Ann Arbor, Michigan.

MISHRILAL JAIN, University of Maryland, School of Law.

FLORENCE KASLOW, Ph.D., Associate Professor and Chief, Forensic Psychiatry/Psychology, Department of Mental Health Science, Hahnemann Medical College and Hospital of Philadelphia.

DAVID LEBOR, Center for Studies in Criminology and Criminal Law, University of Pennsylvania.

ORMA LINFORD, Ph.D., Professor of Political Science, Kansas State University.

JAMES L. MACK, Ph.D., Assistant Professor of Psychology, Department of Psychiatry, Case Western Reserve University School of Medicine.

CLORINDA MARGOLIS, Ph.D., Assistant Professor, Department of Psychiatry, Jefferson Hospital, Philadelphia.

EDWIN I. MEGARGEE, Ph.D., Professor of Psychology, The Florida State University.

MICHAEL MILLS, M.B.A., Department of Psychology, University of Pittsburgh.

WAYNE A. MUGRAUER, Director of Training, Temple University Law Enforcement and Security Academy, Philadelphia.

COURTNEY J. MULLIN, Originator and Co-Director Team Defense Project.

MICHAEL E. PARRISH, Ph.D., Private Practice, Bala Cynwyd, Pennsylvania, and the University of Pennsylvania.

MICHAEL L. PERLIN, Esq., Director, Division of Mental Health Advocacy, Department of the Public Advocate, Trenton, New Jersey.

ANTHONY M. PISA, Ph.D., Chief Psychologist of Admission Services, Norristown State Hospital, Norristown, Pennsylvania, and Consultant to Temple University Center for the Administration of Justice.

MARC REIDEL, Ph.D., Associate Professor and Research Coordinator, Center for the Study of Crime, Delinquency and Corrections, Southern Illinois University.

ELIZABETH ROBERTS, Research Assistant, Department of Psychology, University of Alabama, Birmingham.

R. BARRY RUBACK, J.D., M.S., Department of Psychology, University of Pittsburgh.

ROBERT L. SADOFF, M.D., Clinical Associate Professor of Psychiatry and Director, Center for Studies in Social-Legal Psychiatry, University of Pennsylvania, and Lecturer in Law, Villanova University School of Law.

BRUCE DENNIS SALES, J.D., Ph.D., Director Law-Psychology Graduate Training Program and Associate Professor of Psychology and Law, University of Nebraska-Lincoln.

ANTHONY J. SCOLERI, State Correctional Institution at Graterford, Pennsylvania.

ALLEN E. SHEALY, Ph.D., Associate Professor of Clinical Psychology, Department of Psychiatry, University of Alabama, Birmingham.

RITA J. SIMON, Director, Program in Law and Society and Professor of Sociology, Law and Communications Research, University of Illinois.

ROBERT E. SINNETT, Ph.D., Director, Mental Health Section and Professor of Psychology, Kansas State University.

HENRY J. STEADMAN, Ph.D., Director, Special Projects Research Unit, New York State Department of Mental Hygiene.

MARGERY VELIMESIS, Executive Director, Pennsylvania Program for Women and Girl Offenders.

THEODORE I. WILLIAMS, Norristown, Pennsylvania.

CHAUNCEY E. WILSON, Department of Psychology, University of Pittsburgh.

KENNETH G. WILSON, Ph.D., Assistant Professor, Center for the Study of Crime, Delinquency and Corrections, Southern Illinois University.

PHYLLIS YORK, Private Consultant, Philadelphia.

JAY ZISKIN, Ph.D., LL.B., Professor, Counseling Center, California State University, Los Angeles.

FOREWORD

Almost 18 years ago, a majority of the United States Court of Appeals for the District of Columbia Circuit held for the first time that appropriately qualified psychologists could testify in court as experts on mental disorder.[1] My opinion for the court in that case was not without its critics, however. My dissenting colleagues, for instance, doubted whether "lay psychologists", untrained in medicine, could help the court assess a defendant's mental condition and its possible causal connection to his criminal activity. Nonetheless, in recent years, acceptance of psychologists as expert witnesses has become nearly universal. As the chapters that follow amply document, psychologists now participate in criminal trials and correctional hearings, civil commitment and juvenile court proceedings, and even in major civil lawsuits. Today these experts testify not only on issues of criminal responsibility and treatment of the mentally ill, but also on child custody, prison environments, and the dynamics of witness and jury behavior.

In his introductory chapter to this book, Dr. Cooke asks us all to take a step back from this development and consider once again the fundamental question my court faced 18 years ago: What role, if any, should psychologists and other mental health professionals play in the legal system? This issue has concerned me—some would say consumed me—since I became a judge. Early in my judicial career, I hoped that behavioral scientists called as experts would willingly bring into the courtroom new sources of information on the determinants of human behavior. I believed that they could help the courts by shedding light on cases that raise troubling questions, such as who can be held morally responsible for a crime, who can be forced to enter a hospital for treatment, what forms of treatment can be imposed without the patient's consent, and what are the best interests of a child in a custody dispute. To make responsible decisions about such complex issues, the courts must consider their full social context. I believed that experts could assist the courts in exploring this context by offering information about the psychological, biological, and environmental conditions influencing the behavior of an individual before the court.

I also believed that mental health professionals would help to humanize the law by sharing their information about the well-springs of human behavior. For example, the fundamental assumption of our criminal justice system—that the causes of behavior reside solely within the individual—is markedly at odds with the theories of contemporary psychology. These theories emphasize the degree to which situations, not personalities, control behavior. I thought that information from behavioral scientists would give judges, juries, and ultimately the community at large, the opportunity to understand more clearly the complex nature of criminal responsibility and also the societal conditions that can contribute to criminal behavior. It was my fervent hope that with this information the law could be administered with deeper understanding and humility. I hoped that we would be less prone to apply sanctions to those we cannot morally condemn; those whose choices are patently limited by accidents of birth, such as genetic makeup and environmental conditions. Without insights from the behavioral sciences, society would remain uninformed about appropriate ways to respond to such individuals. With more information, society may be alerted to its own responsibility for their circumstances.

These hopes largely have been unfulfilled. The experts have willingly given their judgments but too often refuse to open up the bases of those judgments, the actual information and reasoning they relied upon, to the scrutiny of the legal process. This pattern became most clear after my court adopted a new test of criminal responsibility in the *Durham* case in 1954.[2] Well-received by the behavioral experts, the *Durham* rule was that a person is not criminally liable if his unlawful act was the product of a mental disease or defect. The purpose of the rule was to permit psychiatrists to share whatever knowledge they might have about the influences on criminal behavior and thereby enable the jury to perform its traditional role of assessing the moral responsibility of persons accused of crimes. Yet in case after case, the purpose of this rule was frustrated. Instead of enriching the information available to the court, the experts often used conclusory labels without revealing the nature of their investigation and theories, or the gaps in their knowledge. Despite out best efforts, the experts resisted the careful examination of their opinions demanded by the adversary process. By failing to reveal the limits of diagnostic judgments, these experts at times hindered rather than enhanced the cause of justice.

Although I joined my court in discarding the *Durham* formula in 1972,[3] I still believe that legal decisionmakers need raw information about the influences on behavior. I have tried to learn from the *Durham* experience why experts often do not share with the court the kinds of information and honest recognitions of the limits of that information so necessary for wise judicial decisions.

I suspect that some psychologists and other behavioral experts do not disclose the considerations behind their conclusions because they would be embarrassed to admit that they had not had enough time for an adequate examination or enough knowledge to reach a definitive diagnosis. Some experts may be defensive because they have allowed "hidden agendas" to interfere with their professional judgment. By "hidden agendas," I mean the institutional pressures and personal biases that can lead an individual to serve unstated interests at the expense of his stated duties. Concern for job security, manpower shortages, and the demands of the employing institution all may impair professional judgment in this way, and yet remain hidden from view. Similarly, personal values may influence an expert's testimony but remain undisclosed to the court or the jury. When this happens, legal decision-makers may place unwarranted trust in the judgment of an expert witness. My experience teaches that in order to assist the court, the psychologist or other expert must be completely candid about the bases of his judgments.

Too many behavioral experts nevertheless believe that they should not disclose the considerations underlying their judgments. They worry that their opinions would lose the mystique that they believe is essential for public acceptance of the profession. But however appropriate mystique may be for therapy, it is antithetical to the adversary process. To play a valuable role in legal decisions, the mental health expert must be a willing participant in cross-examination and other elements of the adversary process that can bring to light the theories and biases that shape judgments, clinical or otherwise.

Furthermore, the psychologist or any other behavioral expert must resist the temptation to substitute his own judgment for that of the law when cases focus upon mental illness, dangerousness, or parental competence. These concepts, however much they resemble psychological terms, are in fact legal terms of art. They invoke issues of morality and legal rights, often involving the fundamental relationship between the rights of the individual and the interests of society. They must be applied and interpreted by individuals who are legally accountable for such decisions, by judges and juries, not by expert witnesses. The role of the witness is to inform those judgments, not to make them.

Thus, for the individual expert, my experience advises candor and willing participation in the adversary process as crucial prerequisites for a helpful role in the legal process. To assist the court, the expert should disclose what course of investigation he pursued. He should explain what he thinks he learned, what facts he found, what conclusions he drew from those facts, and what reasoning process he used. And he should tell the court what he did not or could not discover, either because of limited investigation or the bounds of knowledge in the area. Above all, he must avoid the temptation to make the decision that is rightfully and lawfully the court's.

Some guidelines may help the entire profession to devise a responsible role for psychologists in the legal process. First, the profession should frankly admit the existence of interests that compete with the welfare of the patient when experts act outside of the traditional therapist-patient relationship. To avoid the danger that hidden agendas may influence expert judgments, the profession should develop standards to govern professional conduct in institutional and judicial settings.

Second, mental health professionals who participate in the legal system should keep careful and detailed records of their conduct in particular cases. Reliable records can serve both as a continual reminder of professional obligations and as a basis on which professional conduct may be reviewed.

In addition, peer review mechanisms should be established. The conduct of experts who serve institutional employers should be subject to independent evaluation to ensure a level of performance consonant with the standards of the profession.

I firmly believe that members of the legal profession also have responsibilities to guarantee an appropriate and useful role in the law for psychological experts. Lawyers must learn how to cross-examine experts without simply ridiculing isolated findings or questioning specific test responses. Instead, lawyers should become acquainted with ways to elicit information concerning the significance of test results and the theories and reasoning processes employed to interpret them. Lawyers should also learn when to turn to experts for assistance in reading records and investigating cases. Not only lawyers, but also the courts, the police, and public servants must avoid the temptation to invoke the expertise of psychologists as if it were wizardry that could dispell troubling human problems. The fact is, difficult problems will not go away merely because we turn them over to experts.

Indeed, if psychologists play the role I have described here, courts will be burdened with richly detailed information which makes moral judgments more difficult. Yet only with this kind of contribution by experts can the law stand as a dynamic order built on process, a structure for seeking wisdom. Policies often change as new circumstances and the passage of time bring more information and more experience to bear on particular problems. In this way, the law grows, altering and shedding old conceptions with the help of insights from other fields.

NOTES TO FOREWORD

[1]Jenkins v. United States, 307 F.2d 637 (D.C. Cir. 1962) (en banc). We held that "the lack of a medical degree, and the lesser degree of responsibility for patient care which mental hospitals usually assign to psychologists, are not automatic disqualifications" barring testimony from psychologists. *Id.* at 646. Instead, we ruled that the "determination of a psychologist's competence to render an expert opinion . . . must depend upon the nature and extent of his knowledge." *Id.* at 645. Our chief concern was "whether the opinion offered [would] be likely to aid the trier in search for truth." *Id.* at 643.

[2]Durham v. United States, 214 F.2d 862 (D.C. Cir. 1954).

[3]United States v. Brawner, 471 F.2d 969 (D.C. Cir. 1972) (en banc).

ACKNOWLEDGMENTS

IN 1976 I asked several colleagues to assist me in presenting a symposium at the annual meeting of the American Psychological Association. The topic was the role of the forensic psychologist. The response to the symposium was enthusiastic, and a number of those who attended suggested that there was a need for such a presentation in book form. We began with the six presentations and asked for suggestions for other topics that could appropriately be included in such a book. The planned manuscript grew to its present size, though not every suggested topic could be included.

I would like to express my appreciation to my wife who, in all my work, is a source of original ideas and constructive criticism.

I would also like to express my appreciation to Robert L. Sadoff, M.D. It was he whose enthusiasm for the forensic sciences first got me interested in forensic psychology when I was an intern at Norristown State Hospital in 1966. My contact with him since then has enabled me to learn a great deal.

I thank the Honorable David L. Bazelon, Senior Circuit Judge of the District of Columbia Circuit Court of Appeals for graciously taking time from his busy schedule to review the manuscript and write the Foreword.

I would like to express my appreciation to my colleagues Richard Lonsdorf, M.D., Anthony Pisa, Ph.D., and Michael Parrish, Ph.D. for reviewing parts of the manuscript and sharing their ideas with me. My appreciation also is expressed to all the contributors to the book, many of whom were responsible for suggesting other topics and contributors. I would also like to thank the Regional Forensic Psychiatric Center Director, Joaquin Canals, M.D., for being understanding about the time I had to spend away from the Unit in order to prepare the book.

I am grateful to Karen Couchara who did a lot of typing in a short time under difficult conditions. My gratitude is expressed also to

Joyce Slanker who helped with the typing.

I wish to thank the publishers of the journals who gave permission for the reprinting of three of the chapters.

G.C.

CONTENTS

SECTION III: EVALUATION, SENTENCING, AND TREATMENT OF OFFENDERS

THE ROLE OF THE
FORENSIC PSYCHOLOGIST

SECTION I

GENERAL ISSUES

The first section deals with two types of basic information. The first four chapters should be of interest to psychologists whose professional interests and responsibilities bring them into contact with the legal system. Chapters 5 and 6 have a broader applicability because, though they deal with legal aspects the issues discussed, privileged communication and malpractice, apply to all psychologists, even those who may not wish to become involved at the interface of psychology and law.

study and prediction of human behavior than the use of clinical judgment alone, the psychologist should not lose sight of the limitations of testing. The use of tests provides the psychologist with a tool that may give him data not available to the psychiatrist, yet the psychologist should remember that frequently he will see cases in which there are medical, neurological, or medication issues that require psychiatric evaluation or consultation.

A second important issue concerns the responsibility of the forensic psychologist to the clients. The term "client" is a far-reaching one in forensic psychology. It may include an individual charged with an offense, a person who has suffered an injury, a patient or offender in therapy, an attorney, a court, a police department, a correctional system, or in a sense, society as a whole. In many instances, this responsibility is defined legally; however, in the majority of cases there is no well-defined legal responsibility and it is defined instead by professional and ethical principles. In some areas, such as confidentiality, there is wide agreement *in principle* that the psychologist has responsibility to the client; however, as the Tarasoff case[5] and others have shown, the implementation of the principle becomes a complex issue because of the responsibility to other "clients," e.g. potential victims. There are more subtle responsibilities as well; these are discussed in many of the chapters in this book.

The forensic psychologist who testifies in court has certain responsibilities to the individual and attorney who has requested the testimony, to the court, and to the profession. At times the line between the responsibility to one client and the responsibility to another is a fine one, and the psychologist must rely on a sense of professionalism, ethics, and morality in drawing conclusions. In clinical evaluation and research where an issue such as dangerousness is involved, the forensic psychologist has the responsibility to one client of respecting his civil rights and freedom while simultaneously a responsibility to another, society at large, of respecting the right to protection. In issues such as jury selection, jury behavior, witness behavior, and capital punishment, there is a responsibility to the judicial system and to society to provide an understanding of the factors involved in the determination of guilt, innocence, and punishment so that the outcome is influenced only by factors that are valid and not by irrelevant and/or prejudicial factors.

In providing and evaluating treatment within the mental health and correctional systems, the forensic psychologist has a responsibility to the patient or offender and to the institution to provide adequate and effective treatment while protecting civil rights. There is here, too, a responsibility to society since most patients and offenders do return to society. In working with police departments, again the responsibilities are multiple including not only the responsibility to the department to select and train officers who will have an understanding of human behavior and techniques to deal with that behavior, but also to the officers themselves and to the citizens with whom they come in contact. All of these responsibilities make it incumbent on the forensic psychologist to be a researcher as well as a clinician.

Many terms and concepts will be used in this book with the assumption that the reader will have some basic knowledge. Many of these concepts are quite complex, and the following is meant to provide only a basic knowledge that can be augmented by additional reading.

CONCEPTS IN CRIMINAL LAW
Competency To Stand Trial On Criminal Charges

Most, but not all, states and the federal government have statutes relating to competency to stand trial. Historically, the concept relates back to English law in which a legal case was delayed if, because of physical illness, the accused could not be present to aid in the defense. The concept was later expanded to include persons whose mental condition precluded aiding in their defense. The exact wording of the statute varies from state to state, but the Pennsylvania Statute is representative: "Whenever a person who has been charged with a crime is found to be substantially unable to understand the nature or object of the proceedings against him or to participate and assist in his defense, he shall be deemed incompetent to be tried, convicted or sentenced so long as such incapacity continues."[6] Additional concepts included in some statutes are that the person is to be found incompetent if he does not recognize his relationship to the proceedings, if he is unable to withstand the stress of trial, and if he does not understand the possible consequences of the legal proceedings. The translation of the legal criteria into behavioral variables is complex and somewhat subjective though efforts have been made to develop more concrete criteria. At one time a person found incompetent might be held without trial for many years and in some cases longer than the statutory penalty for the offense. However, in 1972 the Supreme Court ruled in *Jackson* v. *Indiana*[7] that this practice violated due process, and laws now reflect a limitation on the period of incompetency. If the individual is not returned to competency after a specified period of time, the charges are essentially dismissed, and the person is subject to further commitment only if civil criteria are met. It should be emphasized that the issue of competency relates only to mental status at the time of trial and is in no way related to mental status and responsibility at the time the criminal act was committed.

Criminal Responsibility

In law the concept of intent has for centuries been central in determining the degree of culpability for a criminal act. Mental illness is only one of a number of circumstances or conditions that affect the judgment of culpability. Various rules have been developed by which to determine whether an individual's state of mind at the time of the act should lead to a finding of Not Guilty by Reason of Insanity. Even more than in the case of competency, the translation of legal into behavioral criteria is a difficult one that leaves a great deal of room for differences of opinion. The most widely used rule is the M'Naughten Rule[8] formulated in a case in England in 1843. According to this rule a person is not held to be responsible if he was "laboring under such a defect of reason, from disease of the mind, as not to know the nature and quality of the act he was doing or, if he did know it, that he did not know he was doing what was wrong." Many legal and mental health experts find fault with the M'Naughten Rule on a number of grounds, the most prominent of which is that, if strictly interpreted, it relates responsibility only to interference with cognitive processes and not with emotional controls.

Some jurisdictions have attempted to broaden the definition. One such attempt is to add the idea of Irresistible Impulse to the M'Naughten Rule. Under such a rule, the person is not responsible "if he had not the power to resist the impulse to do the act by reason of disease of insanity." The rule that is becoming more and more widely accepted is drawn from the American Law Institute Model Penal Code as stated in *U.S.* v. *Brawner*.[9] This rule states, "(1) A person is not responsible for criminal conduct if at the time of such conduct as a result of mental disease or defect he lacked substantial capacity either to appreciate the criminality (wrongfulness) of his conduct or to conform his conduct to the requirements of the law; (2) . . . the terms 'mental disease or defect' do not include an abnormality manifested only by repeated criminal or otherwise antisocial conduct." For a time an even less restrictive rule, the Durham Rule[10] was in use. This rule stated, "An accused is not criminally responsible if his unlawful act was the product of mental disease or mental defect." Though allowing a wider range of psychological information, this rule has been subject to a great deal of criticism and has not gained wide acceptance. One of the major objections to the rule is that by not being more specific it forces the lay juror to accept the expert witnesses' definition of mental illness and causality without guidance from the law. This has caused a great deal of confusion among judges and jurors alike.

Whatever rule is used, its interpretation varies from jurisdiction to jurisdiction and even from judge to judge within jurisdictions. In recent years, the concept of "diminished capacity" has begun to gain wider acceptance. Here mental status is removed from the question of guilt or innocence, but is relevant in the level of the offense, which, of course, is reflected in the sentencing.

Suppression Of A Confession

According to the Constitution, an individual has the right under the Fifth Amendment not to be compelled to incriminate himself. At the same time, police investigations of alleged criminal behavior usually involve an attempt to obtain a confession from the accused. The guideline *in principle* is that a confession is admissible in court if it is given "freely and voluntarily." Here, as in other areas discussed above, the definition and implementation of the concept is where difficulties arise. According to the Miranda decision,[11] the accused must be made aware of his rights prior to interrogation. These rights include (1) the right to remain silent and the understanding that anything he says can be used against him in court; (2) the right to the presence of an attorney and that if he cannot afford an attorney one will be appointed for him; and (3) the right to stop answering questions at any time. If the accused waives these rights, he must do so knowingly, intelligently, and without pressures, threats, or promises. The forensic psychologist usually becomes involved in such cases where the issue is one of psychological pressure or mental disorder that would preclude a knowing and/or intelligent waiver. For example, a person who is psychotic and acting under a delusion when he confesses would generally not be thought to be knowingly waiving his rights. Similarly there would be a basis for having the confession suppressed for an individual who because of mental disorder or low intelligence cannot understand the words and/or concepts in the Miranda warning.

Decertification From Adult To Juvenile Status

The law holds that a child who commits an offense shall be treated differently than an adult committing the same offense. Though the exact statutes vary in different jurisdictions, the Pennsylvania Statute[12] is representative. For all crimes except murder, a child under age fourteen is to be treated as a juvenile. If the child is over fourteen but under eighteen he may be tried as an adult if (1) the child is not amenable to treatment, supervision, or rehabilitation as a juvenile through available facilities—in determining this the court may consider age, mental capacity, maturity, previous record, and probation or institutional reports—and (2) the child is not committable to an institution for the mentally retarded or mentally ill, and (3) the interests of the community require that the child be placed under legal restraint or discipline, or the offense is one that would carry a sentence of more than three years if committed as an adult. In cases of murder, the child is automatically treated as an adult and it is the juvenile's burden to show that the case belongs in Juvenile Court using the above criteria. The forensic psychologist may play an important role in the evaluation of mental capacity, mental illness, maturity, and amenability to treatment and rehabilitation.

Mitigating Circumstances In Capital Punishment

Death penalty statutes vary from state to state and many are presently being revised by legislators to meet constitutional requirements. However, the statutes will contain lists of aggravating and mitigating circumstances including such factors as the maturity, emotional history, emotional stability, and character of the defendant, and these are issues to which the forensic psychologist can speak.

CONCEPTS IN CRIMINAL OR CIVIL LAW

Prediction Of Dangerous Behavior

In recent years the basis for involuntary commitment and for release have shifted away from mental illness as the primary criteria. The U.S. Supreme Court in *Baxtrom v. Herold*[13] ruled that without a court proceeding on the issues of mental illness and dangerousness, the patient is denied equal protection under the law. The criterion has, therefore, become imminent danger to self or others and most laws require an overt act in the recent past as necessary evidence for a prediction of future dangerousness. The issue is also raised when the forensic psychologist offers an opinion about parole, probation, or bail, though in these instances an overt act is usually not required. The prediction of dangerous behavior and the relationship between behavior within an institution and behavior in society is one that both practicing clinicians and researchers must address. Several of the chapters in the book deal with this issue.

Right To Treatment And Right To Refuse Treatment

In the case of *Rouse* v. *Cameron*[14] the court established that patients have a right to treatment. In *Wyatt* v. *Stickney*[15] the court went further (after evaluating mental hospitals in Alabama) in stating that there was a constitutional right to adequate treatment and set out minimum constitutional standards. A number of other states have since adapted the "Alabama Standards." In *Lake* v. *Cameron*[16] the right to the least restrictive treatment alternative was established. In light of these decisions, persons hospitalized involuntarily, who can demonstrate that these rights are not being realized, have legal recourse. While the right to treatment has now been well established, the right to refuse treatment has not yet been well defined. This issue is usually raised with the more extreme treatments—psychosurgery, electroconvulsive therapy, and psychotropic medication—though in principle it could apply to any form of treatment. Though some cases have granted the right to refuse certain treatments on religious grounds, the more general right to refuse treatment has not yet been established.

CONCEPTS IN CIVIL LAW

Civil Competency

The term "competency" is used in both civil and criminal contexts leading to some confusion. Each type of competency has its own separate criteria, and one type of incompetency does not necessarily imply another type of incompetency. Whether mental illness or mental hospitalization is tantamount to legal incompetence varies from state to state though most authorities feel that incompetence should be a separate issue. In general, civil incompetency means the person is judged incapable of managing his own property or handling his own affairs. In more concrete terms this means that such persons have no capacity to enter into contracts or legal relationships with others; their signatures are meaningless; they may not spend or otherwise distribute their money; they may not enter into debt; they may not obtain a driver's license, vote, marry, or divorce; and they may not execute a valid will. When an individual is declared incompetent, a guardian is appointed to manage the estate. The court criteria by which a person may be declared civilly incompetent are not well defined and, as indicated above, vary from jurisdiction to jurisdiction.

Tort Liability

A tort is a civil, as opposed to criminal, wrong. It is based on the concept that if one injures another, then the author of the injury is responsible for the damages. More specifically, there must be an act that is established to have caused damage to a legally protected interest either intentionally or through negligence. Two aspects of tort liability are of particular interest to forensic psychology. One of these is the evaluation of possible traumatic neurosis; the other is in malpractice cases where the psychologist himself is the object of a tort action.

Traumatic Neurosis

A traumatic neurosis is usually manifested by anxiety, depression, social withdrawal, and somatic symptoms. In a number of cases, the somatic symptoms constitute a hysterical conversion reaction. As in tort law in general, so in the case of a possible traumatic neurosis it must be established that the emotional reaction suffered by the individual was causally related to the particular incident in question. In some cases, such as where a previously well-adjusted individual becomes phobic for riding in automobiles following a serious accident, causality is fairly easily established. However, the establishment of causality is often made more difficult by the fact that the incident is often one (e.g. automobile accident, occupational accident, a fall) that is common, that others experience without developing a traumatic neurosis, and in which the pathology is not so specific as a phobia. Clearly in these cases there are personality factors or life experiences in addition to the specific incident that predispose the individual to develop a traumatic neurosis. A thorough evaluation of the individual's personality through psychological testing can often help to understand why the individual reacted to the incident with a traumatic neurosis. Because the incident is the proximate cause, even though the person was predisposed because of personality features, liability still exists. The forensic psychologist can also be helpful in determining damages. Often the psychological testing provides concrete evidence on how the psychopathology results in deficits in judgment, attention, concentration, and interpersonal and occupational skills.

Malpractice

Malpractice is discussed in detail in Chapter 6. Malpractice torts may be brought against psychologists for a number of reasons. Probably the most well-known case is *Tarasoff* v. *California Board of Regents*[17] where the court ruled that a therapist has a legal obligation to give warning when "in the exercise of his professional skill or knowledge" he determines that a warning is necessary to avert danger. Failure to warn makes the therapist subject to civil liability. A problem here is the determination of "professional skill and knowledge" and whether reasonable care was exercised. This often depends on expert testimony as to the state of the science and prevailing practices. The same issues apply concerning patients who commit suicide. Another basis for tort action against psychologists is found in cases in which therapists use methods, particularly those utilizing touching or sexual behavior, that are unorthodox. Again the issue of prevailing practices is important. Certain types of tort actions that are brought against psychiatrists, such as for false imprisonment, have rarely been brought against psychologists, in part because in most mental hospitals primary responsibility lies with the psychiatrists. However, as this changes, so will the psychologist's vulnerability to additional types of tort actions.

Child Custody

In recent years the psychologist has come to be called upon more frequently to aid the court with a decision on the placement of children in divorce. Changes in societal roles have undercut the assumption that the mother can provide better care, encouraged a greater weighing of the child's preference, and necessitated evaluation of individual factors. The placement is to be in the "best interests of the child" and requires a "fit" parent, but the determination of this is difficult. Clear evidence of criminal behavior, sexual promiscuity known to the child, sexual behavior toward the child, alcoholism, and drug addiction are frequent bases for placement; however, these bases often more prominently involve legal or investigative issues than psychological ones. In fact, it is not always the case that the presence of such behaviors necessarily relates to the ability to be a fit parent. A more obviously psychological basis is where one parent has a diagnosable and established mental illness; however, in some past cases a child has not been taken from a parent even when that parent was found to be psychotic. The same sorts of issues arise in determinations as to whether a child should remain with adoptive parents or be returned to biological parents.

SUMMARY

As is evident in this chapter, the forensic psychologist has the opportunity to participate in a wide range of areas that have an immediate and important impact on society. In order to do so effectively, the psychologist must be well informed and sensitive to ethical and professional issues.

REFERENCES

1. Ennis, B.J. *Prisoners of Psychiatry*, New York, Harcourt Brace Jovanovich, 1972.
2. Cocozza, J.J. and Steadman, H.J. The failure of psychiatric predictions of dangerousness; clear and convincing evidence, *Rutgers Law Review, 29*, 1084–1101, 1976.
3. Ennis, B.J. and Litwack, T.R. Psychiatry and the presumption of expertise: Flipping coins in the courtroom, *California Law Review, 62*, 693–752, 1976.
4. Amicus Curiae Brief for the American Psychiatric Association in Jenkins v. United States 307 F. 2d 6 37, 651, 652 (D.C. Cir. 1969).
5. Tarasoff v. Regents of the University of California 13 Cal 3d 177 118 Cal Rptr 129, 559 P 2d 553 (1974).
6. Pennsylvania Mental Health Procedures Act (143) of 196, Section 402 (a).
7. Jackson v. State of Indiana 92 S. Ct. 1845, U.S. Sup. Ct. (1972).
8. House of Lords 1843, 10Cl. & F. 200, 8 Eng. Reprint 718.
9. United States v. Brawner 471 F. 2d 696 (D.C. Cir. 1972).
10. Durham v. United States 214 F. 2d 862 (D.C. Cir. 1954).
11. Miranda v. Arizona 384 U.S. 436 (1966).
12. Pennsylvania Juvenile Act of Dec. 6, 1972, P.L. No. 33, 11, S28, 11. P.S.
13. Baxtrom v. Herold 383 U.S. 107 (1966).
14. Rouse v. Cameron 373 F. 2d 451 (D.C. Cir. 1966).
15. Wyatt v. Stickney 325 F. Supp. 781 (M.D. Ala., 1971).
16. Lake v. Cameron 364 F. 2d 657 (D.C. Cir. 1966).
17. Tarasoff v. Cal. Bd. of Regents, op. cit.

Chapter 2

ISSUES IN TRAINING
FORENSIC* PSYCHOLOGISTS

BRUCE DENNIS SALES, J.D., Ph.D.

AND

AMIRAM ELWORK, PH.D.

"There is a need for programs designed to improve both public and professional understanding of the relationships between law and social science. Such programs can encourage both law schools and social science departments to develop substantial interdisciplinary training. At the moment, there are only the barest beginnings of programs that provide either training in the social science disciplines for legal scholars, or training in law for social scientists. Yet, both groups need a much deeper understanding of the problems and the capabilities of the other if they are to work together effectively in efforts to produce useful knowledge."

Special Commission
on the Social Sciences of the
National Science Board[1]

---

*Black's Law Dictionary (St. Paul, West, 1968) defines "forensic" to include only court related activities. Yet, it is quite common amongst mental health professionals to use the term to refer to any activity in which the psychologist is involved with the law, legal system, or legal process. For this reason, we have chosen to use the term forensic in its broader, more popular sense in this chapter, It is clear, however, that the psychological community will have to choose a term for this area of work and apply it more consistently. For example, in addition to forensic psychology, such phrases as law-psychology, law and psychology, psycho-legal studies, psychology of law, and legal psychology are also in vogue.

16

W E ARE IN the midst of an "explosion" of interest in the interface of law and psychology (see *e.g.* Tapp[2]). Whereas just ten years ago the number of law-related articles in psychology journals was in the hundreds, today the number is in the thousands. More and more books surveying the field are being published.[3,4,5,6,7,8] There also is a national organization, the American Psychology-Law Society (APLS), and a journal, *Law and Human Behavior*, devoted to this interface. All of these developments are beginning to establish law-psychology as a content area in its own right.

Concurrent with the above mentioned developments, there has been a marked increase in job opportunities for forensic psychologists in research, teaching, and direct services.[9] The market has been so "bullish" in some parts of the country that forensic psychologists are becoming concerned about the need to set professional standards. In fact, the American Psychology-Law Society has formed a committee to investigate the possibility of certifying forensic psychologists. Obviously, the logic behind establishing certification relies on the presupposition that in order to be a forensic psychologist, one must have some specialized expertise that is not in the general repertoire of most psychologists. If that is so, then there is a need to clearly define what are the necessary skills for a forensic psychologist and outline what training psychologists would have to undertake to attain such skills.

This chapter is intended to begin such a discussion. It will be divided into three parts. First, we will present a general outline of the content areas that the law-psychology interface encompasses. This will provide some guidelines as to the possible content areas that could be incorporated in a training program. Second, we will present a general outline of the types of roles that a forensic psychologist may assume. This will suggest further content areas and possible practicum experiences that can also be incorporated into a training program. In the third section, we will discuss different models for administering this type of training.

FORENSIC PSYCHOLOGY AS A CONTENT AREA

The law, legal system, and legal process are in the business of regulating and controlling human behavior. In the past, this control was based upon assumptions about people that often went untested or unstated, simply because human behavior is not in the legal professionals' domain of expertise. Thus, the psychology-law interface is a necessary and a natural development. Its content is the application of all relevant areas of psychological knowledge in order to better understand, evaluate, improve, and administer every branch of the law, legal system, and legal process. It also includes the study of how the law, legal system, and legal process affects the practice of psychology, both as a science and a profession.* While this definition is meant to be encompassing, unfortunately, it might also seem vague. Thus, we will devote the rest of this section outlining more specifically the content areas that can be incorporated in the training of forensic psychologists.

Let us begin with an explanation of the distinctions between the law, legal system, and process. In referring to the law, we include all of the statutes, judicial decisions, and administrative regulations that prescribe appropriate behaviors in our society and within the legal system itself. The legal system is distinguished from the law in that it refers to the legal institutional components (e.g. courts, prisons) in which laws are made and administered. Finally, the legal process refers to the interactions that occur when people are processed through the system and under the law. It also includes the interactions of legal actors (e.g. policemen, judges) in the legal system with each other, with laws, and with society as a whole. As we will show below, each of these components can be further subdivided into many areas to which diverse types of psychological knowledge can be applied.

The law component, as defined above, can be further subdivided into substantive and procedural law topics such as civil procedure, administrative law, commercial law, constitutional law, contract law, criminal law and procedure, family law, labor law, property law, and tort law (personal, property, and business injuries). Since most of today's forensic psychologists have not been trained to appreciate the full spectrum of law as described above, they often have difficulties in recognizing how their expertise can be applied to these different areas. For example, knowledge from clinical psychology on mental disability can have an impact on the administration of criminal law and procedure (e.g. competency to stand trial, insanity defense), contract law (e.g. capacity to enter in a contract), property law (e.g. capacity to buy and manage property), family law (e.g. child custody), and con-

---

*All of our examples are unidirectional; they will be examples of how psychology can affect the law, legal system, and legal process. Our conception of law-psychology, however, is that it is bidirectional and interactive. Unfortunately, a detailed discussion of this point will have to appear elsewhere because of page limitations.

stitutional law (e.g. what constitutes adequate due process). Examples can be equally drawn from other areas of psychology as well. Physiological psychologists can have an impact on drug abuse laws, perceptual and cognitive psychologists can apply their skills to evidentiary questions of law (e.g. eyewitness identification), industrial psychologists can testify on appropriate use of tests in employment discrimination cases, while developmental psychologists can help us decide what limits we want to place on the availability of sex and violence in the media (constitutional and mass communication laws).

Psychological knowledge can also be applied to better understand, evaluate, improve, and administer the legal system. For example, personality and social psychologists can help us understand a great deal about how personality, demographic characteristics, and values of people who work in the legal system affect the administration of the law and its effects on all of us. Organizational psychologists can help us evaluate the efficiency of the institutional components of the legal system. Community, clinical, and social psychologists can help us evaluate the effects that our legal institutions have on our lives.

Finally, various types of psychologists can apply their knowledge to understand, evaluate, improve, and administer the legal process that includes all of the interactions between the individual and the law and legal system. Thus, social psychologists can help us understand and evaluate the adversary process in the courtroom, the deliberation process in the jury room, etc., and personality, social, and clinical psychologists can help us understand and evaluate the hardening effects that prison life has on prisoners and its personnel.

This brief outline of the law-psychology interface should at least suggest the possible content areas that can be included in the training of forensic psychologists. Some of our readers may be overwhelmed by the all-encompassing nature of our conception of this interface and may rightfully ask, "Does this mean that a forensic psychologist has to be trained in all areas of the law as well as in psychology?" The answer is no. We are simply suggesting that the forensic psychologist be at least trained to appreciate the wide range of possibilities for applying psychological knowledge to the law, legal system, and legal process. As with most training programs in psychology, the forensic psychologist then will want to specialize in one or several branches of the law-psychology interface.

THE ROLES OF FORENSIC PSYCHOLOGISTS

In conceptualizing training programs, it is also important to take into account the roles that forensic psychologists play. This will help in two ways: First, the type of job that forensic psychologists want to seek should determine some of the content areas in their training. For example, a forensic researcher needs to be trained much more heavily in applied statistics and experimental design than a forensic clinical practitioner. Second, the recognition of the types of jobs available for forensic psychologists will help in the planning of practicum experiences that could also be incorporated as part of a training program.

There are several ways of categorizing possible roles for forensic psychologists. We prefer the following categorizations: teachers, evaluators-consultants, applied researchers, theorists, and clinical practitioners. Of course, we do not preclude the possibility of a forensic psychologist having a combination of these roles or the fact that activities within some of these roles might overlap.

Forensic psychologists may find themselves teaching their area of expertise in several different environments. The traditional expectation is that a forensic psychologist can find a teaching role at a university or college in a forensic psychology training program, a criminal justice training program, in a traditional psychology training program, in a law school, etc. There are several nontraditional settings available, however. For example, a forensic psychologist can be hired by a police department or a police academy to teach such things as effective methods of riot or crowd control, interviewing eyewitnesses, handling family disputes, anticipating the actions of a criminal, etc. Similarly, a forensic psychologist can be used in training correctional officers, legal agency administrators, judges, lawyers, etc., since each of these personnel have a need for information from the social and behavioral sciences.

Another role that forensic psychologists can play is that of evaluator-consultant. This is a role that requires psychologists to use their expertise to evaluate some aspect of the law, legal system, and legal process and/or use this expertise to advise people within the legal system on how to proceed with some problem. For example, a specialist in social psychology can be called upon to evaluate the effectiveness of punishment as a deterrent to crime or to evaluate the effectiveness of a prison system in rehabilitating criminals. A specialist in clinical psychology can be called upon to evaluate whether a defendant is competent to stand trial or was insane when the crime was committed. In more of a consulting role, this same clinical specialist could be called upon to advise the court or a parole board as to what should be done with a prisoner or, in a custody case, what environment would be most advantageous for a child. Social and personality psychologists can be called upon to consult with lawyers in choosing a jury and/or in presenting a convincing case.

The role of applied forensic researchers is analogous to that of most other applied scientists. That is, while they may use theory in their work, the assigned task is to solve some practical problem. For example, the authors have been involved in research in which we have used knowledge from psycholinguistics and cognitive psychology to improve the comprehension of jury instructions. Industrial psychologists can research ways of improving the selection of police officers while clinical psychologists can be involved in prison reform by researching which therapeutic methods work best in rehabilitating specific prison populations.

Unlike the applied forensic researcher, a forensic theorist is interested in doing research in order to understand and confirm underlying assumptions in and about the law, legal system, and legal process; the work is not necessarily meant to solve practical problems. Most of the theoretical work we have seen thus far has been based on preexisting psychological theories and phenomena. That is, many psychologists have tested traditional psychological theories in legal contexts in order to extend their generalizations (e.g. equity theory in juror decisions). As forensic psychology grows, however, we believe that new theoretical questions that are endemic to the law, legal system, and legal process will arise and become relevant for psychological theory building in general. For example, while the issue of witness credibility is central to a trial proceeding, we have found very scant evidence in the psychological literature on the determinants of lying. We are certain that when this issue is finally researched by forensic psychologists, it will have an impact on general psychological knowledge as well.

Finally, a forensic psychologist can take the role of a clinical practitioner within the legal system. This includes the practice of clinical psychology in terms of providing assessment, therapy, and counseling to populations who are in direct contact with the law and legal system (e.g. prison populations, law enforcement officers, persons undergoing divorce). What makes such work different from other practice is the fact that the legal environment must be taken into account in preparing a successful therapy/counseling plan.

We should add one final comment about the importance of forensic psychologists understanding their roles. As we have been stressing throughout this chapter, the general role of the forensic psychologist is to apply psychological knowledge to the law, legal system, and legal process. In order to perform this role properly, it is imperative that forensic psychologists truly understand the legal context in which they are working and the legal questions that are asked of them. For example, the definition of insantiy for a traditional clinical psychologist may be very different from its legal definition. Thus, a forensic clinical psychologist must be familiar with such legal definitions before expressing opinions in court.

MODELS FOR FORENSIC PSYCHOLOGY TRAINING

There are at least five different models or approaches that could be taken to train forensic psychologists: the disciplinary-unstructured, disciplinary-structured, integrated-interdisciplinary, multidisciplinary, and postdoctoral. Which approach is chosen will depend upon the goals and resources of the trainee. It should be noted that these models are generic and could describe approaches for training in any type of cross-disciplinary area. They are not restricted to forensic psychology.

The disciplinary-unstructured program is one in which the trainee has to learn each discipline independently of the other, with no structure provided to bridge the gap or even encourage the leap. In the case of the psychology student interested in forensics, this approach usually signified the fact that the department has made no accommodation to the student's interest. Thus, in order to get some legal background, the student must seek out one or more law courses to take. Since there is no structured relationship between the psychology department and the law college, enrolling in such courses is often difficult and the student usually winds up taking only those courses in which the instructor gives permission. The problems do not end there, however. Even if the student is allowed to enroll in a particular course, the content is rarely directly on point to the student's needs since there is no reason for the professor to assume that other psychology students will be interested in enrolling, or, if there are some, that the number will be substantial enough to justify modifying the traditional content. This feeling will be bolstered by the fact that the law professors will most likely see their role solely as teachers of law students since no agreement has been worked out between the law college and the psychology department. Finally, problems in enrolling between colleges, transferring credits, being graded on a separate scale from the law students all must be worked out by the students, assuming they can convince the psychology department of the merits of taking such courses in the first place. This characterizes the unhappy state of affairs at the majority of universities today. The financial and time costs to the trainee are large and the energy spent is wasteful. The student must continually act as the integrator with often precious little encouragement. Although the institution incurs no financial costs, society is the true loser here. With a minimum of communication and without incurring the cost of a new program (e.g. hiring faculty), course enrollment between disciplines can increase substantially, and important scholarly training can be developed.

The second approach, the disciplinary-structured model, encourages students to cross disciplinary lines by taking courses in the other discipline for credit within their major department and by offering specially developed courses and seminars that are jointly taught by a psychologist and a lawyer or by one skilled in both fields. These courses also encourage student participation by defining the subject manner in a way that is relevant to both psychology and law students. It provides maximum utilization of existing human and institutional resources without incurring the costs of hiring new faculty or staff. Its inherent flexibility allows growth, diversity, and change in course structure and offerings, or even elimination of them without major concern for problems if the cross-disciplinary program is dropped; the faculty are still committed to their respective departments and areas of original expertise. The disciplinary-structured approach may be used for undergraduate, graduate, and postgraduate training.

The integrated-interdisciplinary model is intended to produce people with a double degree in psychology and law. This approach takes the trainee through both programs as well as a core set of courses and research experiences aimed at bridging the two fields. It requires cooperation between a law college and a psychology department and most likely the hiring of a J.D., Ph.D. to develop courses that will truly integrate the two fields. The benefits of such a program are that it will train scholars with an overview of the entire interface and the ability to identify, understand, and reason in the languages and thought processes of the two disciplines. It should be noted, however, that the double degree is not necessary to ensure quality psychological research and practice within particular areas of law. Its advantage is the breadth of vision it engenders in relating the two fields.

The multidisciplinary model is based on the assumption that problems, especially those of society, need a multidisciplinary approach to reach the proper solutions. The argument for such a program is that since many of the disciplines in the behavioral/social sciences have overlapping concerns, a team of scientists/practitioners representing various disciplines will be better able to solve them. Thus, for example, the faculty for such a program could include people from psychology, law, psychiatry, sociology, and criminology. It is not clear yet that all of these individuals have to reside within one department, although that is one possibility. Rather, a program could be formed using faculty and courses from a variety of disciplines.

In order to contribute to the law-psychology interface, not everyone needs to seek a formal program of study in forensics prior to obtaining their degree. In fact, the history of this field is such that most psychologists probably obtained their forensic expertise after they completed their Ph.D. or Psy.D., or at least after they completed all courses and the dissertation. This is not necessarily a bad system. There are viable postdoctoral options for a psychologist given the high level of training and skill the individual has already attained in psychology. For example, some psychologists may only need a brief excursion into a branch of law in order to gain the minimal insight and skills necessary to direct a specific program of research, teaching, or direct service. A case in point are psychologists interested in doing research on the jury process; they may simply need to audit one or two law courses. Other approaches to getting such brief and specialized training include reading the literature and attending special workshops and paper sessions at universities and annual meetings of national organizations (e.g. the American Psychological Association, the American Psychology-Law Society, and the American Association of Correctional Psychologists) and working in a formal postdoctoral training program under the direct and continuing supervision of a specialist in the field. Finally, clinical psychologists may receive their forensic training as part of their internship since many APA approved internship programs provide such experiences.[10] Obviously, the critical issue is not what type of training psychologists receive but rather that the training has provided sufficient knowledge to truly understand and appreciate the legal problems and the legal context in which they intend to work.

CONCLUSION

As psychologists we are concerned with human behavior and the human condition. Yet for years lawyers and legislators have created laws and legal institutions that were based upon untested assumptions about people's actions. Since the study of behavior is within the domain of psychologists, we have the potential for having a tremendous impact on helping understand, evaluate, improve, and administer the law, legal system, and legal process. The complexity of legal problems demand that some segment of our psychology students be trained in the law-psychology interface. Hopefully, this chapter will encourage the spread of such training.

REFERENCES

1. Special Commission on the Social Sciences of the National Science Board, *Knowledge into action: Improving the nation's use of the social sciences,* Washington, D.C., National Science Foundation, 1969.
2. Tapp, J.L. Psychology and law: A look at the interface. In Sales, B.D. (Ed.), *Psychology in the legal process,* New York, Spectrum Publication, 1977.
3. Bermant, G., Neneth, C., and Vidmar, N. *Psychology and the law: Research frontiers,* Lexington, Massachusetts, D.C. Heath, 1976.
4. Lipsitt, P.D. and Sales, B.D. *New direction in psycholegal research,* New York, Van Nostrand Reinhold, in press.
5. Sales, B.D. *Psychology in the legal process,* New York, Spectrum Publications, 1977.
6. Sales, B.D. *Perspectives in law and psychology, Volume I, The criminal justice system,* New York, Plenum, 1977.
7. Tapp, J.L. and Levine, F.J. *Law, justice, and the individual in society,* New York, Holt, Rinehart and Winston, 1977.
8. Sales, B.D. *Perspectives in law and psychology, Volume II, The jury, judicial and trial processes,* New York, Plenum, in press.
9. Fenster, C.A., Faltico, G., Goldstein, J., Kaslow, F., Locke, D., Musikoff, H., Schlossberg, H., and Wolk, R. In Woods, P.J. (Ed.), *Career opportunities for psychologists,* Washington, D.C., American Psychological Association, 1976.
10. Levine, D., Wilson, K., and Sales, B.D. Legal/forensic experiences in APA approved internship programs, in preparation.

Chapter 3

THE LEGAL STATUS OF THE
PSYCHOLOGIST IN THE COURTROOM*

Michael L. Perlin, Esq.

I N THE PRACTICE of law, just as in the practice of any other profession, trade, vocation or avocation, it is often the folkways, mores,
and customs that deserve the attention usually paid to the written
rules of substance and procedure. Although thousands of words are
written, for instance, about the subtle points of a significant court
decision or statutory revision, usually limited analysis is given to what
can be termed—somewhat inartfully, I am afraid—the socialization of
the law.

Thus, any discussion of "The Legal Status of the Psychologist in
the Courtroom" must begin with the premise that the phrase "legal
status" is really shorthand for at least three bundles of definitions:
The legal status of psychologists as defined by case law (i.e. when can
they give expert testimony) ; the legal roles which psychologists can
fill (i.e., in what kinds of cases can they testify) ; and the social status
of psychologists in the courtroom (i.e. how they are viewed by the
judge, the jury, the parties, other experts and other psychologists
themselves). Although the case law is now becoming relatively uniform and the scope of witness roles is forever widening, it is the social
status of psychologists in the courtroom—a question normally paid
little attention to—which is probably the most important of these
topics to consider. This status—the end product of a mixture of self-
fears, denial, resistance, and the usual gamut of ego defenses we all

---

*This paper was originally presented at the American Psychological Association
Conference, Washington, D.C., September 1976. It is reprinted from the *Journal
of Psychiatry and Law,* 5(1), 41–54, © 1977 by Federal Legal Publications, Inc. 95
Morton Street, New York, New York, 10014.

employ on a daily basis—is the hidden issue that is really worthy of further exploration.[1]

Although a smattering of early cases had held that a properly qualified psychologist could testify in a criminal trial on questions involving mental condition or competency to stand trial[2] or in accident disability cases on questions of extent of neurological impairment,[3] it was not until the 1962 decision of the prestigious District of Columbia Court of Appeals in *Jenkins* v. *United States*[4] that the psychologist's legal status was given firm grounding.

In *Jenkins,* a criminal case in which the defendant on trial for housebreaking with intent to assault raised the insanity defense, the trial judge had ordered the jury to disregard testimony of defense psychologists that the defendant "had a mental disease" when he committed the crimes in question because—according to the judge—"a psychologist is not competent to give a medical opinion as to a mental disease or defect." Following the jury's conviction, however, the court of appeals reversed and remanded the matter for a new trial on a series of grounds, including, *inter alia,* that that ruling by the trial judge was in error, as "some psychologists are qualified to render expert testimony in the field of mental disorder."

Judge Bazelon, speaking for a sharply divided court noted that the appropriate test was "whether the opinion offered will be likely to aid the trier in the search for truth." The answer to this test will not "depend upon the witness's claim to the title 'psychologist,' " the court warned. Rather, the determination must depend "upon the nature and extent of his knowledge." While psychologists otherwise employed in areas such as personnel administration or industrial relations might not qualify to testify as to "mental disease or defect," a Ph.D. in clinical psychology with a psychiatric hospital internship and/or completion of an APA-approved graduate training program and/or Board certification might properly testify.

As indicated, the opinion was far from unanimous. In a special concurring opinion, Judge (now Chief Justice) Warren Burger criticized Judge Bazelon's opinion for its alleged "failure to give adequate guidance as to the scope and nature of the inquiry" on remand and listed seven major areas of questioning—involving such areas as scope of the specific psychologist's clinical education in "physiological and medical subjects," his ability to "prescribe or supervise treatment of mental patients," and the meaning of "clinical experience"—which should be covered on the remand.* Finally, two other judges dissented, urging the court to accept the position of *amicus curiae* American Psychiatric Association, which had argued that psychologists should not be allowed to qualify as experts.[7] According to the dissenters, the majority should have listened to the "wise counsel from the only undisputed experts now at work in the area of medical illness of the mind." That this point of view has not entirely disappeared will be pointed out later.

Following *Jenkins*—a case which, by the way, met with nearly unanimous critical endorsement in the scholarly legal journals[8]— virtually every major criminal decision has echoed its language,[9] thus giving stronger footing to the psychologist's "legal status." More important, however, the acceptance of this approach literally opened the doors to the admission of psychological testimony in a multitude of legal areas.

Thus, psychologists now commonly testify as expert witnesses in civil commitment matters (in cases involving questions of retardation, acceptability of treatment involving behavior therapy, and appropriateness of placements) ,[10] and more increasingly, on such questions as employment discrimination,[11] juvenile placements,[12] accuracy in evaluation of eyewitness testimony,[13] special education assignments,[14] effects of bilingualism on children,[15] postsentencing disposition,[16] extent of neurological injury;[17] even more important, perhaps, they are beginning to testify in class actions involving such fundamental issues as right to education,[18] right to habilitation,[19] and right to vote.[20] By becoming involved in cases such as these, psychologists are continually—and properly—expanding their legal roles. If as has been suggested by Cameron Fincher, the psychological community does, indeed, evince a "consistent concern with the social, cultural and

---

*Burger's views on psychiatry and psychology have been well recorded since. In an article in *Federal Probation,* he stated, "At best psychiatry is now an infant among the family of sciences. Just as the law can lay no valid claim to being truly scientific, neither perhaps can psychiatry and psychology; they may be claiming too much in relation to what they really understand about the human personality and human behavior."[5]

More recently, in a special concurring opinion in the landmark case of *O'Conner v. Donaldson,*[6] he noted, "There can be little responsible debate regarding the 'uncertainty of diagnosis in this field and the tentativeness of professional judgment.' *Greenwood* v. *United States,* 310 U.S. at 375. See also, Ennis, B J. and Litwack, T., Psychiatry and the Presumption of Expertise: Flipping Coins in the Courtroom, 62 *California Law Review,* 693, 697–719."

humanistic issues as well as the professional and technical problems,"[11] then it must critically involve itself in these roles.

However, the simple truism suggested by attorney Bernard Diamond and psychiatrist David Louisell in their article on courtroom psychiatry—"the psychological sciences differ from the biological sciences in that the subject matter of the former is not visible"[21]—is even more applicable to a discussion of forensic psychology and the role of the courtroom psychologist. What are often viewed as the "excess" of flamboyant expert witnesses in public spectacles such as the Hearst or Ruby trials[22] become quickly transformed into sins visited upon *all* expert witnesses: papers are regularly published denying the need for involvement of "adversarial" experts in the legal adversary process,[23] direly forecasting the inevitable prostitution of the profession,[24] questioning the compatibility of psychology, psychiatry and the courts,[25] and recommending that experts only become involved on an amicus (friend of the court) or so-called impartial witness level.[26] Although these positions have been more than adequately responded to by lawyers[27] and psychiatrists,[28] a backlash phenomenon is clearly present.[29]

Beyond this, however, lurks an even more disturbing problem for forensic psychologists; not only must they contend with the same basic antipathy in the courtroom facing the psychiatrist,[30] but they must also contend with what is—sadly—perceived as "second-class expert" status, when compared by judge and/or jury to the medical expert. Thus, a basic legal text points out that "a favorite trick of cross-examination is to bring out the lack of medical education of the clinical psychologist . . . in a voice oozing incredulity or sarcasm."[31] Elsewhere, it has been pointed out that psychologists may be—sometimes effectively—baited by attorneys "indirectly attempting to question their qualifications and competence . . . by addressing them always as 'Mister,' in marked contrast to the consistent and appropriate use of the title 'Doctor'."[32]   One of the post-*Jenkins* decisions, alluded to above, notes, for example, that the trial court had asked the psychologist-witness, "You have never dissected a cadaver, have you?"[33] In another more recent case, in an attempt to discredit a clinical psychologist who had testified as a defense witness, the prosecutor appealed to the jury to disregard the witness's interpretation of a projective test:

> Ladies and gentlemen, then we come to that ink blot. . . .Fourteen
> responses and four of them turned out to be anatomical things—hearts
> or whatever it happened to be. Is there something unusual about

that? Is a man crazy when he sees a heart or something else four times?. . . . After all, they are just blots of ink. Is a man crazy when he sees them? And how about that last one, that rocket one. He says he sees a rocket going off. I asked him, doctor, was there any rocket fired during that period of time that might stick in a man's brain and might suggest it to him? The doctor doesn't know. But there is something explosive about a personality if he sees a rocket on a little ink blot.

Well, ladies and gentleman, there is not much I can say about that; I am not an expert. . . . But I can say one thing; that it is a jury decision. It is your province. It is your function to take that evidence and weigh that evidence and decide whether what that doctor said as far as you are concerned made any sense at all.[34]

In *Jenkins,* itself, in fact, a courtroom observer pointed out that during the course of a psychologist's testimony, the presiding trial judge "literally threw a deck of projective cards onto the floor."[35] Finally, a *Jenkins* analysis concluded by asking rhetorically:

What significance will the jury attach to the defense *psychologist's* testimony when confronted with the conflicting testimony of the state's *psychiatrist?* Will recitation to the jury of the *psychiatrist's* qualifications, which will include a medical degree, have any prejudicial effect on the defendant who produces a *psychologist?*[36] (emphasis added).

The treatment of the problem and answers to those questions must be dealt with openly and completely by forensic psychologists.

In addition, of course, forensic psychologists must also be looking over their other flank at the forensic psychiatrists who are still uncomfortable about the newcomer's involvement (spelled *usurpation* in some quarters). Thus, in the 1972 case I discussed above (where the prosecution said "After all, they are just blots of ink"), the American Psychiatry Association filed an amicus brief, clearly labeling such forensic psychologists as "laymen" in relation to the diagnosis of "mental illnesses or defects."[34] According to the eminent professor of law and psychiatry Richard Allen, the Psychiatric Association's ultimate objective is "quite clear: reversal of Judge Bazelon's decision in *Jenkins*"[34]—this spectre must be a serious subject of consideration for the forensic psychologist.

The progenesis of this attitude, of course, cannot be laid solely, or even, perhaps, predominantly, at the feet of the legal or psychiatric profession. At base, this social status must be seen as a reflection on the self-perceptions held by many psychologists of their potential courtroom role. Although it was a lawyer who noted the traditional limitation in courtroom participation "comes not only from the law, but also from the inhibitions of psychologists,"[31] it is clearly very often the "fault" of the psychologists themselves that their forensic role has been so truncated. Indeed, Louisell's observation some twenty years ago that "psychologists . . . often seem to display an undue hesitancy, *amounting almost to fear,* to taking the witness stand,"[37] is still all too valid in too many instances.[38]

Thus, Douglas Sargent—a psychiatrist—has noted that a forensic psychiatrist is "annoyed by the limitations which legal procedures place on his testimony, impatient with the stilted rituals of courtroom etiquette, intrigued by the law's archaic language" and that this response creates an "unfortunate polarization of attitudes . . . leading to a hostile parody of the truth."[39] The substitution of "psychologist" for "psychiatrist" in that sentence would ring similarly true to many. In addition, forensic psychologists must confront the fact that they cannot "behave in the courtroom as though the issues were settled;"[35] transcripts such as those reproduced by Jeffrey as part of an NIMH project reveal forensic psychological witnesses whose demeanor—in important, otherwise well-prepared, serious criminal cases—ranges from obstinate to condescending to patronizing to omniscient.[35] In the vernacular, some forensic psychologists must "clean up their act."

Louisell's quotation from *Julius Caesar* ("the fault, dear Brutus, is not in our stars,/But in ourselves, that we are underlings"),[32] again, serves as an effective epigram: forensic psychologists must confront the reasons why they have both been treated as second-class citizens in the court and why they see themselves in that role. Thus, the heralded Competency Screening Index, prepared by the Laboratory of Community Psychiatry in conjunction with NIMH, establishes a sentence-completion test for the purpose of "quickly screening defendants" to make recommendations as to their competency to stand trial.[40] It is geared to determine whether an individual defendant meets the three-pronged common-law test for competency (ability to cooperate with counsel, understand nature of proceedings, understand consequences of proceedings), and, in fact, may effectively do so.[40,41] However, a witness who administers and then testifies to the results of a test such as this must be aware of—and must be able to deal with—the pitfalls of probing cross-examination, a skeptical judge, and, on occasion, an incredulous jury. To paraphrase Shakespeare again, the forensic psychologist must be as well-prepared and comprehending as

Caesar's wife needed to be pure.

Although this picture has been, admittedly, somewhat gloomy, it should also be encouraging to the forensic psychologist. The cases which I have referred to—especially the noncriminal ones—can serve as a meaningful opportunity through which psychologists can—and should—push for further involvement in the judicial process, on at least three separate levels.

First, the special assessment, testing, and intellectual/personality evaluation skills and techniques possessed by clinical psychologists uniquely prepare them for much courtroom work,[42] in areas referred to above, as well as such newly emerging areas as ferreting out cultural test biases,[11] a role they will better be able to play if they become—in the phrase of Stanley Brodsky and Ames Robey—"courtroom-oriented" and discard their usual "courtroom-unfamiliar" pose.[43] Second, it is clear that testimony in civil rights/class actions gives forensic psychologists a tremendous opportunity "to contribute to social change"[44] as an "advocate and facilitator"[45] while fulfilling their role as part of a "socially concerned system."[46] As a corollary to both these reasons, it should also be pointed out that forensic psychologists are remarkably *successful* when they go to court—in 70 percent of a group of cases studied, the verdict was in favor of the side on which the psychologists testified.[47]

Finally, it is clear that the courts are more ready for the forensic psychologist. As indicated above, legal barriers to testimony have virtually disappeared.[8,9] One commentator calls the clinical psychologist "worthy of our consideration in the seeking of new and improved trial techniques;[17] another questions how long the law can "lag behind scientific fact and common knowledge";[13] a third argues that the psychologist "can contribute in the courtroom toward a better understanding of emotional illness."[48] Interestingly, this final commentator points out how psychology's struggle for acceptance as a scientific and objective discipline familiarizes the psychologist with ways to overcome the shortcomings of such tools as projective tests and uniquely prepares him/her for the rigors of cross-examination.[48] It thus remains only for the psychological community to openly confront the reasons which have perpetuated the anticourtroom bias and to educate all participants in the litigation process to the need for (and uniqueness of) appropriate psychological testimony.

In a 1961 article, Norma Scheflen—a research psychologist at Temple University—quoted the famous law dean John Wigmore as stating, "whenever the psychologist is really ready for the courts, the courts are ready for him."[48] Although Dr. Scheflen prophesied that "the time is now" fifteen years ago, it is unfortunate that history has not yet truly borne her out. Perhaps now, finally, it will.

REFERENCES

1. Perlin, M. Psychiatric Testimony in a Criminal Setting, *Bulletin of the American Academy of Psychiatry and Law, 3,* 143, 1976.
2. People v. Hawthorne 293 Mich. 15, 291 N.W. 205 (Sup. Ct. 1974); State v. Padilla, 66 N.M. 289, 347 P.2d 312 (Sup. Ct. 1959); Annotation, Qualification of Non-Medical Psychologist to Testify as to Mental Condition or Competency, 78 A.L.R. 2d 919, 920-921, 1961. Contra, Dobbs v. State, 191 Ark. 236, 85 S.W. 2d 694 (Sup. Ct. 1935); People v. Spigno, 156 Cal. App. 2d 279, 319 P.2d 458 (D. Ct. App. 1957).
3. Hidden v. Mutual Life Insurance Company 217 F.2d 818 (4th Cir. 1957).
4. 307 F.2d 637, 643-645, 647-650 (D.C. Cir. 1962).
5. Burger, W.E. Psychiatrists, Lawyers and the Courts, *Federal Probation, 28, 3,* 7, 1967.
6. O'Connor v. Donaldson 422 U.S. 573, 578, 584, 1975.
7. Jenkins v. United States 307 F.2d 637, 651, 652, (D.C. Cir. 1961) (Bastian, J., dissenting).
8. Note. Evidence—Criminal Insanity—Psychologist's Diagnosis Regarding Mental Disease or Defect Admissible on Issue of Insanity, *Villanova Law Review, 8,* 119, 1962; Levitt, E.E. The Psychologist: A Neglected Legal Resource, *Indiana Law Review, 45,* 82, 1969; Lassen, G. The Psychologist as an Expert Witness in Assessing Mental Disease or Defect, *American Bar Association Journal, 50,* 239, 1964. *Cf.,* however, Morse, H.N. Psychologist as Witness on Mental Incompetence, *Journal of the American Medical Association, 198,* 313, 1966.
9. United States v. Green 373 F. Supp. 149, 158 (E.D. pa. 1974). (The critical factor is the psychologist's actual experience and the probable probative value of his testimony); Blunt v. United States 389, F.2d 545, 547 (D.C. Cir. 1967) (repeating "requisite training or experience" language); People v. Lyles 526 P.2d 1332, 1334-1335 (Colo. Sup. Ct. 1974); United States v. Riggleman 411 F.2d 1190, 1191 (4th Cir. 1969) (determination depends on "the nature and extent of psychologist's knowledge"). Contra, People v. Gillian, 16 Ill. App. 3d 659, 306 N.E. 2d 352 (App. Ct. 1974). Most relevant cases are discussed at Pacht, A.R. The Current Status of the Psychologist as an Expert Witness, *Professional Psychology, 4,* 409, 1973.
10. Martin, R. *Legal Challenges to Behavior Modification,* Champaign,

Illinois, Research Press, 1975.

11. Fincher, C. Personnel Testing and Public Policy, *American Psychologist, 28,* 489, 1973.

12. Sussman, A. Psychological Testing and Juvenile Justice: An Invalid Judicial Function, *Criminal Law Bulletin, 10,* 117, 1974.

13. Lezak, M.D. Some Psychological Limitations on Witness Reliability, *Wayne Law Review, 20,* 117, 119, 1973.

14. Kirp, D.L., and Kirp, L.M. The Legalization of the School Psychologist's World, *Journal of School Psychology, 14,* 83, 1976; Katz, L.J., and Bonfield, R.J. The Right to Education: Due Process and the Inner City Child, *Bulletin of the American Academy of Psychiatry and Law, 3,* 70, 1976; Kirp, D.L., Buss, W., and Kuriloff, P. Legal Reform of Special Education: Empirical Studies and Procedural Proposals, *California Law Review, 62,* 40, 1974; Gorlow, L. The School Psychologist as Expert Witness in Due Process Hearings, *Journal of School Psychology, 13,* 311, 1975.

15. Rose, A.M. The Social Scientist as an Expert Witness, *Minnesota Law Review, 40,* 205, 1956; Kendler, T.S. Contributions of the Psychiatrist to Constitutional Law, *American Psychologist, 5,* 505, 1950.

16. Brodsky, S.L. *Psychologists in the Criminal Justice System,* Urbana, University of Illinois, 1973.

17. Gaines, I.D. The Clinical Psychologist as an Expert Witness in a Personal Injury Case, *Marquette Law Review, 39,* 239, 1956.

18. Mills v. Board of Education 348 F. Supp. 866 (D.D.C. 1972); Pennsylvania Association for Retarded Citizens v. Pennsylvania 343 F. Supp. 279 (E.D. Pa. 1972).

19. Wyatt v. Stickney 344 F Supp. 307 (M.D. Ala. 1972), *aff'd sub nom* Wyatt v. Aderholt 503 F.2d 1305 (5th Cir. 1974)

20. Carroll v. Cobb 139 N.J. Super 439, 354 A.2d 355 (App. Div. 1976).

21. Diamond, B. and Louisell, D.W. The Psychiatrist as an Expert Witness: Some Ruminations and Speculations, *Michigan Law Review, 63,* 1335, 1340, 1965.

22. Willis, S.E. Psychiatric Testimony, Trial Gamesmanship and the Defense of Insanity, *San Diego Law Review, 5,* 32, 1968.

23. Suarez, J.M. A Critique of the Psychiatrist's Role as Expert Witness, *Journal of Forensic Sciences, 12,* 172, 1967.

24. MacDonald, J.M. *Psychiatry and the Criminal,* Springfield, Thomas, 1969.

25. Roberts, L.M. Some Observations on the Problem of the Forensic Psychiatrist, *Wisconsin Law Review, 240,* 245, 1965.

26. Van Dusen, F.L. The Impartial Medical Expert System: The Judicial Point of View, *Temple Law Quarterly, 35,* 386, 1961; Balcanoff, E.J. and McGarry, A.L. Amicus Curiae: The Role of the Psychiatrist in Pretrial Examinations, *American Journal of Psychiatry, 126,* 90, 1969.

27. Goldstein, A.S. The Psychiatrist and the Legal Process: The Proposals for an Impartial Expert and for Preventive Detention, *American Journal of Orthopsychiatry, 33,* 123, 1963.

28. Diamond, B.L. The Psychiatrist as Advocate, *Journal of Psychiatry and Law, 1,* 5, 1973; (characterizing the responsible expert role by the phrase "disciplined subjectivity"); Diamond, B.L. The Fallacy of Impartial Expert, *Archives of Criminal Psychodynamics, 3,* 221, 1959; Pollack, S. Observations on the Adversary System and the Role of the Forensic Scientist: 'Scientific Truth' v. 'Legal Truth,' *Journal of Forensic Sciences, 18,* 173, 1973.

29. Robey, A. and Bogard, W.J. The Compleat Forensic Psychiatrist, *American Journal of Psychiatry, 126,* 101, 1969; Sargent, D.A. Problems in Collaboration Between Lawyers and Psychiatrists, *Wayne Law Review, 11,* 697, 1965; Goldstein, J. Psychoanalysis and Jurisprudence, *Yale Law Journal, 77,* 1053, 1968.

30. Robitscher, J. *Pursuit of Agreement: Psychiatry and the Law, 12,* 1966, citing Witlock, F.A. *Criminal Responsibility and Mental Illness,* 1963.

31. Asch, S.H. *Mental Disability in Civil Practice,* Section 12.8 at 292-293, 1973.

32. Schofield, W. Psychology, Law and the Expert Witness *American Psychologist, 11,* 1, 1956.

33. Blunt v. United States 389 F.2d 545, 548, n. 11 (D.C. Cir. 1967).

34. Record at 36, United States v Brawner 471 F.2d 969 (D.C. Cir. 1972), as quoted in Allen, "The Brawner Rule—New Lyrics for an Old Tune" *Washington University Law Quarterly, 67,* 73, 1973.

35. Jeffrey, R. The Psychologist as an Expert Witness on the Issue of Insanity, *American Psychologist, 19,* 838, 1964.

36. Note. *Villanova Law Review, 8,* 124, n. 31.

37. Louisell, D.W. The Psychologist in Today's Legal World, *Minnesota Law Review, 39,* 235, 241, 1955.

38. Schofield, W. supra note 32, at 1 (referring to "sources of stress" residing in the general nature of court proceedings); McCary, J.U. The Psychologist as an Expert Witness in Court, *American Psychologist, 11,* 8, 1956; Rice, G.P. The Psychologist as Expert Witness, *American Psychologist, 16,* 691, 1961.

39. Sargent, D. supra note 29, at 698. For what might charitably be termed bizarre advice to an expert witness faced with such a situation, see Kiger, R.S. The Psychiatrist as an Expert Witness in Criminal Court, *Hospital and Community Psychiatry, 24,* 613, 1973.

40. National Institute of Mental Health *Competency to Stand Trial and Mental Illness,* Washington, D.C., U.S. Government Printing Office, 1974.

41. Group for the Advancement of Psychiatry *Misuse of Psychiatry in the*

Criminal Courts: Competency to Stand Trial, New York, Mental Health Materials Center, 1974.

42. Lezak, M.D.   The Clinical Psychologist in the Litigation Process, In George, B.J. (Ed), *The Effective Use of Psychiatric Evidence in Civil and Criminal Litigation* 137 (P.I.I. ed. 1974); Levitt, E.E.   supra note 16, at 86.

43. Brodsky, S.L. and Robey, A.   On Becoming an Expert Witness: Issues of Orientation and Effectiveness, *Professional Psychology, 3,* 183, 1972.

44. Halleck, S.L.   A Troubled View of Current Trends in Forensic Psychiatry, *Journal of Psychiatry and Law, 2,* 135, 1974.

45. Rollins, B.   The Forensic Psychiatrist: Conspirator, Isolationist, or Advocate?, *Hospital and Community Psychiatry, 24,* 632, 1973.

46. Pollack, S.   Forensic Psychiatry—A Specialty, *Bulletin of the American Academy of Psychiatry and Law, 1,* 1, 1974.

47. Bobbitt, J.M. and Hoch, E.L.   Order—and Psychologist—in the Court, *American Psychologist, 16,* 152, 1961.

48. Scheflen, N.A.   The Psychologist as a Witness, *Pennsylvania Bar Association Quarterly, 32,* 329, 1961.

Chapter 4

FORENSIC PSYCHOLOGIST CERTIFICATION: WHO, FOR WHAT, HOW?

KENNETH G. WILSON, Ph.D.

A N ARTICLE ON THE CERTIFICATION of psychologists is, almost by necessity, bland. However, if one examines the issue of expertise in forensic psychological matters and some of the assumptions underlying this issue, there may be some meat for an otherwise pallid broth.

THE PROBLEMS

Some of the problems accompanying forensic certification are the following: (1) Who do we certify? Psychologists, psychiatrists, social workers, biologists, sociologists, or neurophysiologists? (2) What do we certify them for? Establishing the current mental status of the defendant, the mental status of the defendant at the time of commission of the crime, clairvoyance, the mortal culpability of the defendant, or just the defendant's ability to assist the attorney in the defense? (3) How do we establish the criteria for certification? Who has the ability to establish the criteria? What schools teach forensic psychology? Who can see into the past to certify someone else's ability to do so? Who is so incapable of being fooled by an insanity plea that he can verify another's ability to do so?

EXPERTISE: WHO HAS IT?

If a gynecologist went into the courtroom to testify in a malpractice suit involving neurosurgery, he would probably be laughed from the courtroom after several challenges regarding expertise to testify on that particular subject. Even among very uneducated jurors (and judges and attorneys) the difference between a gynecologist and a neurosurgeon is well known and understood. In psychiatric matters the distinctions among experts are blurred, i.e. not as clearly defined, even among professionals in the field.

Contact with mental health professionals is even more circumscribed than that with health professionals. The result is that laypersons can discriminate among the various health care specialists with relative ease. With mental health professionals the contact is limited (it is still a social taboo to seek psychiatric help) and stereotyping behavior is more likely to occur. Frequently I am asked to prescribe medication or am called a psychiatrist. I patiently explain the difference. The point is that few professionals and even fewer nonprofessionals have the knowledge to discriminate among behaviorists, psychoanalysts, psychoanalytically oriented psychologists, and forensic psychologists. If they cannot discriminate among these subgroups, how can they discriminate among the quite different assumptions and testimony regarding the etiology and mental state of a criminal in a decision-making situation (criminal culpability)?

The problems with forensic psychology are even more complex. There is no unitary theory of the etiology of criminal behavior and neither is there any empirical evidence to support many professional contentions held regarding criminal behavior. Criminals are usually forced into the category of psychoneurotic, character disorder, psychopath, or on occasion, psychotic. Our knowledge (ignorance would be more apropos) regarding psychopaths, character disorders, asocial personalities, sociopaths, and other metaphors we have used to label that which we least understand is extremely limited. We, forensic psychologists and psychiatrists, have not yet developed a comprehensive, empirically tested (or testable) theory regarding individuals in these diagnostic categories. Many still hold the biological atavist theories promulgated by Lombroso. The old wine is in new bottles, disguised as XYY chromosomal research, impulse inhibition theories, pathological sensation seeking propositions, and unresponsiveness to normal rewards and punishments.[1] How many physiologists, biologists, and neurophysiologists are called to testify as expert witnesses?

An area of expertise not usually represented in forensics is sociological. Sociological theories still conceptualize the criminal's behavior from a victimization stance. That is, they view the criminal as a victim of social forces beyond his control. The range of possibilities is extensive, from peer group pressures, learning, and anomie to labelling and the logical response to the disproportionate distribution of wealth. Judge Bazelon, who invited the medical model into the courtroom, has indicted mental health professionals for proposing the diseased mind model as an explanation for criminal behavior. His rationale is that through his continued observation he has concluded that the unequal distribution of and access to wealth is most probably the cause.[2] How many sociologists are called to testify regarding the sociocultural factors producing crime?

Psychologists, on the other hand, range from the behaviorists, who would focus almost exclusively on the reinforcement history and environmental contingencies (which, incidentally, makes the culture, not the individual, culpable), to the psychoanalytically oriented psychologist, who focuses on internal conflicts. Psychiatry focuses on inner conflicts and views criminal behavior as a symptom. The symptom is only the expression of internal hostility toward a parent or sibling, a demand for punishment for internalized guilt, the expression of sexual conflicts (e.g. arson), and concepts such as the repetition compulsion. How do we decide who to certify and for what from among these options?

THE STATE OF THE ART

Forensic psychology and psychiatry are fledgling disciplines in transition. Formal training is scarce and acquired in a tutorial fashion. Most states have forensic units in prisons or state hospitals for court evaluations, the incarceration of successful insanity pleas, and pretrial observation. Few formal programs exist for the training of forensic psychologists and psychiatrists. Indeed, most training, if one could call it that, is acquired on the job. There is only one doctoral level program for the training of correctional psychologists at the University of Alabama. At this point in time, the only fully accepted court expert is the psychiatrist. There is legislation pending to allow psychologists to testify in competency issues, and if other pending legislation permitting psychologists hospital privileges (they must currently admit people for inpatient care under a physician's signature) is passed, the role of psychologists in forensic matters will increase.

Several courts (e.g. California) are removing the forensic issues from the trial proper and utilizing mental health professionals post hoc, i.e. to help settle the issues of appropriate sentencing *after* guilt has been established. The change makes sense since not guilty by reason of insanity implies that the event did not occur because the person who committed the act was not *criminally* responsible.

CURRENT LICENSING

All states now require either licensing or certification for the practice of psychology. Some states recognize psychological specialties such as school, consulting, and clinical. Others have a single classification—psychologist—permitting the practitioner to engage in any aspect of professional psychological practice, with the American Psychological Association's Code of Ethics as a guide to practitioners to offer service only in fields for which they are trained. Most psychologists working for state or federal agencies are not required to be licensed or certified and work under the aegis of the state. The federal government is now requesting that all psychologists in the correctional system be certified in the state they work (where the prison is) so that if expanded responsibilities come with the new legislation they will be able to appear as government witnesses.

There is no national examining agency that is recognized by all states. When a psychologist changes states he must be recertified/licensed in that state. There is, however, an independent and autonomous organization (from A.P.A.) that provides a list to consumers of psychologists who are licensed or certified to provide health care. The *National Register* was established in 1975. General information regarding certification and licensure may be obtained from the American Psychological Association or the Psychologists Examining Board for states in which you wish to apply.

THE FUTURE

Forensic psychology has a bright future. June Tapp has extensively examined the interface between psychology and the law and notes advances from jury research to new dimensions in the understanding of criminal personality.[3] Several organizations are breaching the gap between psychology and the law. The American Psychology and Law Society will meet in the fall of 1978 to examine possible criteria for the certification of forensic psychologists.

The birth of any profession follows a predictable course. The perception of a need, the acquisition of a body of knowledge and research, the growth of professional schools and journals. Forensic psychology is making such an entry, and in the near future we should expect to see forensic psychology as an option in clinical psychology and psychological doctorate programs. I only hope that such programs include some physiology, sociology, and biology.

REFERENCES

1. Hare, R.D. *Psychopathy theory and research,* New York, Wiley, 1970.
2. Bazelon, D.L. Psychologists in corrections—are they doing good for the offender or well for themselves? Appendix A. In Brodsky, S.L., *Psychologists in the criminal justice system,* Marysville, Ohio, American Association of Correctional Psychologists, 1972.
3. Tapp, J.L. Psychology and the law: An overture, *Annual review of psychology, 27,* 359, Palo Alto, California, Annual Reviews Inc., 1976.

EDITORS NOTE: Since this chapter was written the American Board of Forensic Psychology has been incorporated and has begun examining applicants and granting the diplomate in forensic psychology.

Chapter 5

A PRACTICAL GUIDE TO PRIVILEGED COMMUNICATION FOR PSYCHOLOGISTS

Donald N. Bersoff, Ph.D., J.D.

AND

Mishrilal Jain

M R. AND MRS. MIDSON had been seeing Dr. Novice, a psychologist, for several months in family therapy. Their decision to seek counseling was spurred by a series of incidents in which they progressively became more physically violent when disciplining their child. During therapy they revealed many aggressive urges toward the boy, admitted that at times they genuinely hated him, and described several episodes when they beat him with a broom handle. After two years and the apparent resolution of these problems, Dr. Novice and the Midsons agreed that counseling should be discontinued. For the last six months of therapy there had been no overt violence toward their son, the aggressive urges had diminished, and they stated they no longer had strong aversive reactions to him.

Nine months after termination of treatment the child was found dead in a secluded area several miles from the Midson household. He had been beaten to death with a blunt instrument. The Midsons were indicted for murder. At the subsequent trial, Dr. Novice is called by the State to testify about his sessions with the Midsons. Believing that he should not disclose any confidences revealed during the course of the therapy sessions, Dr. Novice refuses to testify as to any communications among the three of them. He agrees only to relate that he did see the Midsons and to state the period when he began and when he completed their professional relationship. The judge orders Dr. Novice to testify, but he refuses. The judge then holds Dr. Novice in contempt of court and remands him to the custody of the county sheriff who places him in jail until he agrees to testify.

We shall spend the next several thousand words analyzing the likelihood of Dr. Novice securing his release. His chances of success will depend primarily on whether he can invoke an element of the law of evidence called privileged communication. Simplistically, the granting of privileged communication permits certain designated persons (usually those who serve others in a professional capacity) to refuse to testify in legal proceedings without penalty concerning matters deemed to be confidential to protect the privacy of those who have sought their help (e.g. clients), if their clients have not waived the right to be protected by the privilege. But, as we shall see, the concept of privileged communication is in reality not so concisely stated. It is complex, controversial, and because it is controlled primarily by state (and federal law), it is by no means uniform. In addition, the existing legal and psychological literature pertaining to privileged communications for mental health professionals is vast and not easily summarized.*[1-40,80] Readers interested in extended discussions of the historical,[41] philosophical, legal, and social policy bases for the privileged communications doctrine should consult those sources.

At best, this chapter can only highlight major principles and offer practical recommendations to psychologists who may find themselves (or, better yet, wish to prevent themselves from being) in Dr. Novice's predicament. To that end, first we will briefly discuss the legal underpinnings of privileged communication. Then we will explain the doctrine in detail and outline its major rules and exceptions through an exploration of some statutory examples. The next section takes the form of a short discussion of the special problem of the law of privilege in group therapy. Next we will summarize major principles and offer some recommendations. Finally we will return to Dr. Novice's problem and raise some questions (and attempt to formulate some answers) concerning his prospects for release from incarceration.

LEGAL AND SOCIAL POLICY UNDERPINNINGS

Undeniably, the protection of client privacy is a laudable aim, but it is in direct conflict with other fundamental interests of society;

---

*Comments, Notes, and Recent Decisions are designations of law student articles published by law reviews. Tradition holds that law students are not given credit, by name, for what they write.

the administration of justice and the ascertainment of truth in legal proceedings. The pursuance of these aims depends upon the court's ability to hear and receive all material and relevant evidence (materiality and relevance are defined later in this chapter). Because testimony is one of the major sources of information in a legal proceeding, justice and truth can only be achieved fully if the government has the broad power to compel persons to testify.

> For more than three centuries it has now been recognized as a fundamental maxim that the public . . . has a right to every man's evidence. When we come to examine the various claims of exemption, we start with the primary assumption that there is a general duty to give what testimony one is capable of giving, and that any exemptions which may exist are distinctly exceptional, being so many derogations from a positive general rule.[39]

Every immunity from the obligation to testify "impedes the achievement of an indispensable requirement of civilized life, the fair administration of justice. Exemptions lessen the fairness of a trial, inasmuch as a trial is only as good as the evidence considered by the court."[33]

However, society also recognizes that there are certain relationships so important to our social system, which depend for their full effectiveness on the total mutual confidence and trust of the participating parties, that the communications between such parties should be considered privileged, i.e. protected against revelation in a formal proceeding as a matter of public policy. Thus, the fundamental consideration as to whether certain information and knowledge can be withheld by witnesses in legal proceedings is "whether . . . the injury to the relationship resulting from disclosure would be greater than the loss to justice if the information were considered privileged."[31]

The conflict between these two interests are apparent in Dr. Novice's case. The determination of guilt or innocence may very well be aided if his testimony concerning the Midsons' interaction with their son is disclosed during their trial. On the other hand, there may be strong countervailing considerations that justify Dr. Novice's refusal to testify about what he learned in the therapeutic relationship.

The primary countervailing consideration that has justified the creation of privileged communications laws involving mental health professionals is the "depth and extraordinarily intimate nature of the patient's revelations"[42] that practitioners hear in psychodiagnostic and psychotherapeutic settings.

The psychiatric patient confides more utterly than anyone else in the world. He exposes to the therapist not only what his words directly express; he lays bare his entire self, his dreams, his fantasies, his sins, and his shame. Most patients who undergo psychotherapy know this is what will be expected of them, and that they cannot get help except on that condition . . . . It would be too much to expect them to do so if they knew that all they say—and all the psychiatrist learns from what they say—may be revealed to the whole world from a witness stand.[14,43,79]

But protection of the client is not the only foundation upon which such privileged communications laws rest.

Inviolability of the confidence is essential to achievement of the psychotherapeutic goal. Without foreknowledge that confidentiality will attach, the patient will be extremely reluctant to reveal to his therapist the details of his past life and his introspective thoughts and feelings. Without the patient's confidence a psychiatrist's efforts are worthless. We believe that the goals of therapy may be frustrated if the privilege would make it doubtful whether either psychotherapists or their patients could communicate effectively if it were thought that what they said could be disclosed compulsorily in a court of law.[17,41]

Some courts have also granted the privilege because of their concern that therapists may be forced to breach ethical codes at the risk of jail.

Because of the special nature of a patient's confidences, the psychotherapist is subject to even more stringent honorable obligation not to disclose, under any circumstances, than are other professionals. We do not wish psychotherapists to be faced with the dilemma of either violating this extraordinary trust or being incarcerated.[41]

In addition to the recognition that "psychotherapy is perhaps more dependent on absolute confidentiality than other . . . disciplines"[44] a few courts have asserted that the "patient's interest in keeping . . . confidential revelations from public purview, in retaining this substantial privacy, . . . draws sustenance from our constitutional heritage."[45] In a series of decisions beginning in 1965, the Supreme Court has found that the right of privacy embedded in the U.S. Constitution prevents certain intrusions by the State into people's private lives. In most cases, these have involved interference into sexual and family privacy (e.g. marital relations, access to contraceptives, the right of parents to educate and rear children, the right of females to secure abortions, the right to possess sexual material, and to satisfy one's intellectual and emotional needs within the confines of one's home). Because it is these very matters that become the subject of diagnostic and therapeutic communications ("Communications between a patient and his or her psychotherapist often involved intimate . . . problems of family, marriage, motherhood and fatherhood, human sexuality, and almost always concern strong emotional needs of the patient"[44] [the dissenting opinion of Judge Hufsteadler]), it has been suggested that the protections afforded by privileged communications laws may be constitutionally mandated.

Thus, it is because society wishes to provide an atmosphere for the revelations of the client's innermost thoughts, to promote a confidential relationship between the client and the therapist, and to protect the privacy rights of the client that some states have chosen to accord the clients of certain mental health professionals the right to prevent the professional from testifying as to confidential communications despite the competing interest of "facilitating the ascertainment of truth in connection with legal proceedings."[45]

PRIVILEGED COMMUNICATION EXPLAINED: STATUTORY EXAMPLES

We have traced the strong social policy reasons and possible constitutional bases for the principle of privileged communications. However, the primary legal source of the privilege comes from state statutes or, in the federal courts, from the federal rules of evidence (which we will consider later in this section). With regard to state legal proceedings, the privilege generally does not exist except as specifically permitted under state law. There are only three reported cases[41,46,47] in which the assertion of the privilege was upheld in the absence of particular legislation. (When judges develop legal rules it is known as common law; law passed by legislatures is known as statutory law.) Those cases should be considered anomalies, and readers should not depend on judges sustaining a refusal to testify unless there is a statute supporting that refusal.

The privilege that psychologists may be permitted to invoke is found in any one of a variety of state statutes. Some privileged communication laws are embedded in psychologist licensure/certification statutes, some in specific psychotherapist-patient statutes (thus according the privilege more on the basis of function than of title), and some in attorney-client privilege statutes when the psychologist acts as an agent of the attorney (i.e. has examined a client under direction of the client's lawyer prior to litigation to enable the attorney to determine whether or not to raise the client's mental condition as an issue).

At this point we will scrutinize a small but representative sample of privileged communication statutes so that readers can better understand the variety, scope, and limitations of such laws.

California: An Example of a Psychotherapist-Patient Privilege Statute

We will take a rather long and involved look at the California law. It has many features found in other state statutes, is very instructive, and has been the subject of two important legal decisions. It is reproduced, in pertinent part, below:[48]

§ *1010. "Psychotherapist"*
As used in this article, "psychotherapist" means:
(a) A person authorized, or reasonably believed by the patient to be authorized, to practice medicine in any state or nation who devotes, or is reasonably believed by the patient to devote, a substantial portion of his time to the practice of psychiatry—
(b) A person licensed as a psychologist . . .;
(c) A person licensed as a clinical social worker . . . when he is engaged in applied psychotherapy of a nonmedical nature;
(d) A person who is serving as a school psychologist and holds a credential authorizing such service issued by the state;
(e) A person licensed as a marriage, family and child counselor . . . .
§ *1011. "Patient"*
As used in this article, "patient" means a person who consults a psychotherapist or submits to an examination by a psychotherapist for the purpose of securing a diagnosis or preventive, palliative, or curative treatment of his mental or emotional condition or who submits to an examination of his mental or emotional condition for the purpose of scientific research on mental or emotional problems.
§ *1012. "Confidential communication between patient and psychotherapist"*
As used in this article, "confidential communication between patient and psychotherapist" means information, including information obtained by an examination of the patient, transmitted between a patient and his psychotherapist in the course of that relationship and in confidence by a means which, so far as the patient is aware, disclosed the information to no third persons other than those who are present to further the interest of the patient in the consultation or those to

whom disclosure is reasonably necessary for the transmission of the information or the accomplishment of the purpose for which the psychotherapist is consulted, and includes a diagnosis made and the advice given by the psychotherapist in the course of that relationship.

§ *1013. "Holder of the privilege"*

As used in this article, "holder of the privilege" means:

(a) The patient when he has no guardian or conservator.

(b) A guardian or conservator of the patient when the patient has a guardian or conservator.

(c) The personal representative of the patient if the patient is dead.

§ *1014. Psychotherapist-patient privilege*

The patient, whether or not a party, has a privilege to refuse to disclose, and to prevent another from disclosing, a confidential communication between patient and psychotherapist if the privilege is claimed by:

(a) The holder of the privilege:

(b) A person who is authorized to claim the privilege by the holder of the privilege; or

(c) The person who was the psychotherapist at the time of the confidential communication, but such person may not claim the privilege if there is no holder of the privilege in existence or if he is otherwise instructed by a person authorized to permit disclosure . . .

§ *1016. Exception: Patient-litigant exception*

There is no privilege under this article as to a communication relevant to an issue concerning the mental or emotional condition of the patient if such issue has been tendered by:

(a) The patient; . . .

§ *1017. Exception: Court-appointed psychotherapist*

There is no privilege under this article if the psychotherapist is appointed by order of a court to examine the patient, but this exception does not apply where the psychotherapist is appointed by order of the court upon the request of the lawyer for the defendant in a criminal proceeding in order to provide the lawyer with information needed so that he may advise the defendant whether to enter or withdraw a plea based on insanity or to present a defense based on his mental or emotional condition.

§ *1018. Exception: Crime or tort*

There is no privilege under this article if the services of the psychotherapist were sought or obtained to enable or aid anyone to commit or plan to commit a crime or a tort or to escape detection or apprehension after the commission of a crime or a tort.

§ *1020. Exception: Breach of duty arising out of psychothera-*

pist-patient relationship

There is no privilege under this article as to communication relevant to an issue of breach, by the psychotherapist or by the patient, of a duty arising out of the psychotherapist-patient relationship.

§ *1024. Exception: Patient dangerous to himself or others*

There is no privilege under this article if the psychotherapist has reasonable cause to believe that the patient is in such mental or emotional condition as to be dangerous to himself or to the person or property of another and that disclosure of the communication is necessary to prevent the threatened danger.

§ *1027. Privilege nonexistent; patient child under 16 or victim of crime*

There is no privilege under this article if all of the following circumstances exist:

(a) The patient is a child under the age of 16.

(b) The psychotherapist has reasonable cause to believe that the patient has been the victim of a crime and that disclosure of the communication is in the best interest of the child.

§ *1028. Criminal proceedings*

Unless the psychotherapist is a person described in subdivision (a) or (b) of Section 1010, there is no privilege under this article in a criminal proceeding.

This statute appears in California's Evidence Code as one of a series of privilege statutes. Sections 1010–1013 are primarily definitional. Because this particular law is limited to psychotherapists and their patients, only those so defined are protected. Under § 1010 licensed and properly credentialed school psychologists are considered psychotherapists. Under § 1011 persons are considered patients if they visit psychologists for purposes of diagnosis or treatment. In some states only information communicated in the course of treatment may be covered.

Section 1012 defines more or less precisely the kinds of information that are potentially privileged. Only those conversations that occur within a professional relationship for the purposes of assessment and intervention may be protected and then only when they are communicated in confidence. Social intercourse is not protected. Further, if the client knows that the message may be communicated to third persons not involved in either the diagnostic or treatment process, such communication is not privileged under California (and other state) law. The importance of the principle that the communications must be uttered in confidence is illustrated by an Oregon case. Prior to a hearing to determine whether their parental rights should be terminated, a psychologist examined two parents who allegedly were neglecting their three children. The assessment was performed pursuant to a Children's Services Division request who paid for the examination. Consent for the evaluation was given by the parents' attorney after consultation with them in which they were told that the results of the examination would be used in the proceedings in which the psychologist would testify. The parents attempted to block his testimony, invoking Oregon's psychologist privilege communication statute, but were unsuccessful, the court concluding the following:

> Counsel gave consent to the psychological examination. He and the parents knew its purpose and that the psychologist would testify as to his conclusion in the termination proceedings. The privilege of (Oregon's law) does not apply, because on the one hand they were not the psychologist's "clients" "in the course of his professional employment," . . . and he was not examined as to any advice he gave them; . . . the circumstances would amount to a waiver of the privilege, if any existed.[49]

Section 1013 lists those who hold the privilege. Although there is some refinement of the matter in §1014, the holder of the privilege is the client, not the psychologist. This rule is a basic provision of privileged communication statutes. A psychologist may feel free not to testify only when clients do not waive *their* privilege to bar the testimony. This principle is reiterated in § 1014, the major provision of California's statute. It is the client who "has the privilege to refuse to disclose, and to prevent another from disclosing . . . " However, as stated in § 1014(c) , the psychologist may also claim the privilege when there is no existing holder of the privilege (i.e. clients or their guardians or personal representatives) or the holder has not *expressly* waived the privilege. For psychologists to attempt to invoke the privilege when the client does not wish the psychologist to do so is to risk being held in contempt of court. Section 1014 contains one further subtlety. The statutes protect more than communications made *by* the client. While clients hold the privilege, they can prevent confidential disclosures made by psychologists in the course of diagnosis or treatment; it is information "transmitted *between* a patient and his psychotherapist" (emphasis added) that is protected.

What is left undefined in the principle provisions of the psychotherapist-patient privilege statute is a statement of the particular proceedings to which the statute applies. The therapist-patient privilege is only one of several relationships California recognizes (among others, attorney-client, physician-patient, clergy-penitent, husband-wife—though not in the same terms as the psychotherapist-patient relationship). It is in the provisions relating to privileges generally that psychologists in California (and other states where statutes are similarly constructed) would have to find the precise settings in which testimony cannot be compelled. In California's Evidence Code, the privilege applies (though attenuated by exceptions) in "any action, hearing, investigation, inquest or inquiry (whether conducted by a court, administrative agency, hearing officer, arbitrator, legislative body, or any other person authorized by law) in which, pursuant to law, testimony can be compelled to be given."[48] Thus, confidential communications are protected in civil and criminal actions, administrative proceedings (e.g. local and state hearings held by education agencies to determine appropriate provision of special education evaluation and placement under Pub. L. 94-142, the Education for All Handicapped Children Act), legislative hearings, grand jury proceedings, coroners' inquests, and arbitration proceedings.

The remaining sections of the statute, which we will discuss extensively, define exceptions to the psychotherapist-patient privilege. We will postpone discussion of the two most important of these § § 1016 and 1024, while we briefly note the others quoted above. Section 1017 illustrates that where there is no expectation of privacy of confidentiality, the privilege does not pertain.* Persons examined under court order cannot invoke the privilege. Section 1018 is popularly known as the "future crimes" exception although the literal language of the provision creates a broad exception. Section 1020 provides protection for both psychotherapists and their clients. If a therapist should sue a client (e.g. for failure to pay a bill) or vice versa (e.g. sexual assault, professional negligence) the defendant in such suits cannot invoke the privilege to prevent relevant testimony

---

*In a suit brought by parents challenging standards used for evaluating and placing emotionally handicapped students in special schools in which plaintiff's sought fifty randomly selected anonymous diagnostic and referral files containing the results of psychological and psychiatric consultations and examinations, a federal court held that the defendant school system's claim of privilege had to yield. The court concluded that an asserted privileged communication standard could not protect the material sought because it was unlikely that there was an expectation of privacy by the students or their families in making their communications and because third parties had access to the data.[50]

as long as the alleged breach of duty arose out of the psychotherapist-patient relationship. Section 1027 is a rather parentalistic limitation on the privilege. Psychotherapists are permitted to disclose confidential information when, in their discretion, disclosure will serve a child's best interest—a vague standard difficult to define. Thus, children under sixteen who have been victims of crimes have less assurance that their confidential communications will be safeguarded than do adults in similar circumstances. Section 1028 clearly distinguishes among the professionals denominated in § 1010 with regard to the privilege in criminal proceedings, demonstrating that the provisions contained within a privileged communication statute may not be uniformly applied to all professionals. Only licensed psychologists and psychiatrists can invoke the privilege in criminal cases; school psychologists can be compelled, therefore, to testify in such proceedings even if their clients order them not to.

The Patient-Litigant Exception

Section 1016 states an important limitation to the general principle of privileged communication. The privilege does not apply to information concerning mental or emotional conditions clients place in issue. For example, in civil proceedings the client-plaintiff may claim that as a result of negligence by the defendant (as in an automobile accident) he or she sustained some psychic as well as physical injury. Or, in a criminal prosecution, the client-defendant may assert insanity as a defense. In both cases, clients have placed their psychological condition in issue and under California law (as in other states) under the patient-litigant exception once clients do this, confidential communications relevant to their mental state are no longer protected.

Psychotherapists have attacked the patient-litigant exception in two landmark California decisions, *In re Lifschutz*[45] and *Caesar* v. *Mountanos*,[44] claiming that it is unconstitutional. Lifschutz, a psychiatrist, was imprisoned by a San Mateo county sheriff after he was adjudged in contempt of court for refusing to obey its orders to answer questions and produce records relating to communications with a former patient. The patient had filed a complaint against a defendant claiming that the defendant's assault caused him severe mental and emotional stress as well as physical injuries. When the defendant found out that Lifschutz had once seen the plaintiff for therapy he subpoenaed the psychiatrist to give a deposition (a pretrial method of discovering information in civil suits). Although Lifschutz appeared for the deposition he refused to produce any of his former patient's medical records, to answer any questions relating to his treatment, or even to disclose whether the plaintiff had in fact been his patient. After a number of rulings by the courts ordering the psychiatrist to testify and his continual refusal to comply, he was held in contempt and arrested. It was in the context of Lifschutz' attempt to attain a writ of habeas corpus securing his release that the California supreme court considered the constitutionality of the patient-litigant exception.

Lifschutz claimed, among other things, that § 1016(a) violated his constitutional right to privacy, unconstitutionally infringed on his right to practice his profession effectively, and failed to protect his client's right to privacy. The court found none of Lifschutz's claims compelling enough to rule the patient-litigant exception unconstitutional. It dismissed the assertion that his personal right to privacy was infringed, finding that the privacy right, if it existed, existed only as part of his client's right: "The psychotherapist, though undoubtedly deeply involved in the communicative treatment, does not exert a significant privacy interest separate from his patient." It also was not convinced that Lifschutz' right to practice was unduly affected by the exception. The court stated that while psychotherapists may suffer some economic loss as a result of the required disclosure, the regulation of economic interests by the government was not unconstitutional *per se* and that "although all compelled disclosure may interfere to some extent with an individual's performance of his work, such requirements have been universally upheld so long as the compelled disclosure is reasonable in light of a related and important governmental purpose." The court found the interference, on balance, justifiable as a means of facilitating the ascertainment of truth and the just resolution of legal claims. It also found that despite the existence of similar laws in other states creating exceptions to the privilege that the practice of psychotherapy had grown, "indeed flourished." While recognizing that clients may be ignorant of these exceptions and thus continue to seek therapy only because they are unaware that their private communications may someday be revealed in a legal proceeding, the court refused to rule in favor of Lifschutz. (Following the ruling Lifschutz did give a deposition stating only that he had seen the client in 1955, ten years prior to the assault, but refused to add any other information claiming that it was irrelevant. When the trial judge studied the patient's records he agreed that it contained no relevant evidence.)[51]

The court did provide some measure of protection to the psychiatrist and his client, however:

> The patient-litigant exception allows only a limited inquiry into the confidences of the psychotherapist-patient relationship, compelling disclosure of only those matters directly relevant to the nature of the specific "emotional or mental" condition which the patient has voluntarily disclosed and tendered in his pleadings or in answer to discovery inquiries. Furthermore . . . trial courts . . . may utilize the protective measures at their disposal to avoid unwarranted intrusions into the confidences of the relationship.

Thus, the waiver of the privilege only encompasses those mental conditions that clients have disclosed as claims or defenses in an action in which they are in issue. Any other disclosures, even though they may be relevant to the civil action cannot be compelled. For example, the court said Lifschutz could not be forced to testify as to aggressive tendencies or other personal attributes that might have been related to the assault (surely relevant to a defendant's self-defense claim) because they were not placed in issue by the plaintiff-client himself: "The patient thus is not obligated to sacrifice all privacy to seek redress for a specific mental or emotional injury; the scope of the inquiry permitted depends upon the nature of the injuries which the patient-litigant himself has brought before the court." As for protective mechanisms to prevent broad, unauthorized disclosure, the California supreme court indicated that the trial judge could issue protective orders during the deposition process to limit revelations and could rule at trial to exclude testimony the evidentiary value of which was outweighed by the probability that its admission would create a substantial danger of undue prejudice.

Six years later, the issues adjudicated in *In re Lifschutz* (1970) were once again considered, this time in the federal courts in a case called *Caesar* v. *Mountanos* (1976).[44] Between 1970 and 1976 the United States Supreme Court had more fully delineated the right of privacy including the principle of patient-physician privacy (at least with regard to abortions) in *Roe* v. *Wade* (1973).[52] In that light, Caesar, also a psychiatrist, who had been held in contempt and sentenced to jail for refusing to disclose any information about one of his clients, apparently believed that the courts might be more inclined to rule that the patient-litigant exception was unconstitutional. Caesar's client had been involved in two automobile accidents, sought therapy for emotional problems she felt she incurred as a result, and was now a plaintiff in an action seeking to recover money damages for her injuries. When ordered to appear for a deposition, Caesar refused to answer any questions regarding his treatment of the client asserting that any revelations could be harmful to her psychological well-being.

Caesar's optimism that *Roe* v. *Wade* and other privacy cases would tip the balance in favor of therapist-client confidentiality was unfounded. The Ninth Circuit Court of Appeals (the middle level court in the federal system that hears appeals from federal trial courts) did recognize that privacy was a substantial, perhaps even fundamental, right and that § 1016 might require "litigants to make some hard choices before bringing a lawsuit and may in fact discourage some legal actions." But, as have other courts, it viewed privacy as a "conditional rather than absolute" right that could be infringed "if properly justified." The justification was once again found in the compelling interest of the state to determine the truth in legal proceedings:

> The . . . questions Dr. Caesar declined to answer all related directly to his opinion whether Miss S. suffered emotional distress or depression from the accidents, whether any condition Dr. Caesar found was the result of a combination of the accidents and other factors in her life, and whether the psychological factors he found played a role in the origin or aggravation of the cervical pain which Miss S. testified she was suffering from. The questions were all clearly relevant and related directly to the issue of her mental and emotional condition which Miss S. herself had raised . . . .
>
> We conclude that . . . § 1016 . . . strikes a proper balance between the conditional right of privacy encompassing the psychotherapist-patient relationship and the state's compelling need to insure the ascertainment of truth . . . . The Plaintiff has placed her mental and emotional condition in issue. By raising this issue she herself has breached the confidential relationship and made her emotional problems known to the public.

While Lifschutz and Caesar have been discussed and criticized[18, 27,28,51,53,54,55] (see also dissenting opinion of Judge Hufsteadler in *Caesar* v. *Mountanos,* 1976) they stand as landmark cases clearly demarcating the limits of the law of privileged communication. They stand only as legal precedents in California and those states that have provisions like California's in the jurisdictional areas of the Ninth Circuit (California, Washington, Oregon, Idaho, Nevada,

Montana, Arizona) but they are of influential import in any jurisdiction in which the patient-litigant exception occurs.

The Dangerous Patient Exception

Section 1024 represents another important and controversial exception to the privileged communication doctrine. On its face, this section permits therapists to take steps to prevent future injury if they believe their clients may be dangerous to themselves, to others, or to the property of others. What is apparently contemplated in this exception is a means for barring the invocation of privileged communication by clients when therapists choose to testify in civil commitment proceedings. As written, this seemingly limited exception is discretionary, prospective, and preventive. That is, it is framed in terms of a *right,* not a duty to disclose; it should be invoked only when therapists believe that their clients *will* be dangerous;[56] the right is triggered only when the therapist believes that disclosure is necessary to *prevent* threatened danger.[57]

However, the "dangerous patient" exception has been given retrospective, not prospective, application in a recent California case. In *People* v. *Hopkins* (1975)[58] the court decided that a client could be barred from invoking the privilege if the court, not the therapist, believed that the client *had been* dangerous. Hopkins, after being assured of confidentiality, told a hospital therapist of his recent participation in certain violent crimes. The therapist then sent him, alone, in a taxi to another branch of the hospital. When Hopkins repeated his story to two nurses they called hospital security personnel who subsequently notified the police. At his criminal trial Hopkins sought to suppress his confession to the therapist but the court admitted it. On appeal, the appellate court upheld the trial judge's decision to deny Hopkins' motion to suppress: "From the evidence the trial court reasonably concluded that the psychotherapist had reasonable cause to believe that Hopkins (was dangerous under the terms of § 1024). Under the circumstances Hopkins held no privilege under the Evidence Code . . . ." The consequences of this judicial interpretation of an existing statute is noted in the following:

> By changing the criterion for the applicability of section 1024 from "disclosure . . . is necessary to prevent . . . threatened danger" to "disclose *was* necessary" the *Hopkins* court altered the orientation of the dangerous-patient exception. The use of the exception in *Hopkins* was not for the purpose of preventing harm; rather, it was

applied retrospectively to defeat a claim of privilege . . . . The determination was made, not by the therapist, but after the fact by the court. Apparently, the therapist's conclusion was that the patient was not dangerous and that disclosure was not necessary . . . . The court may determine the applicability of the exception after the fact, even in the face of a contrary determination by the therapist at the time.[57]

Not only has the prospective nature of § 1024 been changed but so has its apparently discretionary property. In *Tarasoff* v. *Regents of the University of California* (1974, 1976)[59] the therapist's right to disclose has been transformed into a duty. In *Tarasoff,* a college student seeing a psychologist for voluntary outpatient treatment informed his therapist that he was going to kill a young woman he had been dating when she returned from a summer vacation. The psychologist telephoned the campus police to initiate commitment proceedings but the police released the client after he promised to stay away from the woman. The client never returned to the clinic and two months later he carried out his threat. The parents of the victim then filed a complaint against the therapist (and others) claiming that he was negligent in failing to warn their daughter (or her parents) of the threatened danger to her life disclosed by his client. The psychologist moved that the complaint against him should be dismissed on the ground that he had done all that he should have done and that he had no duty to warn private third parties. However, the California supreme court ruled that "the public policy favoring the confidential character of patient-psychologist communications must yield in instances in which disclosure is essential to avert danger to others. The protective privilege ends where the public peril begins." "When a therapist determines, or pursuant to the standards of his profession should determine, that his patient presents a serious danger of violence to another, he incurs an obligation to use reasonable care to protect the intended victim against such danger."[59]

In creating this duty the court relied on § 1024 as evidence of the legislature's intent to counterbalance the important interest of confidentiality in therapeutic communications by what it considered an even more important interest, that of public safety. The reliance on the dangerous patient exception in privileged communication statutes (which deal only with in-court testimony) to establish an obligation to disclose in nonjudicial settings has been severely criticized;[57,60,61] (see also dissenting opinion of Justice Clark in *Tarasoff* v. *Regents,* 1976, p. 357) but the decision exists, has the force of prec-

edent in California, and may be extremely persuasive in other jurisdictions where similar dangerous patient provisions exist. The un-
tenable role in which this places psychologist has been commented
on[61,62] but the decision should alert readers to the fact that naive reliance on both ethical codes encouraging confidentiality and privileged communication statutes is fraught with danger.

Two Briefer Examples: Illinois and New York

Illinois' privileged communications statute is not part of the evidence code but is contained within its Psychologist Registration Act:

> § *406. Disclosure of information by psychologists—Prohibition—Ex-
> ception*[63]
>
> No psychologist shall disclose any information he may have ac-
> quired from persons consulting him in his professional capacity, neces-
> sary to enable him to render services in his professional capacity, to
> such persons except only: (1) in trials for homicide when the disclos-
> ure relates directly to the fact or immediate circumstances of the
> homicide; (2) in all proceedings the purpose of which is to determine
> mental competency, or in which a defense of mental incapacity is raised;
> (3) in actions, civil or criminal, against the psychologist for mal-
> practice; (4) with the expressed consent of the client, or in the case
> of his death or disability, of his personal representative or other person
> authorized to sue or of the beneficiary of an insurance policy on his
> life, health or physical condition; or (5) upon an issue as to the
> validity of a document as a will of a client.

This statute pertains solely to psychologists (not psychotherapists)
certified under the Registration Act and thus accords the privilege
on the basis of title, not function. It does not include school psychologists who have not met the requirements of the Act nor other mental
health professionals not defined as certified psychologists. There is
another notable difference between this and California's law; in Illinois
there is no privileged communications protection for anyone in prosecutions for homicide (murder, manslaughter, negligent homicide)
when the confidential information is directly relevant to the "fact or
immediate circumstances of the homicide" itself. The statute also
reiterates the important principle that only *professional* communications are barred.

New York's law provides yet another method for establishing privileged communications:

> § *4507. Psychologist*[64]
>
> The confidential relations and communications between a psychol-

ogist registered under the provisions of article one hundred fifty-three of the education law and the client are placed on the same basis as those provided by law between attorney and client, and nothing in such article shall be construed to require any such privileged communications to be disclosed.

Like Illinois, only psychologists licensed as private practitioners in New York are within the domain of this statute. Unlike the other two statutes we have surveyed, the precise contours of privileged communication are not set out separately but must be found by referring to the applicable provision of the attorney-client law.[65]

Federal Courts

We have surveyed three major examples of state statutes but these pertain to testimony in state courts only. Many practitioners are called on to testify in federal cases as well where state law may not be applicable. Thus, it would be helpful if psychologists were familiar with the federal rules as well. An advisory committee appointed to formulate rules of evidence for the federal courts recommended that Congress adopt a psychotherapist-patient privilege that would have included psychologists. However, Congress decided not to accept that recommendation and adopted a single general rule instead of the thirteen separate privilege laws drafted by the advisory committee. That single rule, now in force, states the following:

> Except as otherwise required by the Constitution of the United States or provided by Act of Congress or in rules prescribed by the Supreme Court . . . , the privilege of a witness . . . shall be governed by the principles of a common law as they may be interpreted by the courts of the United States in the light of reason and experience. However, in civil actions and proceedings, with respect to an element of a claim or defense as to which State law supplies the rule of decision, the privilege of a witness . . . shall be determined in accordance with State law.[66]

This rather arcane and legalistic language is the result of a compromise between the House and the Senate after they rejected the advisory committee's proposal. The analysis of this statute is far beyond the scope and intent of this chapter but we will attempt a brief explanation of the rule (for a fuller analysis see Weinstein and Berger).[67] In federal criminal cases the application rule is that the right to invoke privileged communication protection are governed by federal judge-made (or common) law. Each federal jurisdiction may develop precedents governing the existence of the privilege even though Congress has not passed any statute to that effect. However, Weinstein and Berger[67] suggest that psychologists may rely upon the proposed (and rejected) federal psychotherapist-patient privilege, not as a law but to create a standard by which to evaluate "reason and experience" cited in Rule 501. Though the psychotherapist-patient privilege was not ultimately adopted by Congress it was proposed by an advisory committee of judges, lawyers, and legal scholars who labored through three drafts and whose work was approved by an eight to one vote of the Supreme Court. The creation of a federal common law of privilege may, however, create inequities. Defendants in a state criminal prosecution may be able to invoke the privilege whereas if they are tried in the same state under federal law in a federal court they may not.[16]

In cases arising under the Constitution or Acts of Congress the federal common law also prevails. But in cases in which a citizen of one state sues the citizen of another (such cases are called diversity suits and most can be heard in Federal Court) or where state law may govern, Rule 501 requires that State privileged communications law controls. The problem with that rule is that it is often ambiguous when a state law "supplies the rule of decision" with regard "to an element of a claim or defense." It is often unclear when a claim or defense is grounded in state law and even judges have difficulty making that determination.

Interpretation of Statutes

The concept of privileged communications did not exist in early legal history. Only the attorney-client privilege was recognized in the common law. Thus, every statute creating the right to invoke the protections of privileged communication is in derogation of the common law. For this reason, they are generally strictly construed and limited in their application by judges who by law are given the responsibility to interpret them. Thus, in a state where there is no psychotherapist/psychologist-patient privilege, psychologists will probably be compelled to testify. For example, a psychologist, but not a psychiatrist, was required to give evidence, although both had treated the defendant because the state in which the case arose only had a physician-patient privilege at the time.[68] Similarly, the protection of a statutory psychiatrist-patient privilege was not extended to a plaintiff who had brought an automobile negligence suit and revealed to his psychologist during the course of treatment that he was responsible for the accident.[69] On the other hand, a psychiatrist was compelled to testify in a divorce action because at the time there was no physician-patient statute in a state where there was a psychologist-patient privilege.[70] The same principles would hold with regard to particular proceedings. If the statute affords protection only in criminal matters, it would not be applicable in child custody disputes, divorce actions, or negligence suits.

However, while courts often narrowly construe privilege statutes to apply in those situations or to those persons specifically named it is probably true that "once a court has determined that a privilege exists, the courts may construe the privilege liberally to protect the patient's interests."[71] For example, a psychologist was ordered to testify in a custody dispute in a Massachusetts court in which the husband contended that his wife was mentally unfit to care for the child. The wife had been seen by the psychologist who was licensed in New York. The psychologist refused to present evidence claiming that confidential communications between him and the defendant-wife were privileged under New York law. The court agreed, citing the New York psychologist-patient law, stating that the "protective statutory bulwark . . . may not be ignored. For it is obvious, that to grant the relief presently sought would be violative of the rights of a citizen of (New York)."[72]

Group Psychotherapy: A Special Problem

Privileged communications statutes primarily protect communications *between* the client and the psychologist and as such may be sufficient to protect confidentiality in the traditional dyadic relationship that occurs in diagnostic and treatment settings. But communications in group therapy flow not only between clients and therapists but among the clients themselves. As we have seen, privileged communications laws are disfavored because they bar the presentation of what may be vital and relevant information in legal proceedings and are thus strictly construed in the great majority of cases. Thus, the term "between" (as in § 1012 of the California statute) may be interpreted so as not to protect client-to-client communications—a common feature of group therapy interaction. Legislatures, as well as the courts, have been resistant to broadening protections to include group therapy. In 1969 the California Law Revision Commission recommended that § 1012 be amended to include information transmitted in confidence between a patient and the psychotherapist "including other patients present at joint therapy."[73]   The commission supported its proposal by stating the following:

> In the light of the frequent use of group therapy for the treatment of emotional and mental problems, it is important that this form of treatment be covered by the psychotherapist-patient privilege. The policy considerations underlying the privilege dictate that it encompass communications made in the course of group therapy . . . . The Commission has been advised that persons in need of treatment sometimes refuse group therapy . . . because the psychotherapist cannot assure the patient that the confidentiality of his communications will be preserved.

However, the Commission's recommendation was never adopted by the legislature.

Nevertheless, the few writers that have contemplated the problem[7,24,34] believe that a plausible case can be made for construing present law to include confidential communications among members of therapeutic groups.   One approach is to consider group members as assistants of the therapist.   For example, in many states in which a physician-patient privilege exists, nurses or technicians who aid the physician in diagnosis and treatment and who are present during the uttering of confidential information are precluded from testifying to the same extent as is the physician:

> It is quite possible that in a liberal jurisdiction a convincing argument could be made demonstrating that psychotherapy patients, being studied under group conditions by a therapist who himself is covered by the patient's privilege, are agents of the therapist and are thereby freed from a judicial requirement of disclosure. . . . They are performing a function of working with the therapist toward the correction of other patients' problems.[24]

Further, the words of California's § 1012 does protect communications to third persons who are present "to further the interest of the patient."   Kansas' privileged communications statute defines confidential communications so as to include "third persons . . . reasonably necessary for the transmission of the information or the accomplishment of the purpose for which it is transmitted."[74]   Given the purpose of group therapy it can be asserted that group members perform functions necessary for aiding, understanding and stimulating behavior change that underlie successful diagnosis and treatment.

Finally, it has been claimed that the word "between" includes client-to-client communication. "Because of the nature of group therapy any communication that the (psychologist) receives from a patient is between them, even though the patient addresses the statement to another patient."[7] The other group members would be considered "mere conduits for communication which, in the end result, are really directed to the therapist in his role as the ultimate producer of ameliorative changes in the patient."[24]

These arguments, however, must be taken for what they are. We have uncovered no judicial decisions in which the issue of the status of group members with regard to privileged communications was considered. While there may be strong policy grounds for the application of the privilege to group members as well as their therapists and ingenious interpretations of current statutes may be resorted to for sustaining the protection, psychologists should not assume that they can rely on existing laws that do not specifically mention group therapy to protect confidential communications among group members.

PRINCIPLES AND RECOMMENDATIONS

As a means of coalescing what we have written, we offer the following summary principles and recommendations:

1. In almost all instances the right to invoke the protection of privileged communications is created by statute. The Constitution may provide its source within the ambit of the right to privacy and a persuasive attorney may be successful in convincing a court of the constitutional demand for the protection of private communications between a psychologist and a client in the absence of a statute but it is risky to rely solely on the Constitution to assert the privilege. Because of the importance of ascertaining truth in legal proceedings, there is significant resistance in the absence of a specific statute permitting the assertion of privileges the consequence of which would be to bar testimony.

2. Privileged communications statutes are diverse in form and substance. While several states have adopted a psychotherapist-patient privilege recommended by the drafters of the Uniform Rules of Evidence,[78] many states still do not protect the clients of psychologist. Those states that do, provide the privilege in several different ways.

3. Psychologist should consult their state's statutory code to learn if a psychologist/psychotherapist-patient privilege exists in their jurisdiction. Such laws can be located by referring to the compilation of statutes found in every law school library, bar library, and most pub-

lic libraries. The collection of laws is found in what is called the *annotated code*. Each code has an index and the specific statute will almost always be printed in full under one of these headings: Psychologist; Privileged Communications; Evidence. The index will refer the reader to the particular Article or Chapter of the code and the precise section within them.

4. It is the ethical and legal responsibility of all psychologists to know the protections and limits of privileged communication statutes. What we have written should not be accepted as legal advice or definitive interpretations of statutes or cases. Authoritative construction of federal and state laws are the work of the courts, not scholars. Psychologists should read the existing statute in their jurisdiction carefully, consult the cases that are cited immediately after the statutory provision in the annotated code, refer to supplements to the code to keep up with amendments to the law and recent cases, seek interpretive help from the licensing or certification boards that regulate the practice of psychology, consult with attorneys expert in these matters, and communicate with state and national psychological organizations for further clarifications.

5. Privileged communication is a legal term embodying one aspect of the ethical concept of confidentiality. The privilege only bars testimony in designated legal proceedings. It neither precludes nor compels revelations in other settings. The protection of confidential communications outside the legal arena is controlled by professional codes of ethics with which psychologists should also be familiar.

6. Even if certain communications or relationships are not protected by a privilege statute, psychologists called upon to testify about private communications are under no compulsion to reveal all information they have received. To overcome the strong privacy interests inherent in a therapeutic relationship, the one who seeks to offer the evidence must show it has a legitimate interest in the information. That legitimacy is tested against the twin principles of *materiality* and *relevance*.

To be material the evidence must pertain to an issue in controversy. For example, testimony as to mental illness is immaterial if the case merely concerns whether someone did or did not sign a contract; it may be material if the issue was whether one of the parties to the contract was legally competent to sign it. If evidence is offered to prove a proposition not a matter in issue, it is immaterial. To be relevant the evidence must logically tend to prove material fact. The evidence must render an inference more probable than it would without it. Evidence as to the provision of psychotherapy ten years prior to a claim that an assault caused psychic injury is likely to be considered irrelevant (see our discussion of *In re Lifschutz*).

It is recommended, therefore, that psychologists called upon to testify request that those who attempt to compel such testimony demonstrate that the potential evidence is material and relevant (actually this and other requests discussed in this section should be made by the client's attorney). Further, to protect the privacy of the communications, demonstrations of materiality and relevancy should be done in judges' chambers (i.e. at an "in camera" hearing).

7. Certain relevant and material evidence can be excluded if the court rules that the probability of its proving a proposition more true than not (i.e. probative value) is outweighed by the probability of undue prejudice to the client. Revelations made by a client during therapy often contain elements of fear, fantasies, impulses, and dreams that may be far removed from the real world making them unreliable yet highly prejudicial communications. (In many instances such revelations would also be immaterial.)

8. Even if evidence is ruled admissible psychologists should seek protective orders limiting the scope of the inquiry so as to best preserve the rights of their clients. Such orders, issued by the court but requested by one of the parties, may strictly restrict the information disclosed, specify what matters, records, or documents must be testified about, and exclude the public during the psychologist's testimony.

9. Psychologists may decide that their own personal moral values and ethics preclude their testifying even if ordered to do so. However, psychologists who make that choice will find little protection in the law.

The American Psychological Association (APA) Revised Code of Ethics do provide some guidelines for the profession. Principle 3(c) states the following:

> In providing psychological services, psychologists avoid any action that will violate or diminish the legal and civil rights of clients . . . .
>
> As practitioners, psychologists remain abreast of relevant federal, state, local, and agency regulations and Association standards of practice. . . . They are concerned with developing such legal and quasi-legal regulations as best serve the public interest and in changing such existing regulations as are not beneficial to the interests of the public and the profession.[75]

The penalty for refusing to comply with a judge's order is citation for contempt of court, which may result in fine and/or imprisonment. The cases of Drs. Lifschutz and Caesar attest to the reality of these sanctions.

10. Psychologists should clearly inform their clients of the limits of confidentiality and privileged communications at the very beginning of a diagnostic or therapeutic relationship. This recommendation comports with both the demands of the APA Code of Ethics and the informed consent doctrine. The latter is an emerging rule of law developed in the context of physician-patient malpractice suits. Generally, among other points not relevant here, physicians violate their obligations to patients and subject themselves to liability for malpractice if they fail to reveal potential dangers and other important facts concerning suggested treatment. The philosophical underpinning to the informed consent doctrine is that everyone has the right to self-determination and as a result is entitled to all the facts necessary to make an informed, intelligent choice prior to consenting to medical intervention. Typically, however, the duty to disclose is not absolute. Rather, the extent of disclosure is determined by the materiality of the risk potentially incurred. Materiality is usually determined by the significance a reasonable person would attach to a risk. The possibility that psychologists can be compelled to testify as to confidential information in legal proceedings that may be harmful to their clients would clearly seem to be a material piece of information requiring disclosure to prospective patients.

The duty to disclose is also embedded in Principle 5(d) of the APA Revised Code of Ethics:

> The confidentiality of professional communications about individuals is maintained. Only when the originator and other persons involved give their express permission is a confidential professional communication shown to the individual concerned. *The psychologist is responsible for informing the clients of the limits of the confidentiality.*[75] (Emphasis added.)

The emphasized portion of the quoted principle makes clear the duty to warn clients. "It is evident that there are ever decreasing guarantees to client-clinician privacy and professional relationships are not immune from the scrutiny of society. Such limits must clearly be conveyed to . . . prospective clients because failure to do so can result in both their loss of liberty and privacy"[62] and to economic deprivation and incarceration for psychologists.

We should point out parenthetically that the nonitalicized portion of Principle 5(d) may lead the unwary psychologist right into jail. As we have discussed, the courts may require certain kinds of information to be disclosed without the express permission of the client, especially where no psychotherapist/psychologist-patient privilege exists. (For other ways in which codes of ethics fail to protect psychologists see Bersoff).[76]

DR. NOVICE REVISITED

We have left Dr. Novice languishing in the county jail during this long discussion and we feel duty bound to try to help him. We can, of course, only ask some questions relative to his case without offering a definitive solution.

1. Does a privileged communication statute exist in his state that includes psychologists? Without one Dr. Novice may be able to develop an argument grounded solely in the constitutional rights to privacy and liberty that he should not be compelled to testify. But, he would be asking the court to balance his client's right to privacy against the strong state interest in determining the truth in criminal proceedings. In the absence of a legislative determination that the balance should favor his clients, the court is not likely to rule in their favor on constitutional grounds alone. (Even a President's assertion of executive privilege did not convince the Supreme Court that the withholding of confidential information could be sustained in the context of a criminal prosecution).[77]

2. If a statute does exist, does it pertain to criminal proceedings? Some statutes exclude the privilege in such cases.

3. If the protective privilege does encompass criminal prosecutions, did the Midsons put their mental state in issue? If the Midsons defend the case by claiming that they were insane during the commission of the homicide or that their capacity to conform to the law was significantly diminished by some mental or emotional problems, confidential communications between them and Dr. Novice may not be protected because of the patient-litigant exception present in most privileged communications statutes.

4. Even if compelled to testify, what is Dr. Novice being asked to testify to? He can seek to limit his testimony to that which is directly and strictly material and relevant to the issues involved. Because there are strong interests protecting psychologist-client privacy, Dr. Novice can request the court's help in restricting what he has to dis-

close. He should be required to testify only to those matters that are material and relevant to the specific issue of criminal responsibility for the death of the Midson child.

5. If Dr. Novice is protected by a statutory privilege should he have agreed to reveal even that he saw the Midsons professionally? It may be appropriate for nonpsychiatric medical practitioners to reveal such information as initiation and termination of treatment and dates of patient visits but the revelation of such information by mental health professionals in the light of the possible stigmatizing function such information can serve may be inappropriate. Dr. Novice, in agreeing to state that he did see the Midsons and offering to disclose when he began and completed their professional relationship, may be unnecessarily violating a confidence as well as breaching the APA ethical code if an applicable privileged communication statute exists in his jurisdiction.

6. Assuming a protective privilege, did the Midsons waive their right to its provisions? The privilege belongs to the client although it may be invoked by the psychologist. But, if the Midsons want Dr. Novice to testify (because, for example, they believe his testimony might help exonerate them), Dr. Novice is precluded from invoking the privilege if the Midsons expressly waive their right to it.

REFERENCES

1. Alexander, J.R. California's new evidence code: Changes in the law of privileged communications relating to psychotherapy, *University of San Fernando Valley Law Review, 1,* 56–60, 1967.
2. Best, B.W. Privilege, in judicial or quasi-judicial proceedings, arising from relationship between psychiatrist or psychologist and patient, *American Law Reports 3d, 44,* 24–162, 1972.
3. Chafee, Z. Privileged communication: Is justice served or obstructed by closing the doctor's mouth on the witness stand? *Yale Law Journal, 52,* 607–609, 1943.
4. Comment. Federal rules of evidence and the law of privileges, *Wayne Law Review, 15,* 1286–1331, 1969.
5. Comment. Privileged communications: A Case-by-case approach *Maine Law Review, 443,* 448–450, 1971.
6. Comment. Underprivileged communications: Extension of the psychotherapist-patient privilege to patients of psychiatric social workers, *California Law Review, 61,* 1050–1071, 1973.
7. Cross, W. Privileged communications between participants in group psychotherapy, *Law and Social Order, 1970,* 191–211, 1970.

8. Diamond, B.L. and Weihofen, H. Privileged communication and the clinical psychologist, *Journal of Clinical Psychology, 9,* 388–391, 1953.

9. Fisher, R.M. The psychotherapeutic professions and the law of privileged communications, *Wayne Law Review, 10,* 609-654, 1964.

10. Fox, S. J. Psychotherapy and legal privilege, *Massachusetts Law Quarterly, 53,* 307–315, 1968.

11. Group for the Advancement of Psychiatry, Confidentiality and privileged communications in the practice of psychiatry, Report No. 45, New York; Group for the advancement of Psychiatry, June 1960.

12. Geiser, R.L. and Rheingold, P.D. Psychology and the legal process: Testimonial privileged communications, *American Psychologist, 19,* 831–838, 1968.

13. Goldstein, A.S. and Katz, J. Psychiatrist-patient privilege: The GAP proposal and the Connecticut statute, *American Journal of Psychiatry, 118,* 733–739, 1962.

14. Guttmacher, M.S. and Weihofen, H. Privileged communications between psychiatrist and patient, *Indiana Law Journal, 28,* 32–44, 1952.

15. Hollender, N.H. The psychiatrist and the release of patient information, *American Journal of Psychiatry, 116,* 828–833, 1960.

16. Louisell, D.W. Confidentiality, conformity and confusion: Privileges in federal courts today, *Tulane Law Review, 31,* 101–124, 1956.

17. Louisell, D.W. The psychologist in today's legal world: Part II, *Minnesota Law Review, 41,* 731-750, 1957.

18. Louisell, D.W. and Sinclair, K., Jr. Reflections on the law of privileged communications—The psychotherapist-patient privilege in perspective, *California Law Review, 59,* 30–55, 1971.

19. Love, G.H. and Yanity, G.J. Psychotherapy and the law, *Medical Trial Technique Quarterly, 20,* 405–429, 1974.

20. MacCormick, A. A criminologist looks at privilege, *American Journal of Psychiatry, 115,* 1068-1070, 1959.

21. McCormick, C.T. *Handbook of the law of evidence* (2nd ed.), St. Paul, Minnesota, West, 1972.

22. McDermott, P.A. Law, liability, and the school psychologist: Systems of law, privileged communication, and access to records, *Journal of School Psychology, 10,* 299–305, 1972.

23. Note. Confidential communications to a psychotherapist: A new testimonial privilege, *Northwestern Law Review, 47,* 384–389, 1952.

24. Note. Group therapy and privileged communications, *Indiana Law Journal, 43,* 93–105, 1967.

25. Note. Psychiatrist-patient relationship: A need for retention of the future crime exception, *Iowa Law Review, 52,* 1170–1186, 1967.

26. Note. A state statute to provide a psychotherapist-patient privilege, *Harvard Journal of Legislation, 4,* 307–324, 1968.

27. Note. Evidence—Privileged communications—A psychiatrist has no constitutional right to assert an absolute privilege against disclosure of psychotherapeutic communications, *Texas Law Review*, *49*, 929–942, 1971.

28. Note. Psychotherapy and Griswold: Is confidence a privilege or right? *Connecticut Law Review*, *3*, 599–606, 1971.

29. Note. Medical jurisprudence—Privileged communications between physician and patient—State regulation and right to privacy, *Tennessee Law Review*, *39*, 515–525, 1972.

30. Rappeport, J.R. Psychiatrist-patient privilege, *Maryland Law Review*, *23*, 39–49, 1963.

31. Shah, S.A. Privileged communications, confidentiality and privacy: Privileged communications, *Professional Psychology*, *1*, 56–69, 1969.

32. Schmidt, L.D. Some legal considerations for counseling and clinical psychologists, *Journal of Counseling Psychology*, *9*, 35–44, 1962.

33. Slovenko, R. Psychiatry and a second look at the medical privilege, *Wayne Law Review*, *6*, 175–203, 1960.

34. Slovenko, R. *Psychotherapy, confidentiality and privileged communication*, Springfield, Thomas, 1966.

35. Slovenko, R. Psychotherapist-patient testimonial privilege: A picture of misguided hope, *Catholic University Law Review*, *23*, 649–673, 1974.

36. Slovenko, R. Psychotherapy and confidentiality. *Cleveland State Law Review*, *24*, 375–396, 1975.

37. Slovenko, R. and Usdin, G.L. Privileged communication and right to privacy in diagnosis and therapy, *Current Psychiatric Therapies*, *3*, 277–319, 1963.

38. Witford, W.C. The physician, the law and the drug abuser, *University of Pennsylvania Law Review*, *119*, 933–969, 1971.

39. Wigmore, J.H. *Evidence in trials at common law*, Vol. 8 (McNaughton rev.), Boston, Little, Brown, 1961.

40. Zenoff, E. Confidential and privileged communications, *Journal of the American Medical Association*, *182*, 656–662, 1962.

41. Allred v. State 554 P.2d 411 (Alaska 1976).

42. United States *ex rel.* Edney v. Smith 425 F. Supp. 1038 (E.D.N.Y. 1976).

43. Taylor v. United States 22 F.2d 398 (D.C. Cir. 1952).

44. Caesar v. Mountanos 542 F.2d 1064 (9th Cir. 1976).

45. *In re* Lifschutz 2 Cal. 3d. 415, 467 P.2d 557, 85, Cal. Rpt. 829 (1970).

46. Binder v. Ruvell Civ. Docket No. 52-3-2535 (Cir. Ct., Cook County, Ill., 1952).

47. State v. Evans 104 Ariz. 434, 454 P.2d 976 (1969).

48. West's Ann Evid. Code § 8901, 1010–1028 (Cum. Supp. 1978).

49. State *ex rel.* Juv. Dept. of Multonomah Cty. v. Black 528 P.2d 130 (Or. App. 1974).

50. Lora v. Bd. of Educ. 77 F.R.D. 159 (E.D.N.Y. 1977).
51. Watson, A. Levels of confidentiality in the psychoanalytic situation, *Journal of the American Psychoanalytic Association, 20,* 156–176, 1972.
52. Roe v. Wade 410 U.S. 113 (1973).
53. Recent Decisions. Constitutional law—Right of privacy—Evidence law of privileges—The patient-litigant exception to the psychotherapist-patient privilege, *Loyola of Los Angeles Law Review, 10,* 695–707, 1977.
54. Suarez, J.M. and Hunt, J. The patient-litigant exception in psychotherapist-patient privilege cases, *UCLA-Alaska Law Review, 1,* 2–20, 1971.
55. Ziskin, J. Privileged communication: A note on the Lifschutz case, *Professional Psychology, 1,* 202–204, 1971.
56. Fleming, J.G. and Maximov. B. The patient or his victim: The therapist's dilemma, *California Law Review, 62,* 1025–1068, 1974.
57. Comment. Discovery of psychotherapist-patient communications after *Tarasoff, San Diego Law Review, 15,* 265–285, 1978.
58. People v. Hopkins 44 Cal. App. 3d 669, 119 Cal. Rpt. 61 (1975).
59. Tarasoff v. Regents of Univ. of Cal. 529 P.2d 553, 118 Cal. Rptr. 129 (1974), 17 Cal. 3d 425, 551 P. 2d. 334, 131 Cal. Rptr. 14 (1976).
60. Note. The dangerous patient exception and the duty to warn: Creation of a dangerous precedent? *University of California at Davis Law Review, 9,* 549–568, 1976.
61. Note. Imposing a duty to warn on psychiatrists—A judicial threat to the psychiatric profession, *University of Colorado Law Review, 48,* 283–310, 1977.
62. Bersoff, D.N. Therapists as protectors and policemen: New roles as a result of *Tarasoff? Professional Psychology, 7,* 267–273, 1976.
63. Ill. Ann. Stat. Ch. 91½ 5406 (Smith-Hurd), Ill. Rev. Stat. Ch 11 § 5306.
64. N.Y. Cir. Prac. Law §4507 (McKinney).
65. N.Y. Cir. Prac. Law § 4503 (McKinney).
66. Federal Rules of Evidence § 501.
67. Weinstein, J. and Berger, M.A. *Weinstein's evidence,* Vol. 2, New York, Matthew Bender, 1977.
68. State v. Bednasek Crim. Cause 2694 (Johnson Cty. Dist. Ct., Iowa, 1950).
69. Elliot v. Watkins Trucking Co. 406 F.2d 90 (7th Cir. 1969).
70. Ritt v. Ritt 98 N.J. Super 590, 238 A.2d 196 (1967).
71. Note. Psychiatrist's duty to the public: Protection from dangerous patients, *University of Illinois Law Forum, 76,* 1103–1128, 1976.
72. Application of Queen 233 N.Y.S. 2d 798 (1962).
73. California Law Revision Commission *Reports, recommendations, and studies,* Vol. 9, California, Author, 1969.
74. Kan Stat. Ann. § 60–427(a)(4).

75. American Psychological Association Revised code of ethics, *APA Monitor, 8,* 22, 1977.
76. Bersoff, D.N.   Professional ethics and legal responsibilities: On the horns of a dilemma, *Journal of School Psychology, 13,* 359–376, 1975.
77. United States v. Nixon   418 U.S. 683 (1976).
78. National Conference of Commissioners on Uniform State Laws Uniform Rules of evidence, In *Federal rules of evidence for United States courts and magistrates,* St. Paul, Minnesota, West, 1975.
79. Guttmacher, M.S. and Weihofen, H.   *Psychiatry and the law,* New York, Norton, 1952.
80. Barbre, E.S.   Communications to social worker as privileged, *American Law Reports 3d, 50,* 563–582, 1973.

Chapter 6

MALPRACTICE IN PSYCHOLOGY: LEGAL AND PROFESSIONAL ASPECTS

ORMA LINFORD, Ph.D.*

AND

E. ROBERT SINNETT, Ph.D.†

O NE OF THE most notable characteristics of American society in the 1970s is the frequency with which Americans go to court. While the law, both as an idea and a system of institutions, has always been held in high esteem in this country, there is a new dimension to the acceptance of decision-making by judges. A major weekly news magazine recently devoted the front cover and lead story to "one of the great unnoticed revolutions in U.S. history": the increasing willingness, "even eagerness," to deal with an ever-expanding range of both public and private problems through the legal system.[1] The "malpractice crisis" is an intense illustration of this trend, and while the concern about being sued is not as acute among psychotherapists as it is among physicians and surgeons, not only is it emerging as an increasingly important factor in the therapeutic relationship between mental health professional and client, but it presents significant public policy questions.

*Orma Linford teaches courses in constitutional law, judicial process and civil liberties at Kansas State University. She received her Ph.D. in political science from the University of Wisconsin, and her articles have been published in law reviews and other scholarly journals.

†E. Robert Sinnett has had varied experience in credentialing, peer reviews, and state association offices in Kansas. He has served on the nonstatutory certification board, has been chairman of the Board of Examiners of Psychologists, is a past president of the Kansas Psychological Association (KPA), and is currently serving as chairman of the Professional Standards Review Committee of the KPA.

73

THE PROBLEM

The American Psychological Association first offered liability insurance through a private carrier in 1955.[2] The levels of insurance ranged from a minimum of $5,000 per occasion to a maximum of $15,-000. The current options for levels of coverage range from a low level maximum of $100,000 per occasion to a higher option of $1,000,000 per occasion. Although there are a few cases that go to court, indications are that there has been a growth in the number of cases in the past twenty years, or so, and that a number of cases have been settled out of court.[3] Expectations are that there will be a continued growth in the number of suits filed.[4,5]

Professional periodicals that provide current news of such activities are the *APA Monitor* and *Psychiatric News,* the official newspaper of the American Psychiatric Association. In addition, some specialized coverage is provided for our medical and psychiatric colleagues in the *Malpractice Digest,* a publication of the American College of Legal Medicine and *Legal Aspects of Medical Practice.* Of more particular interest to psychologists is the recently established *Psychotherapy Finance* (formerly *Psychotherapy Economics*), which offers both a periodical as well as educational tapes.

Although there are no recently published compilations of types of problems for which adjudication is sought, Brownfain's study[3] and those of Kardener, Fuller and Mensh,[6] Holroyd and Brodsky,[7] and a recent survey[8] would indicate that erotic contact between client and therapist is very likely the most common problem. There are indications that physical aggression experienced by the client, particularly in encounter groups,[3,9,10,11] has also been a concern but one of lesser frequency.

Causes

While the increase in the number of lawsuits and other actions against psychotherapists can be attributed in part to the larger trend of increased litigation in general, there are other factors that indicate that the heightened interest in malpractice in the mental health profession is not merely part of the fallout from a spasm in the legal system, but has been generated by marked changes within the profession itself.

To begin with, more people are seeking and receiving the services of therapists. The public is being made aware that mental illness is a major public health problem, and as a result of educational campaigns launched from a variety of public and private sources, society has begun to look upon psychotherapy as an acceptable way to deal with personal problems. At the same time, the mental health professionals have become increasingly specialized, in many respects emulating the medical model, and areas of specialty have proliferated; this increased professionalization has brought about predictable uncertainty about jurisdiction, methods, and standards. These two developments have, inevitably, been accompanied by a steady increase in the cost of treatment. As the provision of mental health services has become more widespread, visible, and expensive, another component of the malpractice picture has been supplied by the consumer movement—patients' rights organizations have emerged to serve as advocates of the rights of clients as consumers.

Further, there is a real attempt being made to solve some of the problems of mental health by providing treatment without confinement, meaning that more mentally-ill people remain in the community. Another development has been the recognition of the constitutional right of a person with mental problems not to be committed to a mental institution without treatment, unless dangerous. While it is true that the U.S. Supreme Court's ruling (based upon the due process clause of the Fourteenth Amendment) in *O'Connor* v. *Donaldson*[12] did not establish an absolute right to receive treatment, it is a landmark decision for advocates of civil rights for a group of people who for too long largely have been considered nonpersons by the law.

Still another development, which came with a built-in guarantee of controversy about standards of professional conduct, was the introduction of nontraditional methods of therapy, such as group sessions, sensitivity training, primal scream, etc. Finally, changes in the moral climate in the United States have prompted entirely new kinds of questions about the role of sex in psychotherapy and the treatment of sexual dysfunction.

All of these factors have increased the probability that questions would be raised about the responsibilities of mental health professionals, questions that end up in the forum Americans seem to trust for finding answers—the legal system and, in the traditional format, the adversary proceeding.

Public Policy Implications

The resolution of questions concerning the law of malpractice, as is true when any question is resolved into law, involves policy decisions that must be preceded by the weighing of the interests involved. Rules of law governing malpractice reflect the balancing of at least three kinds of interests. First, there are the patients' rights: the contractual right to effective treatment, the right to privacy, personal liberty, equal protection, and due process of law. Next, the mental health professional has the right to practice his profession to the best of his ability, to use his knowledge and judgment, free from unreasonable interference and limitations. Finally, the public has a right to be safe from injury that might be inflicted by the mentally-ill, and in addition, possesses legitimate interest in the competent administration of mental health services, in two roles: as consumers and as members of a political society that has made rules requiring professionals to participate in the treatment of mental health problems that affect society. Rules of law governing malpractice, whether the result of decision-making by legislatures, courts, or others acting under authorization, are indeed public policy and the result of striking some balance among these and perhaps other competing interests.

TORT LIABILITY OF PSYCHOTHERAPISTS
Definitions

Authorities agree that "malpractice" is a term of broad significance. It is defined as "any professional misconduct or any unreasonable lack of skill or fidelity in the performance of professional duties." It "may be willful, negligent, or ignorant, and recognizing these elements, it has been defined as improper treatment through carelessness or ignorance, or intentionally."[13] Corpus Juris Secundum also notes that "while the term 'malpractice' is sometimes used loosely to refer to negligence of members of any professional group, legally and technically it is still subject to limited common-law definition which restricts the term to professional misconduct of members of the medical profession."[14]

There are several methods, designed for punitive as well as preventative purposes, for holding a professional responsible for wrongdoing. It should be noted that, generally speaking, one form of proceeding does not bar any of the others, which leads, in a sense, to double or even triple jeopardy. First, criminal charges may be brought if the unprofessional conduct violates some provision of federal or state law or local ordinance. For example, a psychotherapist who uses physical force to have sexual relations with his patient against her will in the name of "therapy" is guilty of professional wrongdoing, but also clearly commits the crime of rape. In fact, the noted authority in the treatment of sexual disorders William Masters has advocated that criminal charges be brought regardless of whether the seduction was initiated by the patient or by the therapist.[15]

Second, the therapist may face disciplinary action by a peer review committee, arbitration officer, or regulatory agency established by professional organization or acting under governmental authority. The resultant action can range from a reprimand to revocation of license, with a variety of other remedies possible. Finally, the therapist might be sued by a patient or others for damages or other relief. This kind of action, a civil lawsuit, is what commonly comes to mind at the mention of a "malpractice case." It should be recognized, however, that a civil suit against a therapist for professional misconduct might be cast in the form of another kind of legal injury; instead of "malpractice" as such, a civil complaint could charge breach of contract, assault and battery, violation of privacy, defamation, or any of a number of other causes of action recognized by law.

Examples

Malpractice might be more accurately termed "professional tort liability," although the common usage of "malpractice" and its practical application sometimes include aspects of contract law, the correct definition of "tort" is a civil wrong done to another person that does not involve a contract. Corpus Juris Secundum describes a tort as a private wrong: "A legal concept possessing basic elements of a wrong with resultant injury and consequential damage which is cognizable in a court of law." Further, while "a mere breach of contractual duty does not constitute a tort," contract may be an element in tort.[16] Further argument about the fine points of definition and the jurisdictional boundaries of contracts and torts is left to legal scholars, and we turn to a more useful inquiry—examples of actual situations that have given rise to liability. It should be noted that the list includes instances of mis– and non– as well as malfeasance:[17]

1. Improper administration of medication.
2. Improper employment of electroshock and surgical techniques.
3. Wrongful action in commitment procedures.
4. Faulty diagnosis.
5. Failure to take precautions against suicide.
6. Breach of confidentiality and privacy.

7. Injury resulting from physical aspects of nontraditional therapy.
8. Abandonment.
9. Failure to warn or otherwise protect third-party victims against dangerous mental patients.
10. Sexual contact between therapist and client.

Several of these contingencies would seem to be directly applicable only to therapists with medical degrees or functioning under the aegis of a hospital or clinic, e.g. the examples involving drugs and surgery, but other professionals might be indirectly involved and thus possibly liable and, in any event, the more complete the list, the better the entire problem is understood.

Elements of Malpractice

In any professional malpractice action, the basic elements are (1) the establishment of the duty of the defendant to give the plaintiff professional services, (2) the plaintiff's reliance on the agreement establishing the defendant's duty, (3) the failure to perform the duty in accordance with professional standards of conduct, and (4) damage caused by that failure.[18]

On its face, a malpractice claim would seem to be identical with an ordinary negligence case, but there are two important differences: the basis of the duty and the standard of the conduct. With regard to the first, in an ordinary personal injury case, the defendant owes the plaintiff only that conduct that would be expected from every other person under the same circumstances, but in a malpractice case, because of the professional relationship with the patient-plaintiff, the responsibility the defendant bears results from the expectation of professional expertise in which the patient-plaintiff has placed his trust. The other distinction concerns the standard of conduct. In any ordinary negligence case, the defendant's performance must only be what any "reasonable man" could be expected to do when faced with the same situation. In a malpractice case, the defendant-therapist must exercise the kind of skill, care, and diligence that members of the profession commonly possess and exercise in similar matters of employment.

Recent Cases

There are two areas of liability that have recently received attention, and both merit consideration and comment here.

In 1976, the California Supreme Court decided *Tarasoff* v. *Regents*[19] in which it ruled that a psychotherapist has a duty to warn third parties of the threat of serious danger posed by a patient under his care.* In *Tarasoff*, the parents of a young woman who was fatally shot by a former mental patient successfully brought suit against the therapist who participated in his treatment at the University of California student health center. It was established that the therapist knew of his pathological attachment to the young woman and that he had purchased a gun, and moreover had concluded that he might be dangerous. The Court held that the *special relationship* between the therapist and patient imposes upon the therapist "a duty to use reasonable care to protect third parties against the danger posed by the patient." The court was not persuaded by the argument that psychotherapists cannot predict "dangerousness" with enough reliability to justify the imposition of such a legal duty. The drastic implications for confidentiality and the patient's right to privacy are obvious; some commentators see *Tarasoff* as a singular threat to the success of the entire therapeutic relationship that exists between professional and client. Further, critics of the decision sadly predict that this ruling will cause therapists, who are already reluctant, to be even less willing to take on "dangerous" patients; ultimately, they say, the public will suffer the damage—the final irony among the consequences of a ruling that was intended in the first instance to protect the public.[22]

The other area concerns intimate contact between professional and client. While there are only a few cases on record, there are indications that the incidence of sexual conduct in the therapeutic relationship is greater than that allowed by popular wisdom and, moreover, is becoming more frequent and reported more often—the fact that one segment of CBS's prime-time "60 Minutes" was devoted to an examination of the subject is evidence in point.

---

*Another recent case involving a therapist's responsibility toward his patient's victim involved a psychiatric clinic and a psychiatrist who authorized the release of a male patient who subsequently killed a girl. The patient had previously pleaded guilty to abduction and received a suspended sentence of twenty years, on the condition that he would continue twenty-four hour treatment at the clinic. He had been released, on an out-patient basis, in violation of the sentencing order that specified that the judge, the probation officer and the clinic were to agree on any future release. In the malpractice suit filed by the dead girl's mother, a federal court of appeals ruled that while the evidence did not show that the psychiatrist's actions violated standards acceptable in the psychiatric community, the release of the patient violated the court order, and as such was itself an act of negligence, regardless of any professional negligence.[20,21]

It has been suggested that malpractice cases involving erotic contact between psychotherapist and patient basically raise a larger question of standards of conduct in the therapeutic relationship, specifically, the standard of closeness.[23] In other words, the therapist owes a duty to his patient to come close enough, but not too close. Professional contact that is too close may involve sex; but the boundary of closeness may nevertheless be overstepped with contact that stops short of sex. Likewise, professional contact that involves sex may or may not be too close; consent to sex, for example, could relax the closeness barrier. It is possible such a shift in perspective might strip the subject of erotic contact in the therapeutic relationship of the moralistic and emotional overtones that hinder objective examination and judgment.

This sort of an analysis provides a somewhat different interpretation of the much-cited case of *Landau* v. *Werner*,[24,25] which ruled that a psychiatrist was liable for injury suffered by his patient after intimate contact. It can be argued that the deeper issue in this case was the "personal abandonment" that resulted after the relationship ended.

The nature of the therapeutic relationship also has implications for defenses against malpractice suits arising from intimate contact. In *Ziplin* v. *Freeman*,[26] the Missouri Supreme Court held that transference made the patient completely dependent upon the therapist; therefore, the patient lacked the free will necessary to support the defendant-therapists's claim of contributory negligence.

PROFESSIONAL REGULATION OF MALPRACTICE

The area of malpractice in psychology is a complex one involving a number of aspects. One of the issues is that a practitioner should have met a defined level of competence such as would be reflected by licensure or certification.[27] Quality of services, providing services that are usual and customary for defined problems and at fees that are reasonable is another issue. Practicing within one's area of competence and conforming to the ethics of one's profession is still a third issue. In terms of regulation by the profession, the bodies that are involved in monitoring and enforcing these standards at the state level are typically the Board of Examiners of Psychologists, peer review committees, (Professional Standards Review Committee and Peer Standards Review Organization), the Ethics Committee of a state psychological association, and the Board of Governors of a state association. At the national level, other organizations might be involved in determining level of competence, such as the American Board of Professional Psychology, the Association of State Psychology Boards, and the National Register of Health Care Providers in Psychology. None of the immediately aforementioned boards are typically involved in imposing sanctions upon the psychologist, but the Committee on Scientific and Professional Ethics and Conduct of the American Psychological Association (APA) might do so when involved by a state association or Board of Examiners. There are regional peer review representatives and the APA counterpart of the state peer review committees is the Professional Standards Review Committee. It should be remembered that in addition to presenting a complaint to authorities within the profession, a client may seek redress through the courts via civil charges as discussed above. Furthermore, both therapist and client can seek to have the courts overturn the actions of state boards and professional associations.

Areas of Malpractice not Associated with Direct Services

Another area that has been of concern to psychologists has been their liability for suit when functioning on professional boards and committees. Coverage has been offered state associations through a private carrier in conjunction with APA for such eventualities and is extended even to nonpsychologist consumer members of committees. From the experience of our medical colleagues, we know that those of us involved as administrators of a service agency may also be named in malpractice suits. Staff, interns, and graduate students might be those delivering the psychological services. Since training and supervision are established functions with psychology and medicine, it would seem that insurance coverage would include such functions. For those of us supervising or providing consultation to paraprofessionals, the situation is unclear for lack of appropriate case law. However, on the face of it, it seems the less training the person delivering the services has, the greater the responsibility of the supervising psychologist unless it were established that: the functions in question were clearly subprofessional or that the psychologist was only responsible for those cases brought to his attention as a consultant in contrast to supervisory responsibilities, which might be considered more comprehensive. Another area of prospective concern would be liability for research subjects. Although there is a paucity of cases in this area, there are possible liability issues concerning exposing the subjects to hazards; the need for truly informed consent from the subject, or his parent or guardian; the need to assure that participation is voluntary and that subjects can indeed freely withdraw from participation; and confidentiality of data.[28]

Procedures for Handling Complaints

For illustrations of the process of adjudicating complaints let us consider in detail cases where a client complains of unwanted physical intimacy that may be offered as therapeutic. A heavily attended symposium at the 1977 meetings of the American Psychological Association cosponsored by five APA divisions reflects the current interest in this controversial approach. A similar symposium was held at the May 1976 meeting of the American Psychiatric Association and followed by a series of six in-depth articles in *Psychiatric News*. Whether such erotic activity is considered therapeutic or not is not the key determinant of complaints, but one source has reported that if the patient and his family are so informed that there is less of an issue of exploiting a weak, dependent client.[15]   In any event it has been established that there is an appreciable incidence of behavior and complaints of this type. Holyrod and Brodsky[7] found that 5.5 percent of male and 0.6 percent of female licensed Ph.D. psychologists reported having had sexual intercourse with patients. A questionnaire study of five hundred psychiatrists reported that 72 percent has experienced attempted seduction by a patient and 70 percent knew of patients or physicians who had engaged in physician-patient sex relations.[8]   In addition to the literature cited above, there have been two in-depth, clinically oriented studies of a series of cases.[29,30]

What constitutes a complaint? One of the authors has had a number of cases in which a significant part of clinical interviews or interviews with family members have been devoted to dealing with the feelings associated with unwanted sexual intimacies between therapist and client. In most of these the client or family member did not wish to make a formal complaint, but assumed the usual condition of privileged communication. The therapist cannot assume that mere presentation of such material in the course of evaluation or treatment implies that the patient or his family wish to make a formal complaint.

In the event that the patient or a member of the family wishes to make a complaint, where do they address it? From the introduction to this chapter it is evident that there are a number of options, e.g.

state association ethics committees, Board of Examiners of Psychologists, peer review committees, or a complaint directed to the courts.

Ethics committees are limited in the sanctions they may impose on a psychotherapist. By themselves they may conduct a hearing and, if the psychologist has violated an ethical principle, they can suggest corrective action, reprimand him, or refer the case to the state association or to the Committee on Scientific and Professional Ethics and Conduct of APA for similar actions. Or they may recommend that the association refer to the Board of Examiners for determination of whether the psychologist's license or certificate should be suspended or revoked. Complaints directed to a district attorney or the attorney general of a state will typically result in a hearing by the Board of Examiners who has the authority to find the charges unsubstantiated or impose sanctions such as suspension or revocation of license or certificate.

What are the risks to the patient of making a formal complaint? Sinnett and Thetford[31] have pointed out that in making a complaint the patient surrenders his privilege. While some attorneys have indicated that disclosure may be restricted to only those portions of the records that are relevant, a defense attorney will typically press for complete disclosure. From the perspective of a therapist, who needs to be protected from unfounded complaints, it is clear that there needs to be sufficient disclosure to defend his position. The client, however, is vulnerable to having testimony impeached as a result of mental illness, as well as subject to damage to his reputation by having his records become exhibits in the transcript of the hearing, which is a public record. For some complaints against practitioners, peer review committees might be the appropriate point of origin, but this body might also consider referral to another such as the Ethics Committee of the Board of Examiners. Consideration should be given to a single source where complaints against therapist could be presented, as is done by the law profession in the state of Kansas. Since there appears to be overlapping jurisdiction of various boards and committees within the APA, the recommendation has been that the Professional Standards Review Committee be designed as the place for presenting complaints initially.

The variety of alternatives for seeking adjudication of complaints is bewildering. One case known to the authors was first presented to the Better Business Bureau. Another disadvantage of multiple authorities is that of multiple jeopardy for the therapist. Although these bodies may communicate with one another via formal complaints or informal liaison, each acts relatively autonomously in imposing sanctions. One unpublished case has come to our attention in which the therapist was deprived of his license, state and national association memberships, and also had to defend his tenured university position for the same violation. Another unpublished case involved a psychologist who initially made disclosures to an Ethics Committee investigating a complaint with the expectation that he would get a peer review. The Ethics Committee imposed sanctions that they felt appropriate and sufficient. Later all records were subject to a subpoena by the Board of Examiners who on review and subsequent to a formal hearing revoked his license.

Furthermore, since many of the hearings are administrative rather than legal proceedings and conducted by psychologists untrained in matters of due process, rules of evidence, and state laws governing administrative hearings, there are some significant problems in conduct of hearings as well as the actions of the administrative bodies. For example, in one of the cases cited in the previous paragraph, the initial ruling by the Board of Examiners was overturned at the district court level for failure of the Board to observe the open meeting law. The advantage of the informal administrative hearing is that more professional input and assessment is possible whereas the legal hearing generates more of an adversary situation.

When we think of malpractice we commonly consider only cases that are prosecuted in courts of law for specific damages. However, in addition to being judged by our peers, we need also to consider that we may need to be sophisticated in order to initiate complaints or to serve on administrative bodies conducting hearings in order to be fair to the therapist and patient. Some sources published by the American Psychological Association that are helpful are the revised Code of Ethics for Psychologists,[32] the procedural guidelines for conducting an ethics committee hearing,[33] the casebook on ethical standards,[34] the ethical principles governing research with human subjects,[28] the standards for providers of psychological services,[35] and the guidelines for psychologists conducting growth groups.[10] In the area of peer review, APA has a procedure manual[36] and there has been a review of similar activities in psychiatry.[37] One of the most elaborate, detailed accounts describing procedures is that governing the APA Committee on Scientific and Professional Ethics and Conduct.[38] Oddly, there does not appear to be any specific literature to orient the new member of a board of examiners. Clearly professional psychology is an evolving field.

CONCLUSIONS AND COMMENTS

Some final observations on the issue of malpractice and psychotherapists are in order. First, there is support for the position that since numerous abuses do exist, "a sophisticated public serves a necessary function in calling attention to malpractice. If lawsuits are necessary to this process, then so be it."[39] However, if the experience of physicians and surgeons is an indication, it is obvious that as malpractice suits become more frequent, the cost of defending against them becomes more expensive, and the cost of therapy will spiral. It would seem prudent to examine alternatives to litigation. A reasonable place to start would be the development of more precise standards of professional conduct, or more careful guidelines for determining standards in specific instances, and the establishment of well-defined procedures consistent with due process for handling abuses within the profession. If the profession does not do it, regulation will come from some other source.

Second, from a more humanistic perspective there is a matrix of intensely unpleasant consequences involved in litigation. Therapists find the prospect of a suit intimidating, and clients may have their competence impugned because of mental illness and suffer from exposure of their records of treatment during the proceedings.

In addition to the role of the accused, psychologists must prepare for other roles in the area of malpractice: that of advocate for the client who wishes to make a formal complaint against another therapist and that of judge. Psychologists must be willing to serve voluntarily, without compensation, on boards and committees involved in peer review and adjudication of complaints.

It has been the authors' observation that many professionals are themselves perplexed and uninformed concerning the legal aspects of malpractice and the possible mechanisms for control within the profession. Many of the administrative bodies require functioning in a quite different capacity. For psychologists who rightfully feel the competence associated with being well-trained in providing services, functioning on a board or committee processing complaints may generate feelings of inadequacy as they learn the operation of the quasi- judicial proceedings of administrative bodies and the exercise of due process in the courts. Even administrative bodies are developing orderly, detailed procedures for hearings in order to insure a fair hearing for the client and the therapist.

Although psychologists need not become amateur lawyers, unless their hearings are conducted in accordance with some established procedures, their decisions are likely to be overturned by the courts. As a matter of fact, courts rarely overturn an administrative body with respect to the area of judgment concerning professional standards of practice, but they may when procedures are arbitrary and capricious.

Finally, psychologists need to view the emerging rules of law governing malpractice in a broader public-policy perspective, to evaluate the total effect of any given decision on the interests involved and existing rules of law, in order to articulate the position of the profession more effectively and responsibly.

REFERENCES

1. Too much law? *Newsweek,* January 10, 1977.
2. Shimberg, B.   Recent developments in APA insurance program, *American Psychologist, 24,* 460–467, 1969.
3. Brownfain, J.J.   The APA professional liability program, *American Psychologist, 26,* 648–652, 1971.
4. Southwestern Psychological Association.   Preventing malpractice suits, *News Bulletin, 10,* 2, 1978.
5. Roche Report.   "Mal-psychotherapy" suits may soon beset psychiatrists, *Frontiers in Psychiatry,* March 1, 1–2, 1978.
6. Kardner, S.H., Fuller, M., and Mensh, I.N.   A survey of physicians' attitudes and practices regarding erotic and non-erotic contact with patients, *American Journal of Psychiatry, 130,* 1077–1081, 1973.
7. Holyrod, J.C. and Brodsky, A.M.   Psychologists' attitudes and practices regarding erotic and non-erotic contact with patients, *American Psychologist, 32,* 843–849, 1977.
8. Hospital Publications, Inc.   Sexual survey #7:   Current thinking on seductive patients, *Medical Aspects of Human Sexuality,* 46–47, February, 1978.
9. American Psychiatric Association.   *Encounter groups and psychiatry,* (Task force report No. 1), Washington, D.C., APA, 1970.
10. American Psychological Association.   Guidelines for psychologists conducting growth groups, *American Psychologist, 28,* 933, 1973.
11. American Psychological Association.   Rage reduction therapy pioneer battles to keep California license, *APA Monitor,* 5, February, 1973.
12. O'Connor v. Donaldson   422 U.S. 563, 1975.
13. 54 C.J.S. Malpractice § 114, 1948.
14. 54 C.J.S.   Malpractice § 114, 1977 Supp.

15. American Psychiatric Association Patient/therapist sex—The legal perspective, *Psychiatric News, 18,* October 15, 1976.
16. 86 C.J.S. Torts § 1–3, 1948.
17. Slovenko, R. *Psychiatry and Law,* Boston, Little, Brown, 1973.
18. Zelle, L. and Stanhope, W.H. Lawyer malpractice: The boomerang principle, *Trial, 13,* 17–19, 1977.
19. 551 P.2d 334 (Calif., 1976). This was the second time the state supreme court had heard the case; it vacated the judgment it had made two years before. 529 P.2d 533 (Calif., 1974). Other defendants were the Regents of the University of California, the psychiatrist who headed the clinic, and the police.
20. Semler v. Psychiatric Institute 538 F.2d 121 (4th Cir.), cert. den. 429 U.S. 827, 1976.
21. Comment. Psychotherapists' liability for the release of mentally-ill offender: A proposed expansion of the doctrine of strict liability, *University of Pennsylvania Law Review, 126,* 204–240, 1977.
22. Stone, A.A. The Tarasoff decisions: Suing psychotherapists to safeguard society, *Harvard Law Review, 90,* 358–378, 1976.
23. Dawidoff, D.J. Insanity, intimacy, and infidelity: Trends in psychiatric malpractice, *Trial, 13,* 27–30, 1977.
24. Landau v. Werner 105 Sol. J.257, C.A., 1961.
25. Brooks, A.D. *Law, psychiatry, and the mental health system,* Boston, Little, Brown, 1077–1080, 1974.
26. Ziplin v. Freeman 436 S.W.2d. 753 Mo., 1969.
27. Bogust v. Iverson 107 N.W.2d. 228, Wis., 1960. The practitioner was cleared of negligence because the court rules that his training did not prepare him to make professional judgments.
28. American Psychological Association. *Ethical principles in the conduct of research with human participants,* Washington, D.C., APA, 1973.
29. Dahlberg, C.C. Sexual contact between patient and therapist, *Contemporary Psychoanalysis, 6,* 106–124, 1970.
30. Taylor, B.W. and Wagner, N.N. Sex between therapist and clients: A review and analysis, *Professional Psychology, 7,* 593–601, 1976.
31. Sinnett, E.R. and Thetford, P. Protecting clients and assessing malpractice, *Professional Psychology, 6,* 117–126, 1975.
32. American Psychological Association. Revised ethical standards of psychologists, *APA Monitor,* 22–23, March, 1977.
33. American Psychological Association. *Proposed procedural guidelines for state association ethics committees,* Washington, D.C., APA, 1972.
34. American Psychological Association. *Casebook on ethical standards of psychologists,* Washington, D.C., APA, 1967.
35. American Psychological Association. Standards for providers of psychological services, *American Psychologist, 32,* 495-505, 1977.

36. Committee on Professional Standards Review. *PSRC procedures manual*, Washington, D.C., APA, 1975.
37. American Psychiatric Association. *Professional responsibilities and peer review in psychiatry*, Washington, D.C., APA, 1977.
38. American Psychological Association. Rules and procedures, Committee on Scientific and Professional Ethics and Conduct, *American Psychologist, 29*, 703–710, 1974.
39. Van Hoose, W.H. and Kottler, J.A. *Ethical and legal issues in counseling and psychotherapy*, San Francisco, Jossey Bass, 1977.

SECTION II

THE COURTROOM

Any breakdown of the topic of forensic psychology is bound to be arbitrary and partially incorrect because evaluation, treatment, and legal issues overlap. Nevertheless, in this section an attempt is made to isolate some of the factors specific to the courtroom. Chapters 7 and 8 present guidelines by two psychologists experienced in testifying. Chapter 9 focuses on the relationship between the forensic psychiatrist and psychologist and the way in which the two can complement each other. Chapters 10, 11, and 12 deal with very specific areas that even many forensic psychologists do not venture into, but provide information on how forensic psychologists may function in highly specialized areas. Chapters 13 and 14 examine the jury system and provide information on its dynamics that can be useful to anyone testifying before a jury, as well as a discussion of the role the psychologist can play in jury selection. Chapter 15 demonstrates the work being done, both in the laboratory and courtroom, to understand the process of eyewitness identification.

Chapter 7

THE ROLE OF THE PSYCHOLOGIST IN CRIMINAL COURT PROCEEDINGS*

GERALD COOKE, Ph.D.

I N 1962 JUDGE Bazelon's court established in *Jenkins* v. *U.S.*[1] that psychologists may be qualified to give expert testimony in the field of mental disorders. Recent appraisals of the legal status of the psychologist (see Chapter 3) demonstrate that this position has been strengthened considerably since that original decision and forensic psychologists have become more and more frequently called upon to conduct psychological evaluations in criminal cases and to present their findings in expert testimony. In past years, a number of psychologists have written on the role of the psychologist in the criminal justice system in general[2] and in the courtroom specifically.[3,4] Some of these authors view the psychologist as having an important role in the criminal justice system, others feel that the present role is inappropriate. As psychologists' legal status has strengthened and the speciality of forensic psychology has developed, psychologists have been gradually moving away from the role of consultant to the psychiatrist and toward more independent roles in which they must relate effectively to psychiatrists, attorneys, and the courts. The present paper focuses on some of the demands of forensic psychologists' emerging role as expert witnesses where they have evaluated a defendant in a criminal action.

Most often referrals for psychological evaluations come from a psychiatrist who has been retained by the defense, prosecution, or the court. In that case, an experienced forensic psychiatrist who is familiar with the use of psychological testing will have specific re-

---

*This paper is a revision of a presentation at the American Psychological Association Convention, Washington, D.C., 1976.

91

ferral questions.   However, as noted above, there is an increasing trend for knowledgeable attorneys and judges to recognize when it is appropriate to have a psychological evaluation in addition to or instead of psychiatric evaluation and to make requests directly.   In these cases, it is incumbent upon the forensic psychologist to discuss with the attorney or judge the relevant questions and whether such questions can be answered by a psychological evaluation.   In this paper we will first define some of the questions that forensic psychologists are called upon to answer and then will present general issues of evaluation and testimony.

The questions that the psychologist is called upon to answer fall into three classes.   First, there are the purely legal questions: Is the defendant competent to stand trial?   Was the defendant competent to waive Miranda rights?   Did the individual have the capacity to form the requisite intent to commit the alleged act?   Is the defendant criminally responsible?   The second class of questions is primarily diagnostic and usually directly related to the legal questions: What are the personality dynamics?   What is the intellectual level and is there evidence of organic brain damage?   Is there an underlying schizophrenic or other psychotic process?   Is the personality pattern consistent with malingering, dissociative episodes, loss of control under the influence of drugs or alcohol, etc?   The third class of questions concerns prediction and is most applicable to disposition: Is the individual in need of and motivated for treatment?   What is the recommended treatment?   What is the prognosis?   Is the individual likely to engage in future dangerous and/or criminal behavior and what controls are most likely to reduce the acting out potential?   Is the individual suicidal?

Before discussing some of these questions in greater depth, it is necessary to review some general issues of evaluation and testimony. First, the forensic psychologist is a clinician with a special tool—the psychological tests.   Though the psychologist should rely heavily on test results, these should be integrated with material from the clinical interview and history.   The term "history" as used here is a broad one and, depending on the specific case, may include police reports, records of prior hospitalizations, incarcerations or evaluations, and testimony of witnesses.   Data from all these sources should be integrated and conclusions drawn in a way that will be understood by the attorney.   If a conclusion cannot be drawn on the basis of the data, this should be communicated as well.

Prior to the actual evaluation, the psychologist must discuss the case with the psychiatrist and attorney so that each clearly understands what is expected of the other and what can be supplied. The attorney should also be aware that the psychologist's task is to perform an evaluation, but that the findings may not be suitable testimony. Many attorneys, particularly those whose practice is wider than criminal cases, will rarely have used a psychiatrist, much less a psychologist, as an expert witness in a criminal proceeding. Many do not understand fully what a psychologist is and does and what psychological tests can and cannot provide. Determine whether the attorney has used a psychologist before and supply a vita with training and credentials. If the attorney has not previously presented psychological testimony, provide some general guidelines. Some of these, such as a reminder that questions should be asked using the term "scientific certainty" rather than "medical certainty," may seem insignificant but often prove to be important. Other guidelines include such things as telling the attorney to present the direct examination so as to allow for a brief explanation to the jury of what psychological tests are and that the witness should not be questioned as to individual test answers or scores but as to general findings and patterns (there are occasional exceptions to this).

Following the evaluation of the client, verbally communicate the findings to the attorney and, depending on the findings, determine whether or not a full written report is appropriate. The report should be written keeping in mind that not all psychiatrists and attorneys are familiar with psychological tests. For example, while psychology reports generally list tests administered without further elaboration, the forensic psychologist must recognize that the attorney needs at least a rudimentary knowledge of the tests if the testimony is to be presented effectively. Therefore, present a brief description of each test. Emphasize certain aspects of a test if it is particularly relevant to the referral questions. For example, if the possibility of malingering is an issue, include in the description of the MMPI that it has validity scales and that there are specific profiles associated with attempts to falsely present oneself as suffering from mental illness when, in fact, no such illness is present. Whether the psychologist is testifying for prosecution or defense, this sets the stage for later testimony as to the presence or absence of malingering.

After the report has been sent to the psychiatrist and/or attorney, a meeting should be held so that the order and method with which testimony will be presented can be discussed. The psychologist should make it clear what he will and will not testify to. Possible cross examination questions should be discussed and the psychologist should indicate what the responses to these questions would be. It is, of course, unethical to distort the data or testimony, but the psychologist does have a responsibility to tell the attorney as precisely as possible what the testimony will be so the attorney can prepare the direct and redirect examination appropriately.

Preparation for testifying is important. Of course the forensic psychologist should thoroughly know the laws governing the legal questions that will be raised. Be able to quote the standards *verbatim;* nothing so damages a witness's credibility as to fumble in this area. Thoroughly know the tests so as not to have to give answers such as "because the norms don't accept that."[5] Be aware of and willing to discuss reasonably the limitations of psychology and psychological testing. Anticipate both legitimate and "tricky" cross-examination questions. Legitimate questions include definitions of the diagnostic categories, aspects of the reliability and validity of tests, etc. Tricky ones are those that question the psychologist's expertise because he does not have a medical degree, ones that suggest that the psychologist is being paid a high fee by the client to bias the testimony, or ones that require complex definitions. For example, once in a case before a jury in which there was a question whether a mentally retarded girl was capable of giving consent to a sexual act or was raped, the issue of whether she loved the man was raised. The witness was asked to define "love." The response to such a question must be scientific without being coldly inhuman.

In presenting testimony, a balance must be struck between professionalism and the layman's knowledge possessed by the judge and/or jury. Jargon should be kept to the minimum and necessary professional terms should be explained. Developing a style of explanation without "talking down" to judge or jury requires experience and sensitivity. Attorney's questions that are not fully understood or that contain multiple parts should be responded to by a request for clarification. The expert witness should not be afraid to indicate that the question was not understood or that the nature of the question precludes a yes/no answer. Such questions may pose a "trap" and, while the psychologist should not be overly paranoid, an expert witness must recognize that the cross-examiner is an adversary whose purpose is to weaken the testimony. The witness must remember, and at times this is difficult to do, that the cross-examination is not a personal attack and the witness should not become angry or upset.

Three of the referral questions will be discussed in some detail: criminal responsibility, malingering, and prognosis with treatment. These have been chosen not because they are necessarily the most frequent or important questions, but because they represent each of the three general classes, demonstrate specific issues, and indicate how the expertise of the forensic psychologist can be most effectively utilized.

The criminal responsibility concept raises many moral, theoretical, and practical problems that have been discussed elsewhere.[6,7] There are many judges, attorneys, and mental health professionals who feel that insanity and guilt should be handled as separate issues and this is beginning to be manifested in some states in the form of the bifurcated trial. But, as long as the law requires such a determination, forensic psychologists must be prepared to deal with this issue. In order to render an opinion about the criminal responsibility of the accused, the witness must assess the accused's mental status at a time often six months to a year before and evaluate behavior that occurred under highly specific circumstances that could not be observed by the examiner. Furthermore, the expert is asked to infer this past mental status from present status and history while realizing that present status has been influenced by the act and all its consequences, including incarceration.

Because of the difficulties inherent in such an evaluation, take a very conservative approach to the issue of responsibility. The psychologist should demand a documented history of emotional problems prior to the criminal act, evidence from witnesses, police reports, etc., consistent with severe mental illness at the time of the act and clinical and test evidence at the time of the evaluation that is consistent with prior severe mental illness. If the psychologist finds such evidence, the findings can be of great use to the attorney because often by the time of trial the individual is no longer overtly psychotic.

Test results can be presented that demonstrate the presence of a psychotic process consistent with the alleged status at the time of the criminal act. An example illustrating this approach is that of a nineteen-year-old male who killed his ten-year-old brother. This man had been hospitalized at a state hospital as an adolescent and though he was not diagnosed psychotic at that time, the records showed severe pathology. Police reports of the incident and his confession given to the police were replete with behaviors and statements that would be viewed as unusual even by the layman and were clearly the product of schizophrenia to a professional. The psychological testing was particularly important in this case because, though the defendant was schizophrenic, he verbalized no hallucinatory experiences, demonstrated little obviously bizarre behavior, and his delusions were not sufficiently systematized and expansive to be labeled as "crazy" by laymen. Psychological testing clearly demonstrated a psychotic thought disorder manifested primarily by concreteness, religious delusions, and autism in which this man felt he was saving the soul of his brother. Though the man was initially found guilty, a new trial was obtained on appeal and he was found not guilty by reason of insanity. Test examples, particularly in terms of extreme MMPI scores and distortion of the Rorschach, were helpful in demonstrating pathology that was not as evident clinically.

The second question is the one of malingering. This question is frequently raised in forensic evaluations, particularly when amnesia is claimed or when an individual is demonstrating psychotic symptomatology of questionable validity. The case to illustrate this point involved a man charged with a number of assaults and robberies. He was verbalizing bizarre delusional material, much of which was of a religious nature. A combination of clinical and test indicators revealed malingering. On the MMPI the man produced a textbook dissimulation pattern; on the Sentence Completion every item was completed with a religious theme, an extreme response set rarely observed even in the most religiously delusional paranoids. From this, one would expect that on interview there would be pressure of speech with religious content; however, such pressure of speech was totally absent. The Rorschach, which is much less amenable to manipulation, revealed none of the distortions that should be associated with psychotic pathology, but showed a characterological pattern. The conclusion of malingering was unavoidable.

The last question has to do with prognosis with treatment. Many individuals request treatment only to escape incarceration. Others are in need of treatment but their lack of insight leads them to deny their mental illness and it is not clear whether their defenses can be penetrated and the anxiety necessary to motivative change can be tapped. The answers to these questions cannot often be determined clinically but may be provided by psychological testing. Certain objective test scales, such as the depression and psychasthenia scales of the MMPI, and a number of indices from projective tests are useful in determining an individual's tendency toward introspection, ownership of responsibility for behavior, and level of anxiety. In the case of the antisocial personality the defense system is often so far developed that the underlying feelings of inadequacy and anxiety cannot be reached, but where offenses stem from other causes, the anxiety may be mobilized for therapeutic purposes.

In summary, the forensic psychologist may provide important information to the court on a wide variety of issues. However, as described above, the credibility of the witness's testimony and the degree to which it is utilized by the court will depend to a large degree upon not only the professional competence of the psychologist but also upon the way in which the expert witness prepares and presents his testimony.

REFERENCES

1. Jenkins, v. U.S. U.S. 307 F. 2d, 637 (D.C. Cir. 1962).
2. Neitzel, M.T. and Moss, C.S. The psychologist in the criminal justice system, *Professional Psychology, 3,* 259–270, 1972
3. Jeffrey, R. The psychologist as an expert witness on the issue of insanity, *American Psychologist, 19,* 843–850, 1964.
4. Ziskin, J. *Coping with psychiatric and psychological testimony,* Beverly Hills, California, Law & Psychology Press, 1970.
5. Kent v. U.S. 401 F. 2d, 408 (D.C. Cir. 1968).
6. Goldstein, A.S. *The insanity defense,* New Haven, Connecticut, Yale University Press, 1967.
7. Glueck, S. *Law and psychiatry: Cold war or entente cordiale,* Baltimore, Maryland, Johns Hopkins Press, 1962.

Chapter 8

GIVING EXPERT TESTIMONY: PITFALLS AND HAZARDS FOR THE PSYCHOLOGIST IN COURT

JAY ZISKIN, Ph.D., LL.B.

F OR THE PSYCHOLOGIST, appearance in court as an expert witness can be a perilous venture in which both his professional and personal selves are vulnerable to polite, but nonetheless deflating, attacks by opposing attorneys. Further, the standing of psychology as a discipline is impaired when a psychologist is made to look foolish on the witness stand.

"STATE OF THE ART" ISSUES

There are several bases for attacking psychological evidence in court that are inherent in the current state of psychological knowledge and method.* These bases include insufficient validation of theories and principles, insufficient knowledge of base rates, deficiencies of the clinical method, negative literature concerning reliability and validity particularly in regard to projective and other personality tests, and negative evidence concerning the effects of experience that in other fields of expertise is an impregnable bastion of the expert. Even if these problems were overcome, it is often difficult, if not impossible, to bridge the gap between psychological findings and legal issues.

It is best for the psychologist to acknowledge areas of deficiency or controversy. Failure to do so may impair credibility, which is the witness's most important asset. Opposing attorneys who are knowl-

*These bases and their use in challenging psychological evidence are extensively discussed in Ziskin, J. *Coping with Psychiatric and Psychological Testimony*, 2nd edition, Beverly Hills, California, Pocket Supplement, Law and Psychology Press, 1977.

edgeable will confront the witness with a considerable body of negative scientific and professional literature or will produce a rebuttal expert who will recite such literature. Obviously, making such acknowledgments will weaken the expert's evidence to the extent that the foundations for such evidence are weakened. However, the personal credibility of the witness is preserved. One approach is to acknowledge deficiencies but assert that, nevertheless, these are the principles and methods that are widely used in the profession and they are the best the profession can offer at the present time.

PERFORMANCE OF THE PSYCHOLOGICAL TASK

The inherent problems described are often compounded by the psychologist's failure to perform the evaluation as well as possible within the limits the "state of the art" allows. The psychologist should be aware of the distinctions between evaluations for clinical purposes and evaluations for legal purposes. In the clinical situation, the goal of the evaluation is usually to provide some hypotheses or guidelines for treatment purposes. In the course of treatment these hypotheses can be checked out and either verified or discarded as the data indicates. In contrast, in the legal situation, the conclusions will be presented; a one-time, all-or-none decision will be made; and it cannot be altered in the light of material that might appear six months or a year later in therapy sessions. Further, any substantive errors or procedural deficiencies will be attacked by a determined opponent in the legal situation.

I have been consulted frequently by lawyers for the purpose of scrutinizing reports or depositions of psychologists to detect any deficiencies or errors. In this role I have observed a number of fairly common practices of psychologists that make them vulnerable in the legal arena. Many of these vulnerabilities, or hazards, could be reduced or eliminated by what might be generally described as a more thorough approach by the psychologist. These deficiencies and the corrective measures, some of which will be obvious, follow.

1. In taking history and getting relevant background information, most clinicians, in my experience, do a job that is woefully inadequate for forensic purposes. It is necessary to thoroughly investigate any potentially relevant area. Particularly, in almost every case, it will be important to obtain information concerning family and social relationships, occupational information, data indicating the manner in which the individual has functioned in society, and an accurate

medical history. It is embarrassing to conclude, as one expert did, that the plaintiff's marriage had broken up due to her loss of sexual interest following an automobile accident, only to be confronted on the witness stand with the fact that she had filed an action for divorce three weeks *before* the accident.

A witness is always vulnerable if his only source of information concerning the litigant or matters at issue, is the litigant himself. Litigants are prone to falsify or exaggerate to further their claim, which makes it urgent that the psychologist obtain confirmatory data on important matters from some other source. Against a knowledgeable opposing attorney, it will not be sufficient to say that in your clinical judgment this person was telling the truth, because such a lawyer will be able to demonstrate there is no basis for concluding that the psychologist is an accurate "lie detector." Medical and hospital records should be obtained and carefully read because frequently they will contain information that requires some modification of conclusions that might otherwise be reached. For example, in one case involving blackouts alleged to have occurred subsequent to injuries in an industrial accident, careful reading of prior records showed the claimant had received a severe concussion some five years earlier with notations by the doctor of blackouts at that time. An expert who learns of such matters for the first time on the witness stand does not make a good impression. Many psychologists will perceive, in connection with this point and others that follow, that taking these precautions will add to the time and effort necessary to do the evaluation and increase its costs. That observation would be correct. My recommendation is that if the expert is unwilling to devote the time necessary to do the job right and if the employing lawyer or party is unwilling to have the job done right, the psychologist is far better off to simply turn down the assignment. Revelation on the witness stand of shoddy work is of no use to the litigant and does nothing to enhance the credibility of the psychologist or his profession.

2. Deficiencies in the scoring of tests are amazingly frequent. An error of a couple of points in scoring an intelligence test may or may not have much significance in the clinical situation, but it will tend to discredit the expert on the witness stand. Failure to adhere to test standardization procedures and proper administration can be glaringly revealed in the courtroom and reduce the professionalism of the expert in the eyes of a jury. For example, I frequently see partial

administrations of the Wechsler Adult Intelligence Scale (WAIS). While this is sometimes defensible, most often it is simply a shortcut and will so appear to the jury. The psychologist on the witness stand will find enough to defend without having to try to explain why he did not administer the full test; and any good lawyer will bring out the fact that the test was meant to be administered in its entirety.

When the evaluation is for legal purposes, it is better to over-test than under-test. For example, one should be very careful not to discontinue a WAIS Sub-Test only to find out later that the next-to-last answer was in fact scoreable and the test should have gone on for several more questions. On the Rorschach, inquiry should be thorough. If the clinician is using the Thermatic Apperception Test (TAT), he should have a rationale for the selection of the particular cards used. In other words, he should be prepared to respond to an inquiry as to why he used these particular cards and not some others. The psychologist should be aware of the psychometric implications of test scores and should not, as happened in one case, state that a scale score of eight on a WAIS Sub-Test represents a deficiency in that area. It should be noted that a single examination, even of two to three hours of duration, is insufficient for legal purposes. Many lawyers are aware that psychological state or condition fluctuates and will bring out that responses and material elicited in a single session might be quite different a week later in the same individual. Therefore, it is advisable to spread the examination over at least two and preferably three sessions.

3. Many clinicians fail to deal with material that is contrary to their conclusions or might be detrimental to the case of the litigant who has employed them. They either fail to note this contrary data or they deliberately ignore it or, in some cases, they note it but gloss over it without attaching any significance to it. For example, in one child custody case, the psychologist noted that the MMPI profile of the father suggested a possible drinking problem and then said nothing further about it in his report in relation to custody recommendations. More significantly, in answer to a Minnesota Multiphasic Personality Inventory (MMPI) question, the father stated that he had used alcohol excessively. This is a matter of obvious importance in a child custody determination and requires, at the very least, an indication that the psychologist has explored the matter thoroughly and on the basis of information obtained has legitimately concluded that it is not a significant problem with an explanation as to why it

is not a problem. It may be worth mentioning here that the MMPI is almost invariably a source of contrary data. The psychologist will be hard pressed, on the witness stand, to maintain his diagnosis of depression where, on the MMPI, the individual has indicated that he is happy most of the time, seldom feels blue, enjoys life, is interested and enjoys many vocational and avocational interests, and so on. The argument that it is only the profile and the accumulation of answers that establishes the diagnoses is not likely to prevail in the face of such overt statements by the litigant. For this reason, while it may be cumbersome, it is necessary to read the individual responses on the MMPI so that one is at least prepared to deal with the contents of those responses.

If there are several instances of denial, avoidance, or ignorance of negative material, a good lawyer will be able to present a very persuasive case for bias on the part of the witness. Related to this problem is the notorious predilection of clinicians to focus almost entirely on psychopathological aspects of the individual. Except in very rare cases, the individual is or has been functioning more or less adequately out in the world, and he must, therefore, have a number of psychological strengths or assets. The psychologist will look foolish on the witness stand if he presents only a one-sided picture of the individual.

4. Many clinicians pay little or no heed to the well-documented phenomena of situational and examiner effects. The mere fact of being involved in litigation is an invariably present situational effect. For almost all litigants, the pending litigation is a source of fear, tension, anxiety, or stress that to some degree affects his interview or test behavior. For example, on the MMPI Sirhan Sirhan indicated that "people were out to get him." That statement might be viewed as having paranoid significance in the normal run of clients seeking psychotherapeutic help for some problem. It has no such significance in Sirhan's case because it simply represents obvious objective truth. The district attorney, if no one else (and there were plenty of others), *was* out to get him. Similarly, at least some of the anxiety observed in a litigant who is hoping to get several hundred thousand dollars for his "psychic injury" must be attributed to the tension and anxiety anyone would be likely to feel with the outcome of such an important event hanging in suspense.

5. Frequently clinicians fail to elucidate the data base for their conclusions. While it is not a requirement that these bases be set forth in a report, the psychologist should nevertheless have in his own

mind a clear basis for his conclusions. Hunches, intuition, or gut re-actions will not get very far in the courtroom. Therefore, before stating conclusions in a report, the psychologist ought to know how he is going to defend and justify them if challenged to do so.

There is one additional vital step in preparing to go into the court-room. It is important to go over the evidence you plan to present with the lawyer for your side of the case to make sure that he under-stands thoroughly what you can say and what you cannot say, so that both you and he know how he plans to elicit your testimony. Some lawyers and/or witnesses prefer some kind of broad open-ended ques-tion that allows the witness to then present his findings in a narrative form. Other attorneys and/or witnesses prefer more interchange be-tween lawyer and witness, with the lawyer asking somewhat narrower questions in a series to bring forth the information. Even in the narrative form it is important that the lawyer make notes as to all the important points he wants you to bring out, so that if under the pressure of being on the witness stand, you should omit some, he will be able to ask you about them. It is important that the direct exam-ination be conducted in as smooth and efficient a manner as possible because that is the portion of the testimony in which the expert is going to look the best that he is going to look. Testimony that might otherwise be effective can be lost or diminished through faltering or clumsy questioning on direct examination.

Similarly, it is advisable to have the attorney for your side put you through a simulated cross-examination. This will prepare you for at least some of the questions that are likely to come up on cross-exam-ination, so that you do not need to deal with them for the first time on the witness stand. It will also make the attorney aware of what your responses are likely to be and allow him to make some plans for re-habilitation if that should be necessary. The expert should be aware that even where weakening or damaging concessions must be made on cross-examination, further explanation to reduce the damage is possi-ble through re-direct examination by the presenting attorney. The expert should also be aware that opposing counsel has the right of re–cross-examination following the redirect examination.

COURTROOM BEHAVIOR

The effectiveness of an expert's testimony is influenced by your behavior and even your appearance in the courtroom. The overriding consideration at all times is to maintain personal credibility regardless of how heavily the expert's conclusions may come under attack. For this purpose the obvious first recommendation is to be honest at all times. Aside from avoiding the pitfall of being exposed in a false statement, the genuine truthfulness of the witness will be communicated to the jury. Do not hesitate to say that you do not know, when that is the appropriate answer. Judges and juries will not expect you to know everything or to be able to answer every question. In some cases it may be possible to rephrase a question in a manner that will then allow you to provide an answer. This is permissible, although a good cross-examiner will point out that you have not really answered the question that he has asked. However, you can still respond that that is the only form in which you are able to answer the question. Similarly, it is best to concede deficiencies in the "state of the art," particularly if they are raised in cross-examination. You may generally be assured that if the cross-examiner is raising these issues, he is armed with sufficient material to establish that they are issues.

It is important to avoid an appearance of partisanship. This may be very difficult to do, as there are a number of publications indicating that there is probably no such thing as an impartial witness. Nevertheless, that is the definition of your role. Your function, as defined, is to provide knowledge and expertise regarding matters in the case for the use of the judge or jury. It is not, at least by definition, your function to try to win the case for one side or the other, or to advance one viewpoint over another. Some lawyers will try to cast the expert as a "hired gun," and this may be difficult to resist. Certainly, there are professional witnesses who function in that role and who have created rather lucrative practices. There are, however, hopeful signs that they may be a vanishing breed. Greater sophistication among lawyers has given them the tools and capabilities of severely diminishing the credibility of such witnesses.

Over the long run, a witness who does his best at least to maintain a neutral stance and provide valid evidence may find his career in forensic psychology more durable if less spectacular. To avoid an appearance of partisanship, it is well to understand the purpose of cross-examination so as to avoid being duly upset or embroiled in argument with opposing counsel. When a cross-examiner challenges your data base, challenges your conclusions, or makes whatever kind of challenge he chooses, you should be aware that there is nothing personal it it; he is merely doing his job. Therefore, you should avoid engaging in some kind of personal intellectual duel with him for the sake of the battle. This does not mean that you should not, when appropriate, provide information negating the point he is trying to make. It does mean that you should avoid sarcasm or a belittling attitude toward the cross-examiner. You should avoid anger because this indicates that you have become somewhat emotionally involved in the case.

There are a couple of tactical matters to consider when on the witness stand. One is to avoid the use of jargon, particularly in jury trials. If your testimony consists largely of a stream of terms from the Diagnostic and Statistical Manual or the esoteric language of psychoanalytic concepts, the jury is not likely to understand what you are talking about and, consequently, may ignore it. If you are unable to describe the individual psychologically in simple everyday language, you should either get out of forensic psychology or go back over your data to determine whether or not you really understand the individual. A good cross-examiner will not let you get away with jargon. He will insist that you reduce the terminology to understandable language and if you are unable to do so, he will urge the jury to disregard it.

A second point has to do with the manner of answering questions, particularly in cross-examination. A good rule is not to answer the question immediately. For one thing, a little thoughtfulness before answering will indicate to the jury that you are giving the matter serious thought. Secondly, the attorney for your side may wish to object to the question; you are not in a position to determine whether it is a proper question or not—the attorney is. If you blurt out an answer before the attorney has a chance to object, even though he may subsequently make objection, the jury will have heard the answer and the objection is relatively useless. Also, it is quite important to be sure that the meaning of the question asked is clear, both to you and to the jury. If you do not fully understand the question, do not attempt to answer it, but simply say that you do not understand it.

Chapter 9

WORKING WITH THE
FORENSIC PSYCHOLOGIST*

ROBERT L. SADOFF, M.D.

A s a forensic psychiatrist I'm called upon to evaluate individuals who are charged with crimes those who have been injured in an accident or at work, those who need civil commitment, those who need involuntary hospitalization, and those involved in domestic relations matters. The extent and scope of the legal psychiatric situations are vast. In a number of cases it is important and necessary to obtain psychological consultation which would aid in resolution of the legal questions.

The average psychiatrist is not trained sufficiently in his residency to conduct forensic psychiatric examinations, and is not fully aware of the intensity and scope of the work. My experience in working with psychologists is similar; i.e., very few psychologists are clearly aware of legal issues that may involve their clients and are not able effectively to apply results of psychological testing and evaluation to the legal questions at hand. A few selected psychologists with experience in working with lawyers and in legal situations have been most helpful in the resolution of legal psychological problems.

Most psychiatrists prefer to conduct a clinical examination based on their interview alone, a unilateral application of their developed skills in interviewing and examining to all patients. The forensic psychiatrist needs to go further and obtain information of a more investigative nature in his efforts to aid the lawyer in the resolution of his case. The forensic expert needs to be an investigator in the true sense of the word by obtaining as much information as he is able

*This chapter was originally presented as a paper at the American Psychological Association Annual Meeting, Washington, D.C., September 1976.

from a number and variety of sources. The forensic psychiatrist, for example, may need school records, may need to speak to witnesses, arresting officers, have information from previous hospitalizations, speak to parents and friends and also obtain special testing, including psychological tests, sodium amytal interview, hypnotic interview, polygraph examinations, etc.

Part of the armamentarium of the forensic psychiatrist is the availability of a good forensic psychologist who is able to apply the skill of a clinical psychologist to legal issues. Like the average psychiatrist, the psychologist usually is content with a clinical examination and an evaluation of a standard battery of psychological tests. For most purposes, as in psychiatry, this would be sufficient. However, in forensic psychology, it is my contention that this is not sufficient and the psychologist needs to have a familiarity with the rules of law and needs also further evidence to support hypotheses and conclusions that he draws. I strongly contend that the forensic psychologist is not merely a consultant to the psychiatrist, who consults with the lawyer, but the forensic psychologist has an equally important role to play with the lawyer, both in evaluation, examination and consultation as well as functioning as an expert witness in court.

There are some psychologists who prefer to conduct the testing blind; i.e., without previous clinical history and without any understanding or knowledge of the legal questions involved. They will give a purely psychological clinical evaluation and assessment, without application to the legal issues. It is my belief from working with all types of psychologists that the most helpful forensic psychologist is the one who is aware of, understands, and is familiar with legal issues and can communicate effectively his findings to the lawyer and help him in preparing his case. Just as the forensic psychiatrist must be a consultant as well as an evaluator, I believe the forensic psychologist must be able also to consult effectively with attorneys and judges in cases involving mental and emotional illness.

In addition, the forensic psychologist must be able to work effectively in court in testifying, must be familiar with the rules of the game and know what is expected of him in the courtroom. The forensic psychiatrist and forensic psychologist can make a most effective team in consulting with attorneys, especially in criminal cases, but also in a number of civil cases, in advising and serving as expert witnesses in court.

One may ask, what if the psychiatrist and psychologist disagree on their conclusions, based on independent clinical studies? Often the case exists where there are subtle differences or disagreements, and sometimes there are gross disagreements, depending on the findings. It is my custom to consult closely with the forensic psychologist with whom I am working and to discuss the matter fully with him or her so that we understand the limitations of each other's professional expertise and on what we base our conclusions. Rarely, but occasionally, the disagreement is so strong that they may not work together effectively for the attorney. In these cases, however, the attorney will accept the one that best fits his needs in that particular case and call him to testify rather than the other who cannot be of help.

Mostly, I enjoy calling in a forensic psychologist who is experienced, whose evaluations I trust, and from whom I want either confirmation or negation of a clinical impression that I may have after one examination. Thus, it is not so much that we would disagree, but whether there would be confirmation or negation of my initial impression based on the clinical tests conducted.

Working with the forensic psychologist, then, implies a comprehensive effort to obtain the best possible examination of the client from different frames of reference, working together to coordinate the findings into a meaningful evaluation. In criminal cases the forensic psychiatrist is generally asked to evaluate the defendant on questions of competency to have made a statement to the police, competency to stand trial, criminal responsibility at the time of the act, and recommendations for disposition. At this point I would exclude the treatment of the offender in a prison and label that role as correctional psychiatry or correctional psychology. The forensic expert is primarily concerned with his role before and during the trial.

In the evaluation of an individual to determine whether he was coerced into making a statement because of his personality, his low intelligence or his use of drugs or alcohol, it may often be helpful to have the consultation of a forensic psychologist. Assessment of intelligence, testing of ego strengths and determination of organic brain damage of a subtle nature requires the expertise of a forensic psychologist.

Another difference between the regular psychiatric patient and the forensic patient is the amount of distortion in criminal cases. The patient does not come to the doctor because he is hurting, he comes because someone else is hurting, or because somebody else requires an examination of him. Thus, he may not tell the truth about his symptoms but may distort in a way that would favor his case.

A more objective method of assessing the degree of illness or the veracity of the patient may be through the psychological testing procedure which one cannot effectively fake throughout. Often one will require psychological testing to determine potential for treatment and underlying psychotic process. Occasionally the testing, especially the projective tests, will show a psychotic element which does not emerge on clinical examination, especially after one or two interviews. Psychological trends and patterns of personality traits are quite helpful in assessing an individual in forensic matters and are best determined by the testing procedure.

Often the defendant in criminal cases will indicate that he does not know the answers to questions that were put to him or that he has forgotten what had occurred at the time of the crime. Mostly the forgetting is convenient rather than amnesic. The amnesia, however, if present, may be due to organic brain damage which may be detected by psychological testing.

Determination of an individual's intellectual capacity and his ability to understand, for example, the Miranda warning at the time of arrest and interrogation, would be helpful in assessing his competence to make a voluntary statement. Testing is also helpful in assessing the defendant's capacity to know the nature and quality of his act and to know at the time of the act whether it was wrong. This is the M'Naughten test for criminal insanity which exists in most jurisdictions, and may be difficult to evaluate in some cases. Often psychological testing is helpful along with other input and data to arrive at an opinion within reasonable certainty.

The forensic psychologist is also helpful in preparing recommendations for treatment, either on probation or within a correctional setting in criminal cases. Assessment of motivation, psychological-mindedness, intelligence and ability to work in therapy is often required for such purposes.

In civil matters, personal injury or domestic relations, the forensic psychologist is most helpful in the evaluation and determination of organic brain disease, intellectual capacity, presence of psychotic thinking, or in resolving such diagnostic problems as malingering, hysterical illness or psychosomatic illness. Often the clinical examination alone is not sufficient to determine whether a person is malingering about illness, but the psychological testing can help in arriving at a valid opinion.

In commitment proceedings the question of dangerousness is quite important, especially with the newer laws requiring involuntary hospitalization to be based on mental illness with dangerousness to one's self or others. Psychological testing may aid in the determination of the potential for self-abuse or acting out impulsive urges.

In summary, the forensic psychiatrist and forensic psychologist may work most effectively as a team in consulting with the attorney in a particular case. The psychologist brings to the case an expertise beyond that of the psychiatrist and together they may complement each other's clinical work in helping the lawyer most effectively with his case. It is quite reassuring for me to have a respected colleague with whom to work and to discuss the matter and with whom to testify in difficult and challenging forensic cases.

Chapter 10

THE USE OF NEUROPSYCHOLOGICAL TESTIMONY IN CIVIL COURT PROCEEDINGS

JAMES L. MACK, Ph.D.

T HE PURPOSE OF THE PRESENT PAPER is to provide an overview of the use of neuropsychological testimony in civil suits and administrative proceedings. Specifically, I plan to discuss the nature and scope of neuropsychological testimony, its value in establishing the presence of neurologically based psychological deficits, and the current status of neuropsychologists as expert witnesses in civil suits. In addition I will provide some general guidelines for preparing neuropsychological testimony and discuss some of the problems commonly arising in the course of such testimony.

In spite of the widespread growth of neuropsychology in recent years, relatively little published information has been made available to facilitate the use of this developing area of knowledge in the courtroom. Psychologists are now licensed by most states and recognized as qualified expert witnesses in most jurisdictions. Furthermore, even those commentators inclined to be somewhat skeptical about the value of mental health specialists as expert witnesses[1] have been impressed by the many objective tests and procedures used in the neurological laboratory. The clinical psychologist, however, may feel somewhat at a loss as to how to incorporate an amount of new information that may be temporarily exceeding his or her processing capacity, while neuropsychologists often prefer to remain safely ensconced in their laboratories rather than be called upon to utter statements within the limits of reasonable scientific or medical certainty.

Certainly there is adequate basis for assuming that such testimony is of considerable potential utility. Neurologic problems in personal injury suits are extremely common. McFarland et al.[2] found that 81 percent of persons who sustained injuries in automobile accidents incurred head trauma. In addition sources of potential neurologic damage are seen in industrial accidents, medical malpractice suits involving complications of such procedures as anesthesia and angiography and a host of other causes of injury. In such cases the evaluation of the nature and extent of the injury frequently requires the assessment of the patient's intellectual and perceptual functioning, and a large number of authors have emphasized the value of psychological testing in providing an objective basis for such findings.[1,3-7]

Beresford[7] has provided an excellent, comprehensive, and candid manual for the neurologist who is about to assume the role of an expert witness. While the general issues he discusses are certainly relevant for a psychologist preparing to give neuropsychological testimony, there is an absence of specific neuropsychological information. Cadwell[4] and, more recently and in greater detail, Lezak[5,6] have provided rather complete descriptions of the nature and value of neuropsychological evaluations in personal injury suits, but their reviews have been directed principally at attorneys.

Lezak's two-part article is sufficiently detailed to provide psychologists with a good general background concerning many of the issues likely to arise in neuropsychological testimony. She discusses the meaning of brain damage, analyzes the various behavioral manifestations of neurologic impairment, and is one of the few authors to take into account emotional as well as intellectual and perceptual effects of head injuries. She provides a basic review of neuroanatomy and the relationship of brain function to behavior and summarizes a large number of neuropsychological tests. Perhaps some of the most significant issues she considers (from the point of view of a psychologist) include her emphasis on the variety of ways in which brain damage may be manifested and the need for a varied battery of tests to determine the extent of the psychological deficits encountered in many patients. In addition she provides a discussion of the various means of estimating the patient's premorbid intellectual level and in terms of the immediate premorbid level of functioning, by evaluating the information that can be obtained from test scores, academic or occupational achievements, school grades, military service records, family reports, and existing records of the patient's premorbid intellectual products, such as letters, inventions, etc. Nevertheless, Lezak's informative article is primarily useful in providing the attorney with a comprehensive picture of what can be obtained from neuropsychological testimony, not as a guide to how such testimony should be given.

The essential purpose of most neuropsychological testimony is to fully describe the nature and extent of the psychological deficit, to provide a differential diagnosis, i.e., to describe the most likely etiology of the deficits reported, within the limits of reasonable scientific or medical certainty, and to offer a prognosis, including a prediction as to the likelihood that the deficits may be permanent and a description of what type of treatment or rehabilitation procedures may be useful in helping the patient recover from or compensate for the deficits. It is important for the psychologist to attempt to relate the neuropsychological test findings to other neurologic evidence in order to increase the credibility of the testimony by demonstrating its consistency with the testimony of medical witnesses and other independent descriptions of the alleged injury.

The most typical use of testimony of the type described above is in the report of the damages received by the plaintiff in a personal injury suit. Essentially the same findings may also be relevant to other civil matters such as divorce proceedings, disputes over contracts, and issues involving testamentary capacity or the management of affairs, where the capacity of one of the litigants has been called into question. Finally, issues regarding the nature and basis of neuropsychological deficits may occur in administrative proceedings, such as workmen's compensation and social security disability hearings. One possible use of neuropsychological testimony that has not been described is on behalf of the defendant in a civil suit to avoid a finding of negligence. While foolish, hasty, or "congenitally defective" behavior, even insanity, does not preclude the possibility that a defendant may be found negligent, transitory unconsciousness or delirium due to illness have commonly been regarded as "circumstances" depriving the actor of control over his or her conduct and thus relieving the defendant of liability. An interesting legal issue may arise in the event that a defendant in a tort action seeks to use neuropsychological testimony to provide a basis for arguing that such deficits constitute circumstances that may attenuate the defendant's liability.

While the use of neuropsychologists as expert witnesses in personal injury cases has not been extensively considered in the medical or legal literature, there appears to be ample support for the use of clinical psychologists for this purpose. Gaines[3] specifically mentioned the use of psychological tests in providing objective evidence of head injuries and reviewed a few early cases outlining the nature and scope of expert testimony given by psychologists in various jurisdictions. Another early review[9] described a number of decisions qualifying psychologists as expert witnesses, although some instances in which testimony in regard to the presence of insanity was restricted to physicians were also noted.

Shulman,[10] in one of the more comprehensive reviews, raised three important points. Because (at that time) the licensing of psychologists was not widespread, it was often difficult to determine the characteristics of a qualified psychologist. Perhaps as a result, Shulman noted, court decisions tended to impose rather high qualifications, including the possession of a Ph.D. degree in clinical psychology, the completion of a one year internship in a facility approved by the American Psychological Association, and postgraduate experience. Shulman emphasized the unique contribution that psychologists had to offer, in that although their final conclusions were similar in character to those of a physician, in particular a psychiatrist, their methods of evaluation were considerably different. The psychologist's use of objective test data, he felt, provided potentially more effective testimony than the more traditional subjective psychiatric opinion. The author then reviewed a number of cases and concluded that psychological testimony could be excluded only if it failed to provide additional or contradictory information to that provided by the testimony of a physician.

Towey[11] reviewed a number of additional cases from widely varying jurisdictions, including a case concerning testimony by a clinical psychologist with regard to the presence of brain damage, and found considerable legal precedent for the use of clinical psychologists as expert witnesses. Deikman[12] has described the details of a case in which a neuropsychologist provided the only basis for a finding of brain damage in a personal injury case. More recently, Pacht et al.[13] have reported the use of clinical psychologists as expert witnesses in a variety of cases and have offered some guidelines concerning their use in such a capacity.

In order to consider more specifically what characteristics a neuropsychologist should possess in order to be qualified as an expert witness, one must first consider in general the state of neuropsychological knowledge. Over the past twenty years a considerable body of evidence has been collected with regard to the extent to which a number of neurological variables may influence psychological functioning. In particular, psychological functions appear to be affected by the locus of the brain lesion, including whether the lesion is generalized, diffuse, or focal. Among focal lesions, effects vary according to whether grey or white matter is damaged, whether the damage is restricted to neocortical areas or involves deeper brain centers, and, within the cerebral cortex, whether the lesion is restricted to a single hemisphere or a single lobe. Lesions may vary in their effects as a function of their time of onset, i.e. whether they are "old," chronic lesions or recently acquired, acute lesions and their course—whether they are static or progressive. The etiology of a particular brain lesion, whether it be vascular, neoplastic, traumatic, infectious, toxic, metabolic, etc., also may influence its behavioral manifestations. Furthermore, the way in which a neurological lesion affects behavior can be influenced to considerable degree by the status of the patient, including the patient's age, personality adjustment, and level of intellectual and perceptual abilities at the time of onset.

At the same time that we have gathered a considerable amount of information concerning relevant neurological variables that must be considered in undertaking a neuropsychological examination, research in the cognitive and perceptual effects of brain damage has demonstrated the importance of independently analyzing a large number of specific abilities in order to carry out a comprehensive evaluation of an individual patient. A number of manipulations of the stimuli presented to the subject have been found to be important—including the nature of the stimulus material, whether it is verbal or nonverbal; the amount of information in the stimulus; the method of stimulus presentation, whether it is presented simultaneously or sequentially; the modality of the stimulus, visual, auditory, somesthetic, olfactory, or gustatory; and the context in which the stimulus is presented, e.g. either isolated from or embedded within an interfering background. The manner in which the subject is asked to respond may also be critical, in that his or her behavior may be considerably affected depending on whether the task requires discrimination, matching, reproduction, spontaneous production, etc. The timing of the response onset is important in regard to whether the subject is asked to respond contemporaneously with the stimulus presentation, immediately following its offset, or following a delay interval during which there may or may not be interfering activity. The duration of the response itself must be considered, i.e. whether it is to a brief, relatively punctate response or a prolonged, stably maintained response.

In addition to identifying a number of crucial neurological and psychological variables that must be considered in the evaluation of a patient with suspected neurologically based psychological deficits, current neuropsychological research has provided an objective basis for the interpretation of psychological deficits through the development of norms on a wide variety of psychological tests for subjects with various ages, backgrounds, and diagnoses.[14,15]

In short, a considerable amount of information has been amassed regarding both the neurological and behavioral aspects of psychological deficits that must be considered if one is to carry out a detailed neuropsychological assessment. Although the literature underlying the basis of the material summarized above is far too extensive to cite in the present paper, there are now available a number of references that provide a broad survey of the present state of neuropsychological knowledge.[16-20] The question remains: How are we to determine the qualifications necessary to provide competent neuropsychological testimony?

Until the present point in this paper, the titles "clinical psychologist" and "neuropsychologist" have been used almost interchangably in regard to the qualifications of an expert witness. When Diekman[12] described a trial in which a neuropsychologist testified, the witness's special experience was used to enhance his credibility, but in no way was it implied that any competent and experienced clinical psychologist could not have taken his place (c.f., for example, Towey[11]). There are no statutory or professional standards for identifying a neuropsychologist, and the assessment of patients with neurologically based deficits has been consistently considered to be within the realm of expertise of a clinical psychologist. As the extent of neuropsychological knowledge and the demands for neuropsychological services have simultaneously expanded, the apprehension of many clinical psychologists has become increasingly evident, as they are called upon to do more and more with patients about whom they seem to know relatively less and less. This picture represents to some extent an exaggeration, since many clinical psychologists have turned to such cases with interest and curiosity and, in effect, have become self-educated neuropsychologists, a necessary adaptation, since until recently, no neuropsychology training programs were available at a postgraduate level and few graduate schools have incorporated such training into their already crowded programs of study.

While no formal standards have been formulated at a national level to define the role and training of a neuropsychologist, a number of informal guidelines have become evident. Many clinical psychologists have taken positions in neurological settings. Professional organizations such as the International Neuropsychological Society and the Academy of Aphasia have accepted large numbers of clinical psychologists as members. Specialized neuropsychological journals, such as *Neuropsychologia, Cortex,* and *Brain and Langauge,* have become available, providing a readily accessible body of knowledge to interested clinical psychologists. Thus consideration of a clinical psychologist's occupational setting, membership in professional organizations, and professional reading provides an informal means of evaluating his or her neuropsychological expertise. Finally, in recent years a number of postgraduate training centers have begun to provide an organized neuropsychological training experience, and some governmental and private agencies have begun to take cognizance of such training as they have searched to develop standards to define health care providers who are competent to carry out special diagnostic and treatment procedures. One might describe the current state of neuropsychology as one of transition. It is highly likely that within the not too distant future there may be formally recognized specialty area of neuropsychology that may or may not require a graduate degree in clinical or experimental psychology as a prerequisite.

In the meantime, we remain in somewhat of a dilemma. Most clinical psychologists without specialized neuropsychological training or experience are loathe to identify themselves as competent to perform neuropsychological assessment, yet within the courtroom, they are quite likely to be considered as qualified to testify as expert witnesses in this regard. Indeed, if they were not so regarded by the courts, there would probably be far greater demand for neuropsychological testimony than there are neuropsychologists to provide such testimony. It seems likely that as attorneys become more familiar with the specialized knowledge provided by neuropsychological research, clinical psychologists will be given increasingly rigorous cross-examinations in regard to the basis of their findings as well as being challenged in terms of their professional credentials.

Having decided to accept the role of an expert witness, the psychologist (clinical psychologist or neuropsychologist) must then set about preparing an adequate presentation of the patient's injuries. Typically the psychologist has been consulted either directly by an attorney or through the suggestion of a physician. In some cases a request is made for testimony in regard to a patient who has been seen in another context but who has subsequently entered into litigation concerning his or her injuries. The material that the psychologist is expected to provide consists of evidence relating to the nature and extent of the injuries the patient has suffered, the causal relationship of the injuries to the negligence that is alleged to have occurred, and the consequences of the injuries to the claimant. The evidence may include medical records, reports of diagnostic evaluations, including results of specific tests, and oral testimony. The expert witness may be asked to submit a report of his or her findings, to give a deposition, and to provide actual testimony in court. In the case of administrative proceedings rather than a civil suit, much the same type of information will be requested, but it will be given in a far less formal setting, in which the primary issues will be the extent of the disability and the compensability of the injury under statutory guidelines; usually no appearance will be necessary.

Fox[21] has discussed in detail what should be included in a medicolegal report, and his general guidelines serve adequately for a neuropsychological report. He emphasizes that the report should include the pertinent medical history, relevant past history, diagnostic findings stated in both medical (read psychological) and lay terminology, conclusions regarding the causal relationship between the injury and the accident, stated within the limits of reasonable scientific or medical certainty, and a prognosis, provided sufficient time has elapsed to allow the formulation of an acceptably accurate prediction. He also includes a discussion of related issues that may be a focus of the cross-examination. In the case of the existence of a previous condition that might produce effects similar to those of the injury in question, he recommends that an explanation be offered as to how the previous condition was exacerbated by the injury. Fox stresses that the emotional aspects of the case should be frankly and fully considered. Too many expert witnesses are inclined to dismiss such findings as subjective and inconsequential when they are not accompanied by objective neurologic findings. In essence, however, when there is evidence establishing the fact that an injury did occur, mental disturbance accompanying that injury is considered to be compensable, since the initial injury establishes a cause of action; such mental disturbance is compensated as "parasitic" damages, even though the injury itself may be negligible.[8]

Postconcussive syndromes and other conditions manifested primarily by either emotional changes or by the persistence of somatic complaints in the absence of neurologic findings provide one of the most difficult issues that must be considered in personal injury suits. Beresford[7] has argued that those symptoms that occur as a direct result of a brain injury and are accompanied by objective neurologic findings are readily supportable in testimony. However, he finds that it is often difficult to testify in regard to those symptoms that are the direct result of brain injury but lack the support of concurrent neurologic findings. In the latter case, Beresford suggests that neuropsychological testing may provide objective findings of deficits that were too subtle to be identified by a clinical neurological examination or other special neurodiagnostic procedures.[22,23] Indeed, there is evidence to suggest that in some instances neuropsychological tests may provide a more accurate diagnostic picture than do standard neurologic tests.[24,25] Beresford, however, avoids the issue of symptoms that are essentially emotional reactions to an injury rather than direct consequences of brain damage, even though such symptoms may well provide an adequate basis for "parasitic" damages. Presumably he would leave the objective description of such findings to psychologists and psychiatrists. Lezak,[5,6] in fact, has addressed this issue and described how standard personality tests may be used to provide a basis for objectively identifying the emotional consequences of brain injury.

After the submission of a neuropsychological report, one is apt to be asked to give a deposition. This proceeding is far less formal than court testimony but is intended to provide opposing counsel with an opportunity to determine what the nature of your testimony will be should the case come to trial. Although the transcript of the deposition is not usually admissible as evidence in the trial, if it contradicts any statements that you might later make at the trial, such contradictions can be used to impeach the credibility of your testimony. Thus a deposition should be prepared for in the same fashion as the trial itself. In fact, it will probably be your last contact with the case since most personal injury cases do not come to trial. To the extent that you are able to impress opposing counsel with the validity of your findings and the manner in which you are able to handle yourself during the deposition, you are likely to reduce the probability that the case will come to trial. Of course, the trial may still occur because issues regarding the negligence of the defendant may be in dispute, even though you have done a superlative job of showing the nature and probable etiology of the injury.

In preparing for a deposition, as for a trial, you should review your records carefully, making certain that statements with your case file do not disagree with your report, since material in the file may well be subpoenaed in a "search and destroy" mission, as opposing counsel attempts to find some possible basis to challenge your findings. In fact, opposing counsel would be well advised to subpoena such information and have it reviewed by another neuropsychologist before deciding whether to accept your findings as unchallengeable. Perhaps the most important aspect of the preparation is to go over your findings with your patient's attorney, so that he may help you anticipate questions that are likely to be asked during the deposition or cross-examination and so that you can outline for him or her the questions that should be asked in order to properly elucidate your findings. Furthermore, it is important that you point out to your patient's attorney any potential weak points in your report or testimony, so that they may be discussed and a means developed for handling them should they be raised by opposing counsel. While you, of course, are expected to openly acknowledge in response to questions of opposing counsel any uncertainties or questions you may have regarding your conclusions, it is important that your patient's attorney have some notion about these possible areas of weakness in the case, so that he or she will not be caught by surprise should the issue arise during the deposition or testimony.

Although you will not be officially qualified as an expert witness during the taking of the deposition, you may very well be questioned about your credentials, and it is appropriate to have a fully prepared curriculum vitae available for opposing counsel (presumably your own counsel will already have been provided with this information). It is particularly important to include in your presentation of your qualifications any specific neuropsychological experience you may have had, including the approximate number of diagnostic evaluations you have carried out, your membership in relevant professional organizations, and the graduate and postgraduate training experiences you have had in the area of neuropsychology, including any relevant research experience as well. Of course, it is also important to state your qualifications as a clinical psychologist since many of the issues that may arise in such a case may pertain more directly to general questions of personality adjustment than to specifically neuropsychological issues.

In preparing for the deposition testimony with plaintiff's counsel and, of course, in the actual testimony, one must cover the following issues:

1. How did you come to see the patient, i.e. by whom was the patient referred and for what reason?

2. When and for how long did you see the patient?

3. What was actually done with the patient, including both interviews with the patient and other relevant family members or friends and testing? At this point, the expert witness should attempt to avoid giving a detailed description of each test administered, although the names of the tests are frequently read into the record. It is usually preferable to describe the nature of the specific tests in the context of describing the patient's deficits. Otherwise, a detailed description of individual tests can become rather boring as well as offer to opposing counsel during the later cross-examination a basis for discussing "normal" tests results, which, while not necessarily relevant to the deficits reported, may successfully (from the point of view of the defendant) cloud the issues and create doubt in the minds of the judge or jury as to validity of the deficits elsewhere described.

4. What was the actual nature of the deficits found as a result of the examination? Emotional difficulties, as well as cognitive and perceptual deficits should be described in detail.

5. The basis of each deficit should be described, including the extent to which the finding was based on test results, interview information, and historical data. When historical information is used as basis for a finding, then the source of this information should be mentioned. Since opposing counsel may attempt to challenge such information as biased or dependent on heresay, it should be stressed that the use of interview and historical information in determining overall findings is in keeping with the usual standard of psychological practice. If you are unable to support the use of such nontest information as an appropriate and standard method of arriving at your diagnosis, then such information may be successfully objected to by opposing counsel. It is, of course, important to emphasize whether interview and historical information is the sole basis for a particular finding or is merely used to substantiate findings that can be independently demonstrated from test results. The test results may also be challenged on the basis of their lack of reliability and validity.[1]

In such instances, the witness must be prepared to defend the use of any particular test instrument. A more clinically relevant means of supporting the use of the tests to arrive at your final conclusions, however, is to demonstrate how several tests independently demonstrated essentially the same findings. It is particularly important to convey that it is the overall pattern of the test results that establish the nature of the deficits, rather than any single test finding.[5,6]

6. Diagnostic findings should then be related to the patient's complaints. Since many of the tests are not obviously related to a particular symptom, this relationship must be explained; when such an explanation can be made in language understandable to a judge or jury, then such corroboration of the patient's symptoms can be of considerable importance in demonstrating that the patient's complaints are justifiable and not simply an attempt on the plaintiff's part to obtain a favorable settlement.

7. The diagnostic findings must be interpreted in terms of the consequences to the patient, both intellectually and emotionally, in terms of his vocational capacities and his ability to carry out and enjoy his daily life.

8. The etiology or cause of the deficits must be spelled out within the limits of reasonable scientific or medical certainty. Although the neuropsychologist may not be considered competent to render a medical opinion regarding the presence of a particular basis for the injury, it is clearly within the realm of neuropsychological competence to relate observed deficits to such neurological factors as the locus of a brain lesion, whether generalized or focal, including the hemispherical and lobular locus of the damaged function, and the likelihood that such a deficit or deficits would arise from a recent or acute etiology or a chronic neurological dysfunction.[26] It is important to realize that recent and generally accepted rules for the demonstration of the cause of an injury do not require the demonstration that the alleged injury is, *sine qua non*, an injury that could not have occurred but for the negligence of the defendant. Rather, it must only be demonstrated that the alleged causal event was a material element and a substantial factor in bringing about the injuries sustained by the plaintiff. Furthermore, the plaintiff is not required to prove his case beyond a reasonable doubt. The evidence is simply required to lead to a reasonable conclusion that it was more probable that the injuries were caused by the action of the defendant than that they were not.[8]

9. The prognosis for recovery from the plaintiff's deficits is an important part of the testimony. Although some have emphasized the importance of avoiding a prognosis early in the course of the injury,[21] since many patients show changes over a period of one to three years following some types of neurological impairment, being too cautious with regard to prediction may cause some courts to rule that permanent injury has not been established, when in fact, it is highly likely.[7] Such predictions are usually based on actuarial information, obtained either from published research or from one's individual case experience, but cross-examining attorneys have occasionally been successful in having such "statistical" data excluded on the basis that it is irrelevant to a particular case. To handle such a possibility, one must be prepared to defend the use of actuarial methods in the prediction of behavior.[27]

10. In addition to prognosis, one must consider to what extent the plaintiff has deficits that may be at least partially remediable given proper treatment, so that treatment costs can be taken into account in whatever settlement is reached. In some cases, appropriate treatment, such as occupational, physical, speech, or psychological therapy, may be readily available. In other cases the plaintiff may have deficits, for which there are no immediately available sources of treatment, and the advisability of seeking treatment at some distance must be considered. In addition to treatment aimed at helping the patient overcome or compensate for his or her deficits, one should also consider the appropriateness and availability of vocational rehabilitation services. General rehabilitation programs must be carefully considered before they are recommended as potential resources since they may not take into consideration specific deficits that are different from those of their typical clients. It is not unusual in this respect to find a patient with a severe nonverbal deficit, such as a visual-spatial organization problem, being enrolled in a rehabilitation program designed to help mentally retarded individuals (most of whom have limited verbal ability) by training them to do assembly line work, hardly the appropriate program for an individual with visual-spatial deficits. In essence, treatment needs should be discussed but only insofar as they are directly related to the plaintiff's deficits.

The essence of handling cross-examination lies in a properly prepared direct examination. One must be able to support one's conclusions with relevant scientific research if called upon to do so, but a trial is not an educational presentation and citing relevant literature is not as effective as a reasoned analysis of the particular case at hand. Because the state of neuropsychological knowledge in regard to cognitive and perceptual deficits is quite objectively based in comparison to our understanding of personality adjustment and emotionality, neuropsychological test findings are often more difficult to challenge and more easily supported by direct citations of appropriate research findings than are subjective psychiatric impressions. Ziskin,[1] in discussing cross-examination of the plaintiff's witness in personal injury cases, suggests that the testimony "is least vulnerable where there is probable damage to the brain, as the psychological consequences of such injury, depending upon the part of the brain injured, have been reasonably well documented." Subsequently Ziskin[28] cited a study in which clinical psychologists were found to be no more accurate in classifying patients as brain damaged or non-brain damaged on the basis of a memory for designs test than were nonpsychologists, but he failed to point out that the psychologists were not neuropsychologically trained and that the classification of patients on the basis of a single test does not represent standard neuropsychological diagnostic procedure.

A note of caution must be injected, however, in regard to supporting diagnostic and etiological conclusions by citations of relevant literature. Such a procedure opens up the possibility that the witness may be cross-examined extensively on the study or studies so cited. One must be prepared to demonstrate a thorough knowledge of any studies thus cited.

There are several issues that are quite likely to be encountered in a cross-examination following neuropsychological testimony, and the expert witness must be prepared to deal with them. Usually the psychologist will be asked to explain how it was determined that the patient's present test results represented a decline from a previously higher level of functioning. Ideally the question can be answered by obtaining evidence from noninterested parties that the patient had previously shown by either educational or vocational attainments a level of functioning that could not have easily been achieved by an individual functioning at the present level of the patient. Thus, uncontested evidence that the patient had obtained an advanced academic degree or had successfully maintained a responsible executive or managerial position in the face of a present IQ of 85 would provide excellent support for the contention that he or she has shown a decline in ability.

Often, however, independent evidence of a previously higher level of functioning is absent and the psychologist is dependent upon reports of the patient or the patient's family members, who may well be presumed to be biased in view of their interest in the outcome of the litigation. In such an instance, the psychologist is wont to turn to tests to answer the question. In Deikman's[12] report of neuropsychological testimony during a personal injury case, the neuropsychologist, among other points, offered as evidence for a decline in function the fact that the patient's Deterioration Index, obtained from the Wechsler-Bellevue Intelligence Scale, indicated a decline. Such an approach is based on the hypothesis that some measures of ability are inclined to be quite stable in the presence of neurological damage while others are sensitive to such injury. Other tests such as the Shipley Hartford-Retreat Conceptual Quotient and the Hunt-Minnesota Test for Organic Brain Damage have been based on a similar premise, but research findings have failed to confirm the use of these procedures in such a fashion,[29] although the underlying premise may not necessarily be incorrect. Lezak[5] has recommended using the highest available estimate of the patient's previous level of functioning, whether it be obtained from historical information or current test findings, in order to determine whether or not the patient's deficits represent evidence of intellectual deterioration. Generally it must be acknowledged that it is difficult to find adequate objective evidence to support such a conclusion, in the absence of unequivocal historical information. Thus there is no easy answer to this question for borderline cases, and the psychologist must depend on using a carefully reasoned analysis of historical and test data in each particular case in formulating a response.

A related issue that is also likely to arise in cross-examination involves the extent to which the patient's deficits may be due to some previously existing injury or disease that is also likely to produce psychological impairment. It must be remembered that such questions are usually introduced by an attorney who has little knowledge of the widely varying ways in which brain damage can affect behavior. In most instances, questions of this type can be successfully answered by carefully describing the effects that the previously existing injury would be likely to produce and contrasting these effects with those observed in the present instance. In the less typical case, in which the previously existing condition produces effects similar to those observed at present, the psychologist must be prepared to contrast the effects of recent brain injury with long-standing injuries.[26] Of course, the possibility remains that the previously existing injury is also relatively recent or the effects of the present injury are relatively mild and therefore not easily discriminable from the effects of a long-standing lesion, in which case the credibility of the testimony will be considerably attenuated.

A final issue frequently encountered during cross-examination involves the extent to which the patient's deficits might be attributed to emotional factors, particularly when there is reason to believe that the patient had experienced emotional difficulties prior to the injury. Of course the fact that previously existing emotional difficulties might have been exacerbated by the injury does not preclude a successful settlement for the plaintiff, but such factors are likely to lead a judge or jury to minimize the nature of the deficits in comparison to deficits that can clearly be attributed to objectively demonstrated brain damage. This line of questioning is particularly likely to arise since many patients who have experienced brain injury show accompanying signs of anxiety or other emotional responses to the trauma they have undergone. Such questions are difficult to answer on the basis of research findings since most studies addressing this issue have compared the responses of brain damaged and emotionally disturbed patients on single tests and found that the two groups are quite difficult to differentiate. Again, the psychologist must depend on a carefully reasoned analysis of the particular case. By spending sufficient time with a patient, the psychologist is often able to demonstrate that even when the patient was showing reduced anxiety, the deficits were still in evidence or that the patient showed impairments on tests that are not likely to be influenced by anxiety, lack of motivation, or other emotional factors that frequently produce impaired performance on testing.

Other general techniques and approaches to handling cross-examination have been discussed elsewhere[7,30,31] and will not be reviewed here. Perhaps a general admonition is appropriate, however: Although the expert witness has been encouraged to spend extensive preparation time in order to give a comprehensive and well-documented presentation of findings and conclusions, it is also important to be able to respond to questions with brief answers, at times even "yes" or "no," rather than appear to be attempting to obfuscate an issue, and to be able to confidently admit the limits of one's knowledge with a firm, "I don't know."

SUMMARY

The present paper has attempted to present an overview of the value of neuropsychological testimony in civil court proceedings and to describe a number of issues that relate to such testimony. Neuropsychological findings hold the promise of providing valuable evidence in personal injury suits as well as in a variety of other civil and administrative proceedings. The issue of what qualifies an individual to be considered an expert witness in regard to neuropsychological matters has been considered, and the difficulties that clinical psychologists may experience in attempting to master a rapidly growing body of highly specialized information have been described. Finally, some guidelines for preparing neuropsychological reports and giving depositions and testimony in personal injury suits have been offered, along with a discussion of some of the issues that are likely to be raised during cross-examination. In general, those individuals who are called upon to provide neuropsychological consultation and testimony in civil proceedings are encouraged to become experienced with the large number of neurological and psychological factors involved in the evaluation of patients with brain injuries and to present a carefully reasoned analysis of their findings and conclusions in each particular case rather than depending on research findings that may not always provide information relevant to the issues that may arise.

REFERENCES

1. Ziskin, J. *Coping with psychiatric and psychological testimony,* 2nd ed., Beverly Hills, California Law and Psychology Press, 1970.
2. McFarland, R.A., Ryan, G.A., and Dingman, R. Etiology of motor vehicle accidents, with special reference to the mechanisms of injury, *New England Journal of Medicine, 278,* 1383, 1968.
3. Gaines, I.D. The clinical psychologist as an expert witness in a personal injury case, *Marquette Law Review, 39,* 239–244, 1956.
4. Caldwell, A.B., Jr. Courtroom use of psychological testing, *Trauma, 1,* 111–164, 1960.
5. Lezak, M.D. Psychological evaluation of brain damage: Part 1, *Trauma, 1,* 4, 5–98, 1972.
6. Lezak, M.D. Psychological evaluation of brain damage: Part 2, *Trauma, 1,* 5, 3-98, 1973.
7. Beresford, H.R. *Legal aspects of neurologic practice,* Philadelphia, Davis, 1975.
8. Prosser, W.L. *Handbook of the law of torts,* St. Paul, Minnesota, West, 1971.

9. Bock, J.A.   Annotation: Qualifications of nonmedical psychologist to testify as to mental condition or competency, *American Law Reports,* 2nd series, *78,* 919–927, 1961.

10. Schulman, R.E.   The psychologist as an expert witness, *Kansas Law Review, 15,* 88–97, 1966.

11. Towey, E.B.   Court testimony by a psychologist on the question of brain damage, In Smith, W.L. and Philippus, M.J. (Eds.), *Neuropsychological testing in organic brain dysfunction,* Springfield, Thomas, 1969.

12. Deikman, E.   Use of cortical function testing in a personal injury trial, In Smith, W.L. and Philippus, M.J. (Eds.), *Neuropsychological testin organic brain dysfunction,* Springfield, Thomas, 1969.

13. Pacht, A.R., Kuehn, J.K., Bassatt, H.T., and Nash, M.M.   The current status of the psychologist as an expert witness, *Professional Psychology, 4,* 409–413, 1973.

14. Reitan, R.M.   Investigation of the validity of Halstead's measures of biological intelligence, *A.M.A. Archives of Neurology and Psychiatry, 73,* 28–35, 1955.

15. Spreen, O. and Gaddes, W.   Developmental norms for 15 neuropsychological tests, *Cortex, 5,* 171–191, 1969.

16. Luria, A.R.   *Higher cortical functions in man,* New York, Basic Books, 1966.

17. Williams, M.   *Brain damage and the mind,* Baltimore, Maryland, Penguin, 1970.

18. McFie, J.   *Assessment of organic intellectual impairment,* New York, Academic Press, 1975.

19. Lezak, M.D.   *Neuropsychological assessment,* New York, Oxford University Press, 1976.

20. Hecaen, H. and Albert, M.L.   *Human Neuropsychology,* New York, Wiley, 1978.

21. Fox, R.M.   *The medicolegal report,* Boston, Little, Brown, 1969.

22. Milner, B.   Residual intellectual and memory deficits after head injury, In Walker, A.E., Caveness, W.F., and Critchley, M. (Eds.), *The late effects of head injury,* Springfield, Thomas, 1969.

23. Teuber, H.L.   Neglected aspects of the post-traumatic syndrome, In Walker, A.E., Caveness, W.F., and Critchley, M. (Eds.), *The late effects of head injury,* Springfield, Thomas, 1969.

24. Spreen, O. and Benton, A.L.   Comparative studies of some psychological tests for brain damage, *Journal of Nervous and Mental Diseases, 140,* 323–333, 1965.

25. Satz, P., Fennell, E., and Reilly, C.   Predictive validity of six neurodiagnostic tests: A decision theory analysis, *Journal of Consulting and Clinical Psychology, 34,* 375–381, 1970.

26. Fitzhugh, K.B., Fitzhugh, L.C., and Reitan, R.M.   Psychological deficits

in relation to acuteness of brain dysfunction, *Journal of Consulting Psychology, 25,* 61–66, 1961.

27. Meehl, P.E. *Clinical versus statistical prediction: A theoretical analysis and a review of the evidence,* Minneapolis, University of Minnesota Press, 1954.

28. Ziskin, J. *Coping with psychiatric and psychological testimony, 1977 pocket supplement,* 2nd ed., Beverly Hills, California, Law and Psychology Press, 1977.

29. Matarazzo, J.D. *Wechsler's measurement and appraisal of adult intelligence,* 5th ed., Baltimore, Maryland, Williams and Wilkins, 1972.

30. Brodsky, S. and Robey, A. On becoming an expert witness: Issues of orientation and effectiveness, *Professional Psychology, 3,* 173–176, 1972.

31. Brodsky, S.L. The mental health professional on the witness stand: A survival guide, In Sales, B.D. (Ed.), *Psychology in the legal process,* New York, Spectrum, 1977.

Chapter 11

THE ROLE OF THE PSYCHOLOGIST IN CLASS ACTION SUITS*

Raymond D. Fowler, Jr., Ph.D.

A SUIT IS DEFINED as action in a court of law to secure justice. An individual who feels unjustly and illegally treated may initiate a suit, and millions do each year. There are times when a great many people have essentially the same complaint, and, in the interest of judicial economy, the most reasonable way to proceed is through a single law suit to deal with their collective complaints. The class action suit, whether initiated by single individuals or a group, seeks to correct an injustice not only for the individual but for the entire group or class of individuals unjustly treated. Individuals or groups have initiated class action suits to prevent water pollution, to block increased utility rates, and to require rebates on breakfast cereal. But the most interesting class action suits, from the point of view of social and behavioral scientists, are those that initiate major social change.

The class action suit had its origin in English law in the seventeenth century, although there is fragmentary evidence that class litigation existed as early as 1309. Until recently, however, class action suits were relatively difficult to initiate, and legal scholars date the birth, for all practical purposes, of the modern class action to a 1966 amendment to the Federal Rules of Civil Procedure.

The principals of law are established by precedents, that is, by the results of litigated cases. A court decision, in effect, establishes law. Even our most fundamental body of law, the Constitution, is subject to continual redefinition by the weight of cases established in

---

*This chapter was originally presented as a paper at the American Psychological Association Annual Meeting, Washington, D.C., September 1976.

federal courts at various levels. Individuals who feel that they are receiving treatment that is contrary to their rights under the Constitution may initiate federal suits. It is often true that class actions are the best vehicles for protesting the constitutionality of the treatment given by states to its citizens, and particularly its most unfortunate citizens.

Of extreme interest to many psychologists are the so-called "right to treatment" cases established in the federal courts over the past several years. By the coincidence of geography and interest, I have become increasingly involved in these cases in a variety of roles. The coincidence of geography is that a remarkable number of cases have been under the jurisdiction of a great district judge, Frank M. Johnson, Jr. of Montgomery, Alabama. My interest in class action "right to treatment" began with the well-known *Wyatt* v. *Stickney*.[1] In this important case, Judge Johnson ruled that mentally impaired persons confined in Alabama state hospitals were denied a constitutional right to treatment.

My initial contact with this case was incidental. I put the original plaintiffs in contact with a talented attorney, George Dean, who devoted most of his time during the next four years to the building of this landmark case. My colleagues at the University of Alabama and I maintained almost continuous contact with the attorneys during this period, serving as resources for technical and professional information, helping to select witnesses, and providing expert testimony. The result of *Wyatt* was the establishment of Human Rights Committees to protect the constitutional rights of the residents of the state's mental health and mental retardation units and to oversee the implementation of the extensive changes ordered by Judge Johnson. The enormous improvement in the state's mental institutions that resulted from Judge Johnson's order convinced me that psychologists interested in social change should look to the courts. Marching with placards, giving lectures, or publishing critiques all have their particular rewards. Similarly, testimony to legislative committees may, on rare occasions, affect decisions. But expert testimony from the witness stand in a federal district court provides immediately usable information to a single individual, the Judge, who has the power to put the information to work. The result of *Wyatt* was a total overhaul of the Alabama mental hospitals and a reduction of the population from 5,200 to 1,600.

My next involvement in Judge Johnson's court came in 1972

in *Newman* v. *Alabama.*[2]   Newman, an inmate in the Alabama
prison system, charged that the medical treatment available to inmates was so poor as to represent an infringement of their constitutional rights.   Judge Johnson included mental health care in his definition of adequate health care, and he ruled that failure to provide
such care to inmates constitutes "a willful and intentional violation of
the rights of prisoners guaranteed under the Eighth and Fourteenth
Amendments."   I was asked by the U. S. Attorney to testify on the
mental health care needs of inmates.   I testified that mental health
care was essentially nonexistent in the prison system, since the system
employed no mental health personnel at all.   The judge ruled that
mental illness and mental retardation are the most prevalent health-
related problems in the Alabama prison system and that the absence
of qualified staff represented pervasive and gross neglect.   The Board
of Corrections, which manages the state prison system, agreed, without
court order, to contract with the University of Alabama Department
of Psychology to develop a plan to establish minimum mental health
standards for the Alabama correctional system.   Under this contract,
we carried out a survey of the existing standards for prison mental
health care in the United States, arranged site visits by correctional
experts from various parts of the country, and designed a program
for the delivery of mental health care throughout the state correctional system.

In partial implementation of this plan, the Board of Corrections
employed several psychologists, established a Division of Professional
Services, and initiated psychological screening as a part of the initial
classification process.

The Newman case resulted in some improvements in medical care
in the prison system, but enormous injustices continued in that area
and in others, and the court received numerous writs from inmates
complaining of the prison conditions.   In June 1975 Judge Johnson
consolidated two cases, one alledging failure on the part of the prison
system to protect inmates from violence on the part of other inmates
and a second alledging that the prison system did not provide adequate
rehabilitation opportunities for inmates.   The case was tried in
August 1975 and a member of our faculty testified to the barbaric
conditions that pervaded the system.

The result of this case was a sweeping decision declaring that the
state prison system actually worsens the physical and mental conditions of inmates and makes them less able to successfully reenter

society. The judge ruled that this constitutes cruel and unusual punishment in violation of the Eighth Amendment. He set down detailed standards that the state prison must maintain in order to comply with the Constitution.

Among the requirements established by the judge in his order of January 20, 1976 was the reclassification of all inmates. He ruled that "there is no working classification system in the Alabama Penal System, and the degree to which this impedes the attainment of any proper objectives cannot be overstated." He specifically ordered the state to contract with the Center for Correctional Psychology, a part of the Psychology Department, to aid in the reclassification. The state objected, and the judge ordered them to submit a plan of their own. He subsequently ruled their plan inadequate, accepted a plan submitted by the Psychology Department, and ordered that it be implemented. His order placed the responsibility for the classification program squarely upon the Psychology Department and allowed us considerable authority in assuring the implementation of our classification decisions.

Since July 7, 1976 my colleagues and I, along with a dozen or so graduate students and recent graduates, have been working full-time at Draper Prison near Montgomery, Alabama. We built, from scratch, a complete classification system with evaluation procedures that protect the rights of the inmates and permit the assignment to appropriate custody level and access to needed services such as education, vocational training, physical and mental health care, and appropriate job placement.

I suspect that our role in this particular case may be unique, and not likely to be duplicated. However, my major point remains: Class action suits can offer a rapid and effective means of applying federal power to remedy some of society's worst ills. Psychologists interested in participating in important social change should seek every opportunity for involvement in such cases.

REFERENCES

1. Wyatt v. Stickney, 325 F. Supp. 781 (M.D. Ala., 1971).
2. Newman v. Alabama, 349 F. Supp. 278 (1972), affirmed in part 503 F. 2nd 1320 (1974).

Chapter 12

THE ROLE OF THE PSYCHOLOGIST IN RAILROAD TORT ACTION CASES*

NEWTON L. P. JACKSON, JR., Ph.D.

B EFORE LOOKING AT THE ROLE of the psychologist in railroad tort action cases, some of the basic legal concepts in this area need to be
reviewed.   In particular, the following questions seem important:
(1) What is a tort?   (2) What is tort liability?   (3) What defenses to
tort liability are railroads confined to?

The word tort comes from Latin, *torquere,* to twist or wrest aside.
It is defined as a civil or private wrong, or injury, independent of contract.   There must always be a violation of some duty owing to the
plaintiff that is usually imposed by general law, not by mere contractual agreement between parties.

For example, if I promise to drive you to work if you pay for the
gas and I later refuse to live up to the agreement, that may be a
breach of contract because we had an explicit arrangement between
us.   However, if while driving you to work, I wreck the car because
I was driving carelessly, that may be a tort.   I never promised you
that I would drive carefully, but the common law holds that I was
implicitly obliged to do so.   You had a legal right under the provisions of general law to expect that I would exercise reasonable care
in transporting you.

Said another way, a tort is a term that has been applied to a "mis-
cellaneous and more or less unconnected group of civil wrongs, other
than breach of contract, for which a court of law will afford a remedy
in the form of an action for damages."[1]   The law of torts is concerned
with the compensation of individuals who suffer losses brought about

---

*This chapter was originally presented as a paper at the American Psychological
Association Annual Meeting, Washington, D.C., September 1976.

by conduct of others that is regarded as socially unreasonable. One might also say that a tort is "one's disturbance of another's rights which the law has created in the absence of contract."[2]

There are then three essential elements in a tort: (1) existence of a legal obligation from defendant to plaintiff, (2) breach of that duty, and (3) compensable damage as a proximate result. When these three elements are proven to have been present, the defendant is unmasked as what is called a tortfeasor.

In contrast to other areas of law, such as contract law, corporate law, criminal law, and so on, there is no Law of Tort. Instead, there are a group of specific cases that continually evolve new standards and definitions of legal rights that people enjoy under common law. These legal rights impose legal duties that, if they are breached and occasion compensable damage to a person, may lead to tort liability. Two kinds of tort liability are particularly germane to this chapter—strict liability and negligence.

Strict liability concepts are relatively new in the law. Until the turn of the century, the focus of law was on limiting liability in tort to "fault" in the sense of wrongful intent or a departure from a community standard of conduct. Newer legal concepts involve imposing liability without regard to "fault," particularly in cases where the defendant's activity is an unusual one involving abnormal danger to others.

For example, if you keep a poisonous snake as a pet and it gets out of its cage and bites someone, you will probably be held strictly liable for that. It does not even matter if you took extreme precautions to prevent the snake from getting out. It did get out, and you have no defense to tort liability. Similarly, if you run an assembly line where there are dangerous machines and one of them explodes and injures someone, you are likely to be held liable. The basis of this concept appears to be in a social philosophy that places the burden of the more or less inevitable losses due to a complex civilization upon those best able to bear them, or to shift them to society at large.

It was such a philosophy that led to workman's compensation acts in the early part of the twentieth century. Under English common law, by far the greater number of industrial accidents remained uncompensated, and the burden fell upon the workman, who could least afford it. Even when a judgment was awarded to a plaintiff, high legal fees, long delays in court, and pressure to settle so as to have money to live on meant small relief. Also, many early decisions about such suits were unfavorable to plaintiffs because courts ruled that workmen "assumed the risk" of their employers violating statutes that would have protected them.

Workman's compensation acts were created so as to "let the cost of the product bear the blood of the workman." The losses of modern industry due to accidents were to be treated like any other cost of production, such as replacement of tools. Workman's compensation acts obliged the employer to carry compulsory insurance that would equalize the cost over the entire industry. These costs would be added to the eventual retail price of the products or services produced, and thus be passed along to the consumer.

Workman's compensation is therefore a form of strict liability. The employer is held liable for injuries to his employees arising out of or in the course of employment. It does not matter if the employee knew the risk and chose to work at the job anyway. It does not matter if another employee, over whom you had no control, was negligent and caused the plaintiff's injury. It does not even matter if the employee got hurt due solely to his own carelessness. The rule is: If an employee is injured on the job, he recovers damages.

This guaranteed assurance that job related injuries would be compensated was balanced by restraints on how much the compensation would be. In Workman's compensation cases, the amount of compensation a person receives for certain injuries is carefully prescribed. For example, for loss of a thumb, the employee will receive 66 and 2/3 percent of his daily wage at the time of the accident for a total of sixty weeks. The injured employee is not allowed to file a tort action suit against his employer as well.

The most important single group of employees *not* covered by Workman's Compensation Acts are those of the railroads. Legislation with respect to railroad workers preceded Workman's Compensation Acts by a decade. In 1906 Congress enacted the Federal Employer's Liability Act, otherwise known as FELA. It was revised in 1908 and again in 1939. Under FELA, like in Workman's Compensation, an employer such as a railroad cannot avoid liability for injuries a railroad employee suffers on the job by claiming the employee knew the risk and chose to take it anyway. It is also no defense to say the employee's co-worker was the one who was negligent and the railroad had nothing to do with it. However, *unlike* Workman's Compensation, FELA allows an employer to reduce its liability by showing that the employee contributed to his own injury.

Contributory negligence is defined as conduct on the part of the plaintiff that contributes as a legal cause to his damage, which falls below the standard to which he is required to conform for his own protection. For example, if hard hats are required of employees in the train yard and an employee does not wear one, and he gets hit on the head by a rock thrown up by the wheels of a passing train (which *if he had been wearing his hard hat* would not have hurt him), the employee will be unlikely to recover for injuries he received.

So where does this leave the psychologist who is going to play a role in railroad tort action cases? Perhaps with the awareness that a civil suit against railroads for damages may involve issues not encountered in other kinds of civil suits where injury to an employee is concerned. There are many causes of action that may be taken against railroads in which psychologists could play important roles, but this chapter will only focus on tort actions brought by employees of railroads who are injured on the job.

Many large industries maintain a claims department that responds to suits initiated against them. In the case of the railroads in this country, there is an association of attorneys who have as a common interest defending railroads against tort actions, this is The National Association of Railroad Trial Counsel, also known as NARTC. Tort action against the railroads involves substantial amounts of money. A single office of a large carrier can easily have many millions of dollars in suits pending against it. The range in dollar amounts asked among these suits runs from as low as a few thousand dollars to as high as several million dollars.

Of the total number of suits pending against a carrier, only a very small percentage will ever go to trial, which is also true for most kinds of litigation. The rest will be settled out of court for some fraction of the original damages asked. One reason for settling out of court is certainly to avoid delay. However, some other good reasons include the following:

1. A trial means that settlement negotiations have been unsuccessful to that point, and the possibility of a million dollar or more judgment against the defendant railroad may now depend upon the juror in the back row who dozed during your best witness' presentation.

2. Most jurors will *say* they understand that the plaintiff must prove the railroad negligent to recover, but then they look at an individual who is injured, is in deep financial trouble, and cannot work

and they feel inside like, "The hell with the fine legal distinctions; this poor guy was injured on the job and now the railroad is trying to say they won't pay a cent toward helping him with his medical bills or feeding his starving family. Well, yes they will." So, according to Workman's Compensation concepts of strict liability, they are likely to find for the plaintiff.

3. Once the finding is made for the plaintiff, however, the jury is not constrained by any schedule of benefits, which should be true if it actually *were* a Workman's Compensation case. Therefore, huge awards can result according to the whim of the jury.

Through both formal and informal contact with NARTC members, some idea of how they view the role of the psychologist in railroad tort action cases can be gleaned. The large majority of trial lawyers who handle railroad defense FELA cases have never employed a psychologist in their legal work at all. Why this should be the case is a matter for speculation. Perhaps one reason is because lawyers have traditionally turned to psychiatrists when they needed a mental health expert. Another may be because they are unaware of how a psychologist could be of help to them.

Some attorneys in this area, however, are quite sophisticated about the potential usefulness of a psychologist to them. They have a rather clear idea of what they think the role of the psychologist in railroad tort action cases should be and use them, for example, to review any protocols or reports generated by opposing psychologists or psychiatrists to discover weak or strong points that should either be challenged or avoided on cross-examination. Very few NARTC members felt opposed to the idea of using psychologists in their legal work. Several believed that a psychologist's principal value to them would be in the area of gathering objective test data upon which an opinion could be based, as opposed to anybody else's *impressionistic* opinion.

Some problem areas in the attitudes of psychologists toward court work were of concern to many of them. Among these were the following:

1. Attorneys feel that psychologists often behave as if they thought it was not ethically permissible or desirable to act as an expert resource in an adversary proceeding. Instead, many psychologists appear to view their role as amicus curiae. Attorneys admit that it is arguable that a better legal system might focus on expert testimony as a contribution from independent and unbiased authorities. How-

ever, the practical fact to them is that their job is to work within the legal system as it is and to win their case. A psychologist who persists in disregarding these facts is a definite liability to them.

2. Attorneys also feel that psychologists sometimes act as if it is shameful for a psychologist to be hired by an attorney whose objective is to defend a large, powerful railroad against the claim of a hapless individual. In point of fact, the apparently large, powerful railroad may be at some disadvantage against an individual at a jury trial because of the sympathy jurors feel for the plaintiff.

3. Attorneys also feel that psychologists often appear to believe their report is sacrosanct and not to be guided in any way lest the psychologist be considered a "defense whore." Attorneys take an alternate view—that the attorney is charged with the management of the case, which includes deciding what material should be introduced into evidence so as to maximize the persuasive power of his argument. For example, the attorney may not wish for a variety of reasons to have the psychologist reach any conclusions at all in the report itself, but instead a simple statement about what kind of examination was performed and what the test scores were. Attorneys view as highly desirable a consultation with them before the report is written (and perhaps a display constructed). Their reason for this is that as one of the few exhibits entered into evidence at the trial, the psychologist's report (and display, if any) may go with the jury into the juryroom deliberations where its impact will be considerable.

Along this same line, attorneys point out that discovery proceedings make the psychologist's report accessible to opposing counsel—there are no written secrets. Therefore, it is not wise to fire off a quick report to an attorney who has retained you as a psychologist. Attorneys want thoughtful, careful, considered reports, not chatty, speculative ones. Similarly, you may be asked by an attorney to review materials from an opposing psychologist or psychiatrist. You may conclude that their deductions are accurate in characterizing the plaintiff as quite emotionally disturbed as a consequence of defendant's negligence. Do not write a letter to the attorney who hired you telling him you think the plaintiff is just as impaired as opposing counsel portrays him to be. Discovery proceedings will put this letter into the hands of opposing counsel, and the attorney for the defendant will have his case seriously compromised. A telephone call is a more secure way to deliver the bad news.

4. Attorneys are also concerned that mental health professionals

in general seem to think their only obligation to a case is to examine the injured individual, write a report, and be ready to testify if needed. Most attorneys feel they would rather work with an expert whose paper credentials are less than they could otherwise obtain if that expert will give them the time to talk about the case and its presentation, where the more qualified expert will not.

A final point might be made about the role of the psychologist in railroad tort action cases. Some attorneys are beginning to view the psychologist as a rehabilitation resource, who can offer treatment to people so they can return to work sooner than they otherwise would, particularly when the alledged injury rested upon psychological damage or trauma alone.

Also, there is some indication that ideas of the role of the psychologist in railroad tort action cases are broadening among attorneys. One law firm that handles railroad defense FELA cases has hired a team of psychologists to train their legal staff—secretaries, paralegals, and associates. This kind of extension of the expertise of the psychologist outside the courtroom into a kind of "preventative" or "anticipatory" role certainly suggests that the potential range of interactions between psychologists and attorneys is not yet known. It seems most likely that attorneys and psychologists will be crossing professional paths more often in the future, to the mutual benefit of both professions and of the public they serve.

REFERENCE

1. Prosser, W. *Law of Torts,* Racine, Wisconsin, Western Publishing Company, 1955.

Chapter 13

JURY SELECTION TECHNIQUES: IMPROVING THE ODDS OF WINNING

COURTNEY J. MULLIN

THE TRUE ENIGMA of the courtroom—Which twelve to select? Much has been written on the jury system[1-4] but, for many attorneys, jury selection remains surely one of the world's great mysteries.

The advent of social science techniques in the courtroom has resulted in the development of tools that provide attorneys a firmer handle to grasp when making decisions concerning jurors.[5-14] Obviously, the problem is complex. To solve the problems, time, effort, patience, and, at times, money are required.

Available to only a few, the gold-plated jury selection system utilizes such pretrial techniques as public opinion polls, computer programming, juror investigation, juror observation, and juror survey and the in-court techniques of evaluating group dynamics, authoritarian personality scaling, and kinesics (body language) analysis and scaling. Because many of these techniques can be used only in lavishly funded civil and criminal cases, I will emphasize the areas that an attorney can reasonably incorporate into everyday practice.

During the past five years, I have talked with hundreds of attorneys about jury selection and have had intensive participation in more than thirty cases as well as a few selected civil cases where hundreds of millions of dollars were involved, and I find that most attorneys regardless of how long they have practiced, believe that they can improve their jury selection skills. The following explanations and examples were put together to give a comprehensive look at these techniques and to illustrate some of them in depth.

First, I will present a brief overview on the value, availability, and costs of the various approaches to jury selection. An extensive discussion will follow concerning the applicability of body language analysis in jury selection and many readers may be surprised at their own abilities in reading the body language of others.

In many trials, most of the information on prospective jurors will be obtained before the first voir dire question is asked.

WHAT DOES JANE BELIEVE?

Public opinion polls provide sound information regarding the opinions held by persons residing in a particular community.[15] Polls expose how people in general feel about the issues involved in the case. The attitudes being surveyed will likely range from general types, e.g. attitudes toward law enforcement personnel, to very specific types, e.g. whether or not people feel the client on trial is actually guilty. Additionally, it is possible to analyze the survey data and obtain a numerical rating as to the favorableness or unfavorableness of any juror. This evaluation is based on specific demographic information (education, marital status, employment, etc.) concerning a particular juror. Further, it is possible to compare this potential juror to other potential jurors.

For example, in a specific case, a potential juror may be old, black, unmarried, live in a rural area, and employed in a local factory. A computer program based on the survey information rates this person as a six on a numerical scale running from one to ten (ten being good or a person who would respond very favorably to the arguments of one side of the case). Then further data analysis can provide information that compares the attitudes held by this person with all of the other persons who also rate six on the scale.

The use of this technique is extremely valuable in three particular situations. First, when the voir dire is limited to a few questions and/or when the voir dire is judge-directed rather than attorney-directed. Second, when the jurors are residents of large cities, a situation may arise involving extreme variability in the attitudes of the people residing in the city. Finally, when a case may have received extensive pretrial publicity. The publicized facts of the case itself may influence people's attitudes and, as a result, attorneys cannot assume that the generally held belief structures would remain intact during a juror deliberation and decision.

However, the financial costs of such an undertaking are extremely high. To insure the validity of the data, the surveyors must contact one thousand persons and the services of a number of experts in the field of survey methodology would be an absolute requirement. Experts would be needed for the running of the public opinion poll, for the data analysis prior to coming into the courtroom, and finally for in-court data analysis during the voir dire itself. Some firms, engaged in civil suits, have paid as much as $125,000 for this service.

Though practical considerations limit the employment of this method to a few celebrated and/or well-funded cases, this tool is not necessarily out of the reach of the average attorney. For example, in cases involving significant social issues, a group of interested attorneys may seek funding for the survey from public or private agencies.

WHAT WOULD SHERLOCK HOLMES SAY ABOUT THE POTENTIAL JURORS?

Juror investigation and juror observation provide valuable information at little financial cost, but at a fairly expensive time cost. The basic requirement for these activities is "person-power." These people need not have any particular training, but should be personable, observant, and reliable. The larger the number of potential jurors, the more people required for the investigation.

Juror investigation, routinely done by many prosecutors and defense attorneys, secures background information from public and private sources thus allowing an attorney to make a pretrial assessment of the kind of person any particular juror may be. An attorney may form prejudgments about the acceptability of a potential juror on the basis of information concerning the person's job, neighborhood, church, and political affiliation.

In large cities, juror investigation may center on an in-depth analysis of various institutions existing within the city. Local planning boards contain a wealth of information. Other good sources of information are university geography or demography departments, HUD offices, the Board of Realtors, church councils, and the like. Thus, when a juror says that she/he belongs to a particular church, information is available concerning the beliefs espoused by that particular church. Or, on the basis of studies that may have been conducted on the neighborhoods in a city, an address will tell you about past, present, and planned changes taking place in that neighborhood, the racial or ethnic mix, and the income spread. To a certain extent, people reflect the attitudes of the institutions to which they belong. A picture of a juror's neighborhood, church, or club may reveal a partial picture of the actual juror.

More specific information concerning individuals is easily obtained from such sources as the Board of Elections office (age, political affiliation, sex, address, length of time registered to vote, and, often, race appear on the voter's cards). Property tax lists provide important information, too. Not only can you estimate the general economic class of the juror, in many instances you can determine the marital status of the person as well.

The jury list should be given to any friends that have contact with large segments of the community (e.g. attorneys, police officers, postal carriers, and precinct leaders). Also the proprietors of local stores, bars, mortuaries, and insurance agencies can provide valuable information. In a recent Georgia murder case, the retired sheriff was able to provide information on 90 percent of the potential jurors.

A trip to actually see the juror's house and to speak with some of the juror's neighbors can also be useful. Homes reveal a great deal about their occupants. What impression might one form by seeing a brick house, ranch style, costing about $50,000; surrounded by an immaculate, manicured lawn with nothing out of place, set among many houses that look just like it; with a Lincoln car in the driveway wearing a bumper sticker, "America, love it or leave it?" Compare this impression with that formed from seeing a small house set among houses costing much more, with toys scattered in the yard, a station wagon in the driveway, flowers growing all over the yard, a cat lying on the windowsill, and children going and coming constantly.

Neighbors provide excellent sources of information. Ask about such issues as juror's background, employment, church affiliation, children, and sociability. They can be helpful in determining how the potential juror might respond to the issues involved in the case, their racial attitudes, their feelings towards crime, towards people in authority, towards the police. Some investigators are able to learn a great deal about potential jurors by talking with neighbors; whereas, other investigators draw a complete blank.

One note of caution—investigators must never speak with the jurors themselves or with members of the jurors' immediate families. However, investigators may speak to anyone else—only their own innovativeness limits them.

SHERLOCK INVESTIGATES FURTHER

Actual observation of the jurors themselves takes place at the courthouse. The observers should arrive before the jurors and take notes on specifics such as: Does the juror come alone or with other jurors? Does the juror come with her/his spouse? With friends? If so, are they the same sex and/or race? With whom do the jurors socialize as they walk in? In the halls? How do they group themselves? Do they appear to know everyone, moving from group to group, or do they appear to be strangers to the rest of the jurors?

It is also useful to note the type cars or trucks the jurors use. Is the vehicle costly? In good repair? High status? A van? Does it have a gun rack? In the courtroom itself, how do they treat each other? With excessive politeness? Is male chauvinism apparent? Do the men occupy the front row? How much do the men and women mix? Watch the jurors as they leave for lunch. Are the groupings still the same? Note any unusual forms of dress. How do the jurors treat others who are of a different race? With excessive politeness? With indifference? With some hostility?

Careful notes should be taken on which persons stand out from the crowd. They may walk at the front of the line, they may ask a question, they may seem to be in charge, ushering others around. Such behavior is indicative of a person who sees themself as a leader, as possessing more power than the other jurors. These persons will likely be elected the foreperson of the jury. The ability of such people to manipulate others makes them extremely risky as jurors.

GIVE THE JUDGE SOMETHING INTERESTING TO READ FOR A CHANGE

Juror surveys, sent out by the court, seek basic background information from each of the jurors. Often a cover letter from the judge is included explaining the purpose of the questionnaire. Covering such basic areas as employment, marital status, prior jury service, and the like, judges often view the questionnaire as a helpful tool in conserving valuable court time. This whole process can be expedited by supplying the judge with a carefully constructed, thoughtful questionnaire. Include as many attitudinal questions as possible. Attitudes may often be elicited through seemingly innocuous questions. "Have you served in the military? Was it an enjoyable experience for you?"

Some attorneys assume that the judges in their area of the country would refuse to send out a lengthy questionnaire. In fact, many judges are cooperative of such an endeavor and find the results very interesting.

This type of juror survey should be standard practice for any major case you try. The surveys are invaluable sources of information in prerating the jurors before they enter the courtroom. You can decide in general terms the probability of this person's being a "good" juror or a "bad" juror.

The rating should be in numerical form (e.g. a scale from one to ten, with ten representing the best possible juror). There will be a tendency for pre-voir dire ratings to evolve into the final rating. Beware. People who seem totally unacceptable on paper may turn out to be the best jurors. One absolute rule exists in jury selection: Never say never.

Public opinion polls, juror investigation, juror observation, and juror surveys—use of some or all of these techniques is effective in providing a solid base upon which juror evaluations can be made. Later, in trial, this information will facilitate the establishment of rapport between the attorney and the juror during the voir dire process. The more that is known about the jurors, the closer the goal, successful jury selection.

I UNDERSTAND WHAT THE JUROR SAID . . . I WANT TO KNOW WHAT THE JUROR MEANT! !

As the establishment of rapport occurs most rapidly in a one-to-one relationship, an individual, sequestered voir dire is best in most cases. Basically, the attorney is attempting to establish good rapport with someone who not only is a total stranger, but who also is placed in an unfamiliar and somewhat frightening situation.

Compounding the problem is the fact that a juror's ultimate decision in the case will rest upon basic feelings and attitudes buried deeply within her/his mind. The expression of attitudes elicited from a surface level of the personality often conflicts substantively with those held at a deeper level.

It is important to determine the value structure that is actually guiding the person's decision process.[16-18] The potential juror should be given space and time to express governing feelings. An individual can be described as many different individuals (the person I believe myself to be, the individual I aspire to be, the individual I want others to think I am, etc.).

During the course of the voir dire, jurors may "speak the truth" on many different levels of their personalities without being aware of the inconsistencies that they might be expressing. If the attorney probes deeply, truer feelings and attitudes often emerge.

I often counsel attorneys to eliminate everything that physically separates them from the juror—this means tables, podiums, and, most importantly, the legal pad filled with notes that has become an extension of their arm. Most attorneys spend more time checking their notes than they do looking at the juror, and the juror is sitting there wondering what else the attorney has written on that pad.

Rapport may be established with the juror by standing behind the client, hands placed upon her/his shoulders, symbolically expressing that the attorney is acting as the client's agent and the fact that the outcome of the trial will be of great consequence.

When attorneys choose to move closer to a juror, they should move up rather slowly and carefully. Many attorneys make use of this mechanism to establish rapport with the juror. However, it is possible to stand so close that the person feels anxious because their sense of personal space has been invaded.

Silence is a powerful tool during voir dire. After a juror has answered a probing open-ended question, the attorney's silence may cause the juror to feel that the answer was incomplete and more information may be volunteered.

Voir dire questions should be the type requiring an explanative answer from the juror. Psychologists have termed such questions, open-ended questions. Open-ended questions begin with such phrases as; "How do you feel about . . .?" "What did you think about . . .?" and "Can you tell me . . .?" Compare this type of question and the amount of information that one will receive from it with such closed-ended questions as: "Have you . . .? "Will you . . .? "Can you . . .?" The questions being asked will obviously vary depending on the facts surrounding the case.

In some instances, the questions will almost always be answered with the socially acceptable response regardless of the person's actual feelings. For example, "Are you prejudiced against blacks?" "Will you presume the defendant innocent until it has been proven beyond a reasonable doubt that she or he is guilty?" These types of questions accomplish little if one is seeking a truthful response. The most racist of persons will answer "no" to the first question, and everyone will answer "yes" to the second question, even though most people believe that if the state has gone to the trouble of holding the trial, the defendant is probably guilty. (Presumption of innocence is a myth).

TRY TO MAKE THE VOIR DIRE A BANQUET RATHER THAN A SNACK

To reach the deeper attitudinal levels, the attorney must "open" the juror. If the voir dire is conversational in tone, the juror is less restrained in expressing true feelings.

The attorney's nonverbal actions will also facilitate the establishment of rapport. Determining meaning from the enormous number of messages (verbal and nonverbal) being sent from a juror is an extremely difficult task for a single person to accomplish—particularly when this person is also involved in asking and formulating questions.

The addition of an observer sitting at counsel table increases the amount of information that is detected concerning the juror's attitudes. Assistance in jury selection may be provided by other attorneys, by social scientists, or by friends whose perceptual expertise is respected. The observer can be of great assistance in picking up on subtle clues the juror sends, in providing the attorney with suggestions for additional questions, in pointing out unexplored question areas, and in evaluating the juror from a more objective standpoint.

Each person connected with the case, especially the client in the case, should evaluate every juror. The final rating for each juror will incorporate all the sources of information that have been obtained both pretrial and during the course of the voir dire. Again, use a numerical scale ranging from one to ten with ten representing a good juror.

Sketches made of the juror's face are also helpful, and reveal much about the person's character, especially when the jury selection requires days or even weeks of court time. Close attention to the mouth, the amount of lip still exposed, and how down-turned the mouth has become often indicate a great deal about the potential juror.

WE WOULD HAVE WON, BUT THE JURORS GROUPED UP

Whenever all potential jurors are voir dired before the exercise of peremptory challenges, attorneys are able to make the best judgments regarding the information of a smoothly functioning jury. This system, termed a struck system, lends itself to the use of information concerning the dynamics of small group behavior. Any jury, considered a "small group" by psychologists, can be expected to be made up of multiple smaller groups and in jury selection, it is possible to construct the most favorable attitudinal group possible, given the choices existing among the jurors who are available.[19-21] Unity between the smaller groups on the jury can be achieved by the selection of bridge persons who can relate to more than one of the groups.

Each of the groups will contain its own leader with a number of clustering people relating to the leader. The clustering people are likely to follow the direction of the leader to whom they are attached. Thus, though the clustering people may hold views that are unfavorable, they will give up their own views and fall under the sway of the leader during the jury deliberations when the views of the leader differ from their own.

Selection of jury members then evolves into the selection of a few key persons whose views are desired and who also possess the ability to become leaders. People whose views are less acceptable may then be clustered around this leader, with reasonable assurance that they will act in accordance with the leader's dictates.

In some instances, the selection of the foreperson causes a true dilemma: Which juror to select when no one person possesses both the required favorable views and leadership abilities. To solve this type of problem, construct a group of persons who will act as the major force of leadership on the jury. Though only one of these persons will be actually elected foreperson, the real power will be held by all of these persons as they act in unison to achieve the result they desire.

In regard to jury dynamics, the key concept is that of power. By this is meant ability to convince others of one's viewpoint. An accurate assessment of the power possessed by each of the jurors selected is crucial. If a truly powerful person holds views contrary to those desired, the negative result of the jury deliberation can be predicted long before any evidence is presented. In one of the Attica trials, two persons who disagreed with the other ten jurors fought for their position unceasingly and were ultimately successful in having their view prevail.

DO YOU BELIEVE OBEDIENCE AND RESPECT FOR AUTHORITY ARE THE MOST IMPORTANT VIRTUES CHILDREN SHOULD LEARN?

Oftentimes, persons possessing leadership qualities are also authoritarians. Authoritarian persons possess a personality structure that is extremely rigid. They tend to be racist, anti-Semitic, sexually repressed, politically conservative, and, important in jury trials, highly punitive. As extreme respect for authority figures characterizes these persons, one can expect them to side with persons who hold socially legitimized positions of authority.[22-26] Their deference to the judge will be obvious. They may admit during the voir dire that they would believe the sworn testimony of a policeman more than the word of a lay witness. They are ideal jurors for prosecutors in criminal trials.

As staunch upholders of the established value system, authoritarians see themselves as the persons most qualified to serve as jurors. Any question concerning their ability to be fair and impartial would never enter their minds. The rigidity of their personality structure allows no space for doubts about themselves and their ability to know what is right and what is wrong.

They may be so out-of-touch with reality that they honestly feel that any prior opinion or bias can be totally erased from their minds and will in no way influence them during their deliberations as jurors. They are mystified when an attorney suggests that their racial bias against a black person would influence them during the trial of a black person.

For them, the world exists as a "should be" place with the traditional norms being upheld, no matter what the cost. Anyone who breaks these traditional rules should expect to be harshly punished.[27-30] No excuses are acceptable as explanations for rule breaking. Authoritarians just are not interested in the *whys* of a situation.

For them, doing one's duty is of paramount importance. Jury service ranks high as a situation in which one should sacrifice anything to perform the duties of a citizen. This exchange took place during the voir dire in a recent trial:

Attorney: "Mr. Jones, I see here that you are the sole proprieter of an oil company."

Juror: (with obvious pride) "Yes, sir!"

Attorney: "Well, sir, it is winter now. I know the oil business must be extremely busy now."

Juror: "Yes, sir. As a matter of fact this is the best year I have ever had."

Attorney: "Mr. Jones, do you have someone who can take over for you, help you out, if you are selected to serve on this jury?"

Juror: "No, sir. There isn't anybody. I keep all the books and everything. No one else would know all my customers and the system for an automatic tank refill that I have established."

Attorney: "Mr. Jones, do you think that if this trial were to last for two to three weeks and you were sequestered, unable to attend to your business, that this would weigh on your mind, that you wouldn't be able to pay as close attention to the trial as you might some other time, for example, if it were summer?"

Juror: "No, sir. It wouldn't affect me at all. I can do my duty."

Attorney: "Is there any question in your mind about this?"

Juror: "No, sir, no question at all. It wouldn't bother me at all."

The bodies of authoritarians often express the rigidity of their personalities with a masklike face topping a ramrod straight body. Men may be seen to assume a "parade rest" position when standing. Clothes are immaculate and shoes are often polished to a high sheen.

The militarism of their personality may also be expressed with the continual "yes, sir," sometimes with an extraordinary emphasis on the sir, to the voir dire questions. Because their minds think only in absolute terms, the language used contains few qualifying words or phrases such as, "I think," "Maybe," "Perhaps." Little time will be necessary to think out their answers to questions. Sometimes, so sure are they of the "right" response to make that the answer comes even before the question has been completed.

White middle-class males, a group of persons significantly over represented in jury pools throughout the country, are most afflicted with the authoritarian personality syndrome. Their social conditioning of leadership roles within the society means that even if they are not elected foreperson, they still will be highly influential and vocal in the jury deliberations. As a general rule, they should be eliminated from juries in cases involving minority persons, social non-conformists, and other controversial persons.[31-39]

Americans are all authoritarians to some greater or lesser degree. They may also express their authoritarianism in regard to some aspects of the syndrome and not in regard to other aspects. What counts is the effect of a juror's own brand of authoritarianism given the issues involved in a case and the amount of personal power a juror may possess. A scale of one to thirty works well in evaluating authoritarianism.

THE BODY SPEAKS TO THOSE THAT TAKE THE TIME TO SEE

As authoritarianism may be read in part through the body, so too may other messages, feelings, and attitudes be expressed through body language. Though a number of popular books have been written on the topic of kinesics, or body language, most of these books are limited by their simplistic approach. The stress on single gestures as indicative of attitudes gives rise to misconceptions on the part of readers. However, the books are generally interesting and may be helpful in assisting the reader in defining various gestures commonly employed by people during communication.[40-47]

A more accurate appreciation of body language is to view it as a component part in a whole system of communication. Gestures can only be evaluated in terms of the totality of the situation in which they occur.

All people are experts in the field of body language. Our problem is to become aware of nonverbal communications and to define meaning from these communications.

Infants are taught to communicate nonverbally at the same time that they learn language. But, contrary to verbal language, body language training occurs at a subliminal level, that is, we simply learn to communicate via bodies without being consciously aware of doing so. The result is that we look at each other, but we do not necessarily "see" in terms of communication.

The word "vibes" comes closest to defining what is meant when discussing body language. We feel each other's vibes in a nonspecific, but fairly accurate, way. There are people who we instantly like and others whom we dislike, without their uttering so much as a sound.

Body language communication awareness training begins with an effort to "see" not just to look. As greater expertise with language results in the ability to express clearly one's thoughts, so too can an understanding of nonverbal language result in more accurate communication between people.

SEEING IS BELIEVING

Television offers an excellent opportunity for the evaluation of nonverbal skills. With the sound turned off, view and then interpret the action being presented. Then turn the sound on to check what is actually happening. Whenever the camera moves in for a close head shot, watch for facial gestures that might have gone unnoticed before.

Go wherever people watching is commonplace. Public places, such as shopping malls, airports, and restaurants all provide ready-made laboratories. Look for patterns in the way that people stand or walk relative to one another. What does this reveal about their relationship? Can you detect which persons are couples by the closeness of their bodies and by the synchronized movement both employ?

Do you notice that people stand side-by-side, relating to each other only via their heads or do the people face each other with the total focus of their bodies revealed to the other? How much space is there between the people? Note the positions of the various parts of the body—arms, legs, torsos, heads. In which direction are these parts facing?

Note closely one part of the body, say the position of the arms. Do the arms serve as shields to keep others from interrupting the communication? Are the legs placed as shields, too? Is there an effort to establish a closer relationship with the arms reaching out toward the other person? Does the head move forward as well? Do the people actually touch? When this happens, what is the expression on the face? Note the amount and intensity of eye contact.

Now ask these questions: What are these people doing? What kind of people are they? What kind of jurors would they make?

Many clues exist to provide answers to these questions. Clothes, hairstyles, items in the possession of the person are informative. Look at the way the clothes fit the body. How is the body held? How rigid or immobile is their body? How about the mobility of the face? Do you feel that there is congruence in the various messages being sent by the person? For example, when viewed carefully, the person may be seen to be expressing the closeness of a relationship with her/his body, but the face may be expressing indifference, boredom, or perhaps even hostility.

Note the face itself. Is the mouth smiling while the eyes do not? Does the smile seem genuine or does it appear to be a Hertz rent-a-smile?

Think of three words which would describe this person. How likeable does this person seem? How open- or closed-minded do they appear to be? How high on an authoritarian scale would they rate? Are they strong-minded, possessing great personal power?

Is there congruence (i.e. consistency or harmoniousness) between the role they are playing and their behavior? Do any of their actions seem out of place, somewhat jarring? What does this mean?

...AND THERE ARE WHOLE CLASSES OF GESTURES

From the start, any serious observation of people reveals the incredible amount of movement they employ. Though confusing at first, classes of movements will gradually emerge as separate and distinct, each with its own meaning, relevance, and relationship one to another within the communicative system.

Cultural, racial, and ethnic differences exist in body language. Certain unique gestures are commonly used by a distinct class or group of people. Spacing and touching behaviors often vary as does body posture and walk.

Not difficult to detect are the class body movements reflecting in-role behaviors. An easily defined and commonly used in-role behavior, listening, may be viewed in its entirety in any school classroom. Though a great many positions are appropriate for listening, all are easily classified as belonging to this group.

Person-specific, on-going, behaviors also occur. This class of behaviors may be termed tension-releasing movements. For some persons, the body charge is excessive and various parts of the body are activated to reduce this charge. The unconscious tapping of the foot or drumming of the fingers occur frequently. Less apparent but also common are shoulder jerks and mouth grimaces.

Tension may also be expressed by the containment of feeling. A clinched fist indicates such a feeling. Characteristically the mouth of such a person turns inward, appears to be clamped shut, and could be described as a pencillike line across the face.

Closer evaluations of the person may reveal a rapid, forceful walk with a strong forward thrust chin and an upwardly tilted head, held in what might be described as a scornful manner. The total image is that of aggression; aggression that is so excessive that it can hardly be contained. The clinched fist is symbolic of an actual desire to hit someone.

I CAN SEE! !

Having defined these broad classes of behaviors, it becomes possible to identify the unique gestures employed by persons to give true meaning to the situation in which they are placed. Often a single primary message is being sent, with a number of amplifying messages and sometimes a message that appears to be entirely different in meaning from the primary message.

Imagine this situation: One person listens raptly to another, the eyes of the listener never leave the eyes of the speaker, a slight smile appears on the lips, and the face appears almost angelic. The listener has thrust the head and shoulders forward from an extended torso facing the speaker with head, torso, left arm, and legs turned to her/

him. The body is immobile—except for the right arm, held behind the back, seen to be frantically gesturing to a third person. Normally, though gestures are more subtle than those described, the message is just as easily interpreted.

Incongruence of gestures often may be detected. In this instance, imagine a mother listening to her child describe a painful bicycle accident that has just occurred to the child. The mother listens, concern registering on her face, particularly in her eyes. As the child continues the description, a quick sadistic smile flashes on the mother's lips.

Congruence is also an important element when evaluating verbal expressions in relationship to the nonverbal messages. Until recently, linguists hypothesized that the only use of gestures was to clarify verbal communications. Now, however, kinesics research has revealed that people use a system approach to communication.

Verbal and nonverbal—the messages often vary and may be communicated simultaneously as well. Though a high degree of congruence may exist between the messages, frequently, the nonverbal message may express an entirely different message from the one portrayed verbally.

Jurors are highly susceptible to expressing incongruent verbal and nonverbal messages. When one appreciates the kinds of problems faced by jurors, this lack of congruence becomes understandable.

Jurors are earnest and dedicated persons. In a sense, they themselves are on trial—they must be judged worthy enough to sit as jurors.

Jury duty bears with it the connotation that the person must be able to be fair and impartial, must be able to understand the courtroom procedure, and must at the end of the trial be able to render a decision in the case. Everyone feels some pressure to think of themselves as possessing the qualities required for jury service, especially when one is aware that evaluation of them as potential jurors will occur in a public place, will be made by a stranger, and may well happen in front of their friends.

Often those called for jury service have never entered a courtroom before. The courtroom procedure, an extremely formal process, is especially inhibiting to jurors. Aware that they will be called upon to participate in these proceedings, that they will have to answer whatever questions lawyers may choose to ask, personal or otherwise, the jurors become anxious, and understandably so.

Most jurors respond to their anxiety in a predictable manner. In answering the voir dire questions, the juror will attempt to present the perfect image of a "good" citizen, a citizen who is entirely capable of performing jury duty ably and well. As responses of this type generally spring from a surface level within the attitudinal structure of the juror, little meaningful information is elicited by the answers to the questions.

However, regardless of how closed-down and carefully thought-out the verbal response, the juror's nonverbal messages will continue to flow unceasingly. Completely unaware of these movements, the juror will reveal some innermost attitudes and feelings; the honesty, the validity, and the importance of such non-verbal messages cannot be questioned.

Optimally, lawyers are allowed to explore with a potential juror all the areas they wish, for as long as they wish. As the voir dire becomes more extensive, so too does the ability to make an accurate assessment of the jurors. Not only does this system make possible the probing of more deeply held values' systems, but also brings about a better, more definitive nonverbal communication between attorney and juror.

To determine meaning from a juror's gesture, an awareness of the exact timing of the occurrence of the gesture is important. Did the gesture occur continuously during the voir dire or did it appear during the voir dire by one side and not during the voir dire by the other side? Was there an appearance of the gesture only when a particular subject was raised with the juror? Did the juror demonstrate the gesture continuously or did it stop at some point? What was happening when the gesture ceased? Did the gesture seem congruous with the verbal message? How much similarity or disimilarity occurred verbally and nonverbally?

Nonverbal expression of rapport between lawyer and juror will be reflected in body movements and gestures. To assess the degree of rapport that has been established between the two, I evaluate five expression areas of the juror's body. These are eye contact, hand movement, body movement, body orientation, and body posture.

When first starting to make these evaluations in the courtroom, it is best to concentrate only on one expression area at a time. Though there is some risk in evaluating gestures singularly, without reference to the other gestures, it is a good way to begin. As mastery of an area occurs, another may be added until all five are observed. Understanding body language in the courtroom is not impossible, but it does take practice.

Of the five expression areas to be evaluated, eye contact has the advantage of being both easy to detect and extremely revealing of the juror's attitudes and feelings. Whenever good rapport is established, the juror's eye contact will be direct, continuous, and somewhat intense. However, generally a juror's eyes move around the room; they may move back and forth between the voir diring attorney and others, establishing contact and then breaking it. They may rest to the side of the attorney's head, not making contact, but looking in the right direction, or they may withdraw entirely to gaze unseeingly at the juror's lap. Sometimes questioning in a particularly sensitive area will cause the juror to glance for support at the opposing attorney, a clear indication that the juror sides with the opposing attorney in this particular matter.

The frequency and type of hand movements exhibited may also indicate rapport. Hand gestures may be expressed in a multiple of movements. Jurors may wring their hands, drum their fingers, play with their clothing, may touch their hearts, heads, or some other part of their bodies. The hands may even cover their mouths when they are lying.

However, hand movements may also reflect a person's internal tensions and the release of those tensions. Thus, for example, when a hand gesture is displayed continuously during the voir dire, it probably expresses this internal tension, rather than a feeling of rapport toward one side or the other.

Body orientation refers to the manner in which potential jurors face their questioner. When there is a close relationship, a juror turns the entire focus of the body to the attorney—legs, torso, arms, head, eyes. However, a number of gradients are also possible. The juror may turn her/his legs away from the questioner, or may turn both legs and upper torso away from the questioner. This action may continue until the juror has turned her/his entire bodily focus away with the exception of sending intermittent eye contact. In some rare instances absolutely no focus occurs at all.

An expression of feelings and attitudes may be made through the body posture, that is, the way in which the body is held. Make note of the body posture: Is the body held in a ramrod straight position indicative of the authoritarian? Does the body "hang loose?" Is the body slumped in a dejected, despondent manner, as though the world has overwhelmed the person? Does the juror lean the body forward in an effort to establish greater rapport? Does a change occur in the body position, to a more upright stance, when there is a discussion of "doing one's duty?"

Body movement may be characterized by squirming in one's chair; a rhythmic rocking of the body back and forth, and involuntary shiver, a shrugging of the shoulders, the movement of the chest during rapid breathing, or the tapping of foot or leg. What matters in all these evaluations is the determination of the timing of these movements making a comparison to them with other behaviors exhibited by the juror.

As one's observational skills develop, it is wise to make use of a form with a scale (one to five) for evaluating juror's nonverbal behavior. The form incorporates the various scalings required, provides space for a sketch of the juror, as well as providing space for any comments or notes concerning the juror's behavior that are relevant.

YES, YOUR HONOR, WE HAVE REACHED A VERDICT

A jury, a representative cross-section of the community, was designed to reflect the standards of the society from which it was drawn. Whenever a class of persons, for example, white males, is overrepresented in a jury pool, jury verdicts will predominantly reflect the attitudes of this class rather than reflecting the attitudes of the entire community. Correcting this situation requires continuous challenges to the composition of the pool until a cross-section of the populace is in fact represented.[48-51] The jury system works and works well, provided that it is what it should be.

HOW DID YOU LIKE THE FINAL ACT?

At the completion of a trial, there often is considerable interest in finding out from the jurors which trial strategies worked and which did not. Though well intentioned, trial workers rarely bother to ask jurors how they voted, much less go to the trouble of writing and administering an in-depth juror questionnaire. Until this is done, routinely, there is absolutely no way to separate the successful trial techniques from those that do not work. Whatever the cost, it is worth it. Ironically, attorneys produce, direct, and act in the courtroom drama; then no one asks the audience how they liked the play. To assess the various aspects of the trial and to provide a data bank about jurors, a scorecard containing information for each juror on age, race, sex, first vote, and last vote, is valuable. The form also has general information on the charges, deliberation time, number of votes, central issues, group dynamics, leaders, etc.

A CRYSTAL BALL

At best, even when using the most sophisticated social science techniques, the gamble involved in jury selection will never be completely eliminated. As clearly seen during the course of any jury selection, jurors who obviously are good for one side stand out from the rest of the jurors and are challenged peremptorily by the other side. There is little difficulty in spotting people whose bias is so obvious. What is more difficult, and what jury selection usually becomes, is the ability to make informed choices among people who differ only slightly from each other in their attitudes and beliefs, those occupying the midpoint on the scale. Social science techniques remove much of the guessing and I believe that adopting some or all of these techniques will result in the ability to be surer that a juror who rates six on an overall favorableness scale is selected more often than a juror who rates a four—a decided advantage in any trial. As many attorneys have told me, whenever the outcome of the trial is 50/50, jury selection techniques push the trial outcome over into the winning category.

Obviously, not all jury selection tools can be used immediately. Learning must take place, too. Not all cases require the use of many of the tools described here; the facts in any case have real bearing in the ultimate outcome of the case. Nevertheless, the techniques work, and they work surprisingly well. The results of better jury selection will mean more effective lawyering and fairer trials for those accused of crimes.

REFERENCES

1. Kalven, H., Jr. and Zeisel, H. *The American jury,* Chicago, The University of Chicago Press, 1966.
2. Katz, L. The twelve man jury, *Trial, 5,* 39–42, 1968–69.
3. Schulman, J., Shaver, P., Colman, R., Emrich, B., and Christie, R. Recipe for a jury, *Psychology Today, 6,* 37–44, 1973.
4. Simon, R.J. (Ed.), *The jury system in America: A critical overview,* Beverly Hills, California Sage, 1975.
5. Bennett, C. Psychological methods of jury selection in the typical criminal case, California Attorneys for Criminal Justice Statewide Law Seminar Syllabus, Los Angeles, California, 1977.

6. Brooks, S. and Doob, A. Justice and the jury, *Journal of Social Issues, 31,* 171–182, 1975.
7. Factor, J., Eisner, J., and Shaw, J. *The jury: A selected annotated bibliography of social science research on juries,* Brooklyn, Center for Responsive Psychology, Brooklyn College, C.U.N.Y., 1977.
8. Gerbasi, K.C., Zuckerman, M., and Reis, H.T. Justice needs a new blindfold: A review of mock jury research, *Psychological Bulletin, 84,* 323–345, 1977.
9. Ginger, A.F. (Ed.), *Jury selection in criminal trials: New techniques and concepts,* Tiburon, California, Law Press, 1975.
10. Kahn, J. Picking peers: Social scientists' role in selection of juries sparks legal debate, *Wall Street Journal, 1,* 13, August 12, 1974.
11. Kairys, D. Juror selection: The law, a mathematical method of analysis, and a case study, *American Criminal Law Reviews, 10,* 771–806, 1972.
12. Saks, M. The limits of scientific jury selection: Ethical and empirical, *Jurimetrics Journal, 17,* 3–22, 1973.
13. Saks, M. Social scientists can't rig juries, *Psychology Today, 9,* 8, 1976.
14. Tapp, J.L. Psychology and the law: An overture, *Annual Review of Psychology, 27,* 258–288, 1976.
15. Boehm, V. Mr. Prejudice, Miss Sympathy and the authoritarian personality: An application of psychological measuring to the problem of jury bias, *Wisconsin Law Review,* 734–750, 1968.
16. Diamond, S. and Zeisel, H. A courtroom experiment on juror selection and decision making, *Personality and Social Psychology Bulletin, 1,* 276–277, 1974.
17. Etzioni, A. Creating an imbalance, *Trial, 10,* 6, 1974.
18. Zehr, H. *A juror evaluation codebook: The keyperson system,* Working paper, Social Science and the Law Project, Talladega College, Talladega, Alabama, 1976.
19. Asch, S. Effects of group pressure upon the modification and distortion of judgments, In Cartwright, D. and Zander, A. (Eds.), *Group Dynamics,* Evanston, Illinois, Row, Perterson, 1953.
20. Collins, B.E. and Raven B.H. Group structure: Attractions, coalitions, communication, and power, In Lindzey, G. and Aronson, E. (Eds.), *Handbook of social psychology,* Reading, Pennsylvania, Addison Wesley, 1969.
21. Tate, E., Hawrish, HM. and Clark, S. Communication variables in jury selection, *Journal of Communication, 24,* 3, 130–139, 1974.
22. Adorno, I., Frenkel-Brunswik, E., Levinson, D., and Sanford, R. *The authoritarian personality,* New York, Harper, 1950.
23. Berg, K., and Vidmar, N. Authoritarianism and recall of evidence about criminal behavior, *Journal of Research in Personality, 9,* 147–157, 1975.

24. Brown, R.   The authoritarian personality, In Brown, R. (Ed.), *Social psychology*, New York, Free Press, 477–546, 1965.

25. Mitchell, H. and Byrne, D.   The defendant's dilemma: Effects of jurors' attitudes and authoritarianism on judicial decisions, *Journal of Personality and Social Psychology, 25*, 123–129, 1973.

26. Sanford, F. and Older, H.   *A short authoritarian equalitarian scale,* Philadelphia, Institute for Research in Human Relations, 1950.

27. Goldberg, F.J.   *Attitudes toward capital punishment and behavior as a juror in simulated capital cases,* Petitioner's Brief, No. 1015, Supreme Court of the United States, Chicago, United States Law Printing, 1968.

28. Jurow, G.   New data on the effect of a death qualified jury on the guilt determination process, *Harvard Law Review, 84,* 567–611, 1971.

29. Mullin, C. and Farmer, M.   Voir dire in a capital case, In *How to try a capital case,* North Carolina Academy of Trial Lawyers, (Ed.) Raleigh, 1977.

30. Mullin, C. and Farmer, M.   Trial — Emphasis on the punishment state of a capital case. In *How to try a capital case,* North Carolina Academy of Trial Lawyers, (Ed.) Raleigh, 1977.

31. Berrigan, D.   *The trial of the Cantonville nine,* Boston, Beacon Press, 1970.

32. Chevigny, P.   The Attica cases: A successful jury challenge in a northern city, *Criminal Law Bulletin, 11,* 157–172, 1975.

33. Ginger, A. (Ed.), *Minimizing racism in jury trials: The voir dire conducted by Charles R. Garry in people of California v. Huey P. Newton,* Berkeley, California, National Lawyer's Guild, 1969.

34. Kairys, D., Schulman, J., and Harring, S.   *The jury system: New methods for reducing prejudice,* Cambridge, Massachusetts, The National Jury Project and the National Lawyer's Guild, 1975.

35. McConahay, J.B., Mullin, C., and Frederick, J. T.   The uses of social science in trials with political and racial overtones: The trial of Joan Little, *Law and Contemporary Problems, 41,* 205–229, 1977.

36. Mitford, J.   *The trial of Dr. Spock, the Rev. William Sloane Coffin, Jr., Michael Ferber, Mitchell Goodman, and Marcus Raskin,* New York, Knopf, 1969.

37. Reston, J.   *The innocence of Joan Little: A southern mystery,* New York, New York Times Press, 1977.

38. Sage, W.   Psychology and the Angela Davis jury, *Human Behavior,* 56–61, January 1973.

39. Salter, K.   *The trial of Inez Garcia,* Berkley, California, Editorial Justa Publications, 1976.

40. Birdwhistle, R.L.   *Introduction to kinesics,* Louisville, Kentucky, University of Louisville Press, 1952.

41. Birdwhistle, R.L.   Kinesics and communications, In Carpenter, E. and

McLuhan, M. (Eds.), *Explorations in communication,* Boston, Beacon Press, 1960.

42. Birdwhistle, R.L.   *Kinesics and context,* Philadelphia, University of Pennsylvania Press, 1971.

43. Goffman, E.   *The presentation of self in everyday life,* Garden City, New Jersey, Doubleday, 1959.

44. Goffman, E.   *Behavior in public places,* Glencoe, Illinois, Free Press, 1963.

45. Goffman, E.   *Relations in public,* New York, Basic Books, 1971.

46. Schflen, A.E. and Schflen, A.   *Body language and social order,* Englewood Cliffs, New Jersey, Prentice Hall, 1972.

47. Schflen, A.E.   *How behavior means,* New York, Anchor Press/Doubleday, 1974.

48. Fowlkes, D., Noble, L.E., and Bray, B.   *Jury selection as political action,* Paper presented at the Annual Meeting of The American Political Science Association, Washington, D.C., 1977.

49. Fowlkes, D. and Noble, L.   *The politics of trial jury selection,* Paper presented at Norfolk State College, Old Dominion University Conference on the Urban South, Norfolk, Virginia, 1977.

50. Levine, A. and Schweber-Koren, C.   Jury selection in Erie County: Changing a sexist system, *Law and Society Review, 11,* 43–55, 1976.

51. Michael, M., Mullin, C., O'Reilly, J., and Rowan, J.V.   Challenges to jury composition in North Carolina, *North Carolina Central Law Review, 7,* (1), 1–24, 1975.

Chapter 14

THE DYNAMICS OF JURY BEHAVIOR

Rita J. Simon

T HE JURY is not held in high esteem by the legal profession. Many of the profession's leading figures who have observed the jury from the bench or from behind the tables of the defense or prosecution have expressed doubt, skepticism, and disdain for the institution and for the abilities and motivations of the individuals who are chosen to perform the work of the institution. The legal profession's esteem drops even more when it considers the responsibility and complexity of the jury's task in cases that are unusually lengthy, complex, or technical. Criminal trials involving a defense of insanity are often cited by the legal profession to illustrate the inappropriateness of having lay persons, ordinary people who lack training in either legal or psychological-psychiatric specialties, make decisions about the sanity and responsibility of the defendant.

This article culls observations of the jury's performance in defense of insanity trials and on the basis of those observations assesses whether the institution deserves the low regard in which it is held by many on the bench and bar. The observations characterize how ordinary people perceive mental illness, what cues they look for and what types of behavior they regard as particularly indicative. They describe how the jurors' perceptions of mental illness affect their determination about whether a defendant was or was not responsible for his behavior at the time he committed the crime for which he is standing trial.

One of the special complexities for the jury in a defense of insanity trial is the testimony of the expert witnesses—usually psychiatrists. If each side has called its own psychiatrist and each witness presents differing and conflicting evaluations of the defendant, it is the jury's task to decide between those opinions. If only one expert has testified, the jury is instructed by the judge that it may disregard the testimony or it may legitimately disagree with the interpretation the psychiatrist offered for the defendant's action.   In this article we describe how jurors have responded to psychiatrists' testimony and how they perceive the division of labor between themselves and the expert witnesses.

Another complexity that a defense of insanity introduces is that it leaves in doubt the defendant's fate should the jury find them not guilty by reason of insanity (NGRI).   In most criminal trials, if defendants are declared not guilty, they are unconditionally released. But in defense of insanity trials, the defendants are almost always taken into custody and detained in a mental institution until such time as medical authorities declare them competent to function in society.   Does the jury consider the consequences of the verdict should it find the defendant not guilty by reason of insanity, and does it understand the practical alternatives between a guilty and NGRI verdict in terms of the length of time that the defendant is likely to be incarcerated?

This article reports three aspects of jury behavior in its role of decision maker for trials involving a defense of insanity—a type of trial that critics of the jury have long urged be removed from the jurisdiction of lay persons and placed in the more competent and technically proficient hands of medical and legal experts.   One, how competently and with what degree of sophistication does the jury discuss mental illness?   What personality characteristics and types of behavior does it associate with mental illness?   Two, how well does the jury understand the experts' testimony and how does it perceive the division of labor between itself and the psychiatrists?   Three, does the jury appreciate the consequences of a verdict that declares the defendant not guilty by reason of insanity?

Much of the information about the jury reported in this article is based on research conducted by the author when she was associated with the Jury Project at the Law School of the University of Chicago. Details about how the data were collected and other information on the design and major findings of the research are reported in *The Jury and the Defense of Insanity*.[1]

THE JURY'S PERCEPTION OF MENTAL ILLNESS

Most jurors perceive mental illness as complex and multifaceted. They do not assume that low IQ is a proxy for determining whether a person is mentally ill nor do they believe that bizarre or violent behavior is a necessary characteristic of all mentally ill people. One juror on an incest case put it as follows:

> I don't think being able to pass a test has anything to do with insanity. As far as his mental knowledge is concerned, he can have all kinds of knowledge about certain subjects, but it does not make him sane.
>
> Did you ever see any of these patients in mental hospitals? There are lots of them that are pretty well. If you saw them anywhere else, you would not think they were insane. And they are not dumb either. Lots of them are not dumb. You can really teach them something like anyone else, and boy, they can be pretty smart at it. They are not a bit dumb.

Another juror who also deliberated on the incest case confessed that his first reaction upon hearing that the charge was incest was "The man must be crazy." But after he listened to the details of the case, which described the number of times the acts were committed, the defendant's use of contraceptives, the facts about his employment record and the steady advances he made in his position, the juror began to doubt his initial reaction. The juror went on to analogize:

> The point is you can have a quirk and still be a member of society as long as you have the mental sense not to allow your quirk to break the law. But, if you break the law, because you have this quirk and still have the mental capacity to know what you are doing and go ahead and do it deliberately, then you are not insane. Then it is no excuse or alibi that you have a quirk. The judge's instructions say that if you think he has a mental illness then you should judge this man insane. If I cut my finger am I ill? I have damage to my body, but is that an illness? I mean is it to the degree that we are trying to judge here?

It was not unusual for jurors to supply personal experiences. In exposing his own experience to the scrutiny of others, a juror not only provided the group with more concrete information about mental illness, but in many instances he obtained therapy for himself. The opportunity to describe one's own involvement with someone who is mentally ill in an atmosphere that is both impersonal and supportive permits expressions of ambivalence about one's own participation. Such expressions often serve two functions. They relieve some of the juror's guilt about his own behavior vis-a-vis the spouse or parent whose commitment he was responsible for, and they reduce some of his negative affect toward the defendant. One juror supplied this analogy:

> He had a mental disorder, but was it of such a magnitude that the man was not responsible for his acts? Can a man have a mental disorder and still have enough free will to make up his mind whether to commit an act or not? You follow me? I mean suppose I like to go out and get drunk on Saturday nights and I love to and I do it lots of Saturday nights. But as long as I make a mental decision ahead of time that that is what I am going to do, and make it, say, in a reasonably sound mind, then I am responsible for going out and getting drunk on Saturday night. I mean, I make the decision of my own free will, I use what is normally deemed as a normal mind to make the decision, because after I am drunk I no longer have a normal mind. But did this man have free will? What I am trying to differentiate is whether this mental disorder or emotional disorder, depending on which man you want to listen to, was such that it denied this man free will in making a decision. If the mental disorder denied him the free will, then he cannot act like an average person on making a decision. See what I am trying to say? Is the act of having a neurosis, and the psychiatrists can tell if there is neurosis, a type of mental disorder that takes away your free will? As long as a person can make a rational decision then the neurosis is not sufficient to say that a man is not guilty of a crime.

In essence, many of the jurors were saying that when all aspects of the defendant's life were examined, his behavior appeared no less rational than their own, except for his incestuous relations with his daughters. They found no other evidence that would support exempting the defendant from responsibility unless the commission of the act itself was sufficient grounds for declaring him mentally incompetent; that criterion they were unwilling to accept.

Another group of jurors deliberated on a defense of insanity trial in which the defendant was charged with housebreaking. In this case the defendant had a long history of mental illness, several suicide attempts, and prior commitments to a mental hospital. A frequent argument used by jurors who believed the defendant's behavior manifested insanity was the nature of the items he was attempting to steal. The fact that they were small and of little value indicated that he was not robbing for profit, i.e. there was no rational purpose behind his behavior. As one juror said:

> Look at it this way. If you were going to go out and break into someone's house, would you take the chance of breaking into some-

body's house and getting caught and spending a couple of years in jail just to steal a cigarette lighter or a pair of cuff-links?

The second most frequently cited fact indicating insanity was the defendant's position of behavior when caught by the police.

> The defendant was hiding in such a childish way, in a corner holding something over his face like an ostrich. His failure to resist arrest by fighting or running away was not the behavior of the normal criminal, who would have been aware of his situation and the consequences of being caught.

Jurors who argued in favor of finding the defendant sane emphasized essentially the same facts as the jurors who favored a not guilty by reason of insanity verdict—namely, the defendant's behavior at the scene of the crime and the items he attempted to steal. The fact that the defendant committed a crime against property rather than a person indicated sanity. The implication is that when the insane commit antisocial acts, they commit acts of violence and not those in which personal gain might be a factor. In this case, not only did the defendant commit a crime for which personal gain might be a factor but he carried it out in a typically criminal fashion.

As one juror observed:

> If in broad daylight, with people watching him, he had thrown a brick through the window and then tried to enter the house, that would have indicated insanity (i.e. uncontrollable, compulsive behavior). But here we have a case in which the defendant broke into an empty house in the middle of the night by fiddling with the lock.

These actions indicated the defendant's ability to plan and carry out purposive behavior, i.e. he must have been watching the house for some time and knew that it would be unoccupied.

Another juror commented:

> When he entered, he did so quietly and at a time when any ordinary burglar would think it safe to break in. Once he was in the house, he didn't turn on any lights, which again is normal for a burglar; and he was selective in the articles he stole; that is, he took small pieces that were easy to carry and negotiable. Later, when confronted by the police, the defendant acted like a normal criminal. Hiding, cowering, playing dumb when you know you're caught is what they all do. In addition, the fact that he was hiding indicated shame, and if you're ashamed, it means that you are aware that you have done wrong.

For jurors who deliberated on the housebreaking case, sane behavior was most often differentiated from insane behavior by the defendant's ability to act rationally and to commit legally punishable
acts in which personal gain was a consideration.

THE JURY'S PERCEPTION OF THE FUNCTION OF EXPERT TESTIMONY

The instructions that juries usually receive from the bench about
expert testimony generally read as follows:

> You are not bound as jurors to accept the testimony of expert
> witnesses. You should certainly consider carefully the qualifications
> of the witnesses, their expriences, their observations of the defend-
> ant and all of the factors that they told you about in their lengthy
> testimony. Then you are to give to their testimony such weight as in
> your judgment it is fairly entitled to receive, with full recognition of
> the fact that while you shouldn't arbitrarily disregard the testimony
> of any witness, yet, if you are satisfied that you don't accept the testi-
> mony of expert witnesses you are not bound to do so.

In the cases we studied the jurors did not always follow the advice
implicit or explicit in the expert's testimony. For example, in the
housebreaking trial when the defendant was described by two psychiatrists as having a psychopathic personality with psychosis and when
the defendant's testimony was jumbled and nonresponsive, and when
his life history showed prior commitments to mental hospitals, 56
percent of the juries found the defendant not guilty by reason of insanity—a verdict consistent with the psychiatrists' testimonies. But in
the incest trial, only 13 percent of the juries found the defendant not
guilty by reason of insanity, even though testimony provided by two
psychiatrists implicitly recommended that the defendant should be so
found.

In the housebreaking case then, a defendant who was patently insane (as determined by his behavior in other contexts, his testimony,
and his prior commitments to mental hospitals) but who had committed a seemingly rational crime (stealing for profit) in an intelligent manner (breaking into an empty house in the middle of the
night) was found not guilty by reason of insanity by a majority of
the juries. In the incest case, on the other hand, a defendant who had
never been committed to a mental institution, who held a responsible
job, and whose condition was described by two psychiatrists as psychoneurotic, i.e. not psychotic, but who repeatedly committed acts that

were unnatural and perverse, was found sane and responsible by almost all the juries.

In listening to the jurors consider the expert testimony, it was not only clear that they understood the technical vocabulary as well as the essence of the testimony, but that they took upon themselves the difficult task of distinguishing how their role in the proceedings differed from or complemented that of the psychiatrists. During the deliberations, the jurors discussed over and over again, "Who should have the final say about what happens to the defendant, a jury of laymen or a group of medical experts?" Most of the time the jury resolved its dilemma by spelling out for itself the separate tasks that the law expected each to perform. In essence, the jury concluded that the experts' testimony emphasized only one aspect of the problem, the clinical part, and that their testimony contributed little to the major dilemma that confronted the jury, that of placing the clinical or purely medical facts about the defendant into a moral–legal context. The jurors reminded each other that the court instructed them that the presence of a mental illness or aberration should not by itself excuse the defendant; that it was the jury's task to decide whether the particular manifestation of mental illness that the defendant exhibited met the norm of nonresponsibility specified by the rule of the law. Thus, the jury could consider the expert's testimony, understand it, choose to reject much of it, and still demonstrate intelligence about the substantive issues involved in the trial as well as the logic of the law they were instructed to apply.

After the jury had completed its deliberation, we asked each juror, those involved in the housebreaking and the incest trials, the following questions:

Which do you believe is the best way of deciding what should be done with a person who has committed a crime and pleads that he is insane?

___ He should be tried before a jury just like anyone else.

___ He should be tried before a judge.

___ He should be turned over by the court to a group of psychiatrists and they should determine what is to be done with him.

Table 14-I describes the percentage of jurors who favored decision by psychiatrists. Since less than 7 percent of all the jurors in both trials chose a judge, the major comparison is between the jury and the medical experts.

TABLE 14-I

PERCENT OF JURORS FAVORING DECISION BY PSYCHIATRISTS

Housebreaking Trial	66
	(360)
Incest Trial	33
	(816)

The percentages in Table 14-I suggest that jurors would be more willing to delegate responsibility to medical experts when the case involves a relatively minor crime and/or when the defendant is psychotic or patently insane.

The data in Table 14-II show that jurors who voted for acquittal on grounds of insanity on the predeliberation questionnaire favored decision by psychiatrists more heavily.

TABLE 14-II

PERCENT OF JURORS FAVORING DECISION BY PSYCHIATRISTS BY VERDICT

	NGRI	Guilty
Housebreaking Trial	71	65
	(238)	(122)
Incest Trial	41	30
	(269)	(547)

The jurors' responses to the question of who should decide tells something about how the jurors perceive the division of labor between themselves and the psychiatrists. We see that the jurors are much more concerned about exercising their responsibility when a defendant has committed a heinous crime and is not patently insane than they are when the defendant has committed a relatively mild offense and is patently insane.

Perhaps the following comment from one of the deliberations captures some of the feelings surrounding this point.

> Just because these doctors are educated and they are way up over our heads, it doesn't mean that we have to accept what they say as truth and that's it. In other words they would be deciding for us. We would not be deciding for ourselves what is right in this particular case. If that were so, then this case should never have gone to a jury. I mean, then we would have to depend upon men specialized in the field of psychiatry to judge this man. The judge said that we could

disregard their testimony, if we wanted to. After all, you can't base your whole opinion on the fact that these people have degrees.

An interesting comparison can be drawn with a national survey I conducted about ten years ago. I asked a sample of lawyers and psychiatrists: In your opinion, with whom should the final verdict in a plea of insanity trial rest? The choices and distribution of their responses are listed in Table 14-III.

TABLE 14-III

PROFESSIONAL OPINIONS ON WHO SHOULD BE RESPONSIBLE FOR INSANITY VERDICTS

	Percent	
	Psychiatrists	*Lawyers*
a. A Jury of Laymen	27.3	39.2
b. A Group of Medical Experts	12.2	11.8
c. A Judge	5.0	7.6
d. A Combined Group of Medical and Legal Experts	53.0	38.0
e. No Answer	2.3	3.9
	N = 139	79

THE JURY'S UNDERSTANDING OF THE CONSEQUENCES OF A NOT GUILTY BY REASON OF INSANITY VERDICT

In most states and in all federal jurisdictions, persons who are acquitted on grounds of insanity are immediately confined to a mental institution until a medical authority determines that they are recovered or restored to sanity. But in many jurisdictions the jury is not instructed as to the consequences of a not guilty by reason of insanity verdict. Many lawyers believe that jurors assume that defendants will go free if found not guilty by reason of insanity and they argue that this lack of information prejudices the defendant's right to acquittal. They reason that a jury is not likely to tolerate releasing a person who had violated the legal and moral code of the community and who might repeat the act.

Some members of the judiciary have recommended that the jury be informed before they begin to deliberate that defendants found not guilty by reason of insanity will be committed until such time as medical authorities believe that they are ready to be released. This information, they believe, would increase the likelihood that a jury would return a verdict of not guilty by reason of insanity.

As part of the experimental design of the housebreaking trial we arranged for half of the juries to be instructed by the judge that if they should find the defendant not guilty by reason of insanity, the defendant would be committed to a mental institution until such time as hospital authorities authorized release. The other juries were given no information about the possible consequences of a not guilty by reason of insanity verdict. We see in the percentages in Table 14-IV that the distribution of verdicts was almost identical between the two sets of juries.

TABLE 14-IV
COMMITMENT INFORMATION BY JURY VERDICTS

Jury Verdicts	Commitment Information	
	Present	Absent
Not Guilty by Reason of Insanity	9	8
Guilty	2	3
Hung	4	4
Total	15	15

The absence of commitment information did not increase, to any significant extent, the likelihood that a jury would find the defendant guilty; nor did the presence of information enhance the likelihood that the jury would acquit the defendant of grounds of insanity. The results are surprising and quite contrary to the expectations of the bench and bar.

However, there may be some puzzle as to how to interpret the lack of differences between the two treatments. Perhaps the jury is after all not concerned with the defendant's disposition? Or perhaps the jury somehow determines by itself, in the absence of specific information, that the court will provide for some period of commitment before it allows the defendant to go free?

We have information bearing on both hypotheses. In the housebreaking trial, the jurors were asked, "In a criminal case like this one, what do you think happens to the defendant when the jury returns a verdict of not guilty by reason of insanity?" The alternatives were the following:

___ Put in a mental institution for a period of time set by the court.
___ Put in a mental institution until, in the opinion of the psychiatrists, the defendant is cured.
___ Put in prison.

___ Placed on probation.
___ Set free.

This question was put to all jurors, those who were given the commitment instruction and those who were not. Ideally, all jurors who were exposed to the commitment instruction version should have checked "Put in a mental institution until, in the opinion of the psychiatrists, the defendant is cured." We would expect a difference in responses to this question depending on the commitment instruction jurors received. But Table 14-V shows that 93 percent of the jurors who received the commitment information checked the correct answer, and 91 percent who did *not* receive the information also checked the "commitment to mental institution" alternative. We see thus that jurors who did not receive the commitment instruction assumed correctly that the defendant would be committed.

TABLE 14-V

JUROR'S EXPECTATIONS ABOUT THE COURT'S DISPOSITION OF THE DEFENDANT BY COMMITMENT INSTRUCTION (IN PERCENT)

Commitment Instruction	Mental Institution*	Prison	Probation or Free	Combined
Given	93	3	4	100 (N = 180)
Not Given	91	3	6	100 (N = 180)

Of those respondents who checked "mental institution," 20 percent (in both treatments) indicated that they believed the length of time defendant remained in the institution was designated by the court. The remaining 71 or 73 percent of the jurors indicated that they believed the defendant "is put in a mental institution until, in the opinion of the psychiatrists, he is cured."

CONCLUDING REMARKS

Probably less than 2 percent of all criminal jury trials in a given year involve a defense of insanity. But the trial in which the insanity defense is offered usually attracts considerable attention from the mass media and the legal profession because of the severity or heinousness of the act that has been committed or because the issues surrounding the case are especially complex and subtle. The jury's performances in such cases provide a severe test of the lay person's competence at understanding and resolving judicial issues. The evidence presented here concerning the jury's treatment of such basic but difficult issues as its characterization of mental illness, its understanding of expert testimony and its perceptions of the likely consequences of a not guilty by reason of insanity verdict consistently demonstrate the jury's competence, resourcefulness, and willingness to fulfill its responsibilities in a manner consistent with the rules of law and evidence.

REFERENCE

1. Simon, R.J. *The jury and the defense of insanity,* Boston, Little, 1967.

Chapter 15

EYEWITNESS IDENTIFICATION AND PSYCHOLOGY IN THE COURTROOM*

ROBERT BUCKHOUT, Ph.D.

I F A PERSON sees an auto accident or is a witness to a murder and is then asked to describe what was seen, there is no one who can create an instant replay in slow motion. The person must depend on memory with all its limitations—a fact which may be of minor importance in ordinary daily activities. If a person is unreliable or shades the truth in reporting what has been seen, it matters little. But when the person is called in as a witness to a crime, the situation escalates in importance. A person's life or an institution's reputation may be at stake, and the witness may be asked to describe what was seen in exact detail as if the person were a videotape recorder. The prosecutor will attempt to show that the person has perfect recall; the defense attorney will try to show, by vigorous cross-examination, that the "tape recorder" is defective. The stakes are high because in modern courts eyewitness testimony is more valued than alibi testimony or "circumstantial" evidence.[1] Uncritical acceptance of eyewitness testimony seems to be based on the fallacious notion that the human observer is a perfect recording device—that everything that passes before his eyes is recorded and can be pulled out by sharp questioning or "refreshing one's memory." My argument, as a psychologist, is that this is impossible because human perception and memory are decision-making processes affected by the totality of a person's abilities, background, environment, attitudes, motives and beliefs—and by the methods used in testing recollection of people and events.

The more I come into contact with the criminal court system the

*Reprinted by permission from *Criminal Defense, 4,* (5). Copyright 1978, National College of Criminal Defense Lawyers and Public Defenders.

more aware I become of a fundamental clash of conceptions between the nineteenth-century viewpoint of the law and public and the twentieth-century viewpoint of psychologists concerning the workings of the human mind. The nineteenth-century view—embodied in psychophysics—asserted a scientific parallel between the mechanisms of the physical world and the mechanisms of the brain. Courts in the United States accept this nineteenth-century thinking quite readily— as does much of the public. However, modern psychologists have developed a conception of a whole human being with an information processing mechanism which is far more complex than the one in the nineteenth-century model. Unfortunately, because research psychologists (who began by studying practical problems) have gone into esoteric areas in their studies, their findings are much less known than they once were.

I regard the human observer as an active rather than a passive observer of the environment. He or she is motivated (a) by a desire to be accurate in extracting meaning from the overabundance of information which affects the senses; and (b) by a desire to live up to the expectations of others in order to stay in their good graces—a factor which makes the eye, the ear and the other senses social as well as physical organs.[2] Perception is thus necessarily selective and much psychological research is concerned with the process by which this selection functions.

In our laboratory experiments on the physical capabilities of the eye and the ear, we speak of an "ideal observer," by which we mean a person who would respond cooperatively to lights and tones with unbiased ears and eyes, much like a machine. But this ideal observer does not exist; it is a convenient fiction. We put great effort into the design of laboratories to provide an "ideal physical environment," free of distractions, in order to enable the observer to concentrate. In the real world such ideal environments are seldom found. The nonmachinelike human observer copes reasonably effectively in uncontrolled environments with a perceptual capability which fits the nature of a social being. When the human observer is witness to a crime, however, the witness is engaged in what can be described as "one-shot perception," that is, the selection and storage of information without an opportunity to rehearse what was seen in order to stabilize his memory.

In a machine we expect that what comes out (the report) will be a direct function of what went in (the input or stimulus). In human perception, however, the whole is actually greater than its parts.[3] That is, the human observer is able to take the fragments of information to which there is time to pay attention (i.e., the information is actively reduced) and reach conclusions based on prior experience, familiarity, biases, expectancy, faith, desire to appear certain, and so forth. Most human observers, for example, look at the moon and see a sphere—despite their inability to verify the shape of the unseen side. The conclusion, in psychological terms, is a decision effectively arrived at and independent of the physical evidence (which is incomplete).

When a person witnesses a crime, the fallible human observer is usually in less than ideal environment. The observer is subject to factors which limit the ability to give a complete account of what took place or to identify the persons involved with complete accuracy.[4] (A complete list of these factors is shown in Table 15-I). Each factor has been shown by laboratory or field research to be an element which

TABLE 15-1
FACTORS AFFECTING THE UNRELIABILITY OF EYEWITNESS
IDENTIFICATION

A. The Original Situation
  1. Insignificance of Events
  2. Shortness of Period of Observation
  3. Less than Ideal Observation Conditions

B. The Witness
  4. Stress
  5. Physical Condition of the Witness
  6. Prior Conditioning and Experience
  7. Personal Biases
  8. Needs and Motives — Seeing What We Want to See
  9. Desire to be a Part of History

C. Testing for Identification
  10. Length of Time from Event to Test
  11. Filling in Details Which Weren't There
  12. Suggestions from the Test Procedure (Line Up, Photo Array)
  13. Suggestions from Test Giver
  14. Conformity
  15. Relation to Authority Figures
  16. Passing on a Theory: The Self-Fulfilling Prophecy

reduces the reliability of eyewitness accounts. I will discuss a selected few of these factors to illustrate how the research and conclusions fit into forensic applications.[5]

The thrust of my research has been to learn about and describe (in a form useful to the criminal justice system) those factors which affect both the recall of events by a witness and his subsequent ability to make an identification. I have participated in some sixty criminal trials where I have discussed the following factors as they relate to eye-witness accounts:[5]

(1) Stress

"I could never forget what he looked like!" This common statement expresses the faith people have in their memories—even under stress. When a person's life or well-being is threatened, a stress pattern known as the General Adaptional Syndrome (GAS) can be expected to occur in varying degrees. This pattern is due to an increase in adrenaline levels and involves increases in heart rate and breathing rate as well as higher blood pressure. The end result is a dramatic increase in available energy which makes the person capable of running faster, fighting with more strength, lifting enormous weight— that is, taking the steps necessary to ensure safety or survival. This is not mere arousal from a quiet state, but a special state which occurs when a person senses that life or well-being is in danger.

However, a witness or victim of a crime who is under stress will be a less reliable witness than if under normal conditions. Research has shown that observers who are under stress are less capable of remembering details, less accurate in reading dials, less accurate in detecting signals.[7] They are paying more attention to their own safety than to nonessential elements in the environment. My research with Air Force flight crew members confirms that even highly trained people become poorer observers when under stress. Events can be remembered, but memory for details, clothing worn, colors, and the like, is not as clear. Time estimates are especially exaggerated under stress.[8]

This idea can be tested by asking a few people where they were when they first heard the news of the assassination of President John F. Kennedy. They will probably recall vividly where they were and who they were with. It is unlikely, however, that they will be able to describe what they or their companions were wearing.

Professors Roger Brown and James Kulik of Harvard made a study of the memories of persons at such critical points in their lives—and found what they call "flashbulb-memories."[9] However, they make the following distinctions between selective perception under stress and the mistaken notion that memory can act as a camera:

> An actual photograph, taken by flashbulb, preserves everything within its scope; it is *altogether* indiscriminate. Our flashbulb memories are not. The second author's crying teacher had a hairdo and a dress that are missing from his memory. The first author faced a desk with many objects on it, and some kind of weather was visible through the window, but none of this is in his memory picture. In short, a flashbulb memory is only somewhat indiscriminate and is very far from complete. In these respects, it is unlike a photograph.

(2) *Prior Conditioning and Experience*

Psychologists have done extensive research on how expectancy is used by human observers to make judgments more efficiently. In an experiment done in the 1930's, observers were shown a display of playing cards for a few seconds and asked to report the number of aces of spades in the display.[10] Most observers reported only three, although there were actually five. Two of the aces of spades were colored red instead of the familiar black. These results were interpreted to mean that, since the subjects were familiar with black aces of spades, they did not waste time looking carefully at the display. Efficiency, therefore, led to unreliable observation. In criminal cases, the prior conditioning of the witness may enable him to report facts or events which were not present but which he thinks should have been. Research also indicates that white observers show better recognition of white people than of black people in a lineup, and vice versa.[11]

(3) *Personal Biases and Stereotypes*

Expectancy in its least palatable form can be found in the case of biases or prejudices held by a witness. A victim of a mugging may initially report being attacked by "niggers," and may, because of limited experience as well as prejudice, be unable to tell one black man from another. In a classic study of this phenomenon, observers were asked to take a brief look at a drawing of several people on a subway train.[12] In the picture, a black man and a white man were seen having a confrontation. The white man held a razor in his hand. When questioned later about what they had seen, the observers tended to report having seen the razor in the hand of the black man.

Prejudices may be racial, religious, or based on physical characteristics such as long hair, dirty clothes, or status. All human beings have some stereotypes upon which they base perceptual judgments—stereotypes which lead not only to prejudice but are also a means of making decisions more efficiently. A witness to an auto accident may save thinking time by reporting his ingrained stereotype about "women drivers." These shortcuts to thinking may be erroneously reported and expanded upon by an eyewitness who is unaware that it is a description of a stereotype rather than the events which actually took place.[13] If the witness's biases are shared by the investigator taking the statement, the report may reflect their mutual biases rather than what was actually seen.[14]

(4) Unfair Test Construction

The lineup and array of photographs used in testing the eyewitness's ability to identify a suspect can be analyzed as fair or unfair on the basis of criteria that most psychologists can agree on. A fair test should be designed so that, first, all items have an equal chance of being selected by a person who did not see the suspect; second, the items should be similar enough to each other and to the original description on the suspect to be confusing to the person who is merely guessing; and last, the test should be conducted without leading questions or suggestions from the test giver.[15]

I have found all too frequently that lineups or photographic arrays have been carelessly assembled or even rigged in such a way as to make the eyewitness identification test completely unreliable.[16] If, for example, a witness is shown five pictures, the chance should be only one in five that any one picture will be chosen on the basis of guessing. Often, however, a single picture of a suspect will stand out. In the Angela Davis case, one set of nine pictures used to check identification contained three pictures of the defendant taken at an outdoor rally, two mug shots of other women showing their names, and one picture of a fifty-five year old woman. It was so easy for a witness to rule out five of the pictures as ridiculous choices that the "test" was reduced to a choice of four pictures—of which three were of Davis. Such a test is meaningless to a psychologist and probably tainted as an item of evidence in court.[17]

Research on memory has also shown that if one item in an array of photos is uniquely different (in dress, race, height, sex, photographic quality), it is more likely to be noticed.[18] A teacher making up a multiple-choice test designs several answers which sound or look alike to make it difficult for a person who does not know the right answer to succeed. Police lineups and photo lay-outs are also multiple-choice tests. If the rules for designing fair tests are ignored, the tests become unreliable.

So far I have presented the research framework on which I build my testimony in court as an expert witness. The framework is built on the work of the past, much of which is familiar to a working psychologist, but is hardly the day to day experience of adult Americans likely to become jurors. Some of the earliest psychologists, notably Muensterberg, had developed the essence of this analysis by the beginning of this century.[19] But there was a gap between the controlled research setting which had yielded data on basic perceptual processes and the real world. In order to close this gap, we have designed tests which evaluate eyewitness accuracy and reliability after having seen simulated crimes where we have a good record of the veridical (real) events for comparison. The following is a description of a version of an experiment first conducted in a more primitive manner by Muensterberg and others over sixty-five years ago.

An Experimental Study of the Eyewitness

In order to study the effects of eyewitness testimony in a realistic setting, we staged an assault on a California State University campus, in which a distraught student "attacked" a professor in front of 141 witnesses.[20] We recorded the entire incident, on videotape, so that we could compare the actual event with eyewitness reports. After the attack we took sworn statements from each witness, asking the witness to describe the suspect, the incident, and the clothes worn. This was essentially a free recall process. We also asked for a confidence rating (0–100%) in the description.

Table 15-II shows a comparison of the known characteristics of the suspect and the averages of the descriptions given by the witnesses. It is clear that the witnesses gave very inaccurate descriptions—a fact which has been demonstrated so often in this type of experiment that

TABLE 15-II

COMPARISON OF AVERAGE DESCRIPTIONS BY 141 EYEWITNESSES
WITH ACTUAL DESCRIPTIONS OF SUSPECTS AND EVENTS

	Known Characteristics	*Averaged Descriptions*
Duration of Incident	34 sec.	81.1 sec.
Height	69.5 in.	70.4 in.
Weight	155 lb.	180 lb.
Age	25 yr.	22.7 yr.
Total Accuracy Score	28 pts.	7.4 pts.

both law and psychology professors use this as a demonstration of the unreliability of eyewitness testimony. People tend to overestimate the passage of time—in this case by a factor of almost $2\frac{1}{2}$ to 1. The weight estimate was 14 percent higher, the age was underestimated, and the accuracy score (made up of points for appearance and dress) was only 25 percent of the maximum possible total score. Only the height estimate was close. This may be due to the fact that the suspect was of average height. People will often cite known facts about the "average" man when they are uncertain. Inaccurate witness's weight estimates correlate significantly with their *own* weight.

We then waited seven weeks and presented a set of six photographs to each witness individually, creating four conditions in order to test the effects of biased instructions and unfair testing on eyewitness identification.

We gave two kinds of instructions: (1) Low Bias, in which witnesses were asked only if they recognized anyone in the photos; (2) High Bias, in which witnesses were told we had an idea who the assailant was and we wanted them to pick him out of the photos. We used two types of photo spreads, using well-lit frontal views of young men who were the same age as the suspect. In the non-leading photo spread, all six photos were neatly set out, with the same expression on all faces and similar clothing on each suspect. In the biased photo spread, the photo of the actual assailant was placed crooked in the array, and he wore different clothing and had a different expression on his face than did the other suspects. We thus violated good testing practice for the sake of comparison.

The results indicated that overall only 40 percent of the witnesses correctly identified the assailant. In fact, 25 percent of the witnesses identified the wrong man—an innocent bystander who had been at the scene of the crime. Even the professor who was attacked picked out the innocent man from the photos as his attacker! Of the witnesses who correctly identified the assailant, the highest percentage came from the group which had been given a biased set of photos and biased instructions. (In some of our recent research we have used the same photo spreads to test non-witnesses. They also picked out the biased picture of the assailant.)

We concluded from this study (1) that the report of most of the eyewitnesses were so unreliable that an investigation begun as a response to these reports would very likely focus on the wrong person; (2) that the presence of biased instructions and leading sets of photos when testing for identification through the use of photographs can increase the percentage of witnesses who pick out the photo toward which the authorities are already biased; and (3) that if the police are biased toward an innocent man, the presence of biased instructions and a leading set of photos could increase the possibility of identifying the wrong person.

As an expert witness and consultant, I have discussed these findings in court as an expert either at a *Wade* hearing or, on some thirty-two occasions, before a trial jury. The story of the fight to get this sort of expert testimony admitted is a long one. Courts have generally upheld the discretion of the trial judge to admit it or not.[21] Even when expert testimony of this nature is not permitted, however, I have been of use in developing a plausible theory for the defense attorney of how mistaken identity or misperception of facts might have contributed to what a witness says in court. In some instances we have measured lighting or directly simulated aspects of the scene of an accident to test how well the average observer would fare under the same circumstances. Our research suggests generally that we cannot take eyewitness testimony for granted even though we shall always be faced with it in the courtroom.

REFERENCES

1. Loftus, E.F. Reconstructing memory: The incredible eyewitness, *Jurimetrics Journal, 15,* 188, 1975. Professor Loftus has shown that the mere presence of eyewitness testimony in a criminal jury trial can change the outcome from a minority to a majority of votes for a conviction.
2. Buckhout, R. Eyewitness testimony, *Scientific American,* December 1974.
3. Miller, G. and Buckhout, R. *Psychology: The science of mental life,* New York, Harper and Row, 1973.

4. Buckhout, R. *The psychology of the eyewitness,* 1975, (Monograph CR-1, Center for Responsive Psychology, Brooklyn College, New York).

5. Buckhout, R. Psychology and eyewitness identification, *Law and Psychology Review, 2,* 75, 1976.

6. Averill, J.R., Opton, E.M., and Lazarus, R.S. Crosscultural studies of psychophysiological responses during stress and emotion, *International Journal of Psychology, 4,* 88, 1969.

7. Levine, E. and Tapp, J. The psychology of criminal identification: The gap from Wade to Kirby, *University of Pennsylvania Law Review, 121,* 1079, 1973.

8. Johnson, C.L. Doctoral dissertation, Oklahoma State University, Stillwater, 1972.

9. Brown, R. and Kulik, J. Flashbulb memories, *Cognition, 5,* 73, 1977. See also Berendt. Where were you?, *Esquire,* November 1973.

10. Postman, L. *Psychology in the making,* New York, Knopf, 1962.

11. Buckhout, R. Eyewitnessing in black and white, 1975, (Monograph CR-21, Center of Responsive Psychology, Brooklyn College, New York)—Luce, T.S. They all look alike to me, *Psychology Today,* November 1974, at 105; Luce, T. S. The neglected dimension in eyewitness identification, *Criminal Defense,* 5, May–June 1977.

12. Allport, G. and Postman, L. *The psychology of rumor,* New York, Holt, 1947.

13. Loftus, E.F. The incredible eyewitness, *Psychology Today,* December 1974, at 116.

14. Buckhout, R. Eyewitness identification: Accuracy of individual v. composit recollections of a crime, *Bulletin of the Psychonomic Society, 8,* 147, 1976.

15. Buckhout, R. and Friere, V. *Suggestivity in lineups and photo-spreads,* 1975, (Monograph CR-5, Center for Responsive Psychology, Brooklyn College, New York).

16. Buckhout, R. and Ellison, K.W. The lineups: A critical look, *Psychology Today,* 82, June 1977.

17. People v. Angela Davis (Superior Court, San Jose, California, May, 1972.)

18. Doob, A. Kirshenbaum, H. Bias in police lineups: Partial remembering, *Journal of Police Science and Administration, 1,* 287, 1973.

19. Muensterberg, H. On the witness stand (1915), edited by Moss, R., New York, AMS Press, reprinting of 1923 edition.

20. Buckhout, R., Figueroa, R. and Hoff, L. Eyewitness identification: Effects of suggestion and bias in identification from photographs *Journal of the Psychonomic Society, 6,* 71, 1975.

21. Katz, M. and Reid, D. Expert testimony on the fallibility of eyewitness testimony, *Criminal Justice Journal, 1,* 177, 1977. See also Buckhout, R.

Nobody likes a smartass, *Social Action and the Law, 3,* 41, 1976 and, Did your eyes deceive you? Expert psychological testimony on the unreliability of eyewitness identification, *Standard Law Review, 29,* 969, 1977.

SECTION III

EVALUATION, SENTENCING, AND TREATMENT OF OFFENDERS

Though this section is titled *Evaluation, Sentencing, and Treatment of Offenders,* it includes some papers only marginally related to this title. An attempt has been made to provide both an overall view on this topic and to pick out specific areas of special interest. Chapters 16 and 17 deal with what may currently be the most critical issue in forensic psychology: the ability or inability of mental health professionals to predict dangerous behavior. Chapter 18, on capital punishment, speaks not only to that specific issue but also to broader questions of disposition of convicted offenders. Chapters 19 and 20 give an overview of treatment within correctional settings and discuss the issue of its efficacy. Chapters 23 and 24 deal also with treatment issues and approach the question of deciding when release is appropriate from two different perspectives. Chapter 28 deals with in-therapy issues with offenders. Chapters 21, 22, and 29 discuss issues relevant to specific offender populations: juveniles, females, and rapists, respectively. Chapter 26 looks at treatment philosophy within state hospital units for offenders. Two chapters that deserve special attention from the reader are 25 and 27, which present how offenders in prisons and hospitals view the treatment provided. Their views should be compared with the views of the providers. Chapter 30 deals with an experimental approach to understanding victim's responses.

Chapter 16

THE PREDICTION OF DANGEROUS BEHAVIOR*

EDWIN I. MEGARGEE, Ph.D.

A T NO TIME has the prediction of dangerous behavior been of great-er concern to mental health professionals and society at large. In addition to the natural concern over preventing violence directed at public figures and ordinary citizens, the problem of predicting dangerous behavior is a common bridge linking the civil and criminal law. As Dershowitz has pointed out, our society has always maintained a system of preventive confinement of potentially dangerous individuals by means of a number of legal strategies including involuntary commitment of the "dangerous" mentally ill individual, denial of bail, probation, or parole to the "dangerous" criminal offender, and confinement of juveniles, "vagrants," and "sexual psychopaths" who appear likely to engage in acts of violence (cited by Stone[1]). Indeed, one libertarian view is that such preventive confinement is the only justification for involuntary civil commitment. According to Stone,

> this progressive approach rejects the medical model, rejects the treatment rationale, and puts forward the narrow John Stuart Mill libertarian point of view, which suggests that in principle civil commitment can be continued if the State can justify the loss of liberty in light of its traditional police function. The emphasis on dangerousness as the salient variable is compatible with the modern jurisprudence of criminal law and is central to the sentencing premises of the American Law Institute Model Penal Code and the Model Sentencing Act. It is also a critical theme in the President's Commission on Law Enforcement and Administration of Justice.

*"The Prediction of Dangerous Behavior" by Edwin I. Megargee is reprinted From *Criminal Justice and Behavior, 3, (1),* 3–21, March 1976 by permission of the publisher, Sage Publications, Inc.

It is easy to understand why Stone concludes, "the generic concept of dangerousness has emerged as the paramount consideration in the law-mental health system."

How well do professionals predict dangerous behavior? The public at large, and law enforcement personnel and legislators in particular, apparently feel mental health personnel advise the release of too many potentially violent individuals to prey upon society. On the other hand, empirical data indicate that clinicians are more inclined to overpredict violence and classify an excessive number of people as dangerous.[12]

In either case, it is clear the prediction of dangerous behavior involves making errors. The purpose of this paper is to present a conceptual framework for examining the process of predicting dangerous behavior, indicating the points at which mistakes can occur, and explaining why such errors are inevitable. Secondly, it will address itself to the implications for social policy and decision making.

"DANGEROUSNESS" VS. DANGEROUS BEHAVIOR

In recent years it has become popular to refer to this problem as the assessment of "dangerousness." "Dangerousness" is an unfortunate term, for it implies there is a trait of "dangerousness" which, like intelligence, is a relatively constant characteristic of the person being assessed. However, the degree of danger an individual represents to himself or others varies markedly as a function of a number of variables. It is better to eschew the term "dangerousness" in favor of discussing the problems involved in "predicting dangerous behavior," to avoid the trap of affixing permanent labels on changeable people.

The term "dangerous behavior," which will be used interchangeably with "violence," will be applied to a relatively narrow range of acts characterized by the application or overt threat of force which is likely to result in injury to people. Although not all dangerous behavior is criminal (since the perpetrator may be lacking criminal intent) this use of the term includes, but is not restricted to, such criminal acts as homicide, mayhem, aggravated assault, forcible rape, battery, robbery, arson, and extortion. Criminal behavior not likely to result in injury to people, such as noncoercive thefts or vandalism, are excluded, as are business practices which, although injurious to people, do not involve the application of force.

BASIC PROBLEMS IN PREDICTING BEHAVIOR

When discussing the accuracy of public opinion polling, laymen intuitively understand that polling a small sample of people to estimate the future voting behavior of the electorate as a whole inevitably involves error. However, it is less often understood that the same problem plagues psychological assessment. Whenever a sample of behavior is used to estimate a larger behavior domain, whether we use high-school grades and CEEB scores to predict college achievement, or case history data and personality tests to estimate the likelihood of dangerous behavior, some errors inevitably occur. Despite our best efforts we will recommend confining some people who, if left free, would not have injured anyone, and will suggest releasing others who will subsequently engage in violence. (If our batting average is perfect for one type of decision, i.e., if none of our released clients ever harms anyone, then the odds are that we are making errors of the other type and confining too many who could have been set free.)

The basic question is how much error can be tolerated and whether more harm is done by predicting inaccurately or by not predicting at all. These value judgments will be considered when we discuss social policy implications. But first the processes involved in predicting dangerous behavior will be discussed to demonstrate why error is inescapable.

THE PROCESS OF PREDICTING DANGEROUS BEHAVIOR

Identifying The Relevant Variables

Although it is axiomatic that behavior is a function of both personality factors and situational variables [B = (P • S)], psychologists typically focus on the former at the expense of the latter. But a recent series of experiments on the prediction of leadership showed that knowledge of both personality and situational variables was essential for accurate prediction.[3,4,5]

Personality Factors

To predict dangerous behavior, the clinician must consider three broad classes of personality variables: *motivation, internal inhibitions, and habit strength.*

Before discussing motivation, or to use a more technical term, *instigation to aggression*, we should distinguish between what Buss[6] termed "angry aggression" and "instrumental aggression." According to Buss, angry aggression is motivated by a conscious or unconscious desire to harm the victim and is reinforced by the victim's pain, whereas instrumental aggression is a means to some other end and is reinforced by the satisfaction of some other drive. Shooting someone you hate is an example of angry aggression; shooting someone in self-defense, in the line of duty, or to fulfill a "contract" would be examples of instrumental aggression. Of course, both types of motivation may be mixed, as in the case of an angry parent who spanks a child partly to help socialize that child and partly to ventilate his or her own feelings.

Instigation to aggression is the sum of both types of motivation and it is necessary to assess not only the degree of anger or hostility but also the extent to which dangerous behavior would be used by the client as a means to some other end. This is particularly true in such violent offenses as armed robbery and forcible rape, which may satisfy acquisitive or sexual drives, and gang fights, which usually satisfy needs for status, affiliation, and territory as well as hostility.

The assessment process is further complicated by the fact that *hostility* and *anger* must be evaluated. Hostility is a relatively enduring characteristic or trait, whereas anger or rage are transitory emotional states which are highly individualized and situation-specific. A client who manifests no anger during the assessment, even when deliberately provoked, may still act out on the street. Although some state-trait scales of anger and hostility have been devised,[7] most are quite obvious and easily dissimulated. The vast majority of the psychometric devices available simply attempt to measure aggressive motivation (or worse yet, "aggressiveness") as though they were enduring traits.[8,9] The case history and interviews with family and friends are more useful in gauging the incidence of transitory states of rage and anger as well as in determining the likelihood that the client will encounter situations or conditions likely to elicit instigation to aggression.

Internal Inhibitions

Internal inhibitions or taboos against engaging in dangerous behavior have received less attention than instigation to aggression. However, they are equally important, because whenever the inhibitions against a response exceed the instigation the response will be suppressed or repressed. Unfortunately for predictors, inhibitions are probably even more specific than instigation. They differ from target to target. Mike LeFevre, a steel worker interviewed by Studs Terkel in *Working*, said, "all day I wanted to tell my foreman to go fuck himself, but I can't. So I find a guy in a tavern. To tell him that. And he tells me to. . . . He's punching me and I'm punching him, because we actually want to punch somebody else."[10] Inhibitions also vary as a function of the act; although Mike LeFevre had few compunctions about hitting the other man, he refrained from using a knife. Distance from the target is yet another factor; a man who would be too inhibited to strangle one individual might well be able to bomb thousands. It is these differences in levels of inhibition as a function of victims and acts that account in part for the phenomena of displacement and response substitution.

Like instigation, inhibitions can vary over time. Moreover, they can be influenced chemically. The association between drinking and violence stems primarily from the fact that alcohol acts to anesthetize the brain areas that mediate inhibitions; chronic as well as acute brain syndromes can also lower inhibitions.

As if these variations in inhibitions did not pose enough problems for the would-be prognosticator, the situation has been further complicated by studies which have demonstrated that some extremely violent people are characterized by excessive inhibitions. In such individuals, suppressed instigation to aggression apparently summated to the point where the massive inhibitions were overwhelmed. (For reviews of these studies and the MMPI Overcontrolled-Hostility scale that helps identify such individuals, see Megargee).[11,12]

Perhaps because of this preoccupation with the chronically overcontrolled assaultive individual, who rarely if ever engages in even mildly aggressive behavior, the author in his previous theoretical writings has neglected a third personality variable which is probably just as important as instigation and inhibitions. This is *habit strength,* the extent to which aggressive responses have been reinforced in the past. An appraisal of habit strength is particularly important when attempting to determine whether an individual will attempt to satisfy his or her needs for sex, power, mastery, wealth, and the like by means of instrumental aggression and in the analysis of socially approved dangerous behavior by people such as policemen and military personnel.

Situational Factors

The importance of situational factors has already been emphasized. These include immediate specific factors such as the availability of a weapon, the presence of onlookers, and the behavior of a potential victim, but more pervasive situational variables such as the level of frustration in the environment, or the social approval of violence in a particular subculture should also be considered.

Situational factors can either facilitate or impede dangerous behavior. A gun in the hand of an angry man can facilitate his committing an act of violence, but if, instead, the gun is in the hand of his potential victim, it is more likely to inhibit his dangerous behavior. One reason behavioral scientists can predict college achievement more accurately than dangerous behavior is that academia presents each student with standard situations and similar stimuli, whereas the situations and milieus to be confronted by mental patients and parolees in the community seem infinitely more variable.

ASSESSING THE RELEVANT VARIABLES

Once the relevant variables have been identified, ways must be found to assess them. The discussion of instigation, inhibitions, habit strength, and situational factors indicated some of the problems involved in their measurement such as the transitory nature of emotional states such as anger, the specificity of both instigation and inhibitions, and the difficulty of obtaining adequate data pertaining to situational variables.

Most of the literature on the prediction of dangerous behavior focuses on the reliability and validity of personality assessment devices. Although many of these instruments can discriminate people who have engaged in dangerous behavior in the past from "normal" nonclinical groups, few, if any, can adequately differentiate violent from nonviolent criminals or patients.[8,9,13,14] Unfortunately, these are precisely the differentiations that practitioners who work in a correctional or mental health setting are usually called upon to make.

Moreover, even if the validity literature showed that our tests could accurately identify people who have been violent in the past, it would not necessarily mean these tests could predict who will behave dangerously in the future. The violent act itself may have created feelings of guilt or relieved pent-up hostility. Also, people who have been identified as having illegally engaged in such acts are inevitably exposed to a variety of judicial and correctional procedures expressly designed to change their personality structure and dynamics. And change they probably do, although the nature of these alterations may be quite different from what was intended.

Psychological tests are neat, efficient, and quantifiable, but they are not always the best samples of behavior for the prediction of violence. Telling a story about a scene depicted in a TAT card or answering a series of true-false questionnaire items are many steps removed from the dynamic interactions that actually result in violence. Case histories are better indicators, but, as already noted, people do change. Institutional behavior may provide some useful data, but it is not infallible. An individual may refrain from violence for years in a facility with strong external controls, particularly if he is receiving chemotherapy and counseling, only to resume violent behavior in a less structured or supportive community setting. By the same token, a person who responded with violence to the peculiar stresses and demands of the institutional subculture might not behave dangerously on the street. Diagnostic role playing sessions in the institution coupled with furloughs might provide useful data. However, such informal assessment techniques are not standardized or quantifiable so it is difficult to determine their reliability or validity.

Whatever the behavior sample the clinician selects, it is no secret that the validity of our assessment techniques is less than perfect, and too often less than satisfactory.[8,9] The clinician can make errors in selecting the variables to assess, but even if he does this perfectly, he is likely to make errors in measuring these variables with the instruments currently available.

DETERMINING THE INTERACTION OF THE RELEVANT VARIABLES

It is not enough to select the correct variables and measure them accurately. Before making a prediction, one must determine how these variables interact. In effect, one must forecast the effects of a rapid internal algebra which determines the response potential for a given dangerous act relative to all other possible behaviors.

Based on the discussion thus far, it would appear, in theory at least, that we could add up the factors facilitating and impeding the expression of dangerous behavior and balance them against one another. One would take the sum of instigation to aggression against victim "x" (M_x), plus the past history of reinforcement (H), and the situational factors facilitating violence (S_f) and weigh them against the sum of the internal inhibitions against a particular dangerous act "a" against victim "x" $(I_{a \cdot x})$ and the inhibitory situational factors (S_i).

If one did go through such a procedure and found that the inhibitions were stronger (i.e., $M_x + H + S_f < I_a ._x + S_i$), then one could safely predict that dangerous behavior against that victim would not occur. (Of course, if the instigation was increased by one more provocation or the inhibitions decreased by one more beer, this balance could be shifted.)

On the other hand, finding that the factors favoring the completion of the dangerous act exceed those inhibiting it (i.e., $M_x + H + S_f > I_a ._x + S_i$) does not mean that poor victim "x" will soon be on the receiving end of dangerous act "a". A predominance of factors favoring the particular response only means that it is *possible,* not that is will inevitably occur. At any given time a number of possible responses are competing for expression and the one actually selected depends upon their *relative response strength.* It may be that the response potential is stronger for some other dangerous act "b" or for act "a" directed at another victim "y". Or, some completely nonaggressive act satisfying competing drives such as hunger, sex, or status might be prepotent.

SOURCES OF ERROR IN PREDICTING DANGEROUS BEHAVIOR

This essay began with the assertion that error is inevitable in the prediction of behavior. It should be clear to any readers who have persevered this far that this is particularly true in the case of dangerous behavior because of the numerous pitfalls along the way. It is easy to make an error in identifying the relevant variables, especially the situational factors, and even easier to encounter difficulties in assessing them reliably or validly. Even if this is done correctly, one can make mistakes as he attempts to determine the interaction of these variables or estimate the relative response potential of dangerous and nondangerous acts.

Unfortunately, once such errors are made, they are greatly magnified by another factor peculiar to dangerous and other infrequent forms of behavior. This is the base-rate problem identified by Meehl and Rosen.[15] Applying Bayes' Theorem, Meehl and Rosen demonstrated that whenever we attempt to predict infrequent events, even a moderate false positive rate will result in large numbers of people being erroneously diagnosed.

In predicting dangerous behavior, we can make two types of errors: "false positives" are those individuals that we erroneously predict will engage in dangerous behavior, whereas "false negatives" are those whom we erroneously predict will not engage in dangerous behavior. Although the public is more concerned about the false negative who are released and later attack someone, it is the false positives who, by sheer weight of numbers, call into question the possibility of accurately predicting dangerous behavior.[1]

Let us suppose that someone devises a method of predicting dangerous behavior that far exceeds any technique currently available and that a validation study shows this new technique correctly identifies 85% of the people who later engage in dangerous behavior (i.e., has a false negative rate of 15%) and 90% of these who do not behave dangerously (i.e., has a false positive rate of 10%). Although the false negative rate exceeds the false positive rate, application of this technique to a random sample of 100,000 U.S. citizens would demonstrate the pernicious effect of false positives. Recently reported data indicates that the base rate for violent crime in the United States is 187 per 100,000.[16] The new test would accurately identify 85% or 159 of the 187 violent individuals. So far so good. But what of the 99,813 citizens who will not behave dangerously? Because of the 10% false positive rate, the test will erroneously predict that 9,981 of these individuals will commit acts of violence. Combining the 9,981 false positives and the 28 false negatives, we see that by using the test we would make 10,009 mistakes. On the other hand, if we had not used the test and had simply predicted no one would be violent, we would have made only 187 errors.

Unfortunately, none of our techniques has a false positive rate as low as our hypothetical example.[2] Follow-up studies of people classified as dangerous who have subsequently been released or transferred show false positive rates of 65%,[17] 76% (women) and 80% (men),[18] and 86–95%.[19] To be sure, Kozol[17] now estimates that with improved techniques his team has been able to lower the false positive rate among previously violent patients to about 50%, but applied to our random sample of 100,000, a 50% false positive rate would result in erroneous predictions of violence for 49,906 people. As Stone[1] has stated, "if dangerousness is the sole criterion for civil commitment or other preventive detention, and if an empirical study demonstrates violence is a rare event (low base rate), then even if we had a very good predictive technique or device, we would end up confining many more false than true positives."

TABLE 16-I
USE OF A HYPOTHETICAL TEST WITH A FALSE POSITIVE RATE
OF 10 PERCENT AND A FALSE NEGATIVE RATE OF 15 PERCENT
TO PREDICT DANGEROUS BEHAVIOR IN A RANDOM SAMPLE OF
100,000 UNITED STATES CITIZENS

PREDICTED BEHAVIOR	*ACTUAL BEHAVIOR* Dangerous	Not Dangerous	Total
Dangerous	159 (true positive)	9,981 (false positive)	10,140
Not Dangerous	28 (false negative)	89,832 (true negative)	89,860
Total	187	99,813	100,000

SOCIAL POLICY IMPLICATIONS

Most mental health professionals will at some time find themselves in a position in which they must decide whether an individual is likely to engage in behavior that is dangerous to him- or herself or to others. Although this question most often confronts clinicians working in criminal justice and in-patient psychiatric settings, others in private practice, in school settings or community mental health centers will also have occasion to make such predictions. Given the current state of the art, what stance should they adopt?

Some may simply refuse to make such predictions on the grounds that the problems discussed thus far make errors inevitable. Although each person must be guided by his individual professional values, the present writer disagrees with this Pilate-like position. It is facile, but correct, to point out that someone has to make these predictions. If there are data that show that better predictions are made without his professional input, then by all means a clinician should decline to participate. Otherwise, as long as predictions regarding dangerous behavior are going to be made, the author feels mental health professionals should contribute to the best of their ability.

More cogent is the fact that in predicting dangerous behavior, the assessor must balance the often-conflicting needs of at least three parties—the person regarding whom the prediction is made (the "predictee" if you will), that person's potential victim, and society at large.[1] In the author's opinion, those who refuse to predict dangerous behavior are letting their concern for the rights and welfare of the "predictee" blind them to their obligations to the potential victim and to society.

One way of crystallizing the issues is to imagine, despite all the evidence to the contrary, that it was possible to identify with complete accuracy those individuals who were going to engage in dangerous behavior. If so, would society have the right to intervene?

The author finds it impossible to cope with such questions without considering the nature of the intervention. Counselors and therapists in some settings are required to warn potential victims if a client appears likely to attack them. Law enforcement agencies can warn individuals likely to engage in dangerous behavior, confiscate their weapons, and, on various legal or psychiatric grounds, usually arrange for a brief period of preventive detention. The present author would have no great reservations about any of these relatively benign interventions if dangerous behavior could be predicted this accurately.

But what if the intervention took the form of confinement for an indefinite period? Such preventive detention would clearly be in the interest of the potential victim but not the potential attacker, except insofar as it might be better in the long run for the latter not to commit a crime of violence. Although the public at large undoubtedly favors the safety of the potential victim over the civil rights of the potential attacker, consideration of the best interest of the third party, society, leads the present writer to adopt a middle course. If the predictee has already engaged in behavior that warrants confinement in its own right, then he would favor preventive detention. For example, if the predictee is hospitalized for mental illness or imprisoned for some crime, then the certainty that the predictee will engage in violence would, in my opinion, warrant continued confinement even though he or she might otherwise be eligible for release or parole. If the predictee is not confined but has engaged in overt behavior that would warrant confinement such as uttering threats, acquiring an illegal weapon, or entering into criminal conspiracy, then the writer would advocate prosecution for that behavior, with all appropriate legal safeguards, and confinement if the predictee were convicted. Similarly, if the individual is committable as mentally ill, this could be undertaken.

However, if the individual is not currently confined and has engaged in no overt behavior or exhibited no other symptoms that would warrant confinement, then the writer would be reluctant to advocate indefinite detention. In my opinion, the harm done to society as a whole for any of its members to be confined indefinitely on the basis of expert opinion rather than overt behavior outweighs the threat to one member of society, namely the victim.

Of course, as we have established, predictions of dangerous behavior are hardly infallible. Examining the problem of predicting dangerous behavior from a purely theoretical standpoint, we saw that errors are inevitable and, when we are working with populations in which dangerous behavior is infrequent, the base rate problem will magnify these errors and result in an excessive number of false positives.

To be right most of the time, a person should go along with the base rates and predict no dangerous behavior will occur. However, rather than be right most of the time, the author prefers a decision model that minimizes the possible adverse consequences for all concerned, the predictee, the potential victim, and society.

A rough screening procedure with literally thousands of false positives is justifiable if the adverse consequences to the predictees are relatively benign. Who can calculate the false positive rate of the psychological screening profiles used by airlines to identify potential hijackers or by the Secret Service to spot potential assassins? But if the only consequences of being classified as a potential air pirate or presidential assassin are being denied access to an aircraft, or proximity to the President, then the writer feels it is better to have a thousand false positives than a single false negative.

But what if the consequences are less benign? What if the prediction that someone will engage in dangerous behavior means that he or she will be denied parole from a correctional institution or involuntarily committed to a mental institution?[2]

The first requirement in such cases is that the prediction should be based on the most complete and valid procedures currently available to minimize errors in general and false positive in particular. Mental health professionals should limit themselves to predicting dangerous behavior in high base-rate populations such as those who have already engaged in repeated violence. Kozol et al.[17] have flatly stated, "No one can predict dangerous behavior in an individual with no history of dangerous acting out." Moreover, predictors should refuse to allow themselves to be trapped into a dichotomous decision model. Instead, they should set cutting scores on both ends, predicting dangerous behavior for those at one extreme, no dangerous behavior for those at the other, and admitting they cannot predict for those in the middle.[3] Thirdly, prediction should be confined to cases for which there is a good understanding of the situation or milieu.

One would expect better prediction of violence inside institutions, where the environment is similar for all, than in community settings, which are more variable.

Despite these measures, it is clear we cannot predict dangerous behavior with absolute certainty. Kozol et al. obtained follow-up data on a sample of patients who were released despite the fact that Kozol's psychiatric team has classified them as dangerous; only 35% actually engaged in violence. On the basis of these data, then, we can believe Harry Kozol and his team if they point to three individuals and say, "If these three people are released, one of them will attack someone, but we do not know which one of the three will do so." Does society have the right to confine two people unnecessarily to prevent violence by a third? Or, on the other hand, does society have the right to release any of the three and thereby knowingly endanger someone else's very life?

Some who would endorse preventive detention if dangerous behavior could be predicted with 100% accuracy will balk at the notion of confining two to prevent violence by a third. The present writer's response would be similar to the guidelines he suggested for the perfectly accurate prediction, i.e., confine only those whose overt behavior would justify confinement even if no prediction had been made. With others take less drastic steps to deter violence such as providing close parole supervision, warning potential victims, or perhaps requiring the posting of peace bonds.

Thus far we have been grappling with these problems on a moralistic basis, balancing the rights of predictees against the safety of potential victims and the preservation of social structure. A "hardheaded" pragmatist might attempt to resolve the dilemma through a cost-benefit analysis. What is the total cost to society of confining 100 of Kozol's patients? This could be calculated by figuring the cost of institutionalizing them (food, buildings, staff, lost earning power, family deprivation, and so on). The same approach could be used to calculate the social cost of the violent behavior-rapes, murdering, child molesting-engaged in by the 35 who became violent, using insurance company estimates of the dollar cost of these crimes to society. The analyst could then determine if society shows a profit or a loss from confining 100 "dangerous" individuals to prevent violence by 35. Although the assigning dollar values to human suffering is morally repugnant, it is one way to resolve the dilemma. However, there is no way to calculate how much it cost society as a whole to curtail the civil liberties of a few.

The public at large is probably not overly concerned about the loss of civil liberties or the unnecessary confinement of people erroneously labeled "dangerous." Clearly most people identify with the victim and place a premium on personal safety, and the professional will experience much more criticism for false negatives than for false positives. Nevertheless, in addition to modifying and improving the prediction process to minimize the number of errors, it is time for mental health professionals to accept the responsibility to consider in each case the ethical and social implications of their predictions. After all, if the predictors do not worry about the consequences of predicting dangerous behavior, who will?

REFERENCES

1. Stone, A.A. *Mental health and law: A system in transition*, Washington, D.C., Government Printing Office, 1975.
2. Monahan, J. The prevention of violence, In Monahan, J. (Ed.), *Community mental health and the criminal justice system*, New York, Pergamon, 1975.
3. Fenelon, J.R. and Megargee, E.I. Influence of race on the manifestation of leadership, *Journal of Applied Psychology, 55*, 353–358, 1971.
4. Fenelon, J.R. and Megargee, E.I. The influence of sex roles on the manifestation of leadership, *Journal of Applied Psychology, 53*, 377–382, 1969.
5. Megargee, E.I., Bogart, P., and Anderson, B.J. The prediction of leadership in a simulated industrial task, *Journal of Applied Psychology, 50*, 292–295, 1966.
6. Buss, A.H. *Psychology of aggression*, New York, Wiley, 1961.
7. Vanderbeck, D.J. An examination of the use of adjective checklists in measuring anger states and hostile traits, *FCI Technical and Treatment Notes, 3*, 1–53, Federal Correctional Institution, Tallahassee, Florida, 1972.
8. Vanderbeck, D.J. The prediction of violence with psychological tests, In Spielberger, C.D. (Ed.), *Current topics in clinical and community psychology*, Vol. 2, New York, Academic Press, 1970.
9. Megargee, E.I. and Menzies, E. The assessment and dynamics of aggression, In McReynolds, P. (Ed.), *Advances in psychological assessment*, Vol. 2, Palo Alto, California, Science and Behavior Books, 1971.
10. Terkel, S. *Working*, New York, Pantheon, 1974.
11. Terkel, S. The role of inhibition in the assessment and understanding of violence, In Singer, J.F. (Ed.), *The control of aggression and vio-*

lence: Cognitive and physiological factors, New York, Academic Press, 1971.

12. Megargee, E.I. Recent research on overcontrolled and undercontrolled personality patterns among violent offenders, *Sociology Symposium, 9,* 37–50, 1973.

13. Megargee, E.I. and Cook, P.E. The relation of TAT and inkblot aggressive content scales with each other and with criteria of overt aggressiveness in juvenile delinquents, *Journal of Projective Techniques and Personality Assessment, 1,* 48–60, 1967.

14. Megargee, E.I. and Mendelsohn, G.A. A cross-validation of 12 MMPI indices of hostility and control, *Journal of Abnormal and Social Psychology, 65,* 431–438, 1962.

15. Meehl, P.E. and Rosen, A. Antecedent probability and the efficiency of psychometric signs, patterns, cutting scores, *Psychology Bulletin, 52,* 194–216, 1955.

16. Hindelang, M.J., Dunn, C.S., Aumick, A.L., and Sutton, L.P. *Sourcebook of criminal justice statistics — 1974,* Washington, D.C., Government Printing Office, 1975.

17. Kozol, H., Boucher, R., and Garofalo, R. The diagnosis and treatment of dangerousness, *Crime and Delinquency, 18,* 371–392, 1972.

18. Steadman, H. and Halatyn, A. The Baxstrom patients: Backgrounds and outcomes, *Seminars in Psychiatry, 3,* 376–386, 1971.

19. Wenk, E., Robison, J., and Smith, G. Can violence be predicted? *Crime and Delinquency, 18,* 393–402, 1972.

Chapter 17

THE PREDICTION OF DANGEROUSNESS—
BAXSTROM: A CASE STUDY

HENRY J. STEADMAN, Ph.D.
AND
JOSEPH J. COCOZZA, Ph.D.

T HE *Baxstrom* decision, "Operation Baxstrom," and the Baxstrom research all take their name from Johnnie K. Baxstrom whose legal battles with the State of New York resulted in the mass transfer of nearly one thousand persons from maximum security correctional mental hospitals to civil state hospitals between March and August 1966. Two reports were produced providing preliminary information about the first year the Baxstrom patients spent in the civil hospitals.[1,2] In 1974 we published a monograph with intensive follow-up on both the hospital and community experiences of the Baxstrom patients during the first four years after their transfers.[3] When this monograph was published it received interdisciplinary review in the psychiatric,[4,5] criminological,[6,7] and sociological[8,9] journals. It was used as support for arguments about psychiatric inabilities to accurately predict dangerousness in a variety of legal briefs such as the Northern California Psychiatric Association's brief to the California Supreme Court requesting a rehearing on the *Tarasoff* case. The research was considered controversial enough to be the focus of the plenary session at the 1976 Annual Meeting of the American Academy of Psychiatry and the Law. Ennis and Litwack[10] in their often-quoted article on psychiatric predictions of dangerousness as coin-flipping, went so far as to say that the Baxstrom research was "Perhaps the most striking evidence" that psychiatrists are inaccurate predictors of violence and consistently overpredict it.

However, as the decision of the U.S. Supreme Court, the mass transfers, and the ensuing follow-up research have been placed in their historicial contexts, one of the core questions that has arisen from various commentaries is the extent to which these situations actually provided a natural experiment to test the accuracy of psychiatric predictions of dangerousness. In his review of our book, *Careers of the Criminally Insane*,[3] which reports the research on the Baxstrom patients to be reviewed below, Halpern asserted, "the refusal by the Department of Mental Hygiene to authorize the transfer (prior to the Supreme Court decision) was on the grounds that the patients were 'objectional', not dangerous, and the decision was an administrative, not a psychiatric one."[11] In contrast, Moran in another review states, "The United States Supreme Court decision in *Baxstrom* v. *Herold* provided a natural experiment in the ability of the psychiatric profession to predict dangerousness in mental patients housed in maximum security mental hospitals for the criminally insane."[6]

Thus, at the outset of this discussion of the Baxstrom research as a case study in the prediction of dangerousness, it is important to determine precisely what was studied so that an accurate estimation may be made as to the place of this research in the sparse empirical literature on the prediction of dangerousness. We will argue that indeed the mass transfers and the research that ensued did provide an opportunity to measure in a natural setting the accuracy of one type of clinical prediction of dangerousness. However, there are a number of qualifications that must be imposed for proper interpretation of the findings; some of which have been overlooked by both the proponents and opponents of the research.

THE BAXSTROM DECISION AND OPERATION BAXSTROM

In February 1966, the United States Supreme Court agreed with the petition of Johnnie K. Baxstrom that he had been denied equal protection as warranted by the U.S. Constitution by his continued detention in Dannemora State Hospital, a maximum security mental hospital run by the New York State Department of Correctional Services. Baxstrom had been arrested in Rochester, New York in October, 1958, for assaulting a police officer. Although the officer was in plain clothes when he got into a fight with Baxstrom in a local bar, Baxstrom was convicted of assault and sentenced to Attica State Prison. In 1961 he was determined to be mentally ill and transferred to Dannemora for treatment. While in Dannemora, his maximum sentence for the assault conviction expired. In December 1961 when this happened he was committed to Dannemora as still requiring psychiatric treatment. Baxstrom then instituted a blitz of habeas corpus briefs, which he completed himself from his study of the law books an uncle had left in his boyhood home in Baltimore. At all state court levels these briefs were denied. What Baxstrom contended was that since involuntary civil mental patients were entitled to jury determination of both mental illness and dangerousness, his continued detention in Dannemora was unconstitutional since he had not been afforded such review at the termination of his criminal sentence.

Baxstrom's legal maneuverings continued until his case reached the U.S. Supreme Court which accepted a brief he compiled himself, and then assigned him counsel from the Legal Aid Society of New York City. After relatively short consideration, Baxstrom's position was supported and the court required that the state review his commitment affording him, if he requested it, a jury trial on both the questions of mental illness and dangerousness. As a result of his efforts, Baxstrom was transferred to Marcy State Hospital in March 1966.

Of more import than the outcome of this case for Baxstrom, was the application of the court's decision by New York State to an additional 966 patients housed in Dannemora and Matteawan State Hospital, the state's other correctional maximum security mental hospital. It was not feasible to provide the review required by *Baxstrom* to all of those patients whose sentences had expired while being retained for mental health treatment in these two correctional hospitals. Instead, Johnnie Baxstrom and 966 other patients were transferred to eighteen state hospitals between March 15, 1966 and August 31, 1966. These transfers, as might be expected, met with tremendous opposition from the civil hospital directors, the hospitals' staff, and the communities surrounding the civil hospitals who feared what were seen as among the most dangerous patients in the state mental health system. The employee unions demanded, but did not get, special training and extra pay for staff members who would have to handle the Baxstrom patients. In at least one facility judo classes were provided to certain staff who were to work with these patients.

In 1968, a one year follow-up on the results of Operation Baxstrom was reported by Hunt and Wiley.[1] Through talking with hospital directors and examining patient discharge and admission records, they provided the first glimpses of what happened after the mass patient transfers. They concluded that, "After one year there have been no significant problems with the patients." White and his colleagues[2] looked more specifically and clinically at the group of patients transferred to one Long Island hospital. In this hospital, which was one of the two facilities that established special security wards for the Baxstrom patients, all but one of the 72 Baxstrom patients had been transferred to an open ward at the end of one year. Overall, they summarized that the Baxstrom "patients have presented no unique problems for the staff of a civil mental hospital." Thus, despite some serious forebodings, initial reports suggested that these supposed dangerous patients appeared to have been not unlike most other civil patients.

Our research extended these one year follow-ups in two ways. First, we followed the Baxstrom patients both in hospital and in the community for their first three-and-a-half years after their transfer from Dannemora and Matteawan. Second, we focused particularly on the level and type of violence in which they were involved after their releases. Our intention was to develop a comprehensive picture of their hospital and community behavior from which inferences might be drawn about the psychiatric abilities to accurately predict future violent behavior. As the design of our research is examined below, the question of what inferences can be drawn from these data and the natural experimental setting will be addressed.

RESEARCH DESIGN

To develop a comprehensive picture of both the backgrounds and outcomes of the Baxstrom patients, records were obtained from both the Department of Mental Hygiene (DHM) and the Division of Criminal Justice Services (DCJS), the agency responsible for compiling all criminal information. From the DMH records it was possible to gather the necessary background information about the individuals such as age, race, and education along with all clinical information about prior and subsequent mental hospitalizations. Likewise, the DCJS information included all criminal activity prior to the Dannemora or Matteawan institutionalizations plus all that during the three-and-a-half year follow-up period. The records of all 967 were gathered, but intensive analysis was done on a sample of 199 of 920 males. The 199 males are an approximately 20 percent systematic random sample from which generalizations may be drawn for all 920 males.

The specific information about the incidence of violent behavior for the Baxstrom patients came both from the DMH and DCJS records. The DMH files recorded incidents of assaultiveness during all civil hospitalizations after transfer and the crime data permitted the enumeration of arrests for murder, manslaughter, and any assaults. These data were of particular interest given what we interpreted to be the primary reasons why the Baxstrom patients had been detained in the correctional maximum security hospitals on the average of fifteen years before their discharges to civil hospitals. Based on the resistances of the state civil hospital staffs, the community fears, and the information in the *Baxstrom* decision, itself, it appeared uncontestable that the main reason they were detained so long was that they were seen as dangerous. They were seen as dangerous by the civil hospital staffs that did not want them in their increasingly open facilities where they might disrupt attempts at more innovative, open programs. They were seen as dangerous by the communities that feared their escape or release and their potential for violence. Finally, they were seen as dangerous by the staff at Matteawan and Dannemora as indicated by commitment statute under which they were being detained. As was noted in footnote five of the *Baxstrom* decision:

> In oral argument, counsel for respondent suggested that the determination by the Department of Mental Hygiene to retain a person in Dannemora must be based not only on his past criminal record, but also on evidence that he is currently dangerous. . . Under this procedure, all civil commitments to an institution under the control of the Department of Correction require a determination that the person is presently dangerous; all persons so committed are entitled to a judicial proceeding to determine this fact except those awaiting expiration of sentence.

Certainly, then, a major criterion for the continued detention of the 967 Baxstrom patients in maximum security facilities was their perceived dangerousness. This is not to say that the Baxstrom follow-up data can be taken as direct evidence to assess the accuracy of specific clinical predictions made on each of the 976 patients that they were dangerous immediately prior to their transfers to civil hospitals. The initial estimations, which tended to become indelible in clinical records, without consideration for recent events, were often made years before their transfers. Statutorily, no person could have been detained after their criminal sentences expired without psychiatric certification that they were dangerous. Quite probably, this statutory requirement was overlooked in some instances. However, the experiences of the Baxstrom patients did, indeed, provide a natural experiment on the accuracy of estimations of psychiatric dangerousness in that they reflect what were then the accepted roles for institutional psychiatry in the state correctional and mental health systems. The inaccuracy of these predictions demonstrated in limited ways the tendencies towards overprediction of dangerousness among the criminally insane.

FINDINGS

Among the first question that this research addressed was who the Baxstrom patients were. Although Hunt and Wiley, and White et al. had provided some useful information, neither provided any information about the demographic characteristics and criminal histories of these patients. It quickly became apparent when these characteristics were reviewed that the Baxstrom patients did not reflect the typical clinical cases presented to the forensic psychiatrist or psychologist today. Rather, they typified patient populations who still inhabit many maximum security state facilities in the United States.

At the time of transfer the males averaged fifty-two years of age and had been incarcerated continuously for an average of fifteen years. Most had never been married (61%) and they had attained on the average a seventh-grade education. The group was about equally divided between whites (47%) and blacks (48%) with the remaining 5 percent Hispanic. Most patients had not been previously hospitalized for mental illness (76%). However, they had many prior arrests, on the average 4.3, and had been incarcerated on the average 2.4 times each. Contrary to popular conceptions, nearly half (48%) had never been convicted of a violent crime prior to their current admission and fully 92 percent had never been convicted of a sex crime.

The offenses for which they had been convicted or charged just prior to their maximum security hospitalizations were predominantly against person (47%), with one third for property, 14 percent for minor offenses, and 5 percent involving sex crimes. At the time of their transfer to the civil hospitals, the most common diagnosis was schizophrenia, paranoid (41%), with all but 22 percent of the group receiving some type of schizophrenia diagnosis.

Thus, the people transferred in Operation Baxstrom were long-term mental patients who had lengthy histories of criminal activity, although this activity was not predominantly of a violent nature. When they were transferred, they had been in correctional settings on the average of fifteen years. Data from a comparison group of patients suggested that had the *Baxstrom* decision not been handed down, they could have been expected to remain in Dannemora and Matteawan on the average another eleven years. Instead, contrary to psychiatric advice and in the face of the active opposition of the civil hospital staffs and the surrounding communities, they were moved to less restrictive settings. Did they, in fact, exhibit the level of dangerous behavior that was expected of them?

This question is hard to answer because the levels expected are difficult to specify. One figure that hospital officials offered was that 25 percent of the patients would prove too dangerous for detention in civil hospitals and would require return to Matteawan. Other officials thought this figure was optimistic. No estimates could be found as to the expected level of assaultive behavior in the civil hospitals, the proportion of patients who would ultimately be released to the community or the percentage of those released that would be rearrested.

It was clear that the actual number returned to maximum security confinement was substantially below the estimates. During the first four years in the civil hospitals, 26 (2.7%) of the total group of 967 Baxstrom patients were returned to Matteawan as either dangerously mentally ill or after reaching the community and being rearrested.* It is sufficient here to note the wide discrepancy between the 25 percent or more estimates of the hospital officials and the less than 3 percent actual figure.

The next factor that was examined as it related to predictions of dangerousness was the proportion of patients who were assaultive after their transfers to the civil hospitals. Over the follow-up period, of the 199 males in the sample, 30 were assaultive at some time. This 15 percent figure for the Baxstrom male patients who were assaultive does not have very many baselines with which to compare it. Among the pre-Baxstrom comparison group, which was eleven years older on the average than the Baxstrom patients, 6 percent were assaultive. There are almost no statistics available on the rates of assaultiveness among civil mental patient populations in general. The only work we have located uses data from Denmark.[12] Among a group of 98 men with an average inpatient stay of twelve years, 22 (22%) were assaultive at sometime. Based on the only two comparisons of which we are aware, evaluating the level of assaultiveness of the Baxstrom patients in the civil hospitals is difficult. Ultimately, the comments of the

---

*More information on the circumstances that led to the return of these patients can be found elsewhere (Steadman, 1974).

hospital directors who responded to our mailed inquiries may be the most instructive. Each of the eighteen directors said "they behaved well," "they adjusted fairly well," or the like. One director stated that he had objected "to receiving patients who were classified as being so disturbed as being obviously unsuited for a civil hospital" but "we had no special difficulties with any of these patients." One director reported that "most of them were good workers and were so highly regarded as helpers by the ward staff that some of the nurses actually came to me and asked for 'their share' of the Dannemora patients."

For the proportion of Baxstrom patients who were released to the community there are even fewer baselines. Before their transfers, officials offered no guesses and the number of patients with similar characteristics released from New York State hospitals during the same time period is hard to estimate. Nevertheless, what estimates can be reasonably made suggest that the Baxstrom patients had release rates higher than those of comparable civil hospital patients. Of the 199 males in the follow-up sample, 23 died while in the civil hospitals. Of the 176 living patients, 98 (56%) were released to the community at some time. Of the pre-Baxstrom comparison group who were transferred in the normal course of events to civil hospitals in the two years prior to the Baxstrom transfers, 49 percent were released at some time. Thus, the Baxstrom patients were released at a higher rate. Likewise, the release rate between 1966 and 1970 of all chronic, i.e. hospitalized for more than two years, adult patients in New York was estimated to be 30 percent, which is about one half of the 56 percent proportion of the living Baxstrom patients. Overall, then, the Baxstrom patients appear to have been released at more rapid rates than the comparable civil hospital populations.

The final area in which the behavior of the Baxstrom patients was examined was criminal activity, especially violent crimes, and assaultive behavior that resulted in rehospitalization. Of the 98 male patients from the sample released to the community, 20 were arrested a total of forty-five times. Seven of the 20 persons arrested were involved in a total of ten assaultive acts. In addition, there were 7 other individuals who were rehospitalized as a result of assaultive acts. The total of the 98 males released to the community who were involved in some reported assaultive act after release was fourteen (15%). Since there are no studies that have compiled behavioral data for both re-arrest and rehospitalization, there is nothing to which this 15 percent figure of the Baxstrom patients is comparable. Looking only at the proportion arrested, which was 20 percent, this was higher than that of the 9.4 percent proportion arrested among all released mental patients in New York State in 1975.[13] However, since this mental patient percentage is for only a nineteen month follow-up period versus the Baxstrom's patients' four years the Baxstrom proportion would be expected to be higher. Regardless of comparisons, these findings demonstrate that four of every five patients never got into serious trouble in the community.

So, on all four measures used in this research (return to maximum security hospital as dangerously mentally ill, amount of hospital assaultiveness, release rates to the community, and criminal activity and assaultiveness in the community after release) the Baxstrom patients were at levels comparable to groups who were not seen as so dangerous as to require special security program or they were below the level of dangerous behavior that was predicted of them at the times of their transfers. Given these findings, the final question remains as to exactly what inferences may be drawn about the predictions of dangerousness.

IMPLICATIONS

We continue to feel, despite the criticism that has been leveled at our inferences, that the court mandated mass transfers of the Baxstrom patients did provide an opportunity for a natural experiment in assessing the accuracy of predictions of dangerousness. The issue that this assertion does not address is the predictions of whom? They were not specific, current clinical predictions of the psychiatrists in the maximum security facilities immediately proceeding the transfers. Certainly, according to state statutes, dangerousness was one of the reasons for commitment to Dannemora and Matteawan, and since the Baxstrom patients were committed to these facilities, some certification of their dangerousness was implied by their initial admissions. Further, based on the court transcripts and the reactions of state hospital staffs to the *Baxstrom* decision, the psychiatrists in the Department of Mental Hygiene felt the Baxstrom patients were dangerous. So, the predictions which were tested by studying the actual outcomes of the Baxstrom patients were global assessments of a group of individuals; not specific, recent clinical work-ups of each of the 967 Baxstrom patients. These predictions might be said to have been made by institutional psychiatry, a generic nonperson and a product of a system of psychiatric practice.

Having thus reconfirmed our belief that the Baxstrom research was a case study of a natural experiment in the accuracy of the prediction of dangerousness, the question arises as to whether or not the predictions were accurate. They were not. On all measures studied, the Baxstrom patients were either below the prediction levels offered or where these did not exist, the Baxstrom patients were at levels comparable to other groups not defined as dangerous. The level of assaultive behavior exhibited by the Baxstrom patients did not appear to warrant their continued detention in maximum security mental hospitals. However, without the *Baxstrom* decision most of these patients would have been expected to remain unnecessarily in Matteawan or Dannemora an average of eleven additional years.

In assessing the usefulness of these findings about the Baxstrom patients in regard to clinical predictions of dangerousness it is imperative to keep in mind the ages and lengths of hospitalization of the group. With an average age of fifty-two and fifteen years of continuous incarceration, the Baxstrom patients are not typical of cases coming in off the street or through the courts and police agencies requiring clinical decisions today. The greatest value of the Baxstrom data is what they provided as a first step in the empirical verification of the clinical inabilities to accurately predict dangerousness. Since the Baxstrom research has been completed, there have been five other studies that have tested clinical predictions of dangerousness with comprehensive follow-up data.[14,15,16,17,18,19] In many ways all of these studies are more germain assessments of the clinical predictions of dangerousness.*

In sum, our Baxstrom research as it relates to the issues of the clinical prediction of future violent behavior is neither as powerful as some of its supporters have posited nor as irrelevant as some of its opponents have contended. It was an important early step, but subsequent research which supported its conclusions ultimately is more pervasive in demonstrating clinical inabilities to accurately predict future violent behavior. As a natural experiment the Baxstrom research, particularly given the strikingly similarities of its findings to those of the follow-up research on the almost identical situation pro-

---

*Most of the studies cited in reviews of the dangerousness literature share one of two characteristics. One is that they present data that have no direct applicability to the questions of accuracy of predictions. Primary in this group is the burgeoning work on the arrest rates of mental patients, which relate at best tangentially to the prediction questions. The other type is the summary of studies that often become cited as empirical verifications, but offer no empirical data beyond the summary of other works, which often on closer inspection are themselves summaries of empirical work. A prime example of this latter type of article is that of Ennis and Litwack.[10]

duced by the *Dixon* case in Pennsylvania,[20] is a useful and important case study in the research on the prediction of dangerousness. However, it must be placed in its historical and empirical context for proper interpretation.

REFERENCES

1. Hunt, R.C. and Wiley, E.D.   Operation Baxstrom after one year, *American Journal of Psychiatry, 124,* 134–138, 1968.
2. White, L., Krumholz, W.B., and Fink, L.   The adjustment of criminally insane patients to a civil mental hospital, *Mental Hygiene News, 53,* 34–40, 1969.
3. Steadman, H.J. and Cocozza, J.J.   *Careers of the criminally insane,* Lexington, Maine, Lexington Books, 1974.
4. Perr, I.N.   Review of *Careers of the criminally insane,* In *American Journal of Psychiatry, 132,* 1340, 1975.
5. Gutman, J.S.   Review of *Careers of the criminally insane,* In *American Journal of Orthopsychiatry, 45,* 898–899, 1975.
6. Moran, R.   Review of *Careers of the criminally insane,* In *Journal of Criminal Law and Criminology, 66,* 516–517, 1975.
7. Sheppard, C.S.   Review of *Careers of the criminally insane,* In *Federal Probation, 39,* 71, 1975.
8. Roucek, J.S.   Review of *Careers of the criminally insane,* In *Social Forces, 54,* 719–720, 1976.
9. Jeffrey, C.R.   Review of *Careers of the criminally insane,* In *Sociology, 2,* 154–155, 1975.
10. Ennis, B.J. and Litwack, T.R.   Psychiatry and the presumption of expertise: Flipping coins in the courtroom, *California Law Review, 62,* 693–752, 1976.
11. Halpern, A.L.   Review of *Careers of the criminally insane,* In *The Bulletin of the American Academy of Psychiatry and the Law, 4,* 187–191, 1975.
12. Ekblom, B.   *Acts of violence by patients in mental hospitals,* Uppsala, Sweden, Almquist and Wiksells, 1970.
13. Steadman, H.J., Cocozza, J.J., and Melick, M.E.   Explaining the increased crime rate of mental patients: The changing clientele of state hospitals, *American Journal of Psychiatry,* in press.
14. Kozol, H.L., Boucher, R.J., and Garofalo, R.F.   The diagnosis and treatment of dangerousness, *Crime and Delinquency, 18,* 371–392, 1972.
15. Thornberry, T.P. and Jacoby, J.E.   *The uses of discretion in a maximum security mental hospital: The Dixon case,* Paper presented at Annual Meetings of the American Society of Criminology, Chicago, 1974.
16. Jacoby, J.E.   *Prediction of dangerousness among mentally ill offenders,*

Paper presented at Annual Meeting of the American Society of Criminology, Toronto, 1975.

17. Levinson, R.M. and Ramsay, G. *Dangerousness, stress and mental health evaluations,* Paper presented at Annual Meeting of the American Sociological Association, Chicago, 1977.

18. Steadman, H.J. A new look at recidivism among Patuxent inmates, *Bulletin of the American Academy of Psychiatry and the Law, 5,* 200–209, 1977.

19. Cocozza, J.J. and Steadman, H.J. The failure of psychiatric predictions of dangerousness: Clear and convincing evidence, *Rutgers Law Review, 29,* 1084-1101, 1976.

20. *The social adjustment of the released criminally insane offender,* Paper presented at the Annual Meetings of the American Society of Criminology, Tucson, 1976.

Chapter 18

CAPITAL PUNISHMENT

MARGARET COOKE

RECENT U.S. SUPREME COURT DECISIONS have reawakened interest in the issue of capital punishment in legislatures, courts, and with the public in general. The impact of the court decisions on law and the social sciences has been far reaching. This chapter will examine the decisions and their implications for psychologists, psychiatrists, social science researchers, and others who may deal with the death penalty either on individual cases or as a broader social issue.

THE MAJOR DECISIONS

In the 1972 *Furman* v. *Georgia* decision[1] the Supreme Court declared capital punishment unconstitutional in the way it was currently being applied; the Court did not, however, declare the death penalty per se unconstitutional, in violation of the Eighth Amendment against cruel and unusual punishment. The Furman decision held that the death penalty was unconstitutional in that it was administered unfairly, in violation of the Equal Protection Clause of the Fourteenth Amendment. Judges and juries were given too much discretion to sentence to life or death. The penalty was applied infrequently and under no clear standards; it was not uniformly applied, thus discrimination (particularly racial) occurred.

In the aftermath of the decision, many states wrote new death penalty statutes. Some statutes followed a mandatory model whereby any individual convicted of a particular crime under certain specified circumstances is automatically sentenced to death. Others followed a limited discretion model where judges or juries could consider a range of aggravating and mitigating circumstances in arriving at their sentencing decision.

In the 1976 *Gregg* v. *Georgia* decision[2] the Court upheld the post-

Furman statutes of Georgia, Florida, and Texas, while striking down those of North Carolina and Louisiana. This reaffirmed that death penalty statutes per se are not unconstitutional. Statutes were declared constitutional if they meet the following requirements:

1. The sentence must be imposed under strictly limited and clearly defined situations.
2. There must be a consideration of the circumstances of the particular crime and of the circumstances and character of the individual.
3. There must be provision for meaningful and automatic appellate review.

A direct result of the Furman decision was the first execution to occur in the United States in ten years and the placing in jeopardy of the 350 people then on death rows.

Table 18-I shows the states with death penalty statutes and the number of people under sentence of death, as of April 1978.[3]

TABLE 18-I

NUMBER OF PERSONS UNDER SENTENCE OF DEATH IN STATES HAVING DEATH PENALTY STATUTES

Alabama	34	Missouri	0
Arizona	25	Montana	4
Arkansas	7	Nebraska	4
California	0	Nevada	6
Colorado	5	New Hampshire	0
Connecticut	0	North Carolina	3
Delaware	0	Oklahoma	7
Florida	99	Rhode Island	2
Georgia	71	South Carolina	5
Idaho	1	Tennessee	4
Illinois	1	Texas	80
Indiana	4	Utah	5
Kentucky	0	Vermont	0
Louisiana	5	Virginia	2
Maryland	0	Washington	3
Mississippi	10	Wyoming	0
	Total Death Penalty States	32	
	Total Sentenced to Death	387	

The decisions and the concurrent carrying out of the death penalty have affected many aspects of the criminal justice system. State legislatures have been faced with the task of considering the death penalty issue repeatedly and of writing bills to conform to Supreme Court and state court decisions. Capital punishment places an added burden on our already overtaxed court system; capital trials are long and expensive and the appeals are endless. Defense attorneys, most of whom have never defended a capital case, are faced with accumulating a whole new level of specialized expertise and/or reliance on outside experts. The personal pressure felt by the defense attorneys who feel an individual's life is in their hands further intensifies the difficulties of a capital case. Juries, too, are faced with extremely complicated instructions as to how to arrive at a decision. The individual juror is faced with the personal moral burden of responsibility for life or death. The existence of the death penalty creates difficult and sometimes tense situations in prisons also.

ROLES OF THE SOCIAL SCIENTIST

The social scientist's expertise may be called upon for individual cases relating to the death penalty as well as for the general social issue of capital punishment. Roles include psychiatric and psychological evaluation and treatment, court testimony on individual cases either alone or as part of a team defense, and research and testimony on social science issues relevant to the death penalty.

Capital Cases

The Supreme Court decisions and their impact on death penalty statutes increases the need for the psychiatrist and psychologist as expert witnesses in individual capital punishment cases. Evaluations and testimony are required to determine competency to stand trial and criminal responsibility. Another role may be involvement in jury selection. In addition, further expert opinion unique to capital cases is required in the weighing of aggravating and mitigating circumstances. Many of the Model Penal Code[4] recommendations for mitigating circumstances, upon which many states have or are about to base their statutes, require expert opinion in their determination. Professionals will be asked to conclude on such issues as the following:

1. whether the murder was committed while the defendant was under the influence of extreme mental or emotional disorder;
2. whether the murder was committed under circumstances that the defendant believed to provide moral justification for his conduct;
3. whether the defendant acted under duress or under the domina-

tion of others (an issue brought to public attention in the widely publicized Patricia Hearst case) ;

4. whether, at the time of the murder, the defendant was capable of appreciating the criminality of his conduct or to conform to the requirements of law (this is essentially the American Law Institute's model penal code in regard to criminal responsibility);
5. whether the defendant was impaired as a result of mental disability or defect or intoxication;
6. whether the defendant is too young or too "immature" to receive the death penalty.

The determination of these mitigating circumstances by an expert witness is rendered difficult by the vagueness of definition of the terms. Such phrases as "extreme" mental or emotional disorder, "domination" of others, and "immaturity" especially will require the development of more precise legal and psychiatric definitions. Legal definitions then need to be translated into psychiatric terminology.

An innovative approach to the utilization of expert testimony in capital cases has been the development of the team defense by the Southern Poverty Law Center.* Attorneys, law students, paralegals and social scientists join in an effort to avoid the death penalty in every stage of the proceedings. The primary emphasis of this approach is on client participation; the defendant is encouraged to assist the defense, testifying, questioning witness, and making arguments to the jury. A standard battery of pretrial motions has been developed; community attitude surveys are utilized in jury selection and jury composition challenges; an offensive strategy of motions is utilized whereby relevant trial motions are injected to destroy the continuity of the prosecution's case; and a model penalty phase of the trial has been developed wherein general arguments against capital punishment, e.g. nondeterrence, moral-religious questions, remorse, and rehabilitation, are introduced.

The expert may also be called upon for the grizzly task of determining if an individual is "fit to die" after being sentenced, because it is widely accepted that no one who is "insane" may be executed. Indeed, many individuals decompensate into psychosis as a

---

*In addition to the Southern Poverty Law Center, Montgomery, Alabama, the following organizations can offer information and assistance, and sometimes provide counsel in capital cases:
A.C.L.U. Capital Punishment Project, New York
NAACP Legal Defense Fund, New York

result of the stress of death row. Another unpleasant task, utilized in some states, is counselling the sentenced in preparation for their executions.

Research

The Supreme Court decisions have increased even more the need for sociolegal research into the issues relating to capital punishment. Such issues as discretion-discrimination, deterrence, rehabilitation, public opinion, and prevention and causation have been and will continue to be examined by the courts in their determinations as to the constitutionality of death penalty statutes.

Discrimination

Evidence as to the discriminatory manner in which the death penalty is applied partially accounted for the constitutional guidelines the Court established in Furman and Gregg.

Studies suggest that post-Furman statutes have not reduced the discretion that results in a disproportionate number of nonwhites being sentenced to death. Currently, 50 percent of people sentenced to death are nonwhite (13% of the U.S. population is nonwhite) and 90 percent of death sentence recipients are poor.[5] Ninety percent of those on death row have court appointed counsel, 60 percent were unemployed at the time of the crime, the majority had no high school diploma, and the mean IQ is below average.[6]

Current research supported by SPLC suggests that further discrimination occurs when the victim's race is considered. Eighty percent of the victims of those who receive the death penalty are white. The most likely circumstance under which one receives the death penalty is the combination of nonwhite defendant/white victim; while white defendant/nonwhite victim accounts for only 2 percent of death penalty recipients.[7]

More research needs to be done to confirm and update the discriminatory aspects of capital punishment in the United States. In addition, further research should explore the entire legal process of the determination of the death penalty to determine at which levels discrimination occurs. Does discrimination take place only at sentencing or is it involved in the whole procedure from charging, through prosecution, and in conviction and the appeal process?

Rehabilitation

Social scientific input is also needed in the current controversy as the purposes of sentencing in general and the death penalty in particular. Should society provide rehabilitation and is rehabilitation possible? Should sentencing play a role in the prevention of crime? Should sentences perform the role of punishment or of mere societal revenge?

If rehabilitation is to be considered, one must consider that persons serving life sentences for murder are generally model prisoners and have the lowest recidivism rate of all parolees. When recidivism does occur, it is almost always for a technical parole violation; the crime of murder is almost never repeated by a parolee.[8] Clearly, if rehabilitation works and is to be an accepted purpose in sentencing, those whose crime is murder have shown that they can benefit and contribute productively to society. Additional updated data on recidivism rates of parolees who have been convicted of murder is needed to support the rehabilitative impact on these individuals. Surely they cannot be rehabilitated if they are put to death.

Deterrence, Causation

If sentencing is to have a preventive function, then the issues of causation and deterrence must be considered and researched. We need to determine the causes of crime in general and murder in particular (e.g. poverty, unemployment, violence, gun ownership).

Much evidence has been presented on the issue of whether capital punishment deters murder; at this point the Supreme Court has chosen to decide that such evidence is inconclusive. Studies have shown the following:

1. In countries with and without capital punishment, the homicide rates are the same.
2. In neighboring states with and without capital punishment, the homicide rates are the same.
3. In the same states, over periods of time during both abolition and retention of the death penalty, the homicide rate remains the same.[9]
4. The rate of murder of police[10] and of prison guards[11] remains the same in states with and without capital punishment.
5. States with capital punishment have the highest murder rates, while states without it have the lowest.[12]

There are several possible explanations for the nondeterrent effect of capital punishment. Any deterrent, to be effective, must be consistently and promptly applied; capital punishment is not. For example, throughout the 1970s there have been approximately twenty thousand homicides per year, whereas there have been about one hundred death sentences per year. Clearly, capital punishment is not consistently applied, so that the threat of execution (the deterrent effect) is nonexistent. Neither is the death penalty applied promptly; the average time spent from the time charges are brought until execution is 32.6 months.[13] The preservation of the already too few legal safeguards render swift and sure punishment impossible.

The fact that murder is rarely premeditated may also account for the nondeterrent effect. In 68 percent of the cases the crime is an irrational, impulsive act committed against a close friend or family member.[14] When impulsive murder against strangers is also considered, the figure rises much higher. Under these circumstances, one does not have the time to stop and consider the consequences of the act.

There is some evidence that capital punishment may even increase the homicidal rate. Recent figures indicate that there is a rise in violent personal crime immediately following an execution. Also, in California from 1946–1955, homicide increased in the days preceding executions.[15] This phenomenon could be explained by the state's setting an example of violence by performing executions. In its acceptance of capital punishment, society says that it is permissible to resolve issues by murder. The state becomes the "parent-model" whose aggressive behavior is imitated. This is supported by the research of Bandura and others in social learning theory, wherein children imitate the aggressive behavior they perceive in adults and on television.[16]

Another indication of capital punishment's role in encouraging killings is the well-documented "murder-suicide" syndrome.[17] Some murders are followed by suicide; sometimes, in the presence of the death penalty, individuals commit murder so that their own suicidal impulses are carried out by the state. There are many documented case histories of individuals who murder and then beg for the death penalty saying they lack the nerve to commit suicide. One man said he would have left California to commit murder had there not been a death penalty in that state. Both Gary Gilmore and Richard Speck left states where there was no death penalty and committed their murders in states that retained capital punishment. It is possible that some murders are committed with the conscious or unconscious wish to be killed by the state.

Public Opinion

Another very important area with which social scientists are involved is studies relating to public opinion regarding capital punishment. The Supreme Court has indicated that the definition of the constitution's prohibition of "cruel and unusual" punishment must draw its meaning from the "evolving standards of decency that make the progress of a maturing society."[18] These standards are to be determined by "enlightened and informed" opinion. Social science surveys are needed as evidence of society's evolving standards and of the development and dynamics of opinion formation in this area. The number of Americans supporting capital punishment has fluctuated through history: 62 percent in 1936, 42 percent in 1966, 51 percent in 1969, and 59 percent in 1973. Those in favor of the death penalty are likely to be older, less educated, Catholic, male, more wealthy, white, urban dwellers, and more religious.[19]

SUMMARY

Quite clearly there is a great need for the social scientist to become involved with the issue of capital punishment on every level. Individual cases, in particular, require the expert testimony of psychiatrists and psychologists. The broader issues such as deterrence, discrimination, public opinion, rehabilitation, causation, and prevention need to be further explored. Previous studies and surveys need to be replicated and new research strategies need to be developed to fully explore the ramifications of the death penalty. Results of individual evaluations and research studies then must be conceptualized in such a way as to be utilized in court decisions.

Sources of information on capital punishment are contained in several major volumes.[11,20,21,22] Research on the subject may be traced through the footnotes and bibliographies of these books.

In addition, the FBI's annual "Crime Reports" and the Justice Department's "National Prisoner Statistics—Capital Punishment" provide up-to-date factual information. The journals have devoted recent issues to capital punishment.[23,24]

REFERENCES

1. Furman v. Georgia 408 U.S., 1972.
2. Gregg v. Georgia 428 U.S., 1976.

3. American Civil Liberties Union. *Capital punishment project report,* New York, A.C.L.U., 1978.
4. American Law Institute. *Model penal code,* 210–216, Philadelphia, A.L.I., 1962.
5. New York Civil Liberties Union. *Legislative memo,* New York, N.Y.C. L.U., 1977.
6. Riedel, M. Differential imposition of the death penalty, *Temple University Law Quarterly, 49,* 261–287, 1976.
7. New York Civil Liberties Union, op. cit.
8. Bedau, H. *The case against the death penalty,* (pamphlet), New York, A.C.L.U., 1978.
9. Sellin, T. *The death penalty,* Philadelphia, American Law Institute, 1959.
10. Sellin, T. In Bedau, H. (Ed.), *The death penalty in America,* Chicago, Aldine, 1967.
11. Sellin, T. (Ed.). *Capital punishment,* New York, Harper and Row, 1967.
12. FBI. Uniform crime reports, Washington, D.C., Government Printing Office, 1974.
13. Bedau, H. op. cit., 1978.
14. FBI. Uniform crime reports, Washington, D.C., Government Printing Office, 1975.
15. Bedau, H. op. cit., 1978.
16. Solomon, G. Capital punishment as suicide and as murder, *American Journal of Orthopsychiatry, 45,* 701-710, 1975.
17. Solomon, G. op. cit., 1978.
18. Trop v. Dulles 336 U.S. 86, 1957.
19. Gelles, J. and Straus, M. Family experience and public support of the death penalty, *American Journal of Orthopsychiatry, 45,* 596–613, 1975.
20. Bedau, H. (Ed) *The death penalty in America,* Chicago, Aldine, 1967.
21. Bedau, H. and Pierce, C. (Eds.). *Capital punishment in the United States,* New York, AMS Press, 1976.
22. McCafferty, J. (Ed.). *Capital punishment,* Chicago, Aldine, 1972.
23. *American Journal of Orthopsychiatry, 45,* 1975.
24. *Criminal Law Bulletin, 4,* 1978.

Chapter 19

DILEMMA IN ADULT CORRECTIONAL SETTINGS: TO TREAT OR NOT TO TREAT AND IF SO, HOW?

Florence W. Kaslow, Ph.D.

PUNISHMENT, PROTECTION, and/or rehabilitation? For many decades a controversy over the purpose of correctional institutions has been evident. Sometimes it flares and burns brightly; other times the embers glow dimly. Which school of thought is in ascendance depends on myriad factors including: who are the eminent criminologists and penologists and what their predilections are; who are the leaders in the legislature and how much they are willing to allocate in the budget for the state department or bureau of corrections; the philosophy and clout of the commissioner of corrections, his top central office lieutenants, and his superintendents of prisons; whether or not mental health professionals are willing to work in correctional settings and in partnership with custodial staff; the attitude of the general citizenry toward offenders; and the temper of prison and ex-prisoner populations.

Historically, one of the two major purposes of the correctional system was to punish those adjudicated guilty of a crime by incarcerating them away from society—"to do time" deprived of liberty and free access to dear ones and the outside world. Since they had erred against society, they were to be isolated from that society; part of the retribution was to house someone in a dreary, barren cell, dressed in prison garb, following a dull routine, being identified more by a number than a name—in sum, a process of depersonalization and dehumanization was, and often still is, part and parcel of the punishment package. Those who are descendants of the law of talion position ask, "How else can one 'pay the debt to society' and atone in some measure for grievous wrongs committed?"

A corollary purpose and another reason for imprisoning someone behind iron bars and a tall wall, segregated from the non-law-violating populace, is to protect society from its most hostile, violent, and dangerous members. The community at large feels safer and sleeps sounder knowing that those who have committed antisocial acts are locked inside maximally secure facilities, preferably located in the hinterlands far from large population centers.

It is illogical to question whether these twin purposes of punishment and protection are valid. They are the fundamental reasons for the existence of the correctional system—and even an enlightened, liberal citizenry is unlikely to be willing to have those found guilty of serious crimes, and who have behaved violently, free to roam the streets. Despite diversionary programs and alternatives to incarceration such as probation and community correctional treatment centers, there appears to be an irreducible group of hard-core, dangerous offenders who need to be contained behind bars for the sanity and protection of society.

But, it would be equally absurd not to confront the glaring fact that the majority of those imprisoned will eventually be released. Since this is true, then it is incumbent upon us to look at what goes on during the prison experience that corrects, that habilitates or rehabilitates, so that when the time for their return to the outside world arrives, they are ready to reenter society and live a reasonably satisfying life in a law-abiding way.

This third and the most recently added, purpose is the one most often debated. Martinson and some associates were hired in 1966 by the New York State Governor's Committee on Criminal Offenders to study through a comprehensive survey what, in fact, works in prisoner rehabilitation. They undertook a six-month survey of all available English language reports on rehabilitation programs in the United States and other countries from 1945 through 1967. Their vigorous criteria for a study's inclusion was that it "had to be an evaluation of a treatment method, it had to employ an independent measure of the improvement secured by the method, and it had to use some control group, some untreated individuals with whom the treated ones could be compared."[1] One measure, the effect of treatment on recidivism, was determined to be the variable that reflected most directly how effective a given treatment program was in accomplishing the rehabilitative task. Their analysis of the data on individual, group, and milieu therapy programs drawn from over 200 studies led them to the conclusion that "with few and isolated exceptions, the rehabilitative efforts that have been reported so far have had no appreciable effect on recidivism." The few studies that did indicate even partial success yielded no distinct pattern regarding the efficacy of any one specific method of treating. They concluded that punishment and not treatment is the major means for deterring incipient offenders and that rehabilitation has been a gigantic failure; they called instead for "something that deters rather than cures, something that does not so much reform convicted offenders as prevent criminal behavior in the first place."

We certainly concur that massive primary prevention efforts were then and still are desperately needed. But that does not obviate the fact that hundreds of thousands of people are already imprisoned and cannot be ignored while the mammoth task of overhauling society is undertaken.

Thus, given the reality that the vast majority of prisoners will return to the outside world and that many rehabilitation programs at the secondary and tertiary levels of prevention are underway—some of them claiming reasonably good results—this author believes we have no choice but to consider again, a decade later, what is being done in the treatment arena. The material is culled from the literature and the author's experience in teaching about and working with correctional systems. Unlike the Martinson study, it is not a review of research studies.

The cautious optimism that permeates this chapter is attributable to the fact that I have seen some offenders make tremendous strides in treatment, and succeed in "going straight," becoming capable, contributing members of society. It is to an ex-student particularly, who was a former supertough con, who served a long sentence in a federal penitentiary, and who after release has gone on to become an outstanding and well-respected human service professional that I attribute my strong interest in correctional rehabilitation and my belief that it can and sometimes does work.

This stance is amply exemplified in Sturup's now classic work on *Treating the Untreatable*[2] in which he recounts the philosophy and nature of the program in existence at Herstedvester Prison in Denmark, a program that encourages and permits inmates to revise their attitudes toward authority. Sturup's approach is predicated on a deep and broad understanding of social psychiatry; he and his staff are convinced of the fundamental humanitarian obligation of society to provide criminals with a prison environment characterized by a psychological climate in which life is bearable and can be constructive. Treatment efforts emanate from the assumption that the "chronic criminal," their designation for an offender who has been sentenced at least three times within a short period (the group that comprises Herstedvester's population), is his own most important therapist and that the major goal of the authorities is to enable him to bring about his own rehabilitation rather than to punish him.

In his stirring, gripping book Sturup relates that they have found since he went to the Detention Center in 1942 that humane treatment can occur within a maximally secure facility and that they have been able to decrease the average length of incarceration from over four years to between two and two-and-a-half years. Simultaneously they have a recidivism rate of about 50 percent for each detention period; thus of 100 inmates, 50 return after the first parole period and 25 after the second parole period.

Herstedvester is a small, closed institution that usually houses from 150 to 200 inmates at any given time. Most have had long histories of interpersonal problems, have low self-esteem, are "deficient in personality for normal social life, are rarely trusted, and feel that they belong to a class of people who are different from the normal." Notwithstanding that such criminals are usually deemed untreatable, Sturup dramatically chronicles that it is "possible to make a criminal *believe* (my italics) that he can *overcome* the difficulties which lie ahead and lead a crime-free life" and that all but 10 percent of his inmates actually are leading law-abiding lives ten years after their first incarceration at Herstedvester. It is the *hope* that the staff transmits that motivates the men to undertake the tedious, taxing ordeal of changing their attitudes, behavior, and life-style. This is done with full regard for security considerations.

They have created a total therapeutic institution in which the milieu is marked by optimism, sympathy, and respect for all members of the community and in which staff efforts are energetic, consistent, and integrated. The staff convey interest in their task and belief in the resident's ability to change through their own efforts and in their own behalf.

They attempt to help inmates reach *realistic* solutions to their problems and in the course of so doing to define and fulfill some of their unmet needs for security, belonging, loving, and being loved.

The approach is rational, clearly communicated at open meetings, and revolves around each person's responsibility for his own behavior since it is "his future which is at stake." Staff attempt to aid an inmate in understanding his own pattern of behavior, assets, and ability to become self-sufficient and independent. Because of the small size of the institution, close collaboration of staff and inmates is feasible and often evolves into a curative alliance in which habit retraining is undertaken. Individual sessions are accompanied by group therapy so that better interpersonal relationships and skills can be fashioned and the men are encouraged to build new patterns slowly and solidly, one step at a time. In all of their milieu-multiple impact therapy, candor with self and others is fostered and "conning" is perceived negatively and handled for what it is.

Through regular case review at periodic intervals during incarceration, evaluation of behavior and difficulties during home visits, and ongoing therapeutic contact after discharge during parole, continued growth is fostered. Who can argue with a documented 90 percent success record for their individualized, integrating growth therapy for people often categorized as "psychopaths" or severe borderline personalities?

Given the space limitations of this chapter, the review of the literature can only be selective and not exhaustive. Different kinds of treatment programs in the United States will be highlighted illustratively and summarized under categorical headings of Individual, Group, Marital and Family, and Milieu Therapies. The major focus is on new and innovative strategies that have received the least attention. It is recognized that vocational, religious, educational, athletic, and work programs can also be rehabilitative in nature and often produce noticeable gains in knowledge, self-awareness, and work and coping skills. It is posited that all of these should be available to inmates. But for purposes of this article, treatment is being defined in the narrower sense of psychotherapy and connotes an intent (1) to help inmates better understand their motivation, needs and behavior; (2) to help them function more appropriately and effectively; (3) to develop awareness and concern for self as well as other; (4) to enable people to use their potential to the fullest, cope effectively with life, and have a sense that it is worth living; (5) to work through resentments, projections, negative injunctions, and life scripts; (6) to help inmates develop realistic positive self-esteem and willingness to be responsible for their own choices and behaviors.

Hopefully this overview will serve to stimulate dialogue, experimentation, and synthesis—since some answers to Martinson's earlier question "What works?" simply must be found.

It is also imperative to keep in mind that whatever intrapsychic, interpersonal, physical, or financial problems a person was plagued by before being incarcerated are likely to be compounded by the very nature and structure of life in prison. The loss of liberty, self-determination, personal possessions, and privacy amidst a routinized regimen in an unattractive, monotonous facility is in and of itself apt to exacerbate one's borderline, neurotic, psychotic, or antisocial behavior and lead to heightened anger, resistance, acting out, or withdrawal. Prisoners enter treatment for a variety of reasons. It may be perceived as almost mandatory because it looks good on their record when they come up for consideration for discharge, or it may provide a break from the tedium—an hour or more a week off the cell block—or there may be tremendous pressure from the administration. Occasionally, some inmates enter voluntarily because they are so disturbed or distressed that they are willing to seek help for relief from overwhelming anxiety, stress, guilt, worry, fear, depression, or suicidal or homicidal impulses. A few gravitate to therapy to find a better way to organize their lives. It is against a backdrop of such a generally unmotivated, captive client population that one must assess treatment philosophies, modalities, and endeavors.

Several other significant areas of concern must be dealt with before specific treatment approaches are elucidated—those of confidentiality, limits to confidentiality, informed consent, and right to refuse treatment. Confidentiality is a basic tenet of all professional practice and should be adhered to in the prison as well as in any other setting. This is clearly spelled out in the Code of Ethics of both American Psychological Association[3] and American Psychiatric Association.[4] But both also delineate the limits to confidentiality allowing for disclosure of information when there is "clear and imminent danger to the individual or society and then only after most careful deliberations." This implies, in the prison context, that patients will be told upon entering treatment that there are limits to confidentiality and what these are likely to be, and advised that they can withold any material that might be self-incriminating. It further implies that the therapist may need to reveal certain information to the person in charge.[5] The "duty to warn" decision handed down in the *Tarasoff* case by the California Supreme Court brings in another element; that is, the responsibility to warn the potential victim if the therapist believes the threat to the person's life is a real one.[6] Judge Tobriner, in his landmark decision, held that "private privilege ends where public peril begins."

Regarding informed consent, the prisoner should be given an accurate idea of what is likely to be entailed in treatment in terms of a time, energy, and emotional commitment and the potential impact of this therapeutic involvement.

Generally, the legislation on right to treatment and right to refuse treatment has been in the arena of mental health and not criminal justice. Three major right to treatment cases, *Rouse* v. *Cameron*,[7] *Wyatt* v. *Stickney*,[8] and *Donaldson* v. *O'Connor*,[9] have established the right to treatment of the civilly committed mentally ill patient. It is quite probable that these decisions also extend these rights to mentally ill prison inmates. Such a right could certainly be argued on either constitutional or statutory grounds. Movement in this direction is apparent in a recent court decision, *Berwanger* v. *State*,[10] in which the Indiana Court of Appeals held that a prisoner is entitled to mental and psychiatric treatment.

It is unlikely that a challenge to the fabric of the correctional system predicated on the prohibition expressed in the Eighth Amendment against "cruel and unusual punishment" will not soon be made in court. If it is, and if such is cogently outlawed, then the correctional enterprise will necessarily undergo a radical transformation.

Prisoners, like mental patients, should be able to refuse to participate in a treatment program—for as we indicated earlier, they are sent to prison to safeguard society and for punishment and not for mandatory rehabilitation.

It is considered essential herein that the kind of treatment a person is offered follow from classification of prisoners, careful assessment, or diagnosis, and then selection of what constitutes the treatment of choice. To the extent possible, the inmate should have a voice in this choice. Where co-therapists are used, as is often the case in group or family therapy, teaming a professional therapist with a specially trained correctional officer is often a wise pairing as it facilitates collaboration between treatment and custody staff.

INDIVIDUAL PSYCHOTHERAPY

Insight oriented psychotherapy is the variety most often utilized by psychiatrists in prison. Social caseworkers and correctional counselors tend to rely on reality oriented and problem solving approaches.

Psychologists, depending on their particular training and philosophy, employ insight oriented methods, behavior modification techniques, and ego supportive and reality oriented approaches. In any given prison, any or all of these theoretical orientations are likely to be in evidence—coexisting with equanimity or in a state of perpetual staff warfare. Which becomes dominant often depends on the preference, background, and flexibility of the director of treatment services. Hopefully, the choice of approach is most often determined by the needs of the patient under consideration. This may sound naive, but it is a goal worth striving for.

Therapists of all persuasions and from each of the helping professions should be on the alert for signs of decompensation so that they can intervene swiftly. All should be able to do crisis intervention since many inmates, who need to appear tough and invincible, will not appear in a "shrink's" presence until a crisis in full blown.

Brodsky[11] provides an excellent discussion of environmental manipulation and behavior modification techniques within the criminal justice system and reports on a number of studies showing authors, settings, subjects, reinforcers, and target behaviors. He indicates that these approaches achieved popularity because (1) there is a well-developed behavioral technology available in the area of social learning theory, (2) the existence of controlled settings for justice clients permits manipulation of external reinforcement variables, (3) to the public, the notion of behavior modification carries the implication of doing something to, rather than for, the offender (this may be highly acceptable to those who believe in a combination punitive and therapeutic approach), and (4) the emphasis on reinforcing immediate, specific, and objective behavior provides an acceptable philosophic, legal, and humanistic position. When this position is adhered to, the individual does not continue to be tried after conviction for the offense and does not have to relive or in some way demonstrate a change in early childhood behaviors. Rather, the focus on current behavior permits an objective evaluation of observed change in immediate behavior.

Yet the behavior modification programs that came into prominence in the 1960s seem to be on the wane in the late 1970s. Perhaps their greatest success, how effective they sometimes proved to be, became the reason for their demise. Detractors criticized the amount of control over another's behavior this placed in the hands of the modifiers. Sometimes the paradigm developed involved initial degradation to stress the prisoner into cooperating more fully.[12] Rarely were prisoners included in designing the behavioral modification system; thus those involved in the prisoners' rights movement and other civil libertarians objected vehemently to what they considered a violation of individual rights and dignity. Utilization of aversive shock, particularly with pedophilic homosexuals, aroused much fury. Some projects supported by federal funds saw the withdrawal of LEAA monies in 1974 and generally token economies have fallen into disrepute.[13]

Schmideberg, in discussing "Some Basic Principles of Offender Therapy"[14] indicates that the therapist must possess a sense of reality in order to aid the patient in this area. Any reality therapy should be symptom oriented. For a long existing symptom to disappear, it is usually necessary for the patient to face it fully with all its implications and consequences, decide to stop it, make a concerted effort to do so, and consider the factors that precipitate it. She holds that a truly nondirective approach is inadequate and inappropriate. Dwelling on the past, ventilation, and catharsis alone do not always help. It is essential to deal with the present and plan for the future.

For individual treatment, as for group and marital therapy, conditions should be clearly explicated and mutually agreed upon. Length and time of session should be consistent since many prisoners need definitive structure and something to count on. Unless custodial staff support treatment efforts, these efforts will fail since it is the correctional officers who must be willing to let an inmate leave the cell block or work area to go to a treatment session. Whether their attitude toward treatment is to denigrate or support it will be a factor in the prisoners' regular attendance.

Just from the few approaches cited above it becomes evident that there is no unanimity on what constitutes the most valid treatment strategy or focus. Diversity and disagreement continue unabated— for better or worse.

GROUP THERAPIES

Innumerable programs utilizing group treatment methods are described in the literature. One finds reference to many therapeutic schools of thought and types of approaches in the literature including psychoanalytic group therapy,[15] transactional analysis,[16] and guided group interaction.[17] A few recent ones will be described as examples of different contemporaneous approaches.

Peer counseling is suggested by Barkley[18] as a solution to the lack of sufficient professional staff to minister to the therapeutic needs of prisoners. He reports persuasively on a program run by and for the inmates at the California Mens' Colony. It is based on transactional analysis and provides a formalized 295 hour didactic training course. The goal for all is self-help; some also strive for the "peer counselor I" certificate, which qualifies the individual as a paraprofessional counselor. This counseling method appears to be successful and has evolved an axiom: "A person will not change until he or she is no longer comfortable being uncomfortable." He concludes that, given the tools for growth and the offer of an alternate correctional life-style, people do modify their own behavior, alter life patterns, and accept responsibility for themselves. This is similar to the findings of Groder alluded to later in the section on milieu therapy.

McCoy[19] describes a self-help project at Parish Prison in New Orleans that utilizes what sounds like a cognitive group therapy packaged in the form of classes six nights a week. Those inmates desirous of joining the project attend four different classes. The names are descriptive and reflect the breadth of the program: (1) Concept Therapy, (2) Tell It Like It Is, (3) Public Speaking and Speech Therapy (to prepare inmates for job interviews and life outside the walls), (4) Goal Setting (related to specific occupational preparation). Since at the time the project was written up only one participant who had been discharged had been returned to prison, the project was deemed successful and efforts were underway to expand the program throughout the Louisiana state prison system.

A somewhat novel approach, that of "fishbowl therapy," is described by Ho[17] and a rather high rate of success is reported with this experiment at El Reno Federal Reformatory in El Reno, Oklahoma. In the fishbowl experience, six clients who want to receive help and the therapist sat in a circle, surrounded by an outer circle of six more clients who were to give help. A specific objective was to find a form of group therapy suitable for application in a prison environment. The fishbowl capitalized on the willingness to receive help and also on the ability of some to provide counseling and guidance. The open sharing atmosphere created by the fishbowl experience appeared to be the single most important contribution of the therapeutic process. Three months after the group therapy terminated, there remained 61 percent fewer disciplinary actions against the fishbowl experimental group members, as compared to a 4 percent increase among the control group.

For prisoners, many of whom have difficulty in the area of trusting, allowing closeness, and interpersonal relations, group methods seem particularly appropriate. Group therapy simultaneously offers access to a therapist, a chance to interact with peers as superficial or as intensively as one is able to, a chance to belong to a group and help shape it, an opportunity to both receive and give help, and to engage in role playing and role taking and thus enlarge one's repertoire of understanding and coping behaviors.

Yet, one must proceed with caution and give serious consideration to the findings reported upon by Sadoff and colleagues in their article on enforced group psychotherapy.[20] Although their study population was sex offenders who had to attend group therapy as condition of probation and not prison inmates, one might expect some of the findings to be applicable. They found that a study of offenders' attitudes toward enforced group psychotherapy revealed that positive attitudes about the experience were correlated with treatment failures. Patients who said the group was helpful were rearrested more often than those who complained about it. The examining psychiatrist was significantly less successful in predicting future criminal behavior than was the psychiatrist who had treated the offender in a group.

MARITAL AND FAMILY THERAPY

Very few prison vocational preparation programs or resocialization programs prepare about-to-be-released offenders to cope with the inevitable interpersonal problems they will encounter with their spouse, children, or parent when they return home. Marital therapy, which recent psychotherapy outcome research literature has shown "to produce beneficial effects in 61 percent of the cases"[21] is beginning to receive some attention as an interventive strategy during incarceration, and during the pre- and post-release periods. A small pilot project with male offenders at Graterford prison in Pennsylvania utilizing family therapy showed much promise and the preliminary results were in keeping with what Gurman and Kniskern recently reported regarding nonprison patient populations—that "every study to date that has compared family therapy with the other type of treatments has shown family therapy to be equal or superior." Their literature review summation found improvement when family therapy was the therapeutic modality in about 75 percent of the families so treated.

After the gates clang shut and the male offender has lost his liberty, he also may feel a tremendous sense of grief at the separation from family members. This may be perceived as his own abandonment of them, as a departure fraught with guilt and sorrow, and there is much apprehension over what will happen to his folks or kids while he is away. How ashamed and angry are they at him for the behavior that got him into difficulty with the law, how furious that he was dumb enough to get framed or caught? What will they do for money? Can they manage without him? Or might they manage so well without him that they will be relieved that he is gone and not eager later to welcome him back? Will his woman be faithful? Will she decide she wants a divorce? What stigma will descend on them? These and many similar family related issues appear to haunt the prisoner's thoughts during the desolate, solitary hours at night in his cell.

Analogous problems vex the family. Why did he get into trouble with drugs, other cons, the street scene? If he loved them, would he not have spared them the agony? While in jail, how will he change? Will he get beaten up by other prisoners? How true are the stories of gang rapes and homosexual attachments?

Major fears of women being incarcerated concern: Who will care for my children? Will the care be adequate? Will they miss me and still love me? Can they forgive me? Can I ever make up for the time I am losing with them? Too little attention has been given to these critical questions and to helping women work out the best possible solution given the scant options available. It is a dilemma that continues to distress mothers and their children throughout the period of imprisonment.[22]

Since the literature on this is recent and sparse, it will be given more comprehensive attention here than other better known and more frequently employed approaches. One excellent, descriptive article by Friedman and Rice, appeared in May 1977.[23] They describe clearly the rationale for and process of "one partner couple therapy" in prison when the therapist has access to only one partner. Imperfect as such an approach may sound, they urge it "when it is the only alternative available to the correctional mental health professional, when the imprisoned partner is in a state of acute pain with both crisis intervention and follow-up treatment critical."

Rice and Friedman advocate that it can and should be used whenever the prisoner is reacting to the stress of separation, loneliness, suspicion, and/or sexual frustration and particularly when divorce action is being contemplated by their mate. They help the inmate cope with finding out about his partner's rejection, handling his feeling of desertion and urges toward self-destructiveness or outer directed violence; they intervene to "forestall any drastic actions by the inmate" to augment his feelings of powerfulness and control, they make him more aware of the wife's problems and conflicts, and they help the inmate and his wife obtain more assistance in the community. When appropriate, these authors recommend using Krantzler's[24] one spouse model of "divorce therapy" to make the experience a growth producing experience, rather than a negative one.

Apparently they view one partner couple therapy as preferable to the more traditional conjoint model because "There is little or no opportunity to practice and generalize the insights and enhanced communication patterns fostered in therapy. The experience of risking, opening up to one another, and then having to sever the closeness experienced can be very painful (when the spouse has to leave)."

Thus therapy with the partner can be efficacious if and when it is not possible to periodically bring in the spouse, or lover. We have also observed that such therapeutic intervention is valuable not only when a crisis caused by illness or threatened divorce erupts, but just because so many inmates have serious problems in the areas of sex role identity, intimacy, activity-passivity, male-female relationships, and parenting behavior.

Certain assumptions were made when the pilot project at Graterford Prison, a state maximum security facility in Pennsylvania, was instituted in conjunction with a graduate psychology student internship unit assignment. It was hypothesized that when family members learn that the offender will be released in the next few months, much ambivalence is felt—relief that the nightmare will soon be over tinged with fear and eagerness about what changes the person's return home will generate and anxiety lest the person recidivate. It is at this point in the prison process that conjoint marital or family therapy should be considered—providing clinical staff possess the requisite knowledge and skills.

If the treatment staff is flexible enough to work evenings and weekends when most visiting occurs, then marital or family sessions can be scheduled at regular intervals. A starting time of three months prior to release has proven workable as this is when going home appears to be in the foreseeable future. Part of the emphasis is on helping family members reconnect with each other. Weekly sessions are advisable, less than biweekly is too sporadic to be effective.

A psychodynamic understanding of all family members involved
is essential. Structural family therapy techniques that incorporate
reality oriented and behavioral approaches, combined with some
illuminating and rewriting of scripts and facilitating open communications, comprises the optimal multi-model treatment strategy.

We have found it important to explore the following themes in
therapy.[25]

1. Feelings of all members about the imprisonment and the reasons for it. Guilt, recrimination, desire to escape from the
   relationship should be handled.

2. Expectations, supports, and demands from the extended family
   and important community members during and after imprisonment.

3. Fear of or desire for return to street life—crime, drugs, hanging
   out.

4. Concerns over the homosexual or heterosexual involvements
   and/or friendships each has formed during the separation.
   This is often hard for people to talk about and must be handled
   tactfully, but it cannot be ignored. Only after this is worked
   through can they face their apprehensions about whether they
   can reestablish (or finally establish) a satisfying sexual relationship together. Sometimes some sex therapy[26] is necessary.

5. Is there space in the family for the ex-offender and, if so, how
   does the role he now will be expected to play differ from that he
   lived before imprisonment? Who may be displaced and how by
   his return? How can their energies and efforts be profitably
   rechannelled and annoyance minimized?

6. What of a job? Can they line one up prior to discharge so
   that the person's self-image is bolstered up by feeling wanted,
   valued, and productive and the family can regain some respect for the husband-father-son's capacity to earn a living and
   be "self-respecting."

7. What other kinds of problems do they anticipate? Frequently,
   because many people who end up in prison fall within the
   "character or personality disorder" classification, they are quite
   impulse-ridden, live for the moment, and cannot plan ahead.
   Introducing queries about what lies ahead, confronting them
   with the fact that inevitably problems will be encountered as
   freedom is not a utopia, and using role play and anticipatory
   guidance approaches can help such individuals project into the

future and begin to develop coping repertoire rather than relying on happenstance and the "I'll cross that bridge when I come to it" logic that has previously plummeted them into trouble.

8. The childrens' understanding of where their parent has been and why and their reactions to this knowledge.

9. Particularly where the father has been away a long time, his homecoming changes the family constellation markedly and the children may be hostile to a perceived intruder. Where mother has been the prisoner, the grandmother or foster mother in charge may be unwilling to relinquish the care-taking role she has held and to lose her pivotal place in the child's affection. These competitive strivings need to be brought out into the open and dealt with to create a favorable milieu for the family's being reunited.

The marital and family therapist can skillfully and tactfully focus on the ambivalences, apprehensions, hopes, and fears and by supporting his patient's ego strengths, optimism, and underlying wish for a better life, make the therapy meaningful.

MILIEU THERAPY

Jails and prisons, as described earlier, are cold, harsh societies. The inmate subculture is often a dominant force and its value system and pecking order are rarely congruent with a rehabilitation philosophy. Thus, in the usual prison environment, the resident who might want to "go straight" and to cooperate with the authorities is perceived as weak, not to be trusted, and finds himself virtually alone in hostile surroundings.

What appears to be needed is nothing short of a total revamping of prison structure and architecture and a rethinking of correctional philosophy. One model might be that established at Herstedvester Detention Center in Denmark. It embodies an enlightened, humanistic philosophy within a clearly articulated and enforced behavioral code. The treatment staff meets daily and functions as a cohesive unit, reenforcing each other's interventions and not permitting inmates to play staff off against each other. They are also highly supportive of growth and change in what is perceived to be a positive direction.[2]

Similar efforts at utilizing a treatment team approach creating in prison an environment comparable to a therapeutic community have been undertaken in this country. Auerbach[27] reports that inmates in their treatment oriented institution in Georgia were more likely to develop positive self-attitudes, a necessary condition for rehabilitative change. Their training team approach entails intensive staff-inmate collaboration. This affords team members the opportunity to get to know the inmate as a whole person during the shift they are on duty; certainly this provides a better, more holistic basis for treating than the weekly, isolated treatment session.

Groder,[16] who pioneered a therapeutic milieu within the federal penitentiary at Marion, Illinois, heavily utilized transactional analysis theory and technique to help the inmates become aware of and diagram their transactions and to comprehend the self-defeating life scripts in which they were enmeshed. Many of the residents of this small community within the larger prison community gradually become able to relate caringly and supportively to one another, to feel a sense of belonging, to share in a mutually beneficial endeavor to trust each other and the dedicated staff who made a tremendous personal investment of time and energy in the project. Upon release from the prison, some returned to work as staff members in the Asklepieion Project, many took additional transactional analysis training.

Given the mammoth task of rehabilitating offenders, who whether one classifies them as sick, disturbed, antisocial, or hapless victims of an unjust society are severely distressed and difficult people, it is incomprehensible that anything less than total milieu therapy in decent surroundings and embodying the best of all the other approaches can prove effective and can significantly cut repeat offender behavior.

SUMMARY

In prisons one finds a variety of theoretical frameworks undergirding clinical practice, thus it is not unusual to find therapy groups run within the same prison according to many different principles and styles. The same potpourri exists regarding the conduct of individual treatment. How confusing it must be to residents when a therapist of one persuasion leaves and is replaced by a leader utilizing a very different treatment approach. Perhaps it is time for state systems committed to rehabilitation to evolve a cohesive philosophy that can permit therapist flexibility but not to such an extreme that chaos results.[12]

How sad that despite all the well-intentioned efforts, innovative and standard, sometimes by quite well-qualified and dedicated staff, so little has been reported that works in a large majority of cases and there are so few replicable and replicated studies. Given the fact that prison budgets are woefully inadequate for the essentials much less for what many legislators consider frills—highly trained treatment personnel and costly therapeutic programs—coupled with the reality that the hard core offenders who make up today's prison populations are among the most difficult to reach and treat, one might be surprised at the number of successful programs reported on the national scene.

When Federal Bureau of Prisons' success in meeting goals set for preparing offenders to reenter society was evaluated, it was found that available rehabilitation programs were not fully utilized because many prisoners were not motivated to improve themselves. Shortages of psychiatrists, psychologists, and social workers meant treatment for some inmates needing help was simply not available. Inmates had only limited opportunities to learn marketable skills. Sufficient stress was not placed on preparing inmates for jobs. It was recommended that the director of the Bureau of Prisons collaborate with federal prison industries to develop and operate a plan to increase opportunities for inmates to acquire marketable skills. Here, as in other endeavors, the critical need to mount programs that include both therapy and job training appears.[28] In our society, the ability to earn a living seems inextricably intertwined with one's sense of self-worth. Working also occupies time and leaves less available time in which to become restless and engulfed in the street culture. Viewed thusly, rehabilitation and resocialization should encompass a two-pronged approach if recidivation is to be diminished.

It does not appear that we have been any more able than Martinson was to report "What Works." Rather the stance taken here is that given that the vast majority of prisoners ultimately return to live in the community at large and given the nationwide acceptance of the principle of the right to treatment, we are legally, morally, and ethically obligated to treat and to do so as efficiently and effectively as we can. This means continued innovation, standardization, evaluation, replication, refinement of technique, and dissemination of our findings.

REFERENCES

1. Martinson, R. What works?: Questions and answers about prison reform, *Public Interest, 35,* 22–54, 1974.
2. Sturup, G.K. *Treating the untreatable: Chronic criminals at Herstedvester,* Baltimore, Maryland, John Hopkins Press, 1968.
3. American Psychological Association, *Ethical standards for psychologists,* (Rev. Ed), Washington, D.C., APA, 1972.
4. Statement of ethics for psychiatrists, *American Journal of Psychiatry, 130,* (9), 1063, September 1973.
5. Kaslow, F.W. and Sadoff, R.L. Unpublished position paper, *Confidentiality for psychotherapists in prisons,* December 14, 1973.
6. Tarasoff v. Regents of the University of California, 1974. See *Atlanta Law Review,* Vol. *36,* pp. 123–128 for full discussion of case.
7. Rouse v. Cameron, 373 F. 2d 451 (D.C. Cir. 1966).
8. Wyatt v. Stickney, 344 F. Supp. 373 (M.D. Ala., 1972).
9. Donaldson v. O'Connor, 493 F. 2d 507 (5th Cir. 1974).
10. Berwanger v. State, 307 N.E. 2d 891, (Indiana) Court of Appeals of Indiana, Second District, March 11, 1974.
11. Brodsky, S. *Psychologists in the criminal justice system,* Champaign, University of Illinois Press, 1973.
12. Kaslow, F.W. Practice trends in corrections and their implications for graduate and professional education, *The Quarterly* (Journal of Pennsylvania Association on Probation, Parole and Correction), *31,* (4), Winter 1975.
13. Trotter, S. Token economy program perverted by prison officials, *APA Monitor,* January, 1975.
14. Schmideberg, M. Some basic principles of offender therapy: II, *International Journal of Offender Therapy and Comparative Criminology, 19,* (1), 22–32, 1975.
15. Steg, J., Wright, L.S., and Peters, J.D. *Psychoanalytic foundations for group, psychotherapy of probationed sex offenders,* Philadelphia, University of Pennsylvania, (mimeographed paper), 1970.
16. Groder, M. Asklepieion: *An effective treatment method for incarcerated character disorders,* Butner, North Carolina, Federal Center for Correctional Research 27509, 1973.
17. Ho, M.K., Fishbowl therapy with prison inmates, *Social Work, 21,* (3), 235–237, 1976.
18. Barkley, B.J. Peer counseling in prison: Do it yourself therapy? *Voices, 11,* (1), 32–34, 1975.
19. McCoy, R.D. Prison rehabilitation, Concept Associates, Inc., *Personnel and Guidance Journal, 51,* (7), 490–491, 1973.
20. Sadoff, R.L., Roether, H.A., and Peters, J.J. Clinical measure of enforced group psychotherapy, *American Journal of Psychiatry, 128,* (2), 116–119, August 1971.

21. Gurman, A.S. and Kniskern, D.P. Research on marriage and family therapy– Progress, perspective and prospect, In S.L. Garfield and A.F. Bergen (Eds.), *Handbook of psychotherapy and behavior change: An empirical analysis* New York, Wiley, 1978.

22. Du Bose, D.G. *Problems of children whose mothers are imprisoned,* Fort Worth, Texas Federal Correctional Institution, (mimeographed paper, no dates).

23. Friedman, B.J. and Rice, D.G. Marital therapy in prison: One "couple therapy," *Psychiatry, 40,* 175–183, 1977.

24. Krantzler, M. *Creative divorce: A new opportunity for personal growth,* New York, Evans, 1973.

25. Kaslow, F.W. Marital or family therapy for prisoners and their spouses or families, *Pennsylvania Prison Journal,* in press.

26. Kaplan, H.S. *The new sex therapy,* New York, Bruner/Mazel, 1974.

27. Auerbach, S.K. Correctional treatment teams, *Georgia Journal of Corrections, 1,* (3), 88–98, 1972.

28. Comptroller General of the United States. *Rehabilitating inmates of federal prisons: Special programs help, but not enough,* Washington, D.C., GAO, 1973.

Chapter 20

THE EFFECTIVENESS OF CORRECTIONAL TREATMENT—ANOTHER LOOK

Marc Reidel, Ph.D.

AND

David Lebor

INTRODUCTION

THE APPEARANCE OF AN ARTICLE by Martinson[1] in 1974 and a subsequent book by Lipton, Martinson, and Wilks[2] in 1975 proclaiming the failure of rehabilitation stimulated a storm of controversy about rehabilitation as the primary goal of criminal justice. On one side were those who asserted that evaluations of numerous rehabilitative or treatment programs had shown no significant impact on recidivism; rehabilitation as a primary goal of criminal justice should be abandoned. Others, opposing this conclusion, pointed to a number of treatment programs that had been successful. This latter group also pointed to the poor quality of evaluation research supporting the conclusion that rehabilitation was a failure.

While it is probably unfair to conclude that the debate over rehabilitation has generated more of the proverbial heat than light, certain issues have been ignored or obscured. First, both the critics and supporters of rehabilitation should be aware that Martinson's conclusions about rehabilitation are hardly an original discovery. As will be apparent in the next section, there have been several important and carefully done reviews of the treatment literature that reach conclusions similar to Martinson.

Second, it is our contention that the rehabilitative perspective has been faulted for failing where no one should have expected it to succeed. It is as unrealistic to expect one perspective to be universally applicable as it is to treat crimes or criminals as a unitary category. What may be effective with one type of offender may be totally inap-

244

propriate with other types of offenders. In addition, the rehabilitation perspective has never explicitly recognized the societal component in punishment. Punishment of crime is only partly a matter of dealing with the individual offender. As we shall see in subsequent sections, the question of the appropriateness of punishment is not limited to its effect on the learned behavior of offenders.

THE FAILURE OF REHABILITATION—SOME OTHER STUDIES

During 1975 one of the authors and a colleague were asked to review the treatment literature and summarize what was known about the effectiveness of the various rehabilitation approaches.[3] A large part of this report was revised and appears in Kusberg and Austin's *The Children of Ishmael.*[4]

After doing an extensive search of the literature we found seven other reviews of the treatment literature. The conclusion reached by the authors was "that there is no systematic evidence that rehabilitation efforts have had a significant impact on recidivism."[4] The reviews of the treatment literature are presented below in an author-by-author fashion to emphasize the different criteria and approaches used. Although he reaches conclusions that are similar to others, we have excluded the oldest review (1954) by Kirby.[6]

Robison and Smith[5]

Robison and Smith reviewed literature relating to the effectiveness of correctional programs in California. They evaluate literature in five critical areas of criminal processing: (1) imprisonment or probation, (2) length of stay in prison, (3) treatment programs in prison, (4) intensity of parole or probation supervision, and (5) outright discharge from prison or release on parole.

Imprisonment or Probation

Robison and Smith indicate that a comparison of recidivism rates between prison and probation does not demonstrate different rates of success, since courts place their best risks on probation, resulting in an inherent bias toward those on probation. One can control for case differences by making a random assignment of cases to either probation or prison, as was done in the California Youth Authority's Community Treatment Project (CTP).* This project, which has

---

*Citations to specific studies in cited reviews are given in the review. Unless otherwise indicated by citation, all references to authors in this paper are cited in detail in the evaluation report under discussion.

been in operation since 1961, has been widely acclaimed for its promise. After random assignment to experimental and control groups, an evaluation was conducted after fifteen months. The results indicated that only 30 percent of the male experimental subjects had violated parole or been unfavorably discharged, while 51 percent of the male control subjects had violated parole or been unfavorably discharged. By the twenty-four month follow-up, 63 percent of the control group failed, as compared with only 43 percent of the experimental group, confirming the efficacy of probation.

However, Robison and Smith found that most of the differences between the experimental and control groups could be explained by the decision-making authority: "In the CTP study the recidivism rates were managed to make the experimentals appear favorable." An analysis indicated that juveniles in the control and experimental groups were handled similarly only when offenses were of a serious nature. Where the offenses were less serious, control subjects were more likely than experimental subjects to have their probationary status revoked. On the basis of this and another study comparing professional casework to a jail or prison term, Robison and Smith conclude that there is no evidence that community supervision is more effective than institutional confinement.

Length of Stay in Prison

Robison and Smith review the research of Jarman, who studied the effect of length of sentence on recidivism. Studies of robbery offenders at six, twelve, and twenty-four month periods indicated that the longer offenders were kept in prison, the more likely they were to recidivate. To counter the argument that poorer risks were kept longer, Jarman introduced extensive statistical controls and found that length of stay was the relevant variable affecting the probability of recidivism. Robison and Smith suggest that administrative needs may be more significant in determining length of stay than the characteristics of the inmates.

Treatment Programs in Prison

Group counseling has been one of the most widely used prison treatment techniques. In reviewing a careful study of group counseling, Robison and Smith agree with Ward, Kassenbaum, and Wilner, who conducted the study. These authors found no significant differences between experimental and control groups and concluded that improvements in offender behavior were not sufficient to warrant continued use of group counseling. Robison and Smith conclude, "Despite the continuing popularization of various treatment programs and the increased attention devoted to more rigorous designs for their evaluation, *there are still no treatment techniques which have unequivocally demonstrated themselves capable of reducing recidivism.*"

Intensity of Parole or Probation Supervision

Numerous demonstration projects have decreased the size of the caseload in the belief that a smaller caseload would mean more intensive supervision and a lower rate of recidivism. Review of the Special Intensive Parole Unit (SIPU) program, initiated in California in 1953, indicated that a fifteen-man caseload did not differ from a thirty-man caseload in terms of parole outcome.

Robison and Smith also look at the results of the 1964 Work Unit Program, in which the size of the caseload was determined in large part by the seriousness of the offense. The Work Unit caseload averaged about thirty-five people, compared to conventional caseloads of seventy people. The small difference of 3.2 percent in favor of the Work Unit becomes insignificant when controls for parolee risk level are introduced. The Work Unit's parolees, in other words, were a better risk. Robison and Smith found that reducing the caseload size was not effective in reducing recidivism.

Outright Discharge from Prison or Release on Parole

Robison and Smith also compare differences in recidivism rates for men officially discharged from prison and those released on parole. Reviewing a study by Mueller, the authors found that during the first two years after release from prison, the discharged offenders are less likely to commit another crime than those paroled. However, after three years there was no difference between the two groups in postinstitutional disposition.

Robison and Smith conclude, after reviewing California studies with recidivism as the dependent variable:

> Analysis of findings in a review of the major California correctional programs that permit relatively rigorous evaluation strongly suggests the following conclusion: *There is no evidence to support any program's claim of superior rehabilitative (sic) efficacy.*

The single answer, then, to each of the five questions originally posed — "Will the clients act differently if we lock them up, or keep them locked up longer, or do something with them inside, or watch them more closely afterward, or cut them loose officially — is: *Probably not."*

We find only minor shortcomings in the Robison and Smith review. Although they claim only to review programs with rigorous evaluations, the authors do not indicate what they mean by "rigorous." While their research judgments are sound, verification is difficult since many of the studies on which their judgments are based are not in readily accessible published sources. Even with these limitations and given that the coverage of studies is limited to California, their results contribute to the conclusion that no program has demonstrated effectiveness in reducing recidivism.

Adams[7]

From his review of twenty-two California studies on the effects of reduced caseload, Adams concludes that thirteen of these programs show either significant reduction in recidivism or a benefit/cost ratio higher than unity. This general conclusion contrasts sharply with the findings of Robison and Smith concerning correctional caseloads. A comparison between the two studies may determine why the authors differed in their conclusions, since in several instances they reviewed the same studies.

The Special Intensive Parole Unit (SIPU) program and related research is divided into five phases. According to Adams, two of the researched phases show negative results, while the latter three display positive results. The fifth and final phase, which is the basis of the Robison and Smith results, was the most elaborate, reflecting knowledge about the research design and program accumulated from previous phases.

After reviewing the major findings of this program, Adams concludes:

> The only variable that made a real difference in parole outcome was the amount of time the parole agent had to devote to supervision. Interaction between agent and parolee characteristics did not appear related to outcome in this phase. Furthermore, the fifteen-man caseloads performed no better than thirty-man caseloads.

These conclusions, which do not differ substantively from those of Robison and Smith, apparently led Adams to classify SIPU as a successful program. But the grounds for his conclusion are unclear.

Adams also reviewed the Work Unit program evaluated by Robison and Smith. Adams concludes that there were significant reductions in returns to prisons for the experimental group. However, Adams did not consider the effect of the parolee risk level. As Robison and Smith indicate, when parolee risk level is introduced as a control, the significant differences disappear.

It is often difficult to assess Adams's claims for the success of programs because he does not clearly delineate what measures of success are used. In some instances, Adams defines success as a reduction in recidivism, while in other cases, he measures success by changes in intervening variables. Frequently success is claimed where there is no difference between experimental and control groups, when the former is less expensive. For example, Adams reports on an evaluation of the Willowbrook-Harbor Intensive Supervision Project, which utilized sixteen-boy community treatment caseloads as the experimental condition and forestry camp placements as a control condition. There was no difference in the success rates, but the average monthly costs for the experimental group was $115, while that for the control group was $326. The argument that although one treatment is no better than another, one is cheaper has frequently been used to bolster conclusions that a particular program is successful. It seems to the authors that when success turns on financial advantages rather than either reduction of crime or rehabilitation, such rationales are an admission of defeat. From an analysis of Adams's review we do not find compelling evidence to reject Robison and Smith's conclusion.

Adams[8]

The review of corrections research by Adams parallels our own efforts, in that he also reviews the results of other evaluations. We and Adams both review evaluations by Bailey,[9] Adams,[8] Robison and Smith,[5] Kassenbaum, Ward, and Wilner,[10] and Martinson.[1] Two reviews examined by Adams—Speer and Berkowitz—were unavailable to us. Adams summarizes the results of these studies as follows:

> D.C. Speer examined twenty-one controlled experimental studies of psychotherapy in corrections and identified eleven that included follow-up data on community performance after treatment. Of the eleven studies, six (55%) indicated a reduction in subsequent arrests and time spent in jail. The most definitive finding was that out of eight studies of juvenile treatment, six showed significant improvement; of the three involving adults, none showed significant improvement.

F. Berkowitz reviewed thirty-eight evaluative studies that were generally representative of 400 LEAA-funded projects under the California Council of Criminal Justice. Specified within the thirty-eight projects were 154 measurable objectives. Of these, 60 (or about 40%) were judged to have been achieved. The reviewer also identified seventy-three methodological deficiencies in the thirty-eight projects. Goal attainment was highest and deficiency rate lowest in the five experimental projects among the thirty-eight studies.

Since we were unable to examine the unpublished reviews, comments about their conclusions must necessarily be tentative. However, we do believe that Speer's conclusion is not supported by other reviewers. It is difficult to evaluate Berkowitz's claims since he provides no clear definition of what he meant by "goal attainment" for each of these projects.

What is significant is Adams's conclusion after reviewing these studies: "There is one sense in which all seven observers agree. Some are much more skeptical than others, but all see research with practical payoff as being a small percentage of the total."

Bailey[9]

The relative effectiveness of action programs is dependent on the quality of the research methodology used to evaluate it. Bailey reviewed one hundred evaluation reports published between 1940 and 1960, all of which were empirical studies. The selection of reports was guided by three principles: (1) the report must be based on empirical data, (2) the treatment evaluated must depend on the manipulation of some form of interpersonal relations as the independent or causal variable, and (3) the behavior to be corrected must be potentially or actually subject to legal sanctions.

Frequency of Types of Reports

Of the one hundred correctional reports only 22 percent were classified as using experimental designs; 26 percent used control procedures with no control group; and 52 percent were empirical studies with no control procedures. In other words, the more rigorous the research, the less frequently it is done.

Frequency of Types of Treatment

As might be expected, group treatment was the most frequently used treatment (58% of the reports), while individual forms constituted 42 percent of the reports. The types of research designs were about equally represented in the evaluation reports of group treatment.

Frequency of Type of Settings

A slight majority (54%) of the evaluations were carried out in correctional settings, in contrast to noncorrectional settings. Only reports using experimental designs or control procedures were used in this comparison.

Professional Identification of Researchers

Focusing only on the reports using experimental designs, ten of the twenty-one reports were authored by psychologists, while sociologists authored six of the reports. Psychiatrists, educators, and social workers contributed one study each, and two could not be classified.

Theories Used in Correctional Outcome Studies

Under the assumption that treatment theory helps to guide treatment, Bailey classified behavioral theories used in the 100 correctional reports into two basic categories. The first, based on "the sick premise," suggests that deviant behavior is symptomatic of underlying psychopathology. The second type, "the group relations premise" assumes that behavior, including deviant behavior, is primarily a function of group relations. Of course, both types of theories may apply to a particular treatment program. Of the 100 reports, 47 percent employed the sick premise approach. A substantial majority (67%) employed both types of theories. Interestingly, despite the finding that over 50 percent of the reports evaluate group treatment, only 9 percent of the reports used the group relations premise as a theoretical justification for intervention.

Effectiveness of Treatment

Of the total sample of reports, 10 percent described the treatments as having either harmful or no effects; 38 percent of the studies reported some improvement;* 37 percent reported statistically significant improvement; and 5 percent could not be classified. "Thus, roughly one-half of the outcome reports" concluded that there was

---

*Some improvement means that the experimental group had better scores than the comparison group, but that the difference was not statistically significant.

considerable improvement.† Of course, it should be noted that Bailey's conclusion does not control for the method used to gauge success.

Bailey reported that as the rigor of the design increases, there is only a slight increase in the number of reported successes. This led him to conclude that the rigor of the research design exerts little influence on the frequency of reported successes. Although approximately one-half of the 100 reports concluded that treatment programs were successful, it is difficult to interpret these findings. Bailey indicates, however, that reports of success are based on the conclusions of the original reports and that a critical evaluation of the actual research designs would decrease the number of successful outcomes. On the basis of his research, Bailey concludes that "evidence supporting the efficacy of correctional treatment is slight, inconsistent, and of questionable reliability."

Logan[11]

More recently, Logan presented a more sophisticated evaluation of 100 studies made since 1940 that used techniques of corrective or preventive treatment. Logan proposed ten criteria for evaluation of the reports:

1. The program of techniques should be adequately defined so that it can be placed in operation and tested.
2. The technique must be capable of being routinized. It must also be possible to implement all its components at various times by different administrators using diverse subjects.
3. There must be provision for a control group.
4. Subjects for experimental and control groups should be randomly selected.
5. Where it is appropriate, the control group should be selected using a matching technique.
6. There must be evidence that the treatment group receives treatment, while the control group does not.
7. Measurements of the behavioral change must be made before and after, with both experimental and control groups.
8. The definition of success must be sufficiently operational that

---

†The percentages, which are presented here as they are given in the original, do not sum to 100. We are relying on Bailey's statement that roughly one-half of the projects were successful.

provides a valid and reliable measurement for determining outcome.

9. Definition of success must be compatible with normal notions of success and should refer to correction or prevention of criminal behavior rather than personal adjustment or mental health.

10. There must be some follow-up measurement in the community for both treatment and control groups.

If we regard the ten criteria as minimal methodological requirements, Logan concludes, none of the studies can be described as completely adequate, since none meet all ten criteria. Only forty-two of the programs attempt to use a control group, only nine use well-defined techniques, and only one study uses a measurable definition of success.

The studies claimed various degrees of success as follows: sixteen claimed high amounts of success; four claimed good to high success; twenty-four studies claimed good success; eleven claimed fair to good success; fifteen claimed fair success; sixteen admitted failure; and fourteen could not be classified. On this basis one might conclude that treatment projects are relatively successful, but Logan's conclusion is somewhat more tempered.

> Thus, there is a strong current of optimism in these studies, with only a small minority (16%) admitting to failure. Perhaps most striking in view of the universal inadequacy of research design is the fact that so few studies insisted on suspending judgment altogether. . . . "Education" programs, as a group, made the highest claims of success while fulfilling the fewest methodological criteria required to support such claims.

Lipton, Martinson, and Wilks[2]

The last review analyzed here is not only the most recent, but certainly the most comprehensive one yet done. Like Bailey and Logan, the work by Lipton et al. employed research criteria to select the evaluation reports. In order to be selected for review the study had to:

1. Be an evaluation of a treatment method.

2. Include empirical data resulting from a comparison of experimental and control groups.

3. Employ an independent measure of the improvement resulting from the treatment.

Studies were excluded for methodological reasons such as the following:

1. Reports had insufficient data or were preliminary or summary reports.
2. Results were confused by the inclusion of extraneous factors.
3. Evaluators used unreliable measures.
4. Descriptions of treatment could not be clearly understood.
5. Evaluators drew spurious conclusions from their data.
6. Samples were either too small or not adequately described.
7. Inappropriate statistical tests were used and insufficient information was presented to recompute the data.

Using the preceding standards, Lipton et al. reviewed every available report published in English that measured attempts at rehabilitation made from 1945 through 1967. From this process, they chose 231 studies that met the criteria proposed for inclusion. These studies were then divided according to the type of treatment used and the success variable that was measured. The treatment categories include probation, imprisonment, parole, casework and individual counseling, skill development, individual psychotherapy, group therapy methods, milieu therapy, partial physical custody, medical methods, and leisure-time activities. The success variables are recidivism, institutional achievement, drug and alcohol readdiction, personality and attitude change, and community adjustment. Since our concern is with recidivism, our discussion will focus on that variable, although the overall conclusions are fundamentally the same for any of the measures.

The major conclusion of the study is that "while some treatment programs have had modest successes, it still must be concluded that the field of corrections has not as yet found satisfactory ways to reduce recidivism by significant amounts." The same conclusion could be made about the success of any of the ten types of treatments in reducing recidivism. Within each of the ten treatment categories, specific types of success can be seen. For instance, a treatment might be more successful for males than females, for a particular age group, or when administered by a certain type of therapist. Results relating to individual psychotherapy provide an example of this type of finding:

> Individual psychotherapy is more likely to be more effective when it is enthusiastically administered to youthful (16 to 20) amenable offenders by interested and concerned therapists with a pragmatic ori-

entation. It is likely to be unsuccessful, and perhaps even harmful, if it is administered to nonamenable or younger offenders by unenthusiastic therapists with a psychoanalytic orientation.

While individual psychotherapy can have positive results in certain situations, for most offenders it has not significantly reduced recidivism rates. The same is also true of the other nine types of treatment strategies surveyed. Though all demonstrate modest success in specific situations, they cannot by and large be considered successful strategies for reducing recidivism.

Moreover, the same conclusion holds for the other outcome measures surveyed by Lipton et al. There is no clearly demonstrated way to improve institutional adjustment, vocational adjustment, educational achievement, the tendency toward drug and alcohol readdiction, personality and attitude change, or community adjustment. In an earlier article one of Lipton's coauthors reached the following conclusion: *"With few and isolated exceptions, the rehabilitative efforts that have been reported so far have had no appreciable effect on recidivism."* That conclusion seems to hold true for the later research as well.

As the review by Logan[11] made clear, evaluation research is of a very low quality. The ten criteria proposed by Logan for evaluation of treatment studies are not unrealistic; we regard them as minimal methodological standards. Yet of the 100 studies reviewed, none met all ten criteria, less than half of the studies used a control group and only one study used a measurable definition of success. The research on the effectiveness of rehabilitation is simply not done well enough to support or not support any general conclusions.

If we cannot make any definitive conclusions regarding the general effectiveness of rehabilitation, other alternatives should be considered. Relying on weak research to support or not support the efficacy of rehabilitation assumes that the most important question is one regarding its general effectiveness. Yet it is just as logical to assume that no one punishment modality is suitable for all offenders and offenses. Given that one of the central limits in criminology is a differentiation of the general category of crime into offense and offender patterns, it also is logical to believe that no one punishment modality will be equally applicable to the wide variety of offenders. If we are prepared to recognize large differences among different kinds of offenders why should we not also be prepared to recognize that all criminal behavior is not changed by rehabilitative approaches? Variety at one stage of the criminal process must be complemented by variety at other later stages of the same process.

Taking the assumption that no one punishment modality is generally applicable means that we need not expect too much from rehabilitation. Rehabilitative approaches, like intensive supervision, may work well with certain types of offenders, but not others, as Palmer[12] has pointed out. If rehabilitation is recognized as one of several approaches to punishment, then failure in one instance does not imply failure in all.

It has only been comparatively recent that alternatives to rehabilitation, such as deterrence, incapacitation and retribution have been considered seriously as a basis for punishment. In the discussion that follows we are not advocating the superiority of deterrence, incapacitation, retribution, or rehabilitation. Our primary interest is in presenting the reader with ideas that are often ignored, but need to be discussed if a real and earnest attempt is to be made at uncovering a workable method of punishment.

THE ROLE OF DETERRENCE, INCAPACITATION, AND RETRIBUTION

The view that no one punishment modality is generally applicable is realistic if we recognize that in practice, rehabilitative approaches have not been followed with any great consistency. To illustrate the point, let us take two cases, a murder and a burglary. In the case of the murder, the offender is presumably given a longer prison sentence than the burglar, other things being equal. Yet this arrangement is not consistent with the rehabilitation perspective. We know from numerous research studies that murderers are excellent, if not the best, parole risks. Particularly where the murder was the result of a barroom or domestic altercation there is a very small probability that the offense will be repeated. Burglary, on the other hand, has a much higher probability of recidivism. Now if the purpose of imprisonment is to have our hypothetical offenders in a place where they can be treated, then the murderer should be given the shorter sentence and the burglar should receive the longer sentence. Indeed, it would not be unreasonable, if we are going to hold these offenders until they are rehabilitated, to postulate that the murderer could be released almost immediately while the burglar may remain imprisoned for a very long time, perhaps indefinitely.

The preceding sentencing practices suggest that the murderer is being rehabilitated too soon and the burglar is being rehabilitated too late. The example also implies that society is not solely interested in rehabilitation of offenders, but is also interested in the larger question of the fairness or appropriateness of the punishment. Murder, the deliberate taking of another person's life, is a very serious offense; it is much more serious than the deliberate removal of another's property and punishment usually reflects the broader societal view. The rehabilitation of the individual offender is of secondary importance.

What we are saying in simple terms is that the disposition of a criminal offender is not just a question of altering his behavior and attitudes so that he can return to society, it is also a question of the claims society makes for violation of the social contract. Violation of criminal law is not a matter of one person having wronged another, it is an offense against a social entity and a violation of shared moral imperatives.

The view that crime is a violation of shared moral imperatives developing and resulting from a social contract leads to different perspectives regarding punishment. The emphasis is placed on the crime and its impact on the victim and broader society. This emphasis is most frequently expressed in perspectives of retribution, deterrence, or incapacitation.

Punishment for crime based on retribution assumes that violations of criminal law represent a threat to the moral integrity of a society. Crime represents a tear in the social fabric that must be mended through appropriate punishment. Society as well as individuals have been victimized and social restitution must be made.

Basing the punishment for crime on a deterrence perspective also assumes the primacy of societal concerns and the criminal act. Deterrence differs from retribution, however, in placing an emphasis on compliance. Punishments are constructed with sufficient magnitude so as to discourage people from committing the particular crime. Punishments serving the goal of deterrence may indeed have a retributive component, just as retributive punishment may have a deterrent effect, but in the former case the deterrent effect is primary.

Finally, incapacitation in its pure form exists simply for the protection of society. One can, of course, put all offenders in prison, but the present criminal justice system could never tolerate such an expenditure of resources. Realistically, incapacitation has been an alternative when all others have failed; incapacitation does not preclude the use of rehabilitative programs, but such programs need not bear any relationship to release from prison. The offender is given a specific sentence that is served. What is done during this period of time may help the offender after he is released, but that is his choice and has little or no impact on time of release.

In discussing the role of society in punishment we are not suggesting that rehabilitation be ignored. Nor, it should be added, are we advocating the superiority of deterrence, incapacitation, or retribution approaches. The four modalities simply represent approaches available to those who create policy and legislation and implement programs.

The crucial question is not the simple one of which punishment modality is generally better. The crucial question is the kind of mix of punishment modalities that will effectively meet the conflicting demands on criminal justice and the task of reducing crime. What has been said about rehabilitation can easily be extended to the other punishment modalities: Any type of punishment will be effective with certain types of offenses and offenders, but not others.

One of the problems that has hampered discussion of the societal view of crime has been the lack of empirical specificity. From a theoretical point of view very cogent explanations of social contract and the moral imperatives can be made. It is intuitively appealing to talk about the need to restore the social fabric through retribution when a crime is committed. However, it is necessary to indicate exactly what is meant by these abstract phrases if any kind of clear-cut correctional policy is to be formulated. We have had only a vague idea of what is meant by the notion of fairness in meting out punishment although we acknowledge it is as important to the victim and society as it is to the offender.

In 1962 Thorsten Sellin and Marvin E. Wolfgang published *The Measurement of Delinquency*,[13] which was an attempt to provide a more useful measure of criminal activity. Because the authors focused on nonstatus offenses and developed a weighted measure of the amounts of injury, theft, and damage for each event rather than relying on legal labels, the product was a measure and a method that is superior to that currently used to collect criminal statistics.

But the development of a superior measure of the amount and kinds of criminal activity, useful though it may be, is not the most important feature of the Sellin and Wolfgang research. The authors developed a measure of perceived seriousness using community judgments and the observable amounts of injury, theft, and damage in each criminal event. The importance of such a weighted scale is that it provides an empirical dimension to discussions about the societal component in punishing criminals. Offenders may be punished in relation to the seriousness of the crime rather than relying upon vague and inconsistent notions about fairness or the appropriateness of a given punishment. The Sellin and Wolfgang seriousness measure provides us with community views of the seriousness of crime in a way that provides a clear-cut basis for policy about punishment.

The measurement of seriousness based on judgments of community members does not resolve the more difficult problem of whether a punishment should be retributive, deterrent, incapacitative, rehabilitative, or some mixture of the above. It does, however, represent an effort to incorporate community views of the gravity of the event into the measurement of crime and a possible guideline for the disposition of the offender.

SUMMARY

In taking another look at the effectiveness of correctional treatment, the following conclusions seem warranted:

First, the controversy over the general effectiveness of rehabilitation is not original with the writings of Martinson. We summarized several other reviews that concluded that treatment programs had no general effect on recidivism.

Second, we contend that it is pointless to believe that rehabilitation should be the only method of processing offenders. Rehabilitative approaches may be successful in some circumstances with some offenders, but to expect more is to expect too much.

Third, we indicated that rehabilitative approaches, although they are the most loudly articulated, are not carried through with any consistency. Claims for fairness to the victim and society force recognition of punishment modalities like retribution, deterrence, and incapacitation.

Finally, the vagueness surrounding discussions of society's and the victim's claims for fairness in punishing the criminal have hampered policy discussion and implementation. We have suggested how the development of a measure of seriousness represents an important first step in ascertaining and implementing community views in the endeavor to develop an equitable and effective system of punishment.

REFERENCES

1. Martinson, R. What works? — Questions and answers about prison reform, *Public Interest*, 22–55, June 1974.
2. Lipton, D., Martinson, R., and Wilks, J. *The effectiveness of correctional treatment: A survey of treatment evaluation studies*, New York, Praeger, 1975.
3. Riedel, M. and Thornberry, T.P. *Measurement and the effectiveness of correctional programs*, Educational Development Center, Wilkes College, 1975.
4. Riedel, M. and Thornberry, T.P. The effectiveness of correctional programs: An assessment of the field, In Kusberg, B. and Austin, J. (Eds.), *The children of Ishmael*, Palo Alto, California, Mayfield, 418–432, 1978.
5. Robison, J. and Smith, G. The effectiveness of correctional programs, *Crime and Delinquency, 17*, 67–80, 1971.
6. Kirby, B.C. Measuring effects of treatment of criminals and delinquents, *Sociology and Social Research, 38*, 368–374, 1954.
7. Adams, S. Some findings from correctional caseload research, *Federal Probation, 31*, 48–57, 1967.
8. Adams, S. Evaluative research in corrections: Status and prospects, In Riedel, M. and Chapell, D. (Eds.), *Issues in criminal justice: Planning and evaluation*, New York, Praeger, 1976.
9. Bailey, W.C. Correctional outcomes: An evaluation of 100 reports, *Journal of Criminal Law, Criminology, and Police Science, 57*, 153–160, 1966.
10. Kassenbaum, G., Ward, D., and Wilner, D. *Prison treatment and parole survival: An empirical assessment*, New York, Wiley, 1971.
11. Logan, C.H. Evaluation research in crime and delinquency: A reappraisal, *Journal of Criminal Law, Criminology, and Police Science, 63*, 378–387, 1972.
12. Palmer, T. Martinson revisited, *Crime and Delinquency, 21*, 133–152, 1975.
13. Sellin, T. and Wolfgang, M.E. *The measurement of delinquency*, New York, Wiley, 1962.

Chapter 21

THE ROLE OF THE PSYCHOLOGIST AS A PUBLIC POLICY PLANNER IN JUVENILE CORRECTIONS*

MICHAEL E. PARRISH, Ph.D.

T HE ASPECTS of the role of a psychologist in public policy planning, as I must discuss them based upon my experiences, are not subtle. I will quickly cover what I think is the basic model of the consultant's role, and then discuss some of the details of a project with juvenile offenders that will elaborate the role.

The model, obviously stated, is as follows: An agency or institution, public or private, contacts the psychologist-consultant and invites his/her participation. The consultant presents his/her proposal based upon research and/or clinical knowledge and to the extent that the proposal influences the outcome of the agency's policy, contingent upon the agency's influence, the psychologist has had an effect on public policy. In my experience the role has been that of a consultant. The agency is not usually composed of peers. They can, however, sense if the proposal meets the kernel needs of the agency, but they are at a disadvantage in evaluating its soundness, i.e. does it reflect a thorough knowledge of the field and is it methodologically feasible? I suspect that the perceived credibility of the consultant is often a deciding factor and this is worrisome. The burden rests with the consultant to articulate the aspects of the proposal that are based upon given types of data. Clinical knowledge and research knowledge should be differentiated and further the reader should be made aware of your confidence regarding the same. In the area of juvenile

*This is a revision of a paper originally presented as part of a symposium at the annual convention of the American Psychological Association, Washington, D.C., September 1976.

offenders, for example, research is most often not experimental. Most common are prediction studies in which attempts to simplify operational procedures have resulted in methodological difficulties, such as the use of statistical procedures that cannot be justified.[1] Your client —the agency—will often choose to extend its offer for your services upon the receipt of this technical feedback. This is essentially what happened in the project to be discussed now.

Dr. Robert Sadoff, a forensic psychiatrist, Dr. William Miller, the Director of Research for the Division of Family Studies, University of Pennsylvania School of Medicine, and I agreed to develop a program, which became known as the Camp Hill Screening Project, for a private agency. This agency, The Center For Community Alternatives, was funded by the Pennsylvania Department of Welfare and Law Enforcement Assistance Agency. The Center for Community Alternatives worked closely with the office of the Pennsylvania Commissioner of Children and Youth who was politically active about the issue of the disposition of juvenile offenders. We were contacted following a decision by the State Attorney General that determined that the incarceration of juveniles at the State Correctional Institute at Camp Hill (SCICH) was in violation of state law. He stated that as of August 31, 1975 no further commitments to that prison were to be allowed. The SCICH is a medium security adult prison with approximately 800 inmates. At the time we were contacted there were 408 juvenile inmates in the prison, representing almost every county in the state. More than one half of the inmates were from the densely populated areas of Philadelphia, Pittsburgh, and Harrisburg.

The Commissioner of Children and Youth strongly advocated that alternative placements for these 408 inmates be determined quickly. It was his opinion that this was a dehumanizing facility for juveniles. The pressure on the existing system that the presence of these 408 inmates, along with those who were now excluded following the Attorney General's ruling, provoked commentary from politicians, bureaucrats, the media, and other citizens around the issue of the "juvenile offender." Simply stated, the issues as they related to our project interacted with the judiciaries responsibility to determine the disposition of juvenile offenders and the various bureaucracies struggles to determine what facilities/programs would be developed and controlled by whom.

That the project would be necessarily involved with public policy was apparent from the outset. The prison was no longer an option.

Alternatives would be made available. Our reports would suggest these alternatives. A brief digression is necessary. An important aspect of the initial contact with the agency emphasized the need to determine which of these 408 inmates were dangerous; specifically which would be assaultive if not incarcerated. They were, after all, in the most secure prison for juveniles in the state. The concern about dangerousness was likely complex in its motivation. But basically the protection of society, the inmates, and prevention of damaging publicity regarding the closing of the facility seemed obvious. We agreed, however, that there was no body of knowledge, clinical or research, in our respective fields that allowed us to predict dangerousness in this population for the individual case. We simply could not predict from group data to the single case.[2] We decided to develop and, if accepted by the agency, to implement a prediction procedure that would summarize the inmates' previous experiences and to determine dispositional recommendations. (The agency's need was for a clinical evaluation and recommendations to be presented to the court for its disposition).

As we considered the magnitude of the project it became clear that a research orientation toward the development of the procedure, training the clinicians, the collection of information that summarized the inmates experiences, as well as the clinical interview would be most effective. Many factors determined this "research orientation" to a clinical task. The agency required that 408 inmates be evaluated within four weeks. We wanted each clinician to devote about three hours to each case. The number of clinicians would approach thirty and interreport consistency would necessitate that the data upon which the reports were based be structured. Also, there were recidivism prediction studies with incarcerated juvenile populations, which, while admittedly predictive for groups, were methodologically satisfactory and included areas of investigation that we wished to consider.[3,4] Furthermore the clinicians we selected were about equally divided between M.D.s and Ph.D.s and while they would have some areas of overlapping professional experience we again needed to insure interreport consistency with regard to the data base as well as the reporting style. Further, we wanted quantifiable information from which to learn more about this population and upon which to base follow-up studies.

One set of forms based upon information available from prison records and one set based upon the interview were developed for the clinician. The information from prison record forms encompassed thirty-five areas that were selected from research articles predicting recidivism based upon record data alone[3] and research that dealt more generally with recidivism.[5] We also relied upon our (Sadoff, Miller, and Parrish) clinical experience in including some areas. The interview information form, which included eighty-one responses, was similarly based upon published research and our clinical experience. While most of the above information could be classified as demographic correlates of delinquency, questions relating to mental status were also included.

The prison records included I.Q. scores. We also had the *Quay*,[6] *Lykken*,[7] *O-H Scale*,[8] and the *Cattel Manifest Anxiety Scale*[9] administered to the entire population. Our research inclinations probably determined the choice of these particular instruments in that we were quite interested to see how typological data (Quay, Lykken) along with demographic data related to current offense history as well as future recidivism.

Given the information from the records and the interview and the tests, the clinician made disposition recommendations that then were the basis for program development around the "juvenile offender" issue. The scope of the possible disposition recommendations was determined by meetings with academicians and practitioners from criminology, psychiatry, and psychology along with individuals who worked at administrative levels in public and private agencies and those who had "line" experience in juvenile facilities and community programs.

But ultimately the recommendations were made by the clinician after he/she had a brief consultation about the case with a peer supervisor, usually Dr. Sadoff or myself. It was then a clinical decision. The decision proper is currently guiding funding requests by state and private agencies. The process involved in that decision has provided information that, when more completely analyzed and published, will be considered in determining policy and will form the basis for follow-up study.

REFERENCES

1. Gottfredson, D.M. Assessment and prediction methods in crime and delinquency, *Task Force Report: Juvenile Delinquency*, Washington, D.C., U.S. Government Printing Office, 1967.
2. Megargee, E.I. The prediction of violence with psychological tests, In Spielberger, C.D. (Ed.), *Current topics in clinical and community psychology*, Vol. II, New York, Academic Press, 1970.

3. Ganzer, V.J. and Sarason, J.G. Variables associated with recidivism among juvenile delinquents, *Journal of Consulting and Clinical Psychology, 40,* 1–5, 1973.

4. Stein, K.B., Sarbin, T.R., and Kulik, J.A. Further validation of antisocial personality types, *Journal of Consulting and Clinical Psychology, 36,* 177–182, 1971.

5. Wolfgang, M., Figlio, R.M., and Sellin, T. *Delinquency in a birth cohort,* Chicago and London, The University of Chicago Press, 1972.

6. Quay, J.C. *Juvenile delinquency: Research and theory,* New York, Van Nostrand, 1965.

7. Lykken, D.T. A study of anxiety in the sociopathic personality, *Journal of Abnormal and Social Psychology, 55,* 6–10, 1957.

8. Megargee, E.I., Cook, P.E., and Mendelsohn, G.A. Development and evaluation of an MMPI scale of assaultiveness in over-controlled individuals, *Journal of Abnormal Psychology, 72,* 519–528, 1967.

9. Cattel, R.B. *Personality and motivational structure and measurement,* New York, World Book, 1957.

Chapter 22

THE MISTREATING OF FEMALE OFFENDERS

Margery Velimesis
AND
Clorinda Margolis, Ph.D.
AND
Phyllis York

SOCIETAL AND INDIVIDUAL PROBLEMS THAT WOMEN BRING TO PRISON

IF, FROM a feminist point of view, women are oppressed, women offenders are doubly oppressed. They not only suffer the prejudices of a male-oriented society; they are too few in number and too widely scattered in the system to protect themselves in a male-oriented criminal justice system. Often they are housed in facilities designed for men—an exposed cell with male turnkeys in a police lock-up, a back wing having no direct outside access in a county jail housing primarily male prisoners. Losing what little respect they have in the eyes of the world as women by becoming offenders, they receive few, if any, of the rehabilitative efforts designed to fill the time and attempt to salvage a few male offenders. Instead, they have a history of sexual exploitation and abuse at the hands of male jailers who complain regularly of the nuisance and bother of having to house such women. If women had no serious mental health problems before incarceration (they do) they would have them during and following incarceration (they do).

This should come as no surprise since national statistics give some indication of the problems that women in general face as a consequence of their place in society and with the medical profession.

In 1975 physicians recorded that women reported 61 percent of

266

psychiatric symptoms and 60 percent of the psychosomatic illnesses of patients seen in their offices.[1] Twice as many women as men were treated for depression in hospitals or out-patient services.[2] Physicians prescribed Valium® and Librium® for twice as many women as men, and 50 percent more women received prescriptions for barbiturates.

Many women question whether physicians are diagnosing their patients on the basis of symptoms presented or by personal bias and sex stereotyping.[3] A study by Difell (1977) showed that 73 percent of psychotropic drug prescriptions were written for women; 27 percent were written for men. But over-the-counter sales for such drugs did not differ by sex.[4] Additionally, there was little consistency between the kinds of symptoms described by women and the type of drug prescribed. While minor tranquilizers such as Valium are viewed as harmless by many, the question arises as to why they are prescribed over long periods of time since their use does not resolve the problem but merely encourages adjustment to it.

The physician is trained to prescribe medications; but accurate diagnosis of the complaints of many women would show that the source of many of those complaints lies in the social and economic forces that affect their lives.[5] In 1976 almost one out of four households was headed by a woman; their average income ($7,749) was only 44.9 percent of that of households headed by men. Of families headed by women, 34.4 percent were below the poverty level while only 7.1 percent of families with male heads were so disadvantaged. The earnings of women employed full-time were only 60 percent ($8,099) that of employed men. Fewer than one man in four (23.6%) with an income lived on less than $4,000 a year, but over one out of two women (53.7%) with an income did so.[6]

Since very few women inherit money or receive alimony sufficient to support a household, the great majority of these women either must work or register for public assistance. Unfortunately, far too many women still are not trained with sufficiently marketable skills to earn an adequate income. Full-time employment is often seen to conflict with the nurturing, child-raising role of women.[7] Yet to go on welfare is considered a kind of disgrace. Not surprisingly, women become anxious and depressed in these circumstances and, while we do not know the income levels of those women treated for depression and who reported psychosomatic symptoms, suffice it to say that one study found that professional and managerial women demonstrated the least depression in the population surveyed.[8] Drugs cannot resolve such

"Catch-22" situations as described above, but appropriate referrals to non-medical resources are often helpful. Better skills and greater income in most instances would materially decrease the complaints of poor women, and such efforts should become a matter of public health policy.

Some studies have shown that incarcerated women come from more distressed families than do incarcerated men.[9] Probably 95 percent of incarcerated women have family backgrounds that manifest one or more of the following: low income status, mental retardation, substance abuse by one or both parents, emotional instability, rigid authoritarianism, or gross physical abuse. About half of the incarcerated women are white in most states. Many (both black and white) were young runaways from abusive family situations, and evidence is mushrooming of the number who were juvenile victims of incest or other rape.[10] (This does not mean that only women from such families break the law, but rather that the women who are imprisoned through the filtering process in the criminal justice system turn out to be the violent, the politically spectacular, but most often the poor) .

Although no hard data yet exist on a national basis, prison figures in Pennsylvania in 1967 (Pennsylvania has one of the lower rates of incarceration in the United States) and contact with women's prisons in other highly populous states indicate that about 5 percent of female inmates are borderline or active psychotics, over 60 percent are substance abusers, 20 percent have previously attempted suicide, and 25 percent have problems serious enough to interfere with adequate functioning as adult women (psychosomatic symptoms, anxiety, depression). These figures are higher for women than for men inmates.

MULTIPLICATION OF THE PROBLEMS IN PRISON

Once in prison women acquire additional problems. About 80 percent are mothers and they are separated, usually by great distance, from their children. Visiting restrictions and conditions are often deplorable.[11] Some of the mothers (especially substance abusers) become anxious about their children often for the first time in some months, but that realization becomes an additional source of worry. The lack of concern about their children on the part of the criminal justice system as a whole is no small worry in itself. Feelings of depression frequently surface as do former physical health problems. Then there is the tension that comes in many prisons from the threats to new inmates by prisonwise inmates in order to obtain money (or its equivalent) or sex.[12] Finally the greater stigma attached to women having been in prison colors most women's anxiety.

Practically any warden in the country will say that women inmates are more difficult to handle than men; that they ask for more medical attention, no matter how much they receive (actually it is usually very little); that they are emotional and impossible to satisfy; that the number of disturbed women he receives is increasing each year; that he would be delighted to have someone take the women out of his institution. Even those who work in all-female institutions seem to be more rigid in attitude than do those who work in male institutions. In spite of the availability of millions of federal dollars since 1968, women's prison programs and staff have not changed substantially.[13] Women's prisons still have far fewer educational, vocational, and recreational programs than men's prisons. Not only is the variety of jobs within the prison more limited, but many prisons that have work or educational release programs for men have none for women. This discrimination is usually rationalized on the grounds that there are too few women to make the program worthwhile and that the level of skills is so low that no jobs could be obtained.

Thus, the boredom and deadly routine of prisons is worse for a woman and gives her many hours to dwell upon her economic, emotional, and psychological problems. Scrubbing floors, helping to prepare large quantities of institutional food, working on a farm, or operating power sewing machines for the benefit of the state with pennies an hour for wages does little to enhance marketable job skills or her self-image.[14] She learns that she is a failure and that subservience and passivity under prison rules is expected of her. Anger and contempt cannot safely be manifested, so new games and skills in manipulation are learned in order to cope with the humiliation that is intrinsic to life in punitive institutions. Childish behavior is punished, sometimes by the use of what is called administrative segregation or even strip cells.[15]* But such behavior is subtly encouraged, too. Women are called "girls" and are treated as children too irre-

---

*Administrative segregation is the term often used to describe cells that are set apart from other cells to keep inmates separated from the rest of the population. Although regular meals are usually served, privileges and participation in programs such as education is restricted. Strip cells are those from which everything except a bolted-down bunk has been removed. Sometimes the inmate must sleep on the bare floor. All privileges such as mail and visiting are suspended and food is often reduced. Such cells exist even in cottage-type institutions.

sponsible to make even simple daily life decisions. Obeying commands is the heart of prison life but rules attempting to regulate the minutae of daily life are far more petty in women's institutions. The resulting stress often erupts into emotional outbursts and fights between inmates. Just as women have been accused of being responsible for their own rape, so does prison punishment for such behavior teach women that they are responsible for their own emotional and psychological problems—truly an illness-inducing situation.

The feeling of helplessness has been identified as one of the factors contributing to depression.[16] In American society women are seen as more helpless than men; their upbringing and traditional socialization has encouraged them to be so. Independent action on the part of girls historically has been ignored or at least discouraged and the preferred stance for young women has been one of dependence on men to solve problems, to take action regarding troublesome family situations, and of course to be the breadwinner. (Such expectations have obviously put a heavy burden on men and have contributed to their mental health problems).

In prison, this female stereotype of helplessness and dependence is reinforced in a hundred different ways even though it almost guarantees increased frustration and depression in women whose life situations have made them have to depend upon themselves for survival. Those who have taken independent actions that they perceived desirable or necessary (thievery, forgery, selling drugs) for economic survival are punished for such actions but they are seldom given good education and training to open up realistic alternatives for their futures. Most prison programs of vocational training are pitiful in comparison with the demands of the job market and scarcely deserve to be titled "education" or "training."[17] Women are figuratively told to go and sin no more and reconcile yourself to a life of poverty and helplessness in the face of mate abuse, joblessness, housing discrimination, and children that you can neither support nor control.

The usual response to advocates who point out the social and economic plight of convicted women is typified by a skeptical judge who commented in 1977, "Well, maybe she *is* living in poverty but that didn't prevent her from appearing in my court in the latest mod boots and leather coat." Now a typical middle-class male attitude condones the pervasive advice (of doctors as well as women) to "Go out and buy yourself a pretty hat or dress and you'll feel better," i.e. overcome a little depression. What level of depression must a woman be experiencing when she trades next month's rent or better food for some outward sign that she is "making it," that she is "somebody?"[18] What is seen as her irresponsibility may simply come from not having the education, the experience, or the realistic opportunity to overcome her sense of failure, frustration, and helplessness in any other way.

Whereas the data available would seem to indicate the need for a full range of reality and ego-building services, the few counselors hired often have little if any training (and less experience) in growth and human-development concepts and methods. Psychiatrists and psychologists, if available at all, come into the prison for a few hours a month to pronounce a diagnosis or to write a prescription for drugs. Their presence frequently is at the request of inappropriately trained personnel.

The dispensing of psychotropic drugs is the prison's answer to all problems: Can't sleep? Feel nervous? Attempted suicide? Assaulted another inmate or a guard? Angry because the Board denied your parole with no explanations or the judge refused to change your sentence? Going out of your mind because a ten-day-old letter says your son was in an accident and now you can't telephone him? Well, here! Valium, phenobarb, thorazine®—whatever—the physician did prescribe it for you (months ago or even last year).

The dispensing of huge quantities of drugs in women's institutions could be anticipated because of the practice of the medical profession as a whole when treating women, as previously pointed out. In prison there is little question that drugs are used to control behavior and to "adjust women" to prison life, just as tranquilizers and more violent treatment such as shock therapy usually result in adjusting women to their situational problems in the community. Since the goal or purpose of prisons has never been that of increasing health or personal growth, the fact that drugs suppress stress symptoms is viewed as quite all right. In fact, the heavy use of drugs is often justified on the ground that women frequently request medications for headache, nerves, and sleeplessness when no physical cause for such complaints can be found. The prison routine and attitude of prison personnel, that increases these complaints is never questioned; it is the women who are weak and at fault.

Although the role of the prison has never been to increase mental or physical health, at least prisons should be prohibited from destroying what health inmates have upon entrance into the institution. High-quality professional studies are needed to determine the state of that health when inmates are received and when they leave the institutions.

Keeping in mind the backgrounds and previous experiences of most women in prison it would seem that prison physicians would work closely with those in education, training, and counseling and those (usually matrons) originating decisions about punishment. However, such cooperation almost never occurs for many reasons, the first being that physicians spend as little time as possible in the prisons. Even in large metropolitan areas, such as Philadelphia, recruitment is difficult; records of time spent in the prison by part-time physicians usually prove to be vague or nonexistent.[19] Physicians together with most prison personnel are not concerned with reducing the stress that women undergo because stress is seen as the inevitable outcome of prison rules and routines that are perfectly acceptable in themselves. The result is an environment that offers the fewest opportunities for personal development and the learning of coping skills that are socially acceptable in the outside world, goals that would seem to be in the interest of public safety.

In carrying out their priorities of punishment and restriction of freedom of movement, prisons succeed in inducing pathology. Physical movement and physical behavior is restricted but the range of emotional and psychological processes is restricted as well. Physical movement is controlled by the bars, walls, doors, and rules of the institution; behavior is controlled by the rules and by massive use of drugs. In a therapeutic situation drugs may provide temporary relief of stress so that the patient may begin to cope. In prison, however, where even the physical health and certainly the mental health of inmates is of minor concern, drugs inhibit psychological growth. By restricting the growth of anxiety, drugs also stifle pathology that would otherwise be the outcome of long stays in prison.

Growth of positive psychological processes often requires the open expression of anger, frustration, and hostility in order to learn how to resolve conflicts, cope with stress, and overcome anxiety. Aggressive, even violent acting-out behavior can often be the result of depression and poor self-image of long standing. But possible growth is restricted by the rules and requirements of the institutional staff and by the prescribing of drugs by the physicians. Instead of encouraging coping skills to handle stress and unproductive responses to crisis situations, inmates are forced into increasingly passive behavior by whatever means are available.

Women sometimes express their deep-seated emotional needs by developing pseudofamilies among their fellow inmates, offering each other support and caring relationships that may, in fact, give them their only positive prison experience.[20] Given the restrictive and judgmental structure and the inmates' own limited positive family relations, this experience is seldom used to help women increase their capacity for intimacy and stability in relationships.

Prison matrons often present the stern, authoritarian mother image, emphasizing the "authority over the child" aspect of motherhood. At the same time, the purposes and priorities of the prison greatly restrict the nurturing, teaching, socializing, and protective aspects of the mother role. That women have seen this authoritarian role as an acceptable one for themselves is within the tradition of women acquiring power by carrying out the orders of men; part of the power and strength of men has been acquired by serving men. Women in such roles suppress female behavior that is nonacceptable to men and the prison encourages the continuation of this type of mothering. While female prison wardens usually adopt such a role it is interesting to note the number of male wardens in all-female prisons. In Pennsylvania when the state prison for women was "reformed" in 1970, a woman superintendent was replaced by a succession of three male superintendents, although no woman has been appointed head of a male prison. (Pennsylvania passed a state ERA amendment in 1971).

Therefore, the inmates who are recommended for early parole, who get the best jobs with the highest pay, who are never assigned to the jobs are those who identify with the norms of this type of staff; ladylike behavior, nonviolent speech and behavior, eagerness to learn what the security-oriented staff deems important.[21] In other words, inmates who demonstrate the surface indications of the personal values of the gatekeepers get along best in prison, but they obviously do not receive assistance or support in personal growth or development. Thus, they, too, leave prison as the same unchanged victims of family violence and social and economic discrimination that they were when they entered; of course they now have the additional handicaps of a prison experience and a prison record.

HOW PRISONS MIGHT BE
Four Groups of Women To Be Served

Until more pretrial release programs are implemented throughout the country, most of the incarcerated women in any given year will be those held awaiting trial because they cannot raise bail. For these women prompt and competent legal services are most needed. In addition they need help from workers in the community to contact their family, to find out what is happening with the children, to bring clothes for the appearance at trial, to assure that rent is paid, that utilities are not discontinued, and that living quarters are secured against vandalism and burglary. The high level of anxiety[22] that prevails at this period usually precludes interest in any other service aside from someone who will listen sympathetically and who can inform the woman of her rights and suggest persons for the woman to contact. Here the emphasis must be on producing a stress-relieving situation. Appropriately trained staff would be able to identify those who are psychotic or epileptic (the latter comprised 10% of the state prison population in Pennsylvania in 1967) and secure medical treatment and transfer if necessary.

A second group of women are those who have been placed on probation. Many of these will be substance abusers for whom the judge has specified treatment, but nonabusers may also desperately need psychological, social, and support services. Professionals and others trained in the special multiproblems of disadvantaged women should be available, with or without court referral. Special attention should be given to reporting procedures that will provide the court with necessary and relevant information including a progress report from the counselor or psychotherapist. However, this must be without access to confidential information disclosed to professional staff whose aim is to develop a therapeutic relationship with the incarcerated women. Included in the support services should be referrals for housing and for jobs. To make this latter a realistic service, a national policy of education, training, and employment that realistically includes women offenders is badly needed.

A third group of women constitute a small but critical number of women who are overtly psychotic or who lapse into psychotic episodes and who are clearly a danger to themselves or others. The needs of these women are ignored in almost every state on the basis that, there being so few of them, there are others more deserving of the treatment and limited resources available. Their bizarre and acting out behavior disturbs other inmates who sometimes mistreat them; this then sets the stage for a ruckus out of which come various disciplinary procedures that take staff time and inmate attention away from more positive efforts. If not actually dangerous, severely disturbed women can still present serious management problems for staff, which sometimes result in unduly restrictive rules for all inmates. Often they are heavily medicated and kept in the regular prison facility because there is nowhere to send them. In those states that have institutions for the criminally insane, a few women will be so diagnosed and packed off, relieving the detention center or prison of their care but in no way insuring the women beneficial or even humane treatment. At best they are warehoused; more likely they will be physically or perhaps sexually abused.

Partial hospitalization programs or day hospitals could provide a few hours of treatment daily, giving the patients structure and supportive assistance, thus allowing them opportunities to rebuild their sense of reality at the same time relieving the prison staff of responsibility for their daytime care. Medication could be carefully monitored reducing the probabilities of excesses. Less disturbed women, or women who begin to reestablish their ego boundaries, who move into remission, could spend less time in the partial hospital program and more time in daily activities and rehabilitation efforts in their place of incarceration. The many women who have emotional problems serious enough to warrant psychotherapy, counseling, and/or medication might go for weekly treatment at the program but would not participate in the daily hospital activities. Once the commitment to supportive treatment for women offenders is made and professional staff is available, a range of group programs could be offered and a therapeutic milieu could be established.

The last group is women sentenced to state prisons and larger county jails for a variety of offenses including violation of probation. If prisons are to serve a positive long-term function for society, a revolution must occur in the purposes, priorities, and staffing of these institutions. Goals of on-going personal growth must take equal priority with that of restriction of freedom. Matrons/guards/correctional officers can no longer simply play the role of turnkeys and enforcers of rules. They must be interested and trained in the issues of authority, interpersonal dynamics, and interpersonal relations in a restricting environment. They must acquire an understanding of institutional settings rather than individual pathologies. They should learn the nature of anxiety and depression and what increases those psychological states. Since many of their charges have never experienced a strong, caring mother it would be helpful if matrons became role models of caring mothers and of competent, responsible women. Matrons could then see the possibility of their helping to alter behavior rather than personally reacting to it. Many of the matrons would welcome the change in role and would be eager for the training that it would require.

Except for the few in prison who have committed either very violent crimes or ones of political prominence, women serve an average of about two years in prison, although time served varies considerably from state to state because of varying sentencing inclinations of judges. This includes those with long histories of drug abuse, alcoholism, petty thefts, and prostitution who serve fairly short sentences and those sentenced on burglary, robbery, forgery, manslaughter, and aggravated assault charges who spend somewhat longer periods of time.

Eighteen months to two years to provide meaningful service and to promote constructive change is manageable for adults if the prison milieu is dedicated to the prospect. Because women's facilities are relatively small and the women few in number, a model center could be set up offering opportunities for change and growth predicated upon a new kind of role for the matrons group.

Women's recidivism is 0 to 2 percent for the most serious crimes (murder and manslaughter) and approximately 50 to 65 percent for the less serious property crimes (bad checks, larceny, drug charges).[23] Experience with women on probation and parole who have received sensitive and skilled services indicates that these latter rates can be significantly reduced. Even if such reductions were not achieved with prisons staffed and managed as has been suggested, at least we could be more assured that women would not be released in a more damaged state than when they entered.

REFERENCES

1. Kravits, 1975 as cited by Fidell, L.S., *Psychotropic drug usage among women*, President's Commission on Mental Health, Panel on Women.
2. National Institute of Drug Abuse, Department of Health, Education and Welfare, 1976, Seidenberg, R. Drug advertising and perception of mental illness, *Mental Hygiene, 55*, 21–31, 1971.
3. Broverman, I.K., Broverman, D.M., and Clarkson, F.E. Sex-role stereotyping and clinical judgment of mental health, *Journal of Consulting and Clinical Psychology, 34*, 1–7, 1970.
4. Fejer, D. and Smart, R., 1973 and Balter, M. and Levine, J., 1971 as cited by Fidell, L.S., op. cit.
5. Weissman, M.M. Depressed women, In Claghorn, J. (Ed), *Successful psychotherapy*, New York, Brunner Mazel, 1976.

6. *Statistical Abstract of the U.S.*, New York, Grosset and Dunlap, 1977.
7. Bradwick, J. *The psychology of women: A study of biocultural conflicts*, New York, Harper and Row, 1971; Gove, W.R. and Tudor, J.F. Adult sex-roles and mental illness, *American Journal of Sociology, 78,* 812–835, 1973.
8. Radloff, L. Sex differences in depression: The effects of occupational and marital status, *Sex Roles; A Journal of Research, 1,* 249–264, 1975; Guttentag, M., Salasin, S., Legge, W.W., and Bray, H. *Sex differences in the utilization of publicly supported mental health facilities*, Washington, D.C., National Institute of Mental Health, 1976.
9. Cowie, J., Cowie, Z., and Slater, E. *Delinquency in girls*, New York, Humanities Press, 1969; Cloninger, C.R. and Guze, S.B. Psychiatric illnesses in the families of female criminals: A study of 288 first degree relatives, *British Journal of Psychiatry, 122,* 607–703, 1973.
10. Tormes, Y. *Child victims of incest*, Children's Division, Denver, American Humane Association, 1966; Benward, J. and Densen-Gerber, J. *Incest as a causative factor in anti-social behavior: An exploratory study*, New York, Odyssey Institute, 1975.
11. *Survey of 41 Court and Correctional Services for Women*, Pennsylvania Program for Women and Girl Offenders, Philadelphia, 1968.
12. Harris, S. *Hellhole; the shocking story of the inmates and life in the N.Y.C. house of detention for women*, New York, Dutton, 1967.
13. *County court and correctional services*, Pennsylvania Program for Women and Girl Offender, op. cit.; Phyllis Chesler, *Women and madness*, Garden City, New Jersey, Doubleday, 1972, p. 39.
14. *Proposed Pennsylvania standards for women's facilities*, Pennsylvania Program for Women and Girl Offenders, Philadelphia, 1976.
15. *Citizen's Task Force Report on the Pennsylvania State Correctional Institution for Women at Muncy*, Pennsylvania Program for Women and Girl Offenders, Philadelphia, 1971.
16. Radloff, L. op. cit.
17. *Citizen's Task Force Report on the Pennsylvania State Correctional Institution for Women at Muncy*, op. cit.
18. Cochrane, R. The structure of value systems in male and female prisoners, *British Journal of Criminology, 11,* 73–87, 1971; Szabo, D. and Landreville, P. Research at the department of criminology, University of Montreal, *Current Trends in Criminological Research*, (Strasbourg, Council of Europe, 1970.
19. *Citizen's Task Force Report on the Pennsylvania State Correctional Institution for Women at Muncy*, op. cit.
20. Gaillombardo, R. *Society of women*, New York, Wiley, 1966; Gaillombardo, R. *Social world of imprisoned girls: A study of institutions for juvenile delinquents*, New York, Wiley, 1974.
21. Hefferman, E. *Making it in prison: The square, the cool and the life,*

New York, Wiley, 1972.
22. Margolis, Clorinda *First impressions in the house of correction,* Paper presented to the American Psychological Association Convention, Washington, D.C., 1973.
23. *Recidivism of Women Sentenced to Probation and Released on Parole in Pennsylvania,* (1971–1973), Pennsylvania Program for Women and Girl Offenders, Philadelphia, 1976.

Chapter 23

PRISON AS AN ENVIRONMENT: THE ROAD TO HELL IS PAVED WITH GOOD INTENTIONS

KENNETH G. WILSON, Ph.D.

THE PURPOSE of this chapter is to provide the reader with (a) the flavor of prison as an environment from the point of view of the inmate, (b) the environment from a psychologist's point of view, (c) my point of view regarding how the prison environment evolved into its current state, and (d) some suggestions about what we might change to make the environment more productive in terms of what we ideally expect it to accomplish. The text is written about male prison environments.

PRISON

In reality and by definition prison is any place (from maximum security institutions to pretrial diversion programs) where custody is maintained under arrest or legal process. For this chapter I shall examine maximum security institutions because they are the definitive case. Whatever exists in maximum security institutions exists in all other custody situations even though to a lesser extent—it is the nature of the beast. Absolute power (over another human being) does corrupt absolutely; the corruption is probably in direct proportion to the level of coercive power held by one individual over another. This characteristic of human beings surfaced in a simple role playing situation[1] where students in a prison simulation experiment actually began to psychologically abuse fellow students who were randomly assigned to the role of prisoner. The abuses became so rampant that there was fear of physical abuse and the experiment had to be terminated. Prison is not just where the body is; it is where the mind is also.

279

ENVIRONMENT

The *Random House Dictionary* (unabridged version, 1966) defines an environment as "the aggregate of surrounding things, conditions or influences, esp. as affecting the existence or development of someone or something." This definition is not sufficiently exhaustive because it ignores the internal environment—it is with reference to this *internal* psychological environment that Huxley stated, "Reality isn't what happens to a man, it is what a man does with what happens to him." It is this bipartite view of the concept environment that prompts a two-level analysis of the environment. First, what are the externally observable schedules of reinforcement that exist to support behavior, what behaviors are supported, what are the reinforcers, and who controls them? Second, what is the cognitive information that is verbally passed from staff member to staff member and prisoner to prisoner?

THE PRISONER'S POINT OF VIEW

The following are excerpts from papers written by students (who happen to be prisoners) about institutional life and how it affected them. The reader must not glean from this section that I am implying maliciousness on the part of the staff. The reader is reminded that under the best of maximum security situations the ratio of staff to prisoner is in the 50 to 1 range, under adverse conditions the ratio may be as high as 251 to 1. In many institutions there are sections of the prison that are covertly "off limits" to staff and the activities that occur there range from drinking, gambling, and drugs to homosexual rape. To a prisoner, in a maximum security setting, he has, in fact, entered a war zone and there are no Geneva Convention rules governing the hostilities. The reader must also remember that the prisoner has no safe place to turn to in prison. One of the favored negative sanctions among prisoners is the "burn out." The "burn out" is accomplished by making a Molatov cocktail from some flammable substance, catching the target inmate locked in his cell and igniting the cell—preferably when he is asleep so that should he survive he cannot identify you. The screams of a human being incinerated are not pleasant and serve as a reminder to the nonconformist (to the dictates of the prison subculture) and "snitch" (one who has given information to the authorities) to cooperate with the dominant prison culture or suffer the consequences. I have given credit for the excerpts by two initials only. Some of the language is coarse but replacing it with "expletive" would deprive the reader of what it is really like to be there. If you are thinking of a career as a correctional psychologist or officer, get used to the lingo. After all, they are only words.

VIEW FROM THE INSIDE
by
J.B., B.K., G.M., M.H., R., D.VB., and E.A.

#1

We have seen movies that make a vain attempt to relate the prison experience . . . written most often . . . from the imagination, not based in the reality of an experience. *Be aware that the prison experience is feelings and it is difficult to comprehend an emotion beyond those you have had firsthand.*

Imagine, if you will, coming into an environment where the basis of interaction is negativity, where it is seldom that you encounter a congenial greeting or nonvulgar conversation. Yet you will find such in this setting, though it will be unusual. Initially the reaction is shock, and very quickly you learn that the way you see others acting is the way to survive. Survival is the order of the day from the moment you enter until the big sliding grill closes behind you as you leave.

Entering a prison as a prisoner is the worst experience any human can encounter. The first person you meet is an officer (hack) who gives you the basic rules: "Stay out of trouble, and follow the rules." "What rules?" "You'll learn." Learning consists of humiliation as a prerequisite to making the subhuman (as perceived), now called an inmate or convict, conform. You must stand in a group of other men naked for an undetermined amount of time to be "Shook down" which is a "bend over and spread the cheeks" inspection to insure you aren't hiding contraband in your anus, which often is the case. Welcome, you are ready to enter the penitentiary population, that is after you spend two or three days in a holding cell containing a basin/toilet combination and a bed. Here you can talk to the inmates who are being held in segregation for violating a rule, like killing a fellow inmate, stabbing or beating someone with a pipe, taking sugar from the mess hall, or just talking back to an officer. Well, turkey, you're now ready to move on to become a true convict.

Now the rules: If you're weak you will be a homosexual, unless you're prepared to kill and can let it be done. You will henceforth use vulgar and profane language, steal anything that you aren't issued from any hack at anytime, never under any circumstances tell a hack anything that a fellow inmate does or doesn't do, learn that from this second on you are blind, deaf, and dumb (if something happens and you're in the general area, like the guy in the next cell yelling for help while he's stabbed twenty-five or thirty times). You know nothing. Just think, this is only an introduction to the penitentiary, where acting out is so high that you will often have a fight for accidently bumping into another inmate in the halls, which could lead to your or his death. For the same thing on the outside, the most that would happen is that you will be cursed or at least receive a frown.

From here things calm down to a regular routine. You get up at the same time, go to breakfast, to your assignment (work), return at 3:50 for lock-up and count, eat from 4:20 to 5:00, hang out until 6:00 when you lock-up again to be counted. This routine doesn't vary five days a week, when it does you know that someone has been hurt or a shakedown is in progress. Three hundred and sixty-five days a year the schedule is set without variation.

What exactly is the prison environment? To me it's having someone give you a baseball, volleyball, handball, basketball, tennisball, golfball, football, or weights. It's having a rigid schedule without variation to get-up, eat, count, move from place to place, work, and sleep. It's having someone think every thought for you, permit you to be an idiot who doesn't know better and make a thousand mistakes on the job, and can't/won't fire you. In essence, it's a two-year-old kid with overindulgent parents who do everything and don't expect or want you to put forth any effort to be responsible. If you attempt to be responsible you're punished because the parents did not tell you to initiate any action.

Prison is a house with one rule—fear. Fear is the order of the day, everyday. Fear is survival—fear of peers, fear of the staff, and most of all fear of self. Who are you, just a number? What are you, man or beast in a cage? Do you think you'll live to leave? Can you still have an independent thought or initiate an independent action? Will someone buy the wolfticket (term to indicate that you have threatened someone with physical violence through a look, glance, minor overt act, or intermediary) you have to sell and you end up with a life sentence, and you only had five or ten to start with? Will the parole board that comes in five or six years let you go back to the streets or tell you to come back to see them after you have two more years in prison? Can you hold on to your sanity, act like the crowd and tell elaborate lies, escape only through dreams and fantasy, and not go insane? Prison is an experience that makes a man doubt his membership in the human race, doubt his eyes, his ears, and his heart, doubt his own existence and self-worth, self-acceptance and ability to last until that unknown day when he will leave prison.

Prison is not only an environment, it's an experience, a voluntary experience because we (me) sent ourselves to prison with the same acting out that we continue to perpetuate here.

#2

In _____ prison there are many similarities but yet it is somewhat different. The same subculture of values exist. Inmates hated informers, took homosexuals for wives and pimped them as prostitutes to others who couldn't get their sexual needs from a woman met. Many who were not prone to such homosexuality before they came to prison became homosexually inclined after they left prison (either as a passive or aggressive homosexual). They wound up molesting kids or became some other sort of sexual dysfunctional. One person, I knew him personally, killed a couple and raped the man. He had begun as a car thief. In prison he found homosexuality. I knew a Vietnam vet with a Silver Star metal that was forced into being a homosexual for another person. But this happened in the joint. . . .

I kind of despise all homosexuals. I hate guy homosexuals whatever role they play, even the guys who are so weak they won't fight back to save their manhood. There are plenty of profiteers in the joints too. I've seen guys buy commissary items, hoard them up in their lockers, and sell them to less thoughtful inmates. There are plenty of drugs around to be had for a price. Most of the killings that go on in the joints are related in someway to drugs and homosexuality. Some are gambling related. A guy will owe too much money and can't pay or refuse to pay and there will be trouble. In the _____ joint plastic money was the medium of exchange, in the _____ joint it is cigarettes. For enough cigarettes you can get a guy's cell burnt out. And for enough greens (U.S. currency) you can have him snuffed out. Or, if you are a big organized criminal, you can have anything done for a promise to give the guy a job once he gets out.

Most inmates who are weak are very gregarious, they join anything for protection. I've seen them in everything from home town gangs to religious groups to avoid being alone. Then use the same group as a power base and carry out their assaults or other vices on others.

There are some guards who are physically sadistic to convicts; but, the Administration is just as hostile to the convicts and they can do it in a more detrimental way by putting disparaging and critical information on your record, and by placing you in solitary confinement on a hard steel bunk. I put twenty-three days in punitive seg. because I asked for a transfer and the major (in the road camp), who I requested it from, thought I was too insubordinate and put me in punitive segregation. He was one of the reasons I escaped from prison. The cockroaches we occasionally found in our bread and cookies was another. But, the central reason was my wife and three kids, I wanted to support (them). My work for the prison department paid heavy dividends for them, but they never tried to see me or any other convict get any monetary compensations in respect to the labor they extracted from us. They even threatened to put me in the hole for unsatisfactory road work, although they never cared if I had adequate basic necessities of sustaining my health and comfort. If I asked for a razor blade I was looked upon as a thief and with scorn and disdain. I don't hate everybody connected with law enforcement and the prison department, but when I escaped it sure felt good to be on the end of the gun they held on me for five years. And I splattered their blood in the streets the way they splattered my life's aims in being with my family and wife, in the bowels of their man-made hell on earth.

If the economical system is changed then the astronomical heights of crime will come down. But more than anything, the way of treating offenders as labels and the dehumanizing penal institutions have to be changed for that's where a person has to be reduced to the lowest common denominator to survive; (e.g.) men having to defend their masculinity by killing somebody or assaulting others to preserve their sexual preference; men having to sell their bodies for money; having to be a profiteer via commissary and drugs or to gamble just to make some money at the expense of the misery of other convicts, just to help support their families because the prison system won't pay even the minimum wage scale for their labor and refusing to let convicts have conjugal visits with their wives or sweethearts. Unless they make some root change in the whole judicial and penal system, crime will further increase in viciousness of every type and be more violent too, because this is the breeding ground for hatred and bitterness.

#3

After years, I'm at last beginning again. Ten years spent undoing the mess I found myself in, mentally and spiritually, after leaving the courtroom of Judge _____.

It is not possible to tell you now what that time has done to and for me in its entirety. It is a two-fold thing, you see, so what I will do is give you what I see/saw and how it affected me and my thinking on Prison Environment.

When I was delivered to the prison, chained and bound like a chattel slave, I knew that I had stepped from life into the inner most chamber of hell on earth. Once inside this chamber, humanity, I saw, moved from the light of day to the valley of the shadow of death. Yet, strange, life did go on, in a way. . . .

After my first week in the iron tomb, I was given a "kit." By whom, I don't know, for I knew no one there nor had I spoken to anyone. I found this kit under my mattress. In it was a knife about thirteen inches long and a pipe of steel about three inches in diameter of equal length. This was wrapped with a rubber band and paper. On the paper was written: "Take care home. . . ." (A term delineating someone from your geographic locale.) I questioned myself. I kept the pipe.

I was given a job in the mess hall and kept to myself for six months. I enrolled in the school. I exercised. I slowly went mad. In this length of time I saw one murder and three homosexual rapes. I withdrew further from what was me. I became a wary beast, watching and waiting for the attack.

I went to the prison industry to work. I fought to hold on to anything that I ever was. It grew darker in the darkness. I had to fight and beat another inmate viciously for a supposed insult (the wolf-ticket mentioned earlier). I was losing.

The racism was great. The officers were truly pigs. Hillbilly to the soul. Black inmates were subhuman. It was truly 1803.

I needed sex, BAD! Not prison homo action, but a real female pussy! My sex drive was terrible. Wet dreams reg. Just the thought of a woman dressed in anything gave a hard-on you would not believe possible. (Now, it's different. The mere thought of my first sex act after nine years gives the feeling of extreme fear. It's a very sick feeling—fear. How the hell do you do it?) I could not seek out a homo, (never did . . .) so it kept building pressure.

In _____ my daughter died. I was not allowed to leave to attend the funeral because of the length of my sentence. I became a time bomb.

I went off into Black Nationalism for many reasons. The main reason being to hold on to a piece of me somehow. To try and understand my people and myself. Since white people were oppressing me and mine, that was the route. White people were the cause, the effect was my being in a prison. So, I threw another log on the fire.

In _____ I blew. I went insane along with a group of black inmates. Resistance. To what? My madness? I was beaten unconscious with axe handles to the point of death and thrown into a concrete strip cell. Without aide of any kind, without water and food for a week, I lived. I came back. Back to what? My hate sat down to a feast.

We were placed at length into what is known as long-term seg. I knew what would be happening. Back to court. What did it matter? I would never be sane again, would I? Prison life on and on. Emotions were willed to death one by one.

While I was in the seg. unit, the officers started a reign of terror—beatings, insults, more beatings. To break a nigger time. To debase a man to the point of suicide or kill him, became the order of the day. The cell started closing in. Six by nine ain't enough space for the mind to deal with day by day, month after month, year after year. But I found out once you can shut the emotions off, you can develop a kind of frozen mindless contentment. You have to. While your body sits in a cell, your brain has to curl up on itself and go to sleep—in deep-freeze, if you will. You must analyze it, question it. You must learn to live inwardly—say in books or building illustrations in your head, say of chess games or women. Build a woman, see every hair, every muscle, every organ; see every part of her, then see her brain and her very thought process, then the thought itself. Knowledge will have to become your narcotic. The alternative is worse. Psychosis. If you're unable to discipline yourself, you'll learn that the inner pain of psychosis is worse than torture. You have to learn to live with time and yet be unaware of it. It's like a cancer. It's always latent, and it can start growing at any time—a cancer of the mind. Time can be like a dripping acid.

The prison environment of seg. made me write to anybody. I wrote to get a grip on things black and most importantly, reality. It started working. I read and wrote. I slowly came back.

Before the days of Bank Robbery were College days and Working days, White people—students, professors, and my daughter's mother. That was over. I no longer wrote to them. I was a strange mixture of Muslim and Black Nationalist.

Every morning I got up, I said to myself—here's another day to look forward to. Every night I went to bed, I said, "that's another day I crossed over and won't get back because of prison questions and thoughts." Like, all any woman wants is a little love. It's always, for some, to have the misfortune to fall in love or with men to have murder or money in their hearts. One's as bad as the other. (Which am I?)

For my trouble and the trouble I caused, I was given an additional two years and sent to _____.

In my summary for this paper, let me say Prison Environment is a number of things and none of them good. I doubt that the Inquisition and the Jesuits could have designed pressures to break the spirit and destroy the moral and intellectual integrity so very thoroughly. To understand punishment calculated to make you feel lost, isolated, hopelessly trapped, you have to feel it and live it. To be deprived of female companionship all the time, to not see or hear children, and at times bereft of even a fellow prisoner's counsel must be seen and lived. You can not understand the debtor-creditor relationship played every day. Oh, yeah! You don't know that one, huh? Dig: The jailor becomes a benefactor to whom the prisoner is indebted for seemingly generous favors. To the man long in jail, the least morsel of compassion, a mere word of encouragement may elicit gratitude. Add a villain (Asshole officer). A role calculated to keep the prisoner in tension and off balance.

#4

Norman Mailer once wrote: "Being a man is the continuing battle of one's life, and one loses a bit of manhood with every stale compromise to the authority of any power in which one does not believe." In prison, one of the ways that *some* (not the majority) of prisoners keep from completely surrendering to the powers of repression while maintaining their humanity and manhood, is to make the prison experience serve them instead of them serving it. In my opinion, the best way to achieve the above (squeezing something positive out of the prison experience) is for the prisoner to convert the prison experience from an agent of humiliation and repression into an agent of growth, into an educational experience by making prison into his Harvard, his Yale, his Howard University.

To me, the prison environment is also the street academy of many of the dispossessed of the world. It is the place that creates and re-

fines everything from professional criminals to dedicated revolution-
aries; it is the place where you can pick your field in the area of crime
to participate in, from pickpocketing to pimping, from petty thievery
to high-class larceny; it is the place where you have the time, plus the
bitterness, to drive you into mastering the difficult revolutionary
works of Marx, Engels, Lenin, Mao, Malcom X, George Jackson, and
others. I tell you, prison is school!

#5

I should begin by saying I came to prison rather late in life, at the
age of thirty plus. I was a businessman, well established in the community, wealthy, and having a fairly happy family life. Then,
gradually I became bored with the everyday scheme of things. This,
I should hasten to add, was my downfall.

Rule number one in prison is not to be around anything taking
place that you are not involved in. Rule number two is, you neither
hear, speak nor see anything that is none of your business. Rule
number three in prison is not to ask anyone what they are doing time
for. The sad part about these three rules, which are the code of most
convicts, is that it is only a dream. You do not have to watch the
man (administration), as you know, he will place you in the hole if
you do something wrong; you have to watch your fellow constituents.

This life is only an existence. It's demoralizing, repressive, and
sick. Homosexuality is rampant, loan sharking, drug dealing, locker
breaking (B & E or stealing), gambling, and drinking are just a few
of the things that make-up everyday life at this place. If you believe
the convicts are bad, the administration is no better, as they allow
these things to exist.

The administration represses speech, outside ties, and visits. The
2nd Circuit Court of Appeals said in a recent decision, "It is not the
job of prisons to punish, the sentence one receives is punishment
enough."

The administration should reward good behavior, praise someone
who attains a college degree, etc., reward those who establish good
work habits and save money, and help those who wish only to do their
time and return to a productive life in society. Counselors, caseworkers, etc. should do their utmost in establishing some sort of
rapport with the inmates to make their stay easier and help with suggestions to improve their standing. They should reward convicts with
early release recommendations and receive inputs from job availability

agencies, so that he may have a job waiting for him on release.

Visits, correspondence privileges, educational, vocational, religious, and psychotherapy programs, to name a few, should be available to all. Every convict participates in a complex set of social relations, bonds, alliances, compromises, and conflicts between hundreds of convicts, guards, administrators, teachers, workers, psychologists, and physicians. Convicts do more than pay society for their crime and "learn their lesson," they *live* twenty-four hours a day in prison. Prison is an education in itself.

When a person enters prison, having hundreds of years of time, there is no incentive for him to do anything constructive, unless he knows with certainty that sometime in the future he will be released. This can be accomplished by goals being set by the administration toward this aim. I believe this would cut down on the violence and give one something to strive for.

In closing, I would like to see one immediate change in the . . . System, realistic goals set by the administration for the individual, so that when he reaches them, he will know that a parole will be forthcoming. This will give each person a goal to reach, knowing at the completion, he can once again enter into society and begin a new life. If he can complete this goal set by the administration, he should have no problem in doing the same in society.

#6

When most people think of home, they have visions of a sweet old lady in a rocking chair with kids playing on the living room floor and the air filled with pleasant aromas of apple pie and fresh baked bread. It would be nice if everyone had this and could return to it in the evenings after a hard day's work. Unfortunately, not everyone has the same vision of home.

There are thousands of us who never leave home for a moment except to go outside for a short while every few years, just long enough to find some judge who is willing to send us home again with a new sentence. This isn't too hard to understand when you realize that "home" to me is prison. Any of the . . . maximum security prisons will fill the bill.

Close examination of the facts show that I commit misdeeds for no apparent reason other than to force society to send me home. Once back home, there are old friends who understand me and welcome me back with open arms. These friends all have an unspoken agreement to listen to and act as though they believe each other's stories about big fancy apartments that come equipped with a half-dozen beautiful girls and a minimum of three Cadillacs.

The agreement calls for each to ignore any discrepancies in the other's stories and not to mention that we burn each other for Bull Durham makings while we tell about the hundred and eighty-eight thousand dollars we have hidden away in a safety deposit box. Though we seldom admit it, we all know that these stories do nothing except hide the ugly truth we each have buried deep inside.

To little boys, home is a haven against the fears, the insecurity, and the everyday tribulations of life. Home is feeling safe from all of these and, in addition, there is food, clothing, and shelter. If he gets sick there is someone to administer to him.

These advantages make it easy to understand why a man will cling to a desire to return home regardless of where his travels may take him. In prison there are few fears and uncertainties over tomorrow, because tomorrow will be a carbon copy of today. It will be very safe and very secure. Prison is a little like a womb where you are nurtured without having to assume any responsibilities. You don't even have to go to the mess hall if you don't want to—you can cuss out a guard and be sent to segregation where food is delivered three times a day.

In eleven years I've finally realized that in fact there are so many things missing in my life that I really don't know what life is all about, and that is why I stay at "home" so much. I have filled my computer banks with irrational and incorrect data and often actually believe that I'm conducting my life in a sensible manner, and that I'm sent home each time I leave by people "out there" who "have it in for me."

My perspective on the . . . correctional system is that it is designed and operated to reinforce the belief systems of all the "scared little boys" who enter into it.

A PSYCHOLOGIST'S POINT OF VIEW

As a psychologist, prisons appear to me to be illogical, irrational, and in many ways insane environments. I am committed to change, and as a change agent I would not design and locate prisons the way they are currently. Those who disagree with me point out that some men are so disturbed, have so much time to do (sometimes hundreds of years) and so little to live for that the maximum security environment is necessary. I agree. I disagree with a sentencing strategy that places individuals in the position that escape is the only viable alternative left open to them.

Maximum security environments are custodial, "human warehouse" situations. The primary function of *all* staff members is containment. The doctor-patient privilege is constantly tested: How does one remain silent about an impending escape attempt that may cost the lives of other patients and co-workers? How does one remain silent about the jealousy of a homosexual affair that is about to result in murder? How does one deal with information about crimes that the patient has not been tried for? How does one deal with obvious inequities in treatment? How does one deal with the frustration when a patient, who is ready for discharge from treatment and prison, is told that "parole at this time would deprecate the seriousness of the offense? Therefore, we are recommending a two-year set off." How does one deal with the systematic resistance of treatment by the custodial staff? How does a psychologist feel about not being included in the decision-making process, being involved in the treatment strategy for each inmate? How does the psychologist feel about having any and all activities cancelled in the name of security? As a psychologist you are considered a softhead, a bleeding heart liberal. You are not really to be trusted because the custodial staff believes you are on the convict's side. That is only half of the prison environment.

How do the inmates perceive you? To many inmates, you are someone to be conned; someone who might write a good report for the parole board; someone who might testify to your sanity or lack of it, depending on their particular need at a particular time. You are the person whom they would like to have intercede with the physician (there is usually not a psychiatrist on regular staff) for some psychotropic medication. You are the person that they would like to intercede with the custodial staff for a job change, a different work assignment. You are the person they come to when they are afraid of being raped or murdered or to help them deal with pressure to engage in some activity they do not want to.

It is difficult for them to turn to the custodial staff because they do not want to be labelled a snitch. The custodial staff is, by necessity, reflexive. They can act after someone has been harmed but not before. Otherwise some unscrupulous and or frightened inmates would have everyone locked up who either was uncooperative or who attempted to sell them a wolfticket. The staff has learned through experience that unless there is overwhelming evidence that an event will occur, let it occur. This rule does not apply to custody issues or contraband issues. If there is the slightest possibility that security will be violated or contraband introduced into the institution, act.

As a prison psychologist some inmates will attempt to use therapy time as a way to avoid work. There is extreme reluctance on the part of anyone to participate in group sessions. Prisons breed paranoia. Not as a delusional system, but as an ego maintenance device. Paranoia in prison is healthy. One does not know who is planning what, that may involve you. Someone overheard you talking about John Doe and only heard the John part and that is his name. Now he thinks you are out to get him. In order to avoid that he must get you first. Keep your back to the wall. The inmates are paranoid about the psychologist also. They may feed you false information to see if it makes its way to the custodial staff. Many of them are professional patients and know psychiatric jargon as well as you do. They will give you the clinical clues to look for problems in the wrong place.

When someone comes to the psychologist, that is a sign of weakness and therapeutic programs are looked upon as places to obtain special favors. Few of the inmates who join a group are interested in helping themselves or others. The first question is "When are we going to have a banquet? How many street people will we have contact with?"

The defensive structure of the hard-core offender is nearly impregnable. Transactional analytic (TA) approaches yielded some inroads[2] into successful treatment through a combination of the Synanon Game, T. A., and a behavioristic total learning environment. The thinking structure of the character disorder is defined as a pretend structure. Character disorders believe that they will never get their needs met like street people, so they adopt the character disorder life-style and then say they like it, and that is the way they want to be. The entire defensive structure is predicated on maintaining those beliefs. That is why they are so hard to treat, not because of some neurological dysfunction. Yochelson and Samenow[3] have done an extensive analysis of the thinking structure of character disorders and should be consulted by anyone dealing with or planning a career in the correctional field.

The picture painted regarding the environment from a correctional psychologist's point of view is bleak. It is painted in black and grey and red—depression, despair, and violence. I would be remiss if I did not point out that there is a small percentage of inmates who actively and seriously seek help and who change their behavior and thinking pattern and become productive members of society. I would also be remiss if I failed to note that there are some correctional administrators and correctional officers who are dedicated to returning these men to productive life. However, I would be a liar if I said there were an abundance of either.

HOW DID THE ENVIRONMENT EVOLVE?

The description in the first part of this chapter and the lamentations of the prisoners might lead the reader to assume that this is just another carping criticism of the prison system. Without some attempt to stand back and attempt to make sense of the relationships that produce the environment, it would be just that.

The way I conceptualize the prison environment is as a three-way interaction or, if you prefer, three vectors with the resultant being the environment. The first vector is the prisoner belief system and the environmental contingencies controlled by them. The second vector is the staff belief system and the contingencies they control. The third vector is external forces such as the parole board, the courts, families, prisoner support groups, etc. and their belief system and the contingencies they control.

Recall for a moment the content of the prisoners' descriptions. The factors that weighed most heavily were (a) prisoner to prisoner violence with the ultimate, immediate sanction—death; (b) the reduction in self-concept by being given a number and having one's decision-making power reduced to the minimum, a label of irresponsibility and coercive power invested in a keeper who has guns and is willing to use them; (c) the lack of definition regarding behaviors that will result in eventual release; (d) the reduction or loss of emotional and familial ties, normal sexual behavior, and a totally "masculine" environment essentially devoid of the emotions typically assigned to females; and (e) loss of hope for the future.

Prison has never approximated a "normal" environment because of beliefs held by correctional thinkers and the line personnel regarding the level of functioning of prisoners. Prisoners are conceptualized as atavistic, subnormal in intellect, possessing insufficient impulse control, and having little or no conscience. They have been assigned these attributes because at times they exhibit them, they are expected of them, and, most importantly, the environment supports those attributes. Psychologists have classic cases of paranoia, catatonia, and hysteria. These classic definitive cases, e.g. *Three Faces of Eve, Sybil,* are used as examples for new students in the field. They enter their practices using these examples as the norm and their reference point. Psychology has recently attacked itself for the misuse of tests and labels because they are not explanations but descriptions. The grand illusion is that naming it explains it. The same process occurs in corrections. Manson, Speck, Whitman, Oswald, and, in the past, Leopold and Loeb have been the exemplars of criminal thinking and behavior. Each new act of violence reinforces these beliefs. With these classic cases as a referent it is no wonder that correctional personnel think they are protecting the people from heinous criminals. I have observed a perverse pleasure among some correctional workers when they have a nationally known criminal in their custody. It adds prestige to an otherwise low status job.

Many of the readers are aware of the classic work of Allyon and Azrin[4] regarding the employee's contribution to the continued "crazy" behavior of mental patients. The cycle was broken when the staff stopped supporting and attending to disturbing behaviors and, instead, reinforced normal prosocial behavior and personal responsibility. Those activities desired by the mental patients (including furloughs and release) were made contingent upon normal behavior. When the staff stopped treating the patients as if they were crazy, they stopped behaving as if they were crazy. The environment obtains the behavior it requests for continued participation in that environment.

The vector representing staff beliefs and the contingencies they control has been described, in part, in the two previous paragraphs. It was suggested that the staff obtains some status from being vested with the responsibility for containing vicious, dangerous, unpredictable criminals. The staff has the expectation that any and all behavior is, or could potentially be, in the service of escape or gaining some strategic advantage over the staff.

I do not think the staff is purposely abusive, informal, aloof, or cold. If one performs a task repeatedly (such as a strip search, interrogation, introduction to the institution, etc.) the task becomes perfunctory. If one trusts, invests extensive energy, and thinks he has helped an inmate change and the inmate returns in six weeks, the staff member becomes cynical. If a new employee finds a prisoner under his care drunk, drugged, engaging in rape, abusing another inmate, or is informed by another correctional staff member that this prisoner has committed a brutal crime or held women and children hostage, he becomes hardened and unsympathetic. When the new staff member has been conned by an inmate he trusted, he protects himself by not trusting again.

The other part of the correctional officer's education is cognitive. The socialization of the correctional officer is directed at "don't be made a fool of." This is accomplished by the internal dialogue of "don't get close to inmates" and "don't trust inmates." The parole board further demeans the role of the correctional officer and correctional staff by ignoring recommendations made by the institution. The institutional staff are intimately aware of the behavior and attitudes of those in their care. Yet, the parole board is under no obligation to follow their recommendation.

To summarize, the correctional officer must present a cold, aloof, implacable visage with a smiling person while harboring the beliefs that he is guarding vicious, malicious, manipulative, hardened criminals who would kill him if necessary to obtain their freedom.

The vector produced by the inmates is well captured in several of the views from the inside. The environment is incredibly calloused. The "convict code" requires that you do not traffic with the staff. The good convict hears no evil, sees no evil, and speaks no truth. The worst violation of the convict code is to snitch. A known snitch has a noticeably short life span unless given a new identity and shipped to an institution where he is not known or locked up in protective custody. The reinforcement schedule among the prisoners is positive reinforcement for engaging in convict activities (gambling, drugs, drinking, escape plans) and punishment (ostracization, physical abuse, and death) for noncompliance, such as being friendly with staff, which could be misconstrued as snitching. The reader may think that being ostracized would actually be a blessing. It must be recalled that anyone alone is vulnerable. Without friends you have no "muscle" and are extremely vulnerable.

The combined effects of the prisoner–staff reinforcement schedules setup a we–they environment. The battle lines are well drawn and communication is kept at a minimum, since talking to the staff could be construed as snitching. From the staff point of view, getting close to prisoners is a setup for disappointment and makes the rest of the staff wonder about your wisdom and commitment to the job. The old maxim "if you aren't with us, you're against us" is reinforced on both sides of the line.

The third vector is produced by external forces. By being deprived of contact with families on a regular and continued basis, the environment inside the prison becomes the real environment and the external world exists in memory and fantasy only. Several of the views from the inside reflect the bitterness that comes from not being able to fill the masculine role in this culture—the role of provider. The result is a decrement in self-esteem. Many wives suffer the privations that come from having an incarcerated husband. Many have "arrangements" whereby the wife is free as long as he is incarcerated. Many simply divorce their husbands.

Another factor in the third vector is the parole board. They may behave capriciously, ignoring several years of good behavior, educational gains, skill acquisition, and a viable parole plan with the old tune "release at this time would deprecate the seriousness of the offense." The result—despair. Ask most prisoners what their prospect for parole is and they will tell you that it makes little sense to engage in programs because the parole board will not seriously consider parole until at least one third of the sentence has been served *regardless* of institutional activities and behavior.

The result of these three vectors is a calloused, hopeless we–they environment, where a life can be purchased for as little as a carton of cigarettes or the promise of a job with organized crime upon release. The environment is not responsive to institutional programs because the parole board can and does ignore programming and institutional recommendations in favor of a fixed interval schedule, based not on responses but on time. The ultimate negative sanction is death and that sanction is controlled by the prisoners not the staff. The institution is not allowed to set goals and release the prisoner upon successful completion; the court (by omission) and parole board (by commission) have stripped the institution of any reinforcement power.

RECOMMENDATIONS FOR CHANGE

One of the nicest aspects of recommending changes is not being charged with the responsibility of implementing them. Since the charge is not implementation, I can be as grandiose as I choose. Some correctional administrators will read these recommendations and assert that I'm not "playing with a full deck." Those responsible for change (policy decisions) need to ask themselves if they sincerely wish for the prison environment to continue as it is or if it is worth the effort to modify the environment. The prison business is no different than any other, inertia is difficult to overcome. It is simpler to continue doing what has always been done than to implement change. There would be massive resistance, on the part of prisoners and line staff alike, to some of these recommendations.

NORMALIZE THE ENVIRONMENT

When men live with other men exclusively they begin to drop social amenities, their language becomes coarse, and they become "real" men. Women do not reinforce the same behaviors that men do, and we call the process socialization. Any of the readers who have lived in an all-male (or for that matter all-female) environment understand what I am alluding to. There are behaviors for social environments (heterosexual) and for restricted (all-male/all-female) environments. The two are unquestionably different. I have observed the introduction of females into juvenile and adult correctional settings. The major changes are the following: appearance improves, language usage changes from expletives to appropriate adjectives, tough veneers soften, incidents of physical abuse disappear, and psychological problems related to women emerge and can be treated. The counterarguments are that rape is a possibility, women make better hostages (psychological effect on public), and they lack the physical strength to control a violent man.

INCREASE THE ROLE OF THE INSTITUTION IN THE PAROLE DECISION

The intent of the Department of Justice, where the Parole Board is concerned, was to provide a review and decision-making system regarding the release of institutionalized offenders. The guidelines specify that a person may be released at almost anytime depending on circumstances and, unless institutional adjustment is extremely poor, the stay should not exceed one-third of the sentence. In 1975 the Parole Board notified the country that it planned to change its rules. Interested parties were invited to respond. In the revised rules, September 5, 1975, of the Federal Register[5] it is stated: "Generally the guidelines were criticized for failing to consider with sufficient emphasis, rehabilitation or institutional progress. However, one comment stated that although prison performance is relevant to the parole decision, the Board's guidelines *correctly deemphasize* (my italics) rehabilitative factors which social science suggests can neither be detected nor measured."

As I recall my appearances in front of the board on behalf of an inmate I become very angry. What I did not realize was that they had already decided that I was not capable of making that assessment and were humoring me. This small section in the parole guidelines substantiates that which was previously implied—bring us (the parole board) one third of the sentence or we will respond with "Release at this time would deprecate the seriousness of the offense." With this as given, where is the motivation or incentive to change? The parole board relies instead on actuarial prediction tables, the salient factor score.[6] What they fail to recognize is that the salient factor score is *determined* when one enters prison for the current offense and there is *nothing* the offender can do to change that score. Where is the motivation to change?

Put yourself in the place of an inmate, caseworker, custodial staff, counselor, psychologist, or psychiatrist and realize that what you say is automatically discounted if not blatantly ignored. I am arguing that if inmates' behavior and staff members' evaluations were influential in the parole decision, wouldn't the motivation to set and meet goals improve? If inmates and staff members were working toward the *common goal* of rehabilitation, wouldn't the we–they attitude that draws one of the battle lines in the war zone shift or even disappear? If institutional performance means something, wouldn't the likelihood of asocial behavior decrease?

EMPHASIZE DIGNITY AND RESPONSIBILITY

If a man's behavior is the factor that controls his release, rather than the amount of time he has served, it is my contention that he will act in his own best interest. If his behavior is poor, if he makes no effort to acquire the skills, attitudes, and behaviors that will facilitate his release success, it is *his* responsibility. Behaviorists have known for years that the worst schedule for high stable rates of performance is the fixed interval schedule. These schedules are like tests in school. Most human beings emit few of the desired behaviors (reading the book and class notes) until a few nights before the examination. A fixed interval of time prior to release has the same effect. What is the use of denying oneself the creature comforts and diversions available in a monotonous ("every day's a carbon copy of the one before") environment if the net gain is zero for doing so? If there is no premium on responsible behavior and the primary concern is on behaving as an automaton (for the sake of an orderly institution), then what is learned other than institutional adjustment? There will be no correctional officer to tell the released prisoner when to shave or get a haircut, control hair length, specify dress, regulate the spending of his earnings, or wake him; and the employer on the streets will fire him if his work performance is below par.

MAKE TREATMENT AND POST RELEASE ADJUSTMENT THE FOCUS OF THE INSTITUTION

It has been argued quite cogently that institutions are not designed for rehabilitation but for punishment. From my observation, I would concur. Martinson[7] has been cited continuously as a justification for everything from the elimination of therapeutic programs to the justice model. Martinson has been sorely misquoted for he did not state that treatment is not effective; he stated that few studies were of scientific merit and of those few that were, there was no clear-cut demonstration of the efficacy of treatment over control comparisons. That is a far cry from stating treatment does not work.

Treatment has never been tried on a large scale, there are few, if any, research dollars available for outcome studies of various intervention strategies; there are several new nonbiological, etiological models of criminal behavior that appear promising for the future[2,3,8] but they have not received the support moneys for assessment of effectiveness. The Federal Bureau of Prisons designed their Butner, North Carolina facility for testing the effectiveness of several intervention models, but public resistance (ignorance and the desire for a pound of flesh) resulted in it being turned into a very comfortable warehouse.

This chapter has presented the prison environment from an extreme, yet I contend accurate, point of view. The environment has been painted as black, grey, and red—depressed, despairing, and violent. From a behavioristic point of view the behavior emitted in an environment is the behavior that is reinforced in that environment. Brehm[9] has argued that when you attempt to change human beings through coercion (negative reinforcement and punishment), a phenomena he labelled *reactance* occurs. Reactance means that if one tells me I *have* to go east then I will go west. It has been argued that the environment is unnatural and fosters irresponsibility. It has further been argued that until that environment becomes normalized and supports and fosters prosocial behavior, it will continue to be a breeding ground for more (sophisticated) asocial behavior. The call has been to revise sentencing practices and turn the prisons into reclamation centers rather than graduate schools in crime ("My Harvard, My Yale, My Howard University").

REFERENCES

1. Haney, C., Banks, C., and Zimbardo, P. Interpersonal dynamics in a simulated prison, *International Journal of Criminology and Penology, 1,* 69–97, 1973.
2. Groder, M. *Asklepieion — an effective treatment method for incarcerated character disorders,* Marion, United States Penitentiary, 1972.
3. Yochelson, S. and Samenow, S. *The criminal personality,* Vol. I, New York, Jason Aronson, 1976.
4. Allyon, T. and Azrin, H. *The token economy: A motivational system for therapy and rehabilitation,* New York, Appleton-Century-Crofts, 1968.
5. *Federal Register, 40,* (173), September 5, 1975.
6. Hoffman, P. and Beck, J. Parole decision making: A salient factor score, *Journal of Criminal Justice, 2,* 195–206, 1974.
7. Martinson, R. What works? — Questions and answers about prison reform, *The Public Interest,* (35), Spring 1974.
8. Glasser, W. *The identity society,* New York, Harper and Row, 1972.
9. Brehm, J.W. *A theory of psychological reactance,* New York, Academic Press, 1966.

Chapter 24

PSYCHOLOGICAL ASPECTS OF PAROLE*

James L. Beck

Parole in the United States serves two functions in the correctional process. First, parole is a system by which incarcerated offenders can be released from prison before the maximum term of their sentence. Secondly, parole is a means of supervising and aiding offenders in the community after release. The present paper is concerned only with the psychological aspects of the decision process involved in granting parole and does not address the area of parole supervision.

There are at present two philosophies of parole. One philosophy can be called a treatment or rehabilitation model of parole. The history of this approach extends back to the earliest uses of parole in the nineteenth century.[1] Adherents of the treatment model hold that protection of society through rehabilitation of the offender is the major goal of the criminal justice process. In this approach, parole is used as a means of promoting the rehabilitation of the offender by releasing those who have shown themselves to be reformed in the opinion of the individuals making the release decision. Punishment as a correctional goal has been held by many of these theorists to be beneath the dignity of an enlightened, democratic society. Menninger, for one, has written that "before we can diminish our sufferings from the ill-controlled aggressive assaults of fellow citizens, we must renounce the philosophy of punishment, the obsolete, vengeful penal attitude."[2]

In contrast to the treatment model, there has developed an alternative parole philosophy that can be labelled a justice or punishment model of parole. This approach is concerned with basing the release

*The opinions expressed in the report are those of the author and do not represent the official position or policy of either the United States Parole Commission or the United States Bureau of Prisons.

from prison on factors other than rehabilitation.   Generally these factors are the seriousness of the commitment offense, extensiveness of prior criminal behavior, and risk to the community when the offender is released.

The motivating forces behind the justice approach to parole have been two-fold. A strong motivation has been the desire of some to use parole as a means of reducing sentencing disparity at the judicial level by "resentencing" offenders at the time of the parole hearing.   A decision to release offenders from prison based on the nature of the offense and/or prior record can have the effect of equalizing inconsistent sentences of varying lengths if the parole decision itself is consistent.   A second motivation behind the justice model has been the backlash to what many view as the excesses of the treatment model. There has been a reaction to the entire treatment approach to corrections on the part of many criminologists, lawyers, and public action groups.   The major indictments of the treatment model have been the following:[3]

A. There is no consensus on the cause of crime or the proper treatment of offenders, so not too surprisingly efforts at rehabilitation have not shown demonstrable success. Reviews of the literature[4] on the effectiveness of treatment have been almost entirely negative.

B. Treatment has, in many cases, been more inhumane than incarceration solely for punishment.

C. Much of what has been done in the name of rehabilitation has not been subject to the same legal constraints as punitive measures.

D. Parole tied to rehabilitation violates a basic individual right by coercing inmates (under the threat of withholding parole) to undergo treatment they might not seek of their own free will.

In addition to the above arguments, others have argued that parole based on rehabilitation has increased the pain of being incarcerated by basing the parole decision on vague criteria thereby making it difficult for an offender to know when he will be released.[5,6,7] In addition, many working in criminal justice have felt that incarcerated offenders themselves are strongly opposed to a system of release based on rehabilitation.[8,9]   Cohen, Cole, and Bailey[10] in a study of prison violence indicated that the abolition of the indeterminate sentence and release tied to rehabilitation is one possible means of reducing violence. Jones[11] found that imprisonment was detrimental to the physical and mental health of those imprisoned. Among the reasons for this, Jones cites the uncertainty of the parole decision and suggests that "prison sentences should be for a time certain, not subject to reduction for vague and subjective reasons such as 'good time' or rehabilitative progress."

Research has recently been conducted contrasting the treatment and justice models of parole. The purpose of this research was an attempt to measure the effect that the two philosophies of parole have on incarcerated offenders' perceptions of the way parole is decided. Offenders being heard for parole under two different parole systems, one a treatment system and one a justice system, were interviewed and asked to evaluate the decision process.

The two parole systems studied were the United States Parole Commission and the Pennsylvania Board of Probation and Parole. The United States Parole Commission makes use of parole decision guidelines to structure its decision making. In the federal system, the amount of time to be spent in prison is specified as a range of time[12] taking into account two major dimensions: seriousness of the offense and risk of committing a new crime. Seriousness of the offense[13] is determined by board policy. Risk of recidivism is measured by an actuarial device,[14] termed a "Salient Factor Score," containing elements primarily related to prior record. For example, in the case of adult offenders, "poor" risk auto thieves can expect to serve twenty-four to thirty months while "good" risk armed robbers can expect to serve thirty-six to forty-five months. Within the specified range, the hearing examiners can take into account institutional discipline and program achievement, either as an indicator of risk, a means of maintaining order in the institution, or to encourage the constructive use of prison time. In addition, the examiners are free to make a decision above or below the guideline range provided they give adequate reason. Although institutional behavior is not ignored, the federal parole board is basically a sentencing panel primarily concerned with assuring that the punishments meted out to offenders for purposes of retribution, deterrence, or incapacitation are equitable and consistent. (The procedures for the United States Parole Commission described are those in effect at the time of the study. Subsequent to the study, some changes were made in the procedures. Under the new procedures, positive behavior in the institution will not, other than in exceptional circumstances, advance a parole date, but negative behavior can extend it.)

The Pennsylvania parole board is typical of many state boards.

In theory, the board can consider any relevant information in deciding parole, but in practice the board considers primarily institutional behavior, recommendations from the institutional staff, and adequacy of release plan. The judge, in most cases, is presumed to have considered offense seriousness and length of prior record in determining the original sentence; therefore, these are not considered to a great extent in deciding parole. The board, however, is not precluded from considering the nature of the offense or prior record and can deny parole on that basis.

Translated into a parole philosophy, the Pennsylvania board is generally treatment oriented, with retribution and incapacitation of secondary importance. If an inmate does well in the institution, he is generally paroled at his initial parole consideration and if he is denied parole, it is usually because his institutional behavior is not judged to be adequate.

The decision in the federal system is a consideration of the length of time to be served based primarily on offense and risk assessment (heavily weighted in favor of prior record). Again, the federal board can be viewed as a sentencing panel designed to equalize sentence lengths based on specified criteria. In Pennsylvania, on the other hand, the decision is a dichotomous parole/no parole decision based primarily on prison behavior with relatively short continuances. "Good" prison behavior is not defined but is rather left to the judgment of the board.

Offender perceptions of the parole decision process were measured on a number of dimensions. Using the research of Moos[15,16,17] measuring the quality of psychological environments in prison as a starting point, the two parole systems being studied were evaluated on three descriptive dimensions felt to measure the quality of parole decision-making. The three dimensions were as follows:

1. *Clarity:* The extent to which the factors on which the parole decisions are based are known to the offender.
2. *Certainty:* The extent to which the offender is able to predict the parole decision in advance for the hearing.
3. *Control:* The extent to which the offender is able to influence the parole decision in his favor.

The dimensions were measured by true/false questions similar in format to those used by Moos in his development of the Correctional Institutions Environment Scale.[15] Typical questions asked were as follows: (1) Do residents understand what the parole board base their decisions on (Clarity)? (2) Do residents know before the hearing whether or not they will be paroled (Certainty)? (3) What the residents do in the institution can help achieve earlier release (Control)? Each question was scored as "one" if the item was answered positively and as "zero" if the item was answered negatively. The responses to each question were then summed to produce a separate total score for each of the three dimensions. An item was not included in the analysis if it was not found to correlate with the score on the dimension it was designed to measure. The scores for each dimension ranged from zero to four on Clarity, zero to six on Certainty, and zero to nine on Control.

In addition to these three descriptive dimensions, offender satisfaction with the parole decision process was also examined. As with the other dimensions, satisfaction was measured by true/false questions that were summed to produce a total score (ranging from zero to four) on a dimension labelled Approval. A typical item was the following: Residents feel that the parole process is basically fair.

Two basic areas of research were addressed. One research question was whether the two philosophies of parole produce different perceptions of the decision process. For example, a justice approach to parole might be expected to result in greater Clarity and Certainty scores because the criteria for parole are not as vague. Likewise, one might predict that the treatment approach would score higher on Control because a parole decision based on rehabilitation is more likely to be influenced by what the offender accomplishes in the institution. A second question was what effect the different philosophies of parole would have on offender self-reported satisfaction with the decision process. In other words, do offenders prefer a treatment or justice model of parole?

The subjects for the study were selected by taking all the names of those appearing on a parole docket for a particular month provided they were adults and scheduled for their first parole hearing. All subjects were interviewed within ten days before the scheduled hearing. In Pennsylvania, 101 subjects were chosen for study. Of these, 91 were interviewed, 1 refused, and 9 could not be interviewed, e.g. subject did not speak English or was not present in the institution on the day of the interview. In the federal system, 141 subjects were identified. Of these, 112 were interviewed, 7 refused, and 22 could not be interviewed.

Using a covariance design to control for differences in the groups, the results showed that the treatment oriented system scored sig-

The Role of the Forensic Psychologist

nificantly (p < .05) higher on the Control dimension (*see* Table 24-I). As might be predicted, those in the treatment oriented system felt that they possessed more personal influence over the parole decision. As one illustrative item that went into the total score on Control, 81 percent of the state subjects agreed that completing program goals in education could help an offender "make parole" compared to 64 percent of the federal subjects.

TABLE 24-I

COMPARISON OF DIMENSION SCORES ADJUSTED FOR SAMPLE
DIFFERENCES: STATE VERSUS FEDERAL

Dimension	State (N = 91)	Federal (N = 112)	F-Value (D f = 1,197)
Clarity	1.85	1.97	.33
Certainty	1.38	1.78	2.62
Control	6.69	5.56	5.85*
Approval**	1.76	.76	17.559†

* = p .05
† = p .001
**D f = 1,196

No differences were found between the two systems on the Clarity or Certainty dimensions. Problems were encountered in attempting to measure Clarity so conclusions are difficult to draw. Both systems, however, appeared to provide an equal degree of predictability. In addition to the fact that there were no significant differences on the Certainty scores, 76 percent state subjects and 72 percent of the federal subjects accurately predicted in advance whether or not they would be paroled.

A marked difference was also found in the degree of hostility expressed by offenders towards the two systems. After adjusting for sample differences, the treatment oriented system scored significantly higher (p < .001) on the Approval dimension designed to measure inmate satisfaction with parole decision-making (*see* Table 24-I). Again, on one illustrative item that made up the total score on Approval, 48 percent of the state subjects agreed that the parole process is "basically fair." Only 20 percent of the federal subjects agreed with that statement.

Not only did the treatment system appear to stimulate greater offender approval of the decision process, but it seemed that a perception of some personal control over the decision was the element that most affected the score on Approval. The correlation between the score on Control and the score on Approval (r = .48; p < .001) was higher than the correlations between other dimension scores. Also, the score on Control was found to be the strongest predictor of Approval in a stepwise regression analysis.

On a more personal level, the comments offered by the federal offenders interviewed also pointed this out. Many of those interviewed complained about the use of the guidelines (47 of 112 federal subjects) and the feeling that what they accomplished in the institution made no difference in being paroled (32 of 112 federal subjects). An inmate publication[18] circulated shortly after the interviews were completed summed up the feelings of many federal subjects: "The Guidelines are based on what you did in the past and no amount of effort to put that past behind you can change what has been done."

The necessity of personal control is supported by more general research in social psychology, particularly the studies reported by Seligman.[19] It is Seligman's hypothesis that a perception of being in control over the major aspects of one's life is essential to a person's emotional and even physical health. Seligman cites numerous studies that dramatize the finding that a lack of personal control leads to emotional deterioration, somatic complaints, and, in extreme cases, death. The central theme of the studies cited by Seligman is that a feeling of personal control is a necessary component for a satisfying, healthy environment. The present research extends this finding as well to the decision process involved in granting parole.

In conclusion, attempting to measure inmate views on a subject as volatile as parole is a tricky business at best. One possible source of bias was the difference in the parole rates between the systems. At the time of the study, the parole rate at the first hearing was approximately 70 percent in Pennsylvania and 20 percent in the federal system, although federal subjects tended to receive shorter sentences and were incarcerated for less time before the initial hearing (seventeen months for federal subjects compared to thirty months for Pennsylvania subjects). Whether the subject expected to be paroled was controlled for statistically in the analyses, but there were other problems that could conceivably bias the results. In federal prisons, the federal parole board functions as a sentencing body in considering the nature of the offense and prior record in deciding parole. In Pennsylvania these factors are considered by the judge in setting the original sentence and are only rarely taken into account by the Pennsylvania parole board.

It is arguable that the hostility directed toward the parole board in the federal system is also present in Pennsylvania. In Pennsylvania, however, the hostility is simply transferred to the sentencing judge. Nevertheless, at this point this remains speculative.

Also the results do not examine the question of whether the use of parole guidelines, per se, increases certainty for the offender. The confounding factor of comparing a treatment system without guidelines and a justice system with guidelines precludes addressing this question. To test the impact of parole guidelines, two similar parole systems, one with and one without guidelines, would have to be studied.

The above problems notwithstanding, it is of interest to note that (at least for the systems studied) the justice approach to parole did not result in greater perceived certainty for the offender before the initial hearing, although the criteria on which the decisions were based were more concrete and more sharply defined. The treatment model, on the other hand, appeared to allow the offender a greater degree of perceived influence over the parole decision. The perception of personal control seemed, in turn, to result in generally less expressed hostility toward the parole system. This, of course, contradicts the views of the authors cited above [5,6,7,8,10,11] who have held that incarcerated offenders are being victimized by the rehabilitation approach to parole and would much prefer to have parole abolished or based on criteria other than rehabilitation. The present study, which may be one of the few to systematically examine the attitudes of offenders about the parole decision process, indicated the opposite.

Nevertheless, these results do not by any means invalidate all the arguments in favor of the justice model. The justice approach to parole is still a useful tool for reducing sentence disparity and the rehabilitation model must always be suspect until some method of rehabilitating offenders has been proven effective. From the viewpoint of the offender, however, the rehabilitation model of parole seems to be the preferred method of deciding when an offender should be released from prison.

REFERENCES

1. Burns, H. *Corrections organization and administration*, St. Paul, West Publishing, 1975.
2. Menninger, K. *The crime of punishment*, New York, The Viking Press, 1968.

3. American Friends Service Committee, *Struggle for justice*, New York, Hill and Wang, 1971.

4. Lipton, D., Martinson, R., and Wilks, J. *The effectiveness of correctional treatment*, New York, Praeger, 1975.

5. Galtung, J. Prisons: The organization of dilemma, In Cressey, D. (Ed.), *The prison: Studies in institutional organization and change*, New York, Rinehart and Winston, 1966.

6. Fogel, D. *". . . We are the Living Proof . . ."*, Cincinnati, Ohio, Anderson, 1975.

7. Sykes, G. The pains of imprisonment, In Petersen, D. and Thomas, C. (Eds.), *Corrections: Problems and prospects*, Englewood Cliffs, New Jersey, Prentice Hall, 1975.

8. Fox, V. *Violence behind bars*, Westport, Connecticut, Greenwood Press, 1956.

9. Kassebaum, G., Ward, D., and Wilner, D. *Prison treatment and parole survival*, New York, Wiley, 1971.

10. Cohen, A., Cole, G., and Bailey, R. *Prison violence*, Lexington, Massachusetts, Lexington Books, 1976.

11. Jones, D. *The health risks of imprisonment*, Lexington, Massachusetts, Lexington Books, 1976.

12. Hoffman, P. and DeGostin, L. Parole decision-making: Structuring discretion, *Federal Probation, 38*, 7–15, 1974.

13. Hoffman, P., Beck, J., and DeGostin, L. The practical application of a severity scale, In Amos, W. and Newman, C. (Eds.), *Parole*, New York, Federal Legal Publications, 1975.

14. Hoffman, P. and Beck, J. Parole decision-making: A salient factor score, *Journal of Criminal Justice, 2*, 195–206, 1974.

15. Wenk, E. and Moos, R. Prison environments: The social ecology of correctional institutions, *Crime and Delinquency Literature, 4*, 591–621, 1972.

16. Moos, R. *Evaluating treatment environments: A social ecological approach*, New York, Wiley, 1974.

17. Moos, R. *Evaluating correctional and community settings*, New York, Wiley, 1975.

18. *Outlook*. Inmate Publication at the Federal Correctional Institution, Danbury, Connecticut, 1976.

19. Seligman, M. *Helplessness: On depression, development, and death*, San Francisco, Freeman, 1975.

Chapter 25

PSYCHOLOGICAL EVALUATION AND TREATMENT: THE OFFENDER'S VIEW

ANTHONY J. SCOLERI

*"They are playing a game. They are
playing at not playing a game. If I show
them I see they are, I shall break the rules
and they will punish me. I must play their
game, of not seeing I see the game."*

"Knots,", R. D. Laing

A TORRENT OF verbiage has been spoken and written regarding the traumatic effect of an inmate's readjustment or reassimilation into society upon his release from prison. Few words, however, have ever been spoken or written about the trauma experienced upon an inmate's reception into prison, an experience that is unquestionably more traumatizing. Deprived of the fundamental privilege of citizenship, an inmate is degraded to the status of a thing, a number, something less than human, subjected to the whim and caprice of indifferent staff and callous custodial officers, as well as predatory fellow inmates. While psychologists have waxed eloquent about the trauma of any new experience, this pertinent fact seems to have been overlooked by psychologists the country over.

Those inmates who are not already embittered over the "production line" brand of justice meted out in the city halls and courthouses soon succumb to the peer pressure criterion of the either/or proposition of "them" and "us." Staff is seen as a mere extension of the political, legal, and/or judicial system that played a part in having them convicted and confined. All staff persons, as well as correctional officers, are therefore feared or distrusted. There are exceptions, of course, but the name of the game to be played in prison, as illustrated

310

in the quote from R.D. Laing's "Knots," is acquiescence. And it never ceases to amaze me how many otherwise intelligent persons allow themselves to believe that acquiescence is synonymous with acceptance.

All new receptions at the correctional institution are confined in quarantine for a period of time ranging from six weeks to three months, in some instances longer. Enduring more restrictions than those imposed upon the general inmate population, with fewer privileges, and with the added indignity of having a number replace one's name—being shunted here and there for a medical examination, x-rays, blood test, educational testing, a social report, *ad nauseam*—a group of new receptions is readied for the standard psychology tests. The tests administered are the Revised Beta to determine one's IQ and the Minnesota Multiphasic Personality Inventory (MMPI) to determine a profile of one's personality. For those who are either illiterate, have some other learning disability, or who are organic, the House-Tree-Person test is administered. Incredulous as it may seem, I have never heard an examiner administering the tests ask whether everyone present could read and write or had any difficulty comprehending what was required of him. It is a moot point though since few adults will make a public admission of illiteracy. Consequently, like the average wayward student who has not prepared for an examination, anyone who is illiterate or who cannot comprehend what is required simply copies from the man next to him. Few inmates balk at taking the Revised Beta or the MMPI. For some reason, however, such is not the case where the House-Tree-Person test is concerned. Hoping to circumvent the purpose of this test, most inmates will draw stick figures, despite admonitions not to, while some adamantly refuse to make any attempt whatsoever. It is surprising that only an occasional inmate will refuse to take any test. Those men who score in the borderline mental defective range or the superior range of the Revised Beta are then administered the Wechsler Adult Intelligence Scale (WAIS) to ascertain the authenticity of the test results. That is, when time and other factors permit.

Surprisingly, despite the trauma experienced by new inmates, despite the testing circumstances, and despite the cheating, a fairly accurate and valid evaluation is made. A good psychological profile is thereby made of each new inmate.

To what avail? For what purpose? Aye, there's the rub! Together with other data compiled by law enforcement agencies, welfare agencies, social workers, and such, the profile or evaluation is duly classified, carefully copied for various departments within the institution, labelled confidential, and locked away in some filing cabinet.

Only when an inmate commits some infraction of the rules of the institution, seeks clearance to work outside the institution, applies for prerelease status, files for commutation of sentence to the Board of Pardons, or comes up for parole is the record looked into or the evaluation considered. For the most part, then and only then is it intimated that an individual has some personality disorder and he is "advised" to become involved in psychotherapy. Any "advice" or "suggestion" by a staff person is correctly interpreted by an inmate to mean a mandate. And a mandate, whether it be called advice, suggestion, or any other word, is still an order. To order or compel a person to participate in either individual or group therapy is diametrically opposed to the basic concept of therapy—a willingness if not a desire to change.

As 99 percent of all incarcerated inmates are eventually returned to society, with or without treatment, we come again to the perplexing and perturbing question: To what avail psychological testing and evaluation? The psychological testing and evaluation of new inmates sentenced to the State Correctional Institutes in Pennsylvania is a farce and a sham. This is so simply because treatment in corrections is as nebulous in deed as it is ludicrous in word. Next to the term "rehabilitation," no word in the lingua franca of corrections irks an inmate more than the word treatment. The psychological evaluation and treatment of inmates can be likened to a medical doctor's examination of an ailing patient, making an accurate diagnosis of the cause of the problem, but making no disclosure to the patient of his findings and offering no treatment for either the symptoms or the cause of the ailment. In a very real way, the testing and evaluation is rendered as superfluous as it is ludicrous by the failure to provide any treatment, let alone any viable treatment. To the administration, however, it does serve a purpose, a dual purpose. The evaluation does disclose those inmates who are prone to violence and those who are considered potential troublemakers. Perhaps of greater import, the pretense of treatment is promulgated and perpetuated.

No critique of treatment in a correctional setting can be considered adequate without taking into account the pervasive factions of Custody. There is a sharp and bitter division in corrections between Custody and Treatment. A constant battle is waged by the factions of Custody against the factions of Treatment. Treatment oriented personnel are subjected to many hassles and harassments, and not a little abuse and disparagement. Of the limited funds allocated for corrections by state legislatures, only 5 percent is allotted for treatment services while 95 percent goes for custodial purposes. It is apparent therefore that Custody has the wherewithal as well as the clout in corrections. As one inmate well puts it, clubs is trump in prison.

Of course, the institution has its various educational and vocational programs. These are, for the most part, showcases for the various groups who are hustled through the institution during meal times when inmates cannot be seen or heard. To illustrate the point, only a very limited number of men can apply for and be accepted into these programs. The typewriter-repair class and the electronics course are presently inactive. The air-conditioning and refrigeration course has three active participants. The automechanics course has six men. At present, the correctional institution has a total population of approximately 1,700 men! A local major university was the first in providing courses for inmates aspiring to an associate's or bachelor's degree—with no remuneration for these courses from the department of education. Only recently was it learned that funds were available for these services. Yet, for the first time in six years, this university was unable to provide any courses this past year because politics evidently had entered into the dealing of the money to an admittedly inferior state college.

Much ballyhoo has been made about the prerelease programs whereby inmates, who have at least nine months residency at a given institution without a major misconduct, have served half of their minimum sentence, and have no outstanding detainers of two years or more, are first granted a temporary home furlough of three days, then become eligible for educational or work release, or placement in a Community Services Center. These programs appear fabulous—on paper. In reality, they shape up as being no more than a papier-mâché facade. More than that, they are a farce. Automatically, inmates with a sentence of life imprisonment are precluded by law from involvement in them. All new receptions are excluded. Likewise for inmates who are serving long sentences. Any major misconduct—and that does cover a multitude of trivial infractions—precludes for a nine-month period anyone otherwise eligible. (It must be added, parenthetically, that avoiding a misconduct in such an environment is like asking a psychiatrist to do his work without asking questions!) Finally, as most of the men have either violation of parole or probation detainers, if not pending cases, the number of men who benefit from the prerelease programs is minimal. I have no idea of the number of men who are eligible for temporary home furlough, but I do know that the total number involved in educational or work release combined is only 34 men.

At any rate, neither education nor vocational pursuits, nor any other accomplishments, constitute treatment or rehabilitation. Some inner change must take place. And what overall treatment is provided to effectuate such change? Precious little. As stated earlier, individual or group therapy may be suggested. Beyond the mere suggestion, however, there is no follow up. While this may seem as inexplicable as it does incredible, the psychology department, consisting of two doctors of psychology, three psychologists, and one psychiatrist, simply cannot accommodate a population of approximately 1,700 inmates, nor can the casework department, with caseworkers carrying a caseload of from 160 to 180 men.

Another factor to be considered is the character and competency of both departments. On balance, the psychology department at the correctional institution performs a monumental task with diligence and dedication. Unfortunately, such is not the case with the casework department. Of the twelve caseworkers at this institution, only two are both competent and caring individuals. The majority are either blatantly incompetent, brutalized by the system, or simply indifferent to the plight of others. The overall attitude may be summed by that universal malady that afflicts mankind—apathy. I was recently told by a staff person that this apathetic attitude was really a case of "burn-out," whatever that may mean. My response to this sophism was to cite the many years of dedicated service of the two caseworkers alluded to above and the several outstanding persons in the psychology department. Perhaps my condemnation of the casework department is unfair; after all, since no real treatment will be provided in any case, a caseworker's reluctance in apprising an embittered inmate that he has certain areas in his personality that require professional help becomes somewhat understandable.

At any rate, little if anything is done with the evaluation of new inmates. Like the acquisition of art work by vandals, there is no appreciable comprehension of the wealth of data at hand. Consider, for example, the following factual matter: In the psychological evaluation of one inmate who had twice attempted suicide while in the army, it was duly noted that this individual "possessed a paranoid ideation and should be watched for any deterioration in his behavior."

But who is to watch him? Certainly not the understaffed and over-worked psychology department. Surely then his caseworker is apprised of the potential for self-destruction? Not unless he has the time or the inclination to read the evaluation. Besides, in most instances, a social report is completed long before the evaluation is made. What about the higher eschelons in the guard force? They have more important matters of custody and security to consider. Well then, surely the officers on the cell block on which he is housed are made aware of this fact? Any such assumption would be laughable if it were not so lamentable.

The treatment prescribed? Nil. No, that is not quite true. Such an individual usually winds up on tranquilizing drugs. Sedated, such an individual is much more tractable. That is the extent of his treat-ment . . . until his condition deteriorates. When this happens, he is usually placed in the Behavioral Adjustment Unit (a whimsical euphemism for the hole or solitary confinement) until he is seen by a psychiatric evaluation team, after which he is usually transferred to a state mental institution.

In the preparation of this paper, a survey was conducted of some twenty-five inmates regarding the testing, evaluation, and treatment. The survey was discontinued because, to a man, the responses were almost all the same, albeit phrased differently. That is, they had taken the tests, no explanation had been given for the purpose of the tests, no one had apprised them of the results, and no treatment had been prescribed or offered.

One inmate, who has a history of violence on his record, including assaults on officers as well as inmates, and who has been a constant thorn in the side of the administration, queried me as to why I was taking the survey. Upon learning it was for this chapter, he volun-teered the information that he had somehow obtained a copy of his evaluation and that it contained a poor prognosis for his adjustment to incarceration. To be specific, the report stated not only that he was self-destructive, but would be destructive to any group or program in which he participated.

Naturally, I eagerly asked what he thought of the evaluation.

"It's right. That's how I am."

"Did anyone offer any treatment or try to help you understand why you were destructive?"

"Like who?" he said.

Who indeed?

Many years ago, I also had an opportunity to "procure" a copy of the evaluation made on my reception into the old penitentiary. I was aghast and infuriated over what had been written about me. Furious, I tore the evaluation to pieces and cursed the psychologist as a pedantic ass. However, despite my anger, despite my protestations to myself, despite the lack of education, despite my "lack of insight," despite my reluctance to face myself as I really was and not as I pretended to be, slowly and agonizingly, I had to come to terms with and accept the truth about myself. Then began a period of self-introspection, the roughest and toughest period of my life, but surely the most rewarding.

A few years ago, I met that psychologist who had tested me and written such as devastating evaluation of me. I quoted to him, in part, his diagnosis.

"Was I correct?" he asked.

"Like you had a crystal ball to help you," I replied.

The smug smile of satisfaction that swept across his face was replaced with a look of bewilderment when I queried, "Will you please explain why I was neither told of the evaluation nor offered any treatment?"

"Harrumph!" he snorted. "Would you have accepted the evaluation back then?"

"I did—back then. But let me ask a more pertinent question: What good is any evaluation if the person about whom it is made is not cognizant of it or apprised of his character or neurotic disorders?"

I have asked the same question of many psychologists since then. To this date, no adequate answer or reasonable explanation has been given.

I submit that incarcerating a person with psychological problems and providing no treatment is like locking a car with some mechanical disorder in a garage and expecting it to be in good running condition after a certain length of time.

From almost thirty years of exposure to the system, I believe I offer more than subjective opinion in asserting that psychological testing and evaluation in a correctional setting, without the provision of any viable treatment, is little more than another weapon in the administrational arsenal by which to enforce its dominion over the inmate population.

Perhaps no treatment is provided because it is not an integral part of the game being played in corrections.

Editors Note: After serving the last 21 years in prison Tony Scoleri was released on parole. Three months later he committed suicide. He will be sorely missed by the many inmates he helped and the professionals who knew him as a friend and teacher.

Chapter 26

TREATMENT OF MENTALLY ILL OFFENDERS IN A STATE HOSPITAL FORENSIC UNIT

GERALD COOKE, Ph.D.

T HE TERM mentally ill offender is used here to include patients who enter the mental health system from the criminal justice system at any one of three levels. Some patients are admitted pretrial, usually on a request for an evaluation of competency to stand trial that may have been raised because of psychotic and/or suicidal behavior while in jail awaiting trial. If these patients are found competent and judged not to be in need of treatment they may be returned to the legal system within a short time. If found competent but in need of treatment or if found incompetent they will remain at the hospital for a period of time determined jointly by their mental and legal status. The next level of entrance is after conviction but pre-sentence. This usually results from a request by the judge for a sentencing recommendation. If in-patient treatment is not recommended, the patient will be returned to the legal system. If in-patient treatment is recommended, the individual will remain at the hospital again for a period determined by mental and legal status. Treatment goals will be different for those whose status requires return to a correctional system and those who will be discharged from the hospital to the community. The third level of entrance concerns convicted offenders who have begun serving their sentences in correctional institutions. They are usually referred to the hospital because of psychotic and/or suicidal behavior. Here, as with second level patients, the goal of treatment depends on whether their status will result in return to the legal system or discharge to the community.

The following description of a treatment program is the author's

317

judgment as to what would constitute an ideal program. We have strived toward this at Norristown, however, probably few programs, including our own, approach this ideal for a combination of reasons including staff shortages, inadequate relationships with judges and community groups, and political pressures. The description will focus on adult male mentally ill offenders for several reasons. First, this is the author's principle experience. Second, there are few state hospital programs specific to the treatment of female forensic patients or juvenile forensic patients. Unquestionably, the facilities for these two groups need to be greatly expanded as many mentally ill women and juveniles now languish in correctional institutions without adequate care. The following description also applies to what is generally classified as minimum to medium security. In many states the maximum security facility is located far from other facilities and from the major population centers. This removes those patients from easy access to attorneys, courts, family and community support systems, and competent professionals. Such individuals often receive inadequate treatment, even abuse, and often remain incarcerated for longer than necessary. It is the author's opinion that maximum security facilities should be located adjacent to medium security facilities that, in turn, should be near the state's population centers. Further, maximum security placement should be regarded as a temporary measure, justifiable only by repeated overt assaultive behavior and/or serious escape attempt in a medium security facility. The patient's right to the least restrictive alternative should be protected by a commitment type hearing with legal representation before placement in a maximum security unit. Continued placement in maximum security should be based only on repeated overt acts and, in their absence, return to the medium security unit should be at the earliest possible time.

As indicated above, treatment goals and priorities for mentally ill offenders depend greatly on whether return to a correctional facility or discharge to the community is anticipated. When return to the correctional facility is anticipated, the goals should be much more limited and focused primarily on alleviating the psychotic and/or suicidal behavior that resulted in hospitalization. This can often be accomplished by the use of medication, mileu therapy, and supportive psychotherapy. The goal of treatment here is to help the patient accept the reality of incarceration and prepare him to deal with the stresses of prison. Insight therapy emphasizing self-revelation, expression of feeling, and giving and receiving interpersonal feedback is strongly contraindicated. Such behaviors can get a man killed in prison. It is the author's contention that prison is a dehumanizing antitherapeutic experience and that inmates who show improvement in prison do so in spite of, rather than because of, incarceration. For these reasons, whenever possible the goal of treatment should be for return to the community and the following treatment program makes that assumption.

When an individual is admitted to the hospital acutely psychotic or suicidal, the initial phase of treatment consists primarily of appropriate medication, the more therapeutic milieu of the hospital, orientation to hospital surroundings, rules, and routine, and supportive therapy provided in a group and/or individual context. As the more acute symptoms subside, a wider range of treatment becomes appropriate. Each treatment modality will be discussed separately.

MEDICATION

Medication needs to be reviewed weekly or, in cases where the patient has side effects, even more frequently. Patients often complain of side effects and every effort should be made to keep this at a minimum through adjusting the type and dosage of medication or adding other medications that inhibit side effects. Misuse of medication often occurs when it is used to control rather than to treat, and overmedication should be avoided for several reasons. First, it is medically unsound and dangerous; second, it causes resentment in the patient and he is less likely to cooperate with treatment; and third, the overmedicated patient cannot adequately participate in therapies that are the means through which long-term personality and behavioral changes may be accomplished.

MILIEU THERAPY

This term has so often been a euphemism for custodial care that it now has a negative connotation. However, real milieu therapy can take place in a number of ways. First, if security aides interact with patients in a respectful, empathic, and supportive way, a less stressful environment is created. This can occur in the day-to-day running of the ward, in informal talks, or around activities such as pool, ping pong, cards, games, etc. that should be available on the ward. Orientation to the ward and discussion of ward concerns in weekly (or more frequent) ward meetings adds to the quality of the milieu and allows the patients a voice in the administration of the ward.

An important aspect of the ward milieu, and one often neglected with forensic patients, is a privilege system. For security and treatment reasons when patients first are admitted they may have to be placed in seclusion rooms or under observation in a day hall. However, as the patient's mental condition improves and the staff comes to know the patients, they can begin to move up the privilege system.

At first the patient is restricted to the ward. Then he obtains building privileges that allow for participation, if appropriate, in a range of activities including occupational therapy, recreational therapy, academic school, etc. Patients who have not yet been to their first major staff conference (this usually occurs in from 30–40 days) or for whom the recommendation is to return to the legal system do not receive privileges off the building. However, patients retained at the hospital are begun with grounds privileges with security staff escort. This usually consists of two hours on the grounds on a visit to the canteen, library, recreation building, etc. These outings may also be used for walks on the grounds, bicycling, tennis, or fishing. The patient may earn up to seven outings a week, i.e. one outing per day.

At the next two privilege levels the patient may be escorted by other members of the staff besides security aides or by volunteers. In order to proceed to the sixth level, which is daytime ground privileges without staff escort but with escort by a patient with a higher level, permission must be granted by the court. The patient then moves up to daytime ground privileges without escort, evening with patient escort, and evening without escort.

Permission is then requested for off ground privileges and these are given at first for days under supervision and then for increasing amounts of time with decreasing levels of supervision. The patient may, prior to discharge, have off ground privileges on his own for work, school, and/or recreational activities. Granting of increases in privileges depends on ward behavior, attendance in therapy, and mental and legal status. A "model patient" with a cooperative judge and a short sentence would take approximately ten months from admission to extensive off ground privileges; however, in most cases the period of time is considerably longer. The purpose of the privilege program is to provide incentive and reward for appropriate prosocial behavior so that there is a gradual increase in freedom and responsibility in preparation for return to the community.

Where a unit is divided into admission and advanced treatment wards, as at Norristown, patients at the higher levels (patient escort and above) can form a therapeutic community within which the patients develop and enforce rules and grant privileges by voting. This is aimed at providing a cooperative atmosphere with peer feedback and increased responsibility for self and to the community.

GROUP AND INDIVIDUAL THERAPY

It is this author's opinion that for state hospital patients with characterological features, group therapy is superior as a treatment modality to individual therapy. Such patients often come from lower socioeconomic level minority group backgrounds and have a history of conflict with authority. They are, therefore, unlikely to be able to form close relationships with and accept feedback from professional therapists who generally come from white middle-class backgrounds and have not experienced the kinds of problems that the patients have. Group therapy in which the therapist acts as a facilitator laying the groundwork for peer feedback seems to have more potential for insight and behavioral change.

Various kinds of groups can be formed and an ideal program should provide at least the following categories: (a) Ward groups, groups on each ward to discuss conflicts and problems that arise on the ward. These may be divided into high level and low level groups depending on mental status, ability to develop insight, and intelligence. (b) Personality problems groups, for these groups patients are drawn from all wards and an effort made to concentrate on personality and behavioral characteristics. Again they may be divided into high and low level groups with the former focussing more on developing insight and the latter on basic social skills and techniques for coping with stress. (c) Special problem groups, these would include groups for persons found incompetent, which might involve information giving and role playing; groups for patients returning to prison; groups for persons with drug problems, alcohol problems, and sexual problems; family groups for those with family conflicts; and an exit group for those soon to return to the community. (d) Special technique groups, these sometimes overlap with special problem groups. For example, an assertiveness training group would include persons who are too passive and those who are too aggressive. Other special technique groups include psychodrama and the use of videotape feedback. (e) Reality orientation and resocialization, current events groups for regressed patients. (f) Groups in which therapeutic interaction is based around an activity such as bible study, chess, jogging, etc. (g) Activities of daily living in which patients learn basic skills such as cooking, washing, etc.

For reasons discussed above and because of staff shortages, only a limited amount of individual therapy is available and the patients with the most favorable prognosis are, with few exceptions, the ones usually chosen.

OCCUPATIONAL THERAPY, MUSIC THERAPY, AND RECREATIONAL THERAPY

These activities are important parts of the treatment program for several reasons. First, they often provide a good first therapy because they introduce the patient to the idea of therapeutic activities in a nonthreatening way. Second, many forensic patients have problems with frustration tolerance and perseverance that can be addressed by these therapies. Finally, accomplishments in these areas help in building the self-concept.

Many forensic patients have a high activity level and require an active recreational program to burn off energy that might otherwise be expressed in destructive ways.

ACADEMIC AND TECHNICAL SCHOOL

Though a hospital's orientation is usually toward behavior change, therapies probably affect the probability of further criminal behavior less than training in academic and technical skills. No matter how much the patient learns about himself if he cannot find work because of academic or occupational deficiency, he is likely to regress to his previous behavioral patterns. Hence, a full academic school program providing education for everyone from total illiterates through those who want to obtain a GED to those who want to do college work is extremely important. A technical school that can teach such things as electrical work, TV repair, plumbing, janitorial work, carpentry, furniture repair, automobile mechanics, etc. is also essential.

VOLUNTEERS

The use of volunteers in paraprofessional therapeutic relationships, particulary those who come from a background similar to that of patients, is extremely valuable. Volunteers provide a nonthreatening source of feedback that is uncomplicated by the kinds of administrative issues often surrounding the professional therapist. Also volunteers provide an opportunity for contact with people living in the community.

SUMMARY

In summary, it should be emphasized that no matter what treatment is offered on paper, in order to be effective it must be given in a way that shows respect for the individual's worth as a human being no matter what his mental condition or past history of criminal behavior. It should be clear that this ideal of treatment is rarely reached and is often consciously or unconsciously sabotaged by those who lack this fundamental respect. As a result, the patient's perception of the treatment offered is frequently far different from that of the staff.

Chapter 27

PSYCHOLOGICAL EVALUATION AND TREATMENT IN A STATE FORENSIC HOSPITAL—THE PATIENT'S VIEW

Joseph B. Centifanti*
AND
Theodore I. Williams†

O NCE UPON A TIME three blind men came upon an elephant in the forest. Not being able to identify what it was before them by sight, the blind men sought to do so by touch. The first man, by happenstance, grasped the animal's trunk and exclaimed that they had surely found a huge, old snake. However, the second touched the front leg of the beast and concluded just as firmly that it was a trunk of a large tree. Finally the third man felt the sides of the elephant and announced conclusively that they were before a long, high wall. They argued for some time, each from his own position and then, failing to agree, they went to reexamine the beast. The elephant had by then moved on. The three blind men retired in confusion.

The moral to that fable is one that we think can be applied to our evaluation and treatment as patients in a forensic unit of a state mental hospital. We are not sure whether anyone can really expect to understand the whole of such an experience or the whole of an elephant. All that we can expect to do is grasp at all the parts we can.

As we thought about what we had seen and experienced, the question we asked, as did the blind men, was what exactly was it that was going on around us?

---

*Mr. Centifanti was a patient from October 1975 to January 1978.
†Mr. Williams was a patient from August 1976 to September 1978.

First and most basically, were we patients or prisoners? No, we are not playing word games. We believe that many of the answers to the other questions we have about evaluation and treatment follow from that first question of our status, for example: Is the forensic unit of a state mental hospital more hospital or more prison? Are the staff physicians, psychologists, nurses, and aides acting more as a treatment team or as warden and guards? Is the thrust of the forensic unit psychological program rehabilitative treatment or punishment? The question of our status seemed all-important to us as a kind of two-way street.

Before walking through the door of the unit, we had already been processed by the prison and/or court system. If we came from the prison system we were sure we were still in jail. If we came from the courts directly, any doubts we had were not resolved. The prison analogy seemed reasonable enough at first glance by such security precautions such as locked doors, barred windows, and "counts."

After taking some time to observe what was going on from the "inside," the blur between the types of lock-ups increases. We are not sure anyone can fulfill the role of both guard and therapist. The relationships between us as inmates and those assigned to help us never seemed to be very stable. On one hand the caring and nurturing role assigned to, and assumed by hospital personnel was regularly undercut by the responsibilities of the "turnkey." We wanted to be able to know the people who were trying to help us as people. It is axiomatic that you cannot be close to your guard or the person you are guarding. Our desire for rapport with our therapists was further frustrated by the fact that we often saw and experienced a single individual almost simultaneously acting in both roles. Added to the on-going uncertainty about the role of the staff of the forensic unit there was a kind of cycle to the style of the unit as a whole. Depending on the type of patients, the level of violence and other incidents, and public and political pressure, the unit tended alternately to become more like a hospital or more like a prison. In such a changing environment both staff and patients were at the mercy of a "we-they" mentality. We felt that this attitude was counterproductive to our treatment.

Perhaps all of this confusion cannot be completely removed. However, we saw a tremendous amount accomplished where the staff person is sensitive to the dual role and its effect on the relationships with patients. Some staff seemed to understand this and resolved the matter by adopting primarily one role or the other. To us, even if the staff person chose the guard role, this was often preferable to the ambiguity that otherwise made any relationship impossible.

Secondly, middle-class, white-oriented values of family, work, and behavior were sometimes held up didactically by the staff as models where our own real-life situations were totally outside such patterns. Perhaps that kind of thing is inevitable anywhere just because people are people. The fact is, however, that when coupled with the confusion about our own status, staff roles, and our ongoing legal problems this unintended assault upon the wider range of values was particularly untimely. We felt that the staff that understood this problem reached us with less wasted effort and greater effect than those who did not. Those that did practiced a kind of neutral nonjudgmental approach to us as people. Having seen it done in group, individual, and milieu therapy we are convinced it can be done in other units such as ours. It made a lasting impression on us.

And what about the staff attitudes toward patients generally? We thought that the staff were often as confused as we were about the nature and purpose of the forensic unit. When we arrived, we were told that we were there to be helped. Yet at other times it was implied and suggested that we were all getting an undeserved break by being hospitalized rather than simply jailed.

Indeed, one of the constant factors of our hospitalization from referral to release, was the repeated challenge from the staff to justify our stay in the unit. Partly, at the beginning at least, this was understandable given the demand for the scarce spaces in the unit. Our acceptance of a need for treatment and for being there was in a sense a rite of passage like an initiation or boot camp. We realize that we could not have it both ways; either we were sick and needed treatment or we were not and could be safely returned to the legal system. However, the constant questioning of the genuineness of our problems was, in the end, a distraction and roadblock to our treatment. Having made in our own way our individual commitments to getting treatment, the die was cast. The repeated justifications only raised the same paradox for each of us: How could we ever return to the real world if the idea of treatment and illness was not even accepted at the institution? Perhaps the depth of our feeling on this issue cannot be appreciated by anyone who has not had the experience of being on the horns of this particular dilemma. At first we did not want to admit our sickness; when we were finally able to, we were called liars and fakers. It seemed that we, not the staff, were the only believers in the myth of mental illness.

Coupled with the challenge to our honesty were the repeated threats of a return to the legal system in response to a variety of our behaviors. Again, as before, the basic economics of the unit seem to dictate that its spaces be allocated to those who will cooperate with the treatment available to them. Those who cannot or will not participate in the program must necessarily be transfered elsewhere. We accept that reality for ourselves and those who were "inside" with us. However, we must note that there seems to be an especially subtle kind of triage at work here. Some of those who are really ill and dangerous are either returned to prison or to the streets because they are beyond help in units like the one where we were. In particular, we felt factors such as age, race, and type of offense seem to affect the decision of who should continue to be treated and who sent back to be punished. We feel we were lucky to have been selected and treated over a long-term; we know many who were not so fortunate. We cannot forget that throughout the process the spectre of returning to jail was raised to control our behavior. Perhaps that was another vestige of the real world come to haunt us. If so, it hardly seemed necessary after a time and, like the staff role confusion, there was a lot of wasted emotion and effort attached to these threats.

We are not sure but that some special set of rights should attach to forensic patients along the lines already developed for mental patients generally. Specifically, we might all promote the basic right to treatment of persons who are mentally ill and who also have legal problems.

Once again, the question of the nature of the creature seems all important in the area of discipline and right to treatment. If we are prisoners in a jail called a forensic unit, then we have one kind of rights and obligations. There is a well-settled body of law applicable to the rights of those in state prisons. If, however, we are really more than prisoners, then a different series of rights and rules would seem preferable. While we were "in," no one, least of all us, was quite sure what exactly the thing was that we were "in." We resented the uncertainty since we felt it made us that much more helpless. Our observation was that many of the staff, particularly the nonprofessionals, also wanted some idea of how they were to treat us when disciplinary problems arose. We believe that some basic guarantees of the due process are appropriate in the hospital discipline and transfer system. We are hopeful that the increased interest of the community and particularly the bar should encourage and accelerate such developments. With the advent of "Patient Bill of Rights" and "Human Rights Committees" effective changes are already coming for mental patients.

Together with the staff personalities, roles, and attitudes, we came into contact with the treatment program. As with the other elements, we often could not be sure whether we were being punished or helped by treatment. A primary example of this confusion about treatment was in the area of medication. It would be clearly dishonest for us to say medication was uniformly bad. However, it is equally clear that the medication we received and saw was not all to the good. We ourselves recognized the need for medication and accepted that little could be accomplished without drugs in many cases. However, in some instances we saw medication (including the major tranquilizers) used for control where control was clearly punitive. The range of reasons for giving such drugs as a part of treatment ranged from verbal abuse to overt violence. In some instances the use of heavy medication was justified but in others it was used for other than therapeutic purposes, influenced by personal and even sometimes racial bias.

One situation that we observed deserves reporting here even though strictly speaking it does not relate to the propriety of the particular medication itself. Briefly, the situation begins with the medication being prescribed by the staff psychiatrist and taken by the patient more or less without protest. The administration of the drug, however, over a period of time, becomes onerous because of the attitude of the institution staff toward medication. The experience that we had suggests that medication is often perceived by staff and patients as the ultimate threat for misbehavior. Perhaps, because of a general attitude toward drugs, we also thought that both patients and staff viewed medication as a "crutch." These attitudes worked against the kind of patient-staff contract about this most important part of treatment. The best results that we saw occurred where the patient accepted the medication and understood its effects. This is important especially since we have had to continue medication on our own after release from the institution. We came to believe in our own need for our medication only after overcoming the negativism attached to it initially. We believe that such an understanding came to be shared by other patients in our unit who were handled as we were.

After personnel and medication, the third part of this elephant is the treatment programs themselves. We viewed the therapies offered by the hospital as the most important and beneficial part of our experience. As there were a variety of programs, there were a variety of reasons that we felt we benefitted.

First and foremost we benefitted from group therapies run by experienced therapists and kept reasonably stable in membership. Trust, a scarce commodity at best in our situation, developed in these groups. With a little guidance from the staff, we found that we could help each other. Despite the difference in patient backgrounds in our unit, there really seemed to be more gained from our diversity than lost. We benefitted particularly from the groups that concentrated on particular problems such as sex problems, alcoholism, and drug addiction. We thought that individual therapy was also helpful. However, it is here that a constant theme of our treatment experience becomes most apparent—staffing. Since individual therapy is the most costly treatment in terms of personnel time it was always in short supply in our institution. At best such treatment even when available was short-term, hardly the most beneficial approach. As we noted in connection with the remarks on group therapy, we thought long-term therapy relationships produced the most benefits for us while institutionalized. We recognize the sad fact that without more staff psychiatrists and psychologists, there can be no real change in this area. But it does seem clear to us that no other single change could provide greater benefit.

To some extent the benefit from many of our treatment programs was a function of the respect and understanding shown by the therapist to us as patients. The one really discouraging thing to us about the whole experience was the extent to which racism and to some extent sexism were still unstated conditions for the operation of the hospital. It was obvious that while the nonprofessional staff was largely black, the professional staff were almost completely white. More and more of the professional staff seemed to have backgrounds other than American and, either from ignorance or indolence or whatever, racial problems within the staff or among patients or between these groups were ignored. The black patients were, we think, largely not best treated by a white staff that despite all of its good intentions did not share their language, culture, or experience. There was no single area of treatment that could not have been improved by the addition of black staff. Beyond black professionals, this includes black occupational therapists, alcohol counselors, even black barbers and hospital volunteers. If the keystone of our benefitting from therapy was trust, the building blocks had to be on our sense of accepting and being accepted as human beings. For black patients, we think the process of building trust is retarded by a white treatment team. The availability of sufficient black staff is, of course, the first hurdle in dealing with this problem. We merely mean to underscore the need as we perceived it.

Balanced off against the forensic unit's treatment program was the general lack of understanding of the court system. This ignorance was shared by patient and staff alike. In Pennsylvania, where we were institutionalized, we recently had a new statute to try to understand in addition to the usual problem of trying to integrate two different systems and vocabularies. It seemed to us that neither the legal system nor the hospital wanted to accept ultimate responsibility for us, our incarceration, and our treatment. As though in support of that theory, communication between court and forensic unit was often slow and mistake-ridden. The legal process seemed not to be fully comprehensible to anyone on the treatment end and our experience in court even before knowledgeable judges seemed to show that the courts did not fully understand the treatment end either. It seemed to us that some designated liaison post at the court and hospital would ease some of the frustration and anger we felt as the court and hospital "waited" for each other to act or blamed the other for poor judgment. Again, it is a question of confusion and distraction that undermine the therapy and positive rehabilitative efforts of both systems. As we used to assure each other and the staff, patients may be crazy but they are not dumb. Many of us have been in the armed services, worked in business, and been in other institutions. Besides, we all have a basic ability to recognize a "run around." So do well-meaning staff members trying to cut through the red tape. It seemed to us in our own cases, *sui generis* as each seemed to be, that the interface between the court and the hospital needed rearrangement. At a minimum, a professional skilled in mental health law and treatment could save innumerable physician and lawyer and judge hours now spent explaining the law, the treatment, and every other facet of many otherwise standard cases. Note that we are not advocating speedier releases or easier treatment plans: we are merely seeking some clarity for everyone concerned. It seems to us that the present system grew topsy-turvy with each part passing the buck. Too often we felt the buck stopped at the patient. Where a particular

D.A.'s office in our unit's catchment area appointed an attorney and/ or paralegal to specialize in commitments to our unit, the system seemed to work more efficiently. Our idea of a kind of ombudsman for the D.A. and the hospital merely takes this idea one step further.

Finally, we have no idea where the hospital went after we last had contact with it. It is as though the creature was never really there at all. By the nature of the unit and our offenses, many of us who were treated there were there a year or more. As we have said, the duration of our stay was one of the factors that made our treatment there valuable. The same reasons that made long-term treatment useful serve to create the human relationships naturally arising from treatment of that type. Inevitably, after release, we found our real-world problems taking shapes and dimensions that we had not forseen while in the hospital. The trust and communication we had with our former therapists exceeded that of any casual referral to mental health centers. However, the fact is that staff time and the delivery system set up (at least in our system) does not readily accommodate seeing our old therapists. Nor are there readily available facilities for out-patient therapies for former forensic patients. Along the line of AA, we think that with a little help, we and our fellow patients can best help ourselves by continuing to help each other on the "outside." The closed-door model of psychological treatment in the forensic unit should be opened just a crack to provide an opportunity for continuing out-patient contact. We think we benefitted from the experience of psychological evaluation and treatment. We are both on probation now, as is usual in most cases from our unit. That probation mandates continued treatment. One of the incidental benefits of having been in a worthwhile program is that we can tell when we have been helped. Our joint observation of the present system since our release from hospitalization is that help, like that elusive elephant, is often what and where you yourself find it.

Chapter 28

TREATMENT OF OFFENDERS*

JAMES T. BARBASH, Ph.D.

IT SEEMS ALMOST CERTAIN that mental health specialists will be called upon increasingly to treat persons who violate the law. Federal and state agencies have focused attention on community needs, including crime. Greater psychological sophistication on the part of law enforcement personnel, attorneys, and judges is becoming a reality. Correctional institutions, probation departments, and parole boards are placing greater emphasis on a need for psychotherapy. The cumulative effect of these modifications has already resulted in unmet requests for diagnostic and treatment facilities.

UNPOPULAR PATIENTS

In general, persons with antisocial patterns do not prove to be popular cases with treatment specialists. Because of a variety of irritating resistances, seeming lack of gratitude, and relatively little anxiety over offenses, many such persons have been erroneously diagnosed with labels that indicate exceedingly poor prognosis. Passive resistance, attempts to manipulate for ulterior motives, verbal attacks upon society's systems and upon values held by therapists further add to their lack of popularity. Many offenders possess an unusual capacity to arouse feelings of uneasiness, if not outright hostility, within specialists accustomed to more conventional patients.

The picture, however, is not unilateral. Unconscious attitudes of the public have a great impact. In a sense, they seem contradictory because these attitudes are both ambivalent and highly punitive. Ambivalence about good law enforcement is reflected in an almost un-

---

*Adapted from an earlier article that appeared in the *Pennsylvania Psychiatric Quarterly, 9,* 1969.

believable number of ways. While demanding better police protection for themselves, "average" citizens shoplift millions, perhaps billions, of dollars worth of goods each year. Store losses from this type of theft far exceed those incurred from hoodlum activity. Politicians, union officials and others who have been convicted of offenses connected with their duties are returned to office by voters. Attempts at income tax cheating are common. Professionals of all varieties remain silent about incompetent colleagues. Thus, by silence, they expose clients to both fraud and danger. Illegal price fixing, by respected business personnel of large corporations, bilk both individuals and governments. False advertising and shoddy products are not the exclusive province of fly-by-night entrepeneurs. In the United States, drunken driving is directly related to twenty-five thousand deaths a year. An intoxicated driver has greatly increased his potential for assault and murder. Yet those who drive and drink excessively seem no less punitive toward others who commit similar crimes while sober. Driving at an excessive speed is not uncommon, especially for certain CB operators who have the "bears" (police) spotted for them by other radio operators. Legally executing a person in order to uphold a law against killing is a classic example of the confusion that surrounds our legal system. Use of technical loopholes to free dangerous offenders does not seem to bother many attorneys. The list of public inconsistencies goes on and on until it reaches trivia. For instance, use of tricks to cheat telephone companies out of a dime is common practice. Pens, pencils, paper, and other material from the office or shop seem to find their way to private homes. In one sense, it is necessary for therapists to resolve some of the ambivalences that occur in our own lives.[1]

As therapists, it is occasionally difficult to recognize and resolve our own feelings toward offenders, particularly when certain types of crimes have been committed. Reinforcing one's super-ego by punishing others who violate codes is a well-known unconscious desire not always limited to an unenlightened public. It is sometimes easier to identify with a victim than with the offender.[2] An opposite approach, perceiving most criminals as ill in the traditional sense, may make us more comfortable when treating but is not a tenable position.

In our opinion, most recidivists can be viewed simply as persons who use antisocial behavior as a vehicle for other underlying problems. There are, of course, the socioculturally induced delinquent who fits well into his own environment and the psychobiologically impaired individual who can not compete in free society.[3]   The term offender in this section includes a majority of individuals who are often diagnosed as suffering from either character and behavior disorders or from neurotic criminality.   Our description of offender treatment attitudes intentionally emphasizes those aspects that seem most troublesome.   Obviously, universal attitudes can never be found, and we are admittedly painting with a broad brush.   This does not preclude the existence of frequently found similarities within a group or some general differences between offenders and other patients. These will be defined in later sections.

IMPORTANCE

The necessity for psychiatric, psychological, and case work attention is reflected in our enormous crime problem, low success rate of punishment as a deterrent, increasing number of referrals for treatment while on probation or parole, and in current literature.[4,5,6,7] The need for attention is further supported when one considers that numerous innocent persons are injured by commission of an offense. The impact upon victims and their families of murder, rape, child molesting, or even theft adds another dimension to the need. Thought must also be given the family of an apprehended offender and to the inmate himself who often has no conscious recognition of his underlying motives.   Early treatment can also serve as a preventive measure, particularly for those who tend to commit increasingly severe offenses.

Our standards of justice specify limits to the punishment courts can impose.   As a result, it has been approximated that 95 percent of all current prison inmates will eventually be released by law.   Therefore, simple incarceration affords society only a limited form of relief.

In the long run, community protection can be secured best by helping offenders change.   Adequate psychotherapeutic facilities must be an integral part of that protection.   However, antisocial individuals are apt to present therapists with unaccustomed challenges that require special attention.   The efficacy of treating so-called character and behavior disorders has been questioned for many years.

Our own findings indicate that psychological therapy is feasible, provided adjustments in orientation and techniques are made.   A ten-year follow-up study conducted in the Pennsylvania Bureau of Correction[8] revealed that recidivism rates were modified by therapy and under certain conditions were even reversed.   Using completion of parole and absence of rearrest for even minor offenses as criteria, statistically significant differences were found between fifty-one treated cases and fifty-one control cases. Only 25 percent of the untreated group remained successful. The experimental (treated) group showed 72 percent success when positive transference and identification with the therapist took place. When it did not, only 26 percent were successful. Nature of offense, length of criminal record, and other similar factors proved of little consequence or lost their statistical meaning because of attentuating circumstances. Similar results are being secured at the Penn Foundation for Mental Health, Inc., Sellersville, Pa.

SUSPICION, PROVOCATION, AND RESPONSIBILITY

Unlike most clinic and private patients, many offenders beginning treatment view the therapist as an adversary, or at least with much ambivalence. He is perceived as being less a source of help than a parent-community surrogate who will inflict further rejection, loss of self-esteem, inequity, or punishment. Just as frequently he is seen as being incapable of really understanding, easily manipulated, and naive. To the offender, these are realistic assumptions, based on his experiences as he perceived or misperceived them and usually reinforced by others like himself in school, gangs, and prisons. Unconsciously, he may hope these assumptions prove untrue.

Failure to assume responsibility for one's own therapeutic progress is a second common characteristic of offenders entering treatment. Many are highly attuned to even slight signs of rejection or gullibility and will frequently provoke rejection as a test of the specialist. His negative reaction reaffirms the offender's expectation of finding an adversary relationship and justifies him in thereafter avoiding responsibility for growth through treatment. A variant of this is found in those cases that assume help to be some form of total need meeting, no matter how irrational or unjustified the need. Failure to meet these insatiable expectations of support results in the specialist being perceived as rejecting and perhaps threatening. Again, the offender can rationalize his therapeutic irresponsibility. In general, clinic and private patients attempt to modify their behavior to secure approval and symptom relief. Many offenders beginning treatment make use of unintentional slights, disapproval, and provoked rejection in the opposite manner to justify resistances. The same type of rationalization is applied to therapists who are easy to manipulate. They are perceived as incompetent and therefore incapable of helping.

Methods of provoking rejection vary with other concomitant needs. A particularly interesting method is to attack the treatment specialist verbally. This may be done directly or by attacking society and its values, in which the specialist has more emotional investment than he recognizes. His need to overtly challenge an offender's view of police, school teachers, physicians, religious leaders, morality, etc. often makes the therapist feel quite threatened. Assuring a psychotic that his hallucinations are not reality can have very different motivation than defending middle– and upper-class values. Therapists have considerable investment in concepts concerning human life, honesty, fairplay, justice, and so on. Furthermore, the same community that advocates these values supplies the treatment specialist with status and income. Many offenders are quick to sense these vested interests and to rationalize their resistances on the basis of the therapist's "insufficient concern" for patients. We are not suggesting that appropriate confrontation over unacceptable behavior be avoided. However, to be meaningful, it must be in terms of the offender's needs, not the therapist's. Good timing and a positive relationship greatly enhance its chance of success.

ACCEPTANCE AND CONFRONTATION

The concept of personal acceptance without necessarily condoning behavior is particularly important in this respect. Here again, therapists may face unaccustomed problems. Because most offenders do not exhibit traditional symptoms of disturbance, specialists tend to forget that certain aspects of reality require special recognition. Reality, as experienced and perceived by the offender, can be quite different than for the public at large. For example, his life may have been full of experiences that led him to view conventional standards and values as a sham. Poorly timed confrontation results only in a specialist being viewed as insincere or unrealistic. Conversely, implied agreement with the sham concept suggests that the specialist has been trapped in a similar perception with a resultant loss of treatment effectiveness.

Verbal attacks serve many functions besides avoiding treatment responsibility, as do the more subtle techniques like passive resistance, manipulation, and surreptitious misbehavior during periods of seeming progress. These functions may be viewed at various levels. Among the more common are adolescent limit-testing, counterphobic reactions to dependency needs, avoidance of emotional attachment to a therapist, avoidance of emotional material, and problem denial. Some offenders find communicating very difficult and require special assistance in this area. Others mislead the therapist because they are sure rejection will follow his discovery of what they "are really like." Confusion about adult life roles is particularly common. Men exhibit concern about being treated like a child, about being "a man," and are apt to view aggression as proof of masculinity. Underlying all these functions are obvious dynamics that not only reveal familial patterns of interaction, but suggest what is expected of the therapist as a parent surrogate.

ENTRAPMENT

A third common characteristic of offenders is an unusual capacity to entrap others in their own anxieties and hostilities. The list of techniques used is long and includes both conscious manipulation and unconscious motives. Demands or pleas for intercession with the authorities, employers, or family members, threats to become involved in dangerous situations, or descriptions of misbehavior since beginning treatment, are but few. Therapists' unconscious ambivalences toward authority may be particularly vulnerable in such situations. The specialist who becomes entrapped, and shows it, is of little value because then the therapist appears less able to handle anxiety and hostility than the patient and reinforces the problem. In group treatment, cotherapists unaccustomed to offenders may find themselves manipulated into competing with each other or with a vocal patient for acceptance from the group.

The type of provocative behavior already described is another example of entrapment technique. When successful, the offender is not only reinforced in his assumption about himself and society but the therapists may even begin to question their own motives in terms of masochistic needs. Here we can only suggest that as long as resistances are perceived in their dynamic context and a reasonable success rate is secured, the specialist probably need not be concerned.

GUILT FEELINGS, LOYALTY, AND GRATITUDE

It has been contended that many offenders lack guilt feelings, are ungrateful, and exhibit little loyalty to others. Certainly this description fits a few but, by and large, it has not proven consistent with our experiences over a thirty-year period. The question is loyalty to whom and guilt feelings about what? Generally speaking, offenders entertain more than their share of feelings of worthlessness and guilt. However, guilt is more often centered unconsciously around reasons for parental rejection, interpersonal relationships, and personal failures than antisocial behavior. Loyalties tend to be on a juvenile level and extend largely to others who are perceived as fellow outcasts and victims of society. These two relatively common attributes can be exploited therapeutically. Dwelling upon antisocial acts during treatment is rarely constructive whereas uncovering and resolving conflicts over self-esteem and guilt usually is. Once the outer defensive resistances have been penetrated, the therapist may become an object of childlike loyalty and gratitude. These factors represent a fourth common characteristic of offenders.

UNDERLYING MOTIVES

Descriptions of the motives underlying criminal behavior vary with the level upon which they are focused. Listed below are some of the ones we have found to be of functional value in treatment. They represent a range of levels from conscious to deeply repressed. Many, of course, overlap.

1. Inappropriate attempts to retaliate against loved ones by victimizing surrogates, provoking punishment, or causing embarassment by being apprehended.
2. Escaping to jail.
3. Acting out unconscious wishes of one or both parents.
4. Autonomy-dependency conflicts in which crime serves as erroneous proof of adulthood and arrest means of avoiding precipitating agents.
5. Attempts to prove others care by self-injurious methods.
6. Unrealistic expectations of interpersonal life, usually on an all-or-none basis. Failure to secure idealized relationship resulting in various intrapunitive and extrapunitive actions.
7. Repeating with current authority the distorted patterns established with parental authority.
8. Inability to withstand normal frustrations of everyday living either because of overprotection and control or emotional deprivation during childhood.
9. Parental example.
10. Feelings of unworthiness and guilt dynamically requiring self-

punitive behavior. Frequently disguised with compensatory actions or pseudoindifference to self.

11. Overt or near surface oedipal problems, particularly in rape cases.

PARENT SURROGATE AND DIAGNOSIS

Our fifth characteristic deals with therapy and perceived parental roles. Probably no group of patients view therapists as parent surrogates more intensely than offenders. It can be anticipated that attempts will be made during treatment to repeat parent-child patterns with the specialist. On this basis alone, it is usually not difficult to draw tentative broad diagnostic conclusions. However, these have only limited functional value compared to underlying motives as exemplified in the preceding section. Unfortunately, offenders are adept at disguising such motives. If there is a diagnostic rule of thumb, it would be to look in a direction opposite to the patient's verbalizations. Expressions of hatred for a parent usually mean quite the opposite, coupled with an inability to win over that parent. When lengthy accounts are given about the hardships of jail, careful questioning will often reveal that crimes were committed in a manner unconsciously designed to ensure arrest. Devoted assistance by family members during arrest and confinement periods may be offered as proof of familial concern but may also indicate that these are the only times concern is expressed. We know of forgers who seemingly made unusual progress in therapy, but forged checks against the specialist and town mayor. Needless to say, their first victims had been their own fathers.

The therapist's ability to pick out patterns quickly, particularly those relating to parental interaction, has much to do with establishing a successful treatment relationship. It protects the therapist against entrapments that neither the therapist nor the offender can afford and establishes the therapist's competence in the eyes of a skeptical patient. It also allows management of cases that might otherwise seem prognostically impossible.

ONE TECHNIQUE

To note that therapists contribute something of themselves to each patient is axiomatic. Techniques vary with training and personality. Our own experiences point to saying very little during the first three to six appointments. We offer no comments on police, victims, judges, moral codes, employers, parents, guilt or innocence of the offender, reasons for being in therapy, reasons for not being in therapy, attorneys, wives, girlfriends, husbands, boyfriends, accomplices, sexual habits, etc. We have no way of knowing what is intentional prevarication, what is unconsciously distorted, or the reasons for either. When necessary, we will ask questions but give no indication of whether we accept or reject the response. At the end of allotted time we intentionally give a show of friendship by commenting on some neutral subject or perhaps a slap on the back or anything else that the subject seems able to accept. This maneuver is repeated occasionally. In essence, we are beginning the process of saying "I like you but do not necessarily believe what you say."

The patient on the other hand usually goes through a series of complaints dealing with the authority figures that are listed above and finds no response from the therapist. In time he is apt to try several different "persecutors" to no avail. In the interim, the therapist listens carefully for dynamics. Are the complaints mostly against male or female authority? Were they real, untruthful, or imagined? What underlies the verbalizations? Who were his victims, past and present? Was there no seeming pattern at all? Was he caught in a way that the therapist thinks he may be escaping to, not from jail? Did he have accomplices and what dynamic stimulation were they? Is he attempting to retaliate by provoking punishment or acting out wishes of a parent? Parental example? Self-punitive behavior for marked feelings of inadequacy or guilt? What are his real views of parents or their substitutes? In some form of theft, he could probably earn as much by working or being on welfare. What he says is not psychotic but delivered like a "normal" person. In the long run, antisocial behavior is the responsibility of the person acting it out. However, the essential causes are found in a person's dynamics as a rule.

After three or four sessions, we have enough of the dynamics and have listened to enough extraneous jargon to pointedly interrupt our subject, list and give reasons for what would seem to be some of the real causes. The reactions may be slight, or as it is in many cases, profound with blushing, squirming, fingernail biting, etc. It is then that the therapeutic process actually begins. No technique is universal but the system is usually effective whether the subject is relatively sincere and insightless or the opposite. Their reasons for coming do not matter.

It is not uncommon for offenders to break appointments, and therapists should be prepared. In the long run, a large percent will eventually return.

QUANTITATIVE AND DIRECTIONAL

In many ways, we view treatment difference between offenders and nonoffenders as quantitative rather than qualitative. Certainly conventional patients can also become resistant, provocative, suspicious, manipulative, entrapping, etc. Offenders are simply apt to do it more effectively. We also see differences in the direction in which offenders express their hostilities, specifically toward the therapist's values and society's codes. However, essential personality patterns and defenses resemble those of other patients. Recognition of both differences and similarities forearms the therapist and encourages the examining of motives, codes, and values normally taken for granted. Finally, it reduces the entrapment potential of provocative behavior by their beginning treatment.

NONVOLUNTARY PATIENTS

Many nonconfined offenders seek treatment for conscious ulterior motives. To do otherwise is to admit being "crazy," a usually unfounded allegation particularly intolerable to the patient. Not infrequently, defense attorneys who urge therapy are perceived by the offender as only suggesting a manipulative technique to soften the judge. Other face-saving rationalizations are often applied to courts sympathetic to treatment, parole authorities, and family members.

Traditional methods of evaluating motivation for therapy can rarely be applied to offenders. Holt[9] has raised questions concerning motivation in all types of cases. His conclusions coincide with our own experiences—that offenders pressed into therapy by the authorities generally proved as successful as self-referrals, provided three conditions were met fairly early. First, the specialist had sufficient skill to communicate his interest, concern, and respect for people in general. Second, the therapist communicated sufficient psychological sophistication to understand and help the offender, despite the latter's conscious resistances. Third, the therapist had sufficient "strength" to avoid being trapped in competitive reactions or duped into sympathy. These three conditions are obviously important in any therapeutic relationship, but particularly so with skeptical, defensive, rationalizing offenders.

REFERENCES

1. Barbash, J.T.　Compensation and the crime of pigeon dropping, *Journal of Clinical Psychology, 8,* (1), 92–94, 1952.
2. Barbash, J.T.　*Correctional counseling,* Camp Hill, Pennsylvania Bureau of Correction, 1964.
3. Barbash, J.T.　*An investigation of the predictability of prison adjustment,* Microfilms, Ann Arbor, Michigan, 1956.
4. Glasscote, R., Sanders, D., Forstenzer, H., and Foley, A.　*The community mental health center: An analysis of existing models,* Baltimore, Maryland, Garamond/Pridemark, 1964.
5. Hartman, K.B.　G.P.'s pioneer a community center, *SK&F Psychiatric Reporter,* May–June 1965.
6. Sadoff, R.L., Polsky, S., and Heller, M.S.　The forensic psychiatry clinic: Model for a new approach, *American Journal of Psychiatry, 123,* (11), 1402–1407, 1967.
7. Snake pits give way to new clinics, *Business Week,* November 5, 1966.
8. Barbash, J.T.　A study of psychological therapy and post-release adjustment, *American Journal of Correction, 25,* (1), 26–29, 1963.
9. Holt, W.E.　The concept of motivation for treatment, *American Journal of Psychiatry, 123,* (11), 1389–1394, 1967.

Chapter 29

THE FORENSIC PSYCHOLOGIST AND THE RAPIST: DISPOSITION AND TREATMENT

JAN C. GROSSMAN, Ph.D.

INTRODUCTION

As I am writing this article, there is some controversy in the Philadelphia area over a common pleas court judge who sentenced a twenty-one-year-old man convicted of raping a sixteen-year-old girl at knifepoint to seven years probation. When the victim, who was in court at the time of sentencing, expressed unhappiness over the judge's leniency, he severely reprimanded her for questioning his judicial prerogative. Ten days after his release, the convicted rapist was rearrested after a forty-year-old woman positively identified him as the man who had just attacked her. The jurist involved has since been the subject of the most vitriolic media attacks for his conduct of the case.

In some circles, however, this judge is considered "enlightened." He decided on probation even though the presentence probation report recommended incarceration. The results of psychiatric and psychological reports were not made public. His stated reason for probation was the fact that the defendant has no previous adult contact with the law. He probably felt that a prison experience would only serve to expose the young man to professional criminals and to the possibility of prison rape, either as the perpetrator or victim. He told the accused at the time of sentencing that he was a reasonable candidate for rehabilitation and made specific recommendations in that regard.

Increasingly, forensic psychologists find themselves in a similar position as the judge. They are asked to assess the convicted rapist, use their knowledge, clinical skills, and psychological instruments (and usually intuition) to make an assessment, a diagnosis, and a "scientific" recommendation to the court as to case disposition. In this chapter, we will accept that forensic psychologists can adequately analyze their test and interview data and report on personality findings in a cogent and meaningful way. The personality, psychodynamics, demographics, and psychiatric history are discussed at length by Rada,[1] Amir,[2] and Abramson.[3] We will then turn our attention to the problems of disposition recommendation and rehabilitation.

All too often the forensic psychologist has only two recommendation alternatives: prison (and all the problems that go with it) and "psychiatric" or "supervised" probation (which can mean as little as one to four hours of professional contact a month). Happily, some states, such as New Jersey, provide by law for a third alternative, a special facility for housing and treating sex offenders. Some communities have special treatment centers for rapists, such as the Center for Rape Concern in Philadelphia, but these treatment options are available only in a minority of areas. It also is not clear that any given treatment program is going to be successful. Later in this chapter we will look at various psychological treatment approaches that have reported some success in reducing rape recidivism.

At the "recommendation" part of his report, the forensic psychologist may have a crisis of conscience. Does he opt for recommending probation, with perhaps little or no treatment but protecting the rapist from the prison experience, or does he "protect the community" by recommending incarceration? This decision might depend, in part, on the "psychiatric" diagnosis established, but the psychiatric labeling process has well-known reliability, social, and predictive drawbacks.[4] This recommendation might depend, in part, on test or interview results but there seems to be some question as to which examination variables, if any, are predictive of rape recidivism or success of sex offender rehabilitation. This recommendation might also consider details of the crime and the "type" of rapist involved, as there are now rapists taxonomies, but has it been clearly established that one kind of rapist is a better community risk than another? Whatever conclusions are arrived at, how do alcoholism and drug abuse affect the outcome? Many rapists are intoxicated at the time of the rape. In this chapter we will explore these questions.

SOME BRIEF STATISTICS

In 1975 the FBI published statistics relating to rapist recidivism.[5] Of the national sample of 930 arrested for forcible rape, between

1970 and 1975, it was the first rape offense for only 36 percent of the subjects. The survey further revealed that 20.5 percent had one other rape arrest, 11.6 percent had two prior rape arrests, and 31.1 percent had three or more prior rape arrests. Of those convicted rapists released in 1972, 75 percent had been rearrested at least once by the end of the survey period in 1975. Recently, Growth and Burgess[6] reported the following:

> The compulsive nature of rape behavior was reflected in the discovery that 53 percent of the 133 offenders had at least one previous conviction for rape. . . . In addition, a good many "first offenders" admitted to a number of previous assaults even though their most recent offense was their first conviction. Further. . . . 63 percent showed an increase in force and aggression during their assaults over time; none showed a decrease (p. 403)

These figures might well lead the forensic psychologist to the assumption that the odds strongly favor the possibility of rape or criminal recidivism in the rapist he is examining. It is just this belief that leads many professionals to expect continuing criminal involvement from the rapist and then look for some evidence to the contrary when considering recommendations to the court.

DIAGNOSIS

The final diagnosis of the rapist may well determine the disposition of the case. Recent studies agree that one third to two thirds of rapists most closely fit into the category of antisocial personality or related personality disorders.[1,2,7,8] This diagnosis itself can be extremely pejorative in the mental health community. It infers an ingrained pattern of hostile acting out that is relatively immune to traditional therapeutic rehabilitation.[9] It has been described as the "kiss of death" that will elicit the strictest penalties from judges who look to psychiatric data before pronouncing sentence. Because of this, some forensic psychologists are reluctant to attach the antisocial personality label to young rapist first offenders.

Psychotic diagnoses are found in about 10 percent of convicted rapists.[1,7] Rada[1] points out that this diagnosis is important because of the following:

1. Amelioration of the psychotic condition may lead to the cessation of rape activity.
2. The presence of an acute psychosis at the time of the commission of the offense may have important legal implications; for

example, the rapist may be found to be not guilty by reason of insanity.

3. Rape offenses by psychotic rapists are likely to be bizarre, violent and exceedingly terrifying experiences for the victim (p. 121).

Though a diagnosis of psychosis infers the possibility of remission, there is also an inference, particularly with schizophrenics, of the possibility of regression and further psychotic acting out.   One judge, after attending a seminar for legal personnel on diagnostic classification put it this way, "It looks like anti-social personalities never get better and schizophrenics may get better and then get worse."

It is usually assumed that the minority of rapists with a clear diagnosis of neurosis, situational disorder, retardation, or "other" are the most fruitful grounds for rehabilitation.   Such men present little or no criminal history and have clear and workable therapeutic issues relating to their masculine identification, relations with women, dealing with stress, etc.[1]   It should be pointed out at this time that this author has never seen any systematic research correlating rapist diagnosis with recidivism or rehabilitation.

PSYCHOLOGICAL TEST DATA

Rada[1] in a thorough review of over thirty different studies since 1950 found much ambiguity relating to the psychological test data of rapists.   Some studies did not isolate rapists from other sex offenders. Others did not have adequate normal controls, while others were case histories or had a small number of subjects.   Results that were obtained were disappointing for those who would like to believe in a "'rapist profile" on tests.   After reviewing results on the Rorschach, the Figure Drawing Tests, the Thematic Apperception Tests, and the Minnesota Multiphasic Personality Inventory, Rada concludes the following:

> Reports of psychometric studies of the rapist are few and the data is inconsistent. . . .   In the last ten years there are even fewer reports, possibly because previous inability to adequately correlate personality types with specific criminal behavior has led to apathy and dissatisfaction with these techniques (p. 32).

Rada also concluded that there was similar ambiguity when it came to rapists' intellectual functioning as measured by standard adult Intelligence Quotient (IQ) tests.

Nowhere in Rada's summary was any study done using psychological test data to predict success of rehabilitation or recidivism. This author has never come across one of any note. It seems that the test data of the rapist should be viewed less for the crime and more for the person. Interpretation should be based on basic well-proven clinical indicators and signs and not with any rapist profile in mind. If a forensic psychologist has some general test indices he looks for to indicate recidivism risk in criminals, he may choose to apply them to the rapist at his own judgment and risk, bearing in mind the aforementioned 75 percent rapist recidivism rate. It seems safer to use the test data to obtain a reasonable description of the subjects' personality, conflicts, defense, psychopathology, and intelligence and to avoid using them as the sole basis for any definitive predictions.

ALCOHOLISM, DRUG ABUSE, AND THE RAPIST

It is quite often that one has to remind an inexperienced psychology student or intern that the "sincere," "insightful," "remorseful" (often tranquilized) rapist that he has just examined was not quite the same man who committed a vicious rape a month previously. At our forensic unit at Philadelphia State Hospital, 60 percent of the rapists we examine report alcoholic intoxication at the time of the offense. It is more than a useful exercise to attempt to reconstruct an intoxicated picture of the rapist from test data and interview material because, especially in the case of the alcoholic, it is likely to expect that he will be that way on the outside again. It is quite common to find the following line in our reports to the court: "In the testing situation, Mr. X demonstrated adequate social controls and insight into his problems but based on past history and test data we can make no guarantee about his controls under reduced states of consciousness while in the community."

Alcohol has long been recognized as a contaminating variable in the rape situation. Abramson[3] reported that over half of the 102 rapists he studied were drinking at the time of the offense. Amir[2] reported that one third of his 646 cases were intoxicated at the time of the offense. Rada[10] studying 77 convicted rapists, reported 48 percent were under the influence at the time and 35 percent could be considered alcoholic. Rada has suggested three types of alcohol rape situations. In the first type of situation, a nonalcoholic rapist uses alcohol to bolster his ego, overcome his timidity, and release an underlying rape dynamic. In the second situation, an alcoholic rapist manifests rape behavior as part of a series of manifestations of social disorganization. In the third situation, alcohol appears to trigger a different associational pattern between sexual and aggressive impulses that is then reflected in the conscious fantasies of the rapist. In some rapists, the desire to rape is always associated with alcohol and is never, or hardly ever, present in the sober state.

In some alcoholic rapists, it seems reasonable to make a tentative prediction for recidivism with the likelihood of continued drinking and rehabilitation with correction of the alcoholic condition. In many cases, probation, even "psychiatric probation," means a return to the same friends and same community where strong alcoholic consumption is the expected norm and a requisite for social functioning. Under such pressure, it is reasonable to be pessimistic about the future of even the most well-intentional alcoholic-rapist. Whenever possible, we opt for recommending a *live-in* alcoholic rehabilitation setting for the alcoholic-rapist with strong community follow-up, rather than probation.

A survey of research indicates that very little research has been conducted to explore the connection between drug abuse and rape. At Philadelphia State Hospital we find about 20 percent of our rapists were under the influence of illegal drugs (usually marijuana) at the time of their rape but most of these men had also been drinking. Rada[10] found only 3 of the 77 rapists in his study were on drugs at the time of their crime. Gebhard et al.[11] discuss the connection between drugs and sex crimes and find little or no correlation. DeLeon and Wexler[12] interviewed 31 heroin addicts and found a marked decrease in sexual interest and the quality and quantity of the sexual act. It can be tentatively concluded that at least some drug abuse is not clearly correlated with rape and in some cases may even contraindicate it.

CLINICAL INTERVIEW

A review of the literature reveals no studies correlating the specific clinical interview behaviors of the rapist with recidivism or probability of rehabilitation. Indeed, our clinical experience at the forensic ward of Philadelphia State Hospital has shown us that some convicted rapists who gave the "best," most remorseful, insightful interviews and were subsequently released to the community, were quickly rearrested for another rape or similar offense. Others with similarly "good" interviews went on to successful community adjustment. What we can be more definite about, however, is that convicted rapists who perform "poorly" in the interview are much more likely candidates for recidivism. In other words, the interview, by itself, should not be used to predict therapeutic success, but can be used in some cases, to effectively anticipate an active community risk.

What we center on in the rapist interview, aside from a thorough mental status examination, psychiatric history, and assessment of current life functioning, is (if the subject cooperates) an in-depth verbal recreation of the rape situation from the time of its inception in the mind of the rapist to its conclusion. Subjects we view as definite community risks have histories of sexual offenses and often a diagnosis of antisocial personality or related disorder. They can and do become pleasurably involved in the retelling of their crime—smiling, seeming to enjoy the retelling with a marked lack of anxiety or remorse. Some may verbally express guilt while obviously enjoying the memories. Such subjects often have a marked lack of empathy for the victim of the rape, they downplay any suffering on her part and/or unrealistically view her as an active participant or initiator of the sexual act. In more brutal rapes, the victim can be viewed as deserving or being "turned on" by the violence.

We have also found that the rapist who commits his act while psychotic can be a poor candidate for rehabilitation. During the interview, his recreation of the crime can be totally unrealistic from gross denial of the act to delusional stories of the victims "evil purposes" to attribution of the act to "other forces." Even during remission of psychosis, recollection of the crime can be defensively repressed or distorted so that the subject cannot therapeutically deal with his criminal behavior. During subsequent psychotic episodes, we find the rapist can experience a recurrence of similar reality testing loss with similar criminal results.

RAPIST TYPOLOGIES

Based upon an accurate description of the rape situation and some psychological understanding, the forensic psychologist might wish to relate the subject to one of the rapist classification systems currently in use. These systems attempt to establish a taxonomy of the rapist to account for his style, motivation, and psychodynamics. In the uncooperative convicted rapist this means that the courtroom accounts of the rape, by themselves, can lead to some psychological understanding of the offender leading to appropriate disposition recommendations.

Cohen's Typology

In 1971, Murray Cohen and his associates published the first well-defined and recognized system of rapist classification based on their study of 600 offenders committed to Bridgewater Treatment Center in Massachusetts.[13] Cohen et al., listed four basic types of rapists and clinical descriptions to go with each. Cohen's work is also significant because it clearly postulated that many rapists' primary motives for their act are aggression not sexuality. This idea has recently enlisted support and elaboration and has become more accepted.[14]

The first type of rape that Cohen identified is the *aggressive aim rape*. The primary purpose of this assault is to brutalize and cause pain to the victim out of a dynamic or displaced rage from primary female relationships. Such men have an extremely stereotyped masculine presentation and describe their primary feelings during the assault as anger. Cohen's second type of rapist has primarily a *sexual aim*. Men who commit this type of rape are often weak and ineffectual in their heterosexual life with a history of sexual deviation. There is a minimum of violence and if women resist actively, the rapist frequently discontinues the act. These men are frequent recidivists with rape fantasies as an active part of their mental life and masturbatory activity. The third kind of rapist described by Cohen is subject to *sex-aggression defusion* in that there is a strong sadistic element needed for the production of sexual excitation. This is the rarest type of rapist and men in this category most frequently fall into the category of antisocial personality. Occasionally, this rape leads to murder or severe maiming. In this category the rapist often projects enjoyment of the violence on the victim. Cohen's last rape classification is that of the *impulse* rapist. These are essentially antisocial personality types who commit a rape as an adjunct to another crime such as robbery or burglary. He takes the sexual satisfaction because it is there and not out of any specific rape psychodynamic.

Power and Anger Typology

As an outgrowth of the recognition of hostility as a primary motive in rape, Growth, Burgess, and Holstrom[14] proposed a rape classification based on their examination of rape accounts taken from 133 offenders and 92 victims. In this classification system, Growth et al. totally deemphasized sexuality as the primary motive labeling the act of rape as "pseudosexual." All rapes, according to these researchers, stem from motives of anger or power and can be classified accordingly. In *power rapes* "the offender seeks power and control over his victim through intimidation by means of a weapon, physical force or threat of bodily harm. Physical aggression is used to over-power and subdue the victim and directed toward achieving submission. The aim of the assault usually is to effect sexual intercourse as evidence of conquest" (p. 1240). This type of rapist uses the power of the rape to compensate for real interpersonal and heterosexual life inadequacies. These rapes are usually premeditated with much fantasy related to the conquest. There are two types of power rapists. The *power-assertive* rapist sees rape as an "expression of virility and mastery and dominance." He feels entitled to "take it" or sees sexual domination as a way of keeping "his women in line" (p. 1240). The *power-reassurance* rapist attempts "to resolve disturbing doubts about his sexual adequacy and masculinity. He wants to place a woman in a helpless, controlled position in which she cannot refuse or reject him, thereby showing up his failing sense of worth and adequacy" (p. 1241).

Growth et al. state that the other basic type of rape is the *anger* rape in which the rapist can vent his rage toward women on his victim through extreme violence, far more than would be needed just to force her into submission. The anger rapist has extremely conflicting hostile heterosexual relationships. He finds the punitive sadism of his rape extremely exciting. Anger rapists are primarily responsible for rape-homicides. There are two kinds of Anger rapists. The *anger-retaliation* rapist's primary motive is the clear release of sadism and rage with the goal of "degradation and humiliation." The *anger-excitation* rapist receives pleasure from the pain he inflicts on a victim. There is a definite fusion of sexual and aggressive drives.

Clinical Typology

Rada[1] suggests what he calls a *clinical* classification system of rapists based on symptoms and characterological types. A plurality of his cases fall into what he calls the *sociopathic* category. These are impulse rapists who rape as part of a pervasive pattern of antisocial behavior. There need not be, and usually is not, any particular rape psychodynamic. The *psychotic* rapist category covers the bizarre rapes that are committed by men at various stages of the decompensation process. These rapes often represent blatant acting out of primitive psychosexual conflicts, particularly relating to the maternal environment. The *situational* rapist commits his act as a result of intense stress problems or loss in his life. When not stressed, he presents a normal/neurotic clinical picture with a history of some work and social adjustment, but when pressured gives the impression of undergoing an agitated depression. This type of rapist is likely to express guilt to his victims, feel honest remorse for his behavior and respond to outpatient psychotherapy. The *masculine identity conflict* rapist feels basically insecure in his masculine identification and plans his rape enjoying the fantasy of conquest and humiliation of his victim to bolster his sexual image of himself. This rapist is a frequent recidivist but is often apprehended when his masculine self-aggrandizement and bragging to his victim bring about his capture. The smallest category of rapist is the *Sadistic* rapist. He requires degradation and pain from his victim to meet his sexual needs. His sexual and aggressive drives are clearly fused. His rapes are planned to meet his needs.

Summary on Diagnosis and Disposition

It seems clear that when making a disposition recommendation for a convicted rapist, the forensic psychologist should keep in mind the FBI's 75 percent three-year criminal recidivism rate. This includes only the men who were caught. If you assume that others acted out and were not apprehended we are estimating that perhaps only 10 percent of rapists are good risks for direct release in the community. The men who might possibly be good risks would have no history of rape or antisocial behavior, present a neurotic/normal clinical picture, be nonalcoholic, and have no history of rape/sadistic fantasies. These men committed their one rape during a period of intense stress in their lives and have some therapeutic distance or insight and guilt in relation to their behavior. They will have a job and family in the community and will seek out therapeutic support.

Bad risks include men who present an antisocial or recurrent-psychotic clinical picture with a history of rape recidivism and sadistic/rape masturbatory fantasies. Also, clearly bad risks are men of mixed diagnosis with chronic masculine identification conflicts requiring victimization of women for some of psychic equilibrium as well as men who are clearly fused in the area of sexuality and aggression, requiring violence toward a woman to achieve sexual excitation. Alcoholism, of course, multiplies the risk factors in the above individuals.

The ideal disposition placement for rapists with a high recidivism probability is a special live-in intensive treatment center for sex offenders available in some states or areas. At the very minimum, if these men are given community placement, they should be in high intensity therapy programs with well-supervised lives. Examples of promising therapy programs for rapists will be given in the next section. If no adequate treatment is available, the forensic psychologist might well consider the probabilities and statistics when making a recommendation of prison or probation.

RAPIST TREATMENT APPROACHES

In this section, we are presenting brief summaries of rapist treatment programs from a variety of psychotherapeutic perspectives from behavioral, to analytic, to emotive. All claim high (70–100%) success rates, that is, low recidivism rates after program completion.

Behavioristic Approach

Abel et al.[15,16] list five important elements in most successful rapist rehabilitation programs. They are the following:

1. The establishment of an empathic therapeutic relationship.
2. Confronting the rapist with the responsibility for his behavior.
3. Skill and behavior training in heterosocial and heterosexual situations.
4. Promoting arousal to "normal" adult female stimuli situations.
5. Decreasing the urge to rape and its concommitant arousal.

Though Abel et al. call their treatment an "integrated" one, theirs along with the work of Cooke[17] can best be classified as behavioral, in that it makes use of modern behavior therapy techniques at every point in the treatment process.

Cooke[17] and Abel et al.[15] point out that before the therapy process can begin, total assessment must be made regarding the pathological, sexual, and social thoughts and behaviors to be reduced and the deficits in positive social and heterosexual behaviors to be overcome. Such an assessment should be done in some detail in order to pick up and relate to the specific individual stimuli causing deviant arousal and the specific individual thoughts and fears contributing to social dysfunctioning.

Reduction of deviant arousal has been accomplished by two established techniques: electrical aversive conditioning and covert sensitization. Electrical shocks can be applied to the rapist as punishment as he goes through the specific deviant thoughts and fantasies in regards to his rape behavior. This can serve to reduce his stimulation. Cooke[17] describes the use of covert sensitization[18] in which the rapist is taken on a fantasy experience of his rape behavior, followed by vivid descriptive imagery of him getting sick and vomiting—imagery so vivid that it often leads to nausea and regurgitation. Callahen and Leitenberg[19] report that shock and covert sensitization are equally effective in reducing deviant sexual behaviors. Cooke[17] also uses "thought stopping" in which the patient is asked to verbalize deviant fantasies, at which point the therapist yells, "Stop!" The patient, in this way, can learn to stop himself cognitively.

Systematic desensitization[20] is a behavior therapy process that allows the subject to associate fear stimuli on a fantasy level with verbally induced relaxation. Cooke[17] uses it with rapists to reduce fears in four general areas that often inhibit normal social and sexual functioning:

1. Fear of rejection in social and sexual situations.
2. Fear of inadequacy in social and sexual situations.
3. Fear of constructive expression of anger.
4. Fear of homosexuality, which is often found in connection with rape.

Abel et al.[15] and Cooke[17] then describe behavioral techniques for creating normal heterosocial arousal and conditioning positive social and heterosexual behaviors. Orgasmic reconditioning is used where appropriate and has the rapist masturbate, substituting normal heterosexual thoughts for deviant masturbatory fantasies. The rapist is also encouraged to go through many role playing and behavior rehearsal sessions to polish much lacking assertive social and heterosexual skills.

Emotive Release Therapy

Prendergast[21] reports the development of a highly successful rapist rehabilitation program he calls "Re-education of Attitudes (and) Repressed Emotions (R.O.A.R.E.)" R.O.A.R.E. therapy has been conducted exclusively on sex offenders of all types who are sent by state law to the Adult Diagnostic and Treatment Center in Avenel, New Jersey. He reports a two-year recidivism rate of only 12 percent.

R.O.A.R.E. involves a series of intensive therapeutic emotional experiences whose goal "is the release of dynamic emotions of pain, fear, anger, and hurt which are then replaced with love, acceptance and support." R.O.A.R.E. also facilitates the recall, release, and reliving of repressed trauma. These reexperiences are extremely real to the subject in that he can feel "pain, pleasure, heat, cold, orgasm, etc." It is clear from Prendergast that the adult rapist who has performed much violence upon his victim relives during R.O.A.R.E. sessions childhood violence done upon him. Descriptions of R.O.A.R.E. therapy reactions are reminiscent of Janov's primal scream therapy.[22,23]

R.O.A.R.E. sessions are held in groups over periods lasting four to six hours. Patients must volunteer for R.O.A.R.E. therapy as it is adjunctive to the regular therapies required for offenders. Sessions are videotaped with the opportunity for self-observation afterwards, when he has the intellectual and emotional distance to observe himself. From this observation much insight is gained as the patient, whose defenses are down from his session, can clearly look at himself.

"Re-education" is the ultimate goal of the treatment and results in permanent changes in "behavioral attitudes and trends." The reeducation results in what Prendergast calls a "new identity" and new values and attitudes relevant to an adaptable successful social existence.

Group Psychoanalytic Approach

Steg et al.[24] report success working with sex offenders (including rapists) in an analytic group situation at Philadelphia's Center for Rape Concern. Peters et al.[25] report that offenders attending a mean of twenty-six weekly sessions had only a 3 percent criminal recidivism rate during a two-year follow up. Patient attendance in groups was mandatory as a requirement for probation.

The therapy of the group was based upon the fact that most men fit into the diagnostic category of character disorder. This is manifested by severe ego function deficits, including problems in psychosexual development, poor social adaptation, and impaired secondary process functioning. The therapeutic process encouraged resolution of these problems by identification with the functioning group and its leaders. As a result of the identification process, infantile demands and needs for immediate gratification yield to more ego control and socially acceptable behaviors. Peters et al.[25] reports three phases of the sex offenders participation in the analytic group. The initial phase consists of denial, silence, resistance, and withdrawal, combined with suspicion of the group and its authority figure therapists. During the middle phase, the members become more verbal and active, speaking frankly and responsibly of sexual issues and assuming group leadership. In the terminal phase of treatment, positive feelings are expressed toward the group, men realistically deal with their sexual fears and feelings as well as expressing here and now feelings toward the group. Peters and Roether[26] state that one of the main benefits of such a process is to dilute the offenders intense reaction to authority by working through peers in the group setting, thus overcoming any cultural gap between subject and therapist.

Summary on Rapist Treatment Approaches

It is clear from the aforementioned that treatment using a number of different theoretical approaches can lead to a marked lowering of the rapist recidivism rate. It is not clear how much marked personality change is accomplished in one program as opposed to another as the criterion for success is extremely narrow, namely no further arrests for sexual offenses. When available, a rapist treatment program with a good history of success seems to be a preferable dispositional alternative.

REFERENCES

1. Rada, R. Alcoholism and forcible rape, *American Journal of Psychiatry, 132*, 444–446, 1975.
2. Amir, M. Patterns of forcible rape, In Chnard, D. and Quincy, R. (eds.), *Criminal behavior systems*, New York, Holt, 1967.
3. Abramson, D. *The psychology of crime*, New York, Columbia University Press, 1960.
4. Mahrer, A.R. *New approaches to personality classification*, New York Columbia University Press, 1970.
5. Kelly, C. *Crime in the U.S., 1975*, Washington, D.C., Government Printing Office, 1976, pp. 42-47.
6. Growth, A.N. and Burgess, A.W. Rape: A sexual deviation, *American Journal of Orthopsychiatry, 47*, 400–406, 1977.
7. Henn, F.A., Herjanic, M., and Vanderpearl, R.H. Forensic psychiatry: Profiles of two types of sex offenders, *American Journal of Psychiatry, 133*, 694–696, 1976.
8. McCaldon, R.J. Rape, *Canadian Journal of Corrections, 9*, 37–46, 1967.
9. Coleman, J.C. *Abnormal psychology and modern life*, Glenview, Illinois, Scott, Foresman, 1975.
10. Rada, R. Alcoholism and forcible rape, *American Journal of Psychiatry, 132*, 444–446, 1975.
11. Gebhard, P.H., Gagnon, J.H., Pomeroy, W.B., and Christenson, C.V. *Sex offenders*, New York, Harper and Row, 1965.

12. DeLeon, G. and Wexler, H.K.   Heroin addiction: Its relations to sexual behavior and sexual experience, *Journal of Abnormal Psychology, 81*, 36–38, 1973.

13. Cohen, M.L., Garofalo, R., Boucher, R., and Seghorn, T.   The psychology of the rapist, *Seminars in Psychiatry, 3*, 307–327, 1971.

14. Growth, A.N., Burgess, A.W., and Holmstrom, L.   Rape: Power, anger and sexuality, *American Journal of Psychiatry, 134*, 1239–1243, 1977.

15. Abel, G., Blanchard, E., and Becker, J.   An integrated treatment program for rapists, In Rada, R. (Ed.), *Clinical aspects of the rapist*, New York, Grune and Stratton, 1978.

16. Abel, G., Blanchard, E., and Becker, J.   Psychological treatment for rapists, In Brodsky, S.L. (Ed.), *Sexual assault*, Lexington, Massachusetts, Lexington Books, 1976.

17. Cooke, G.   *The behavioral treatment of the rapist*, presented at The Faces of Rape: A conference on the medical, legal, psychological and cultural aspects, Philadelphia, Pennsylvania, 1978.

18. Cautela, J.   Treatment of compulsive behavior by covert sensitization, *Psychological Records, 16*, 33–41, 1966.

19. Callahan, E.J. and Leitenberg, H.   Aversion therapy for sexual deviation, Contingent shock and covert sensitization, *Journal of Abnormal Psychology, 81*, 60–73, 1973.

20. Wolpe, J.   The systematic desensitization treatment of neurosis, *Journal of Nervous and Mental Disease, 132*, 189–203, 1961.

21. Prendergast, W.   *R.O.A.R.E.*, presented at The Faces of Rape: A conference on the medical, legal, psychological and cultural aspects, Philadelphia, Pennsylvania, 1978.

22. Janov, A.   *The primal scream*, New York, Dell, 1970.

23. Casriel, D.   *A scream away from happiness*, New York, Grosset and Dunlap, 1972.

24. Steg, J., Wright, L., and Peters, J.   *Psychoanalytic foundations for group psychotherapy of probationed sex offenders*, presented at the American Psychiatric Association Meeting, Boston, 1972.

25. Peters, J., Pedigo, J., Steg, J., and McKenna, Jr.   Group psychotherapy of the sex offender, *Federal Probation, 32*, 41–45, 1968.

26. Peters, J. and Roether, H.   Group psychotherapy for probationed sex offenders, *International Psychiatry Clinic, 8*, 67–80, 1972.

Chapter 30

THEFT VICTIMS' DECISION TO CALL THE POLICE: AN EXPERIMENTAL APPROACH*

Martin S. Greenberg, Ph.D.
AND
R. Barry Ruback, J.D., M.S.
AND
Chauncey E. Wilson
AND
Michael K. Mills, M.B.A.

T HE EFFECTIVENESS of the criminal justice system is contingent on citizen cooperation. As Black and Reiss[1] have shown, citizen notification accounts for about 85 percent of the crimes investigated by police. That citizens exercise their discretionary power is shown by recent victimization surveys conducted jointly by the Law Enforcement Assistance Administration (LEAA) and the Census Bureau. According to these surveys less than half of the crimes committed in the United States are ever reported to the police.[2] Other data indicate that when crimes are reported to the police, victim delay in reporting is the major reason for the police's late arrival on the scene.[3] It was, perhaps, for these reasons that Hindelang[4] labeled the victim "the gatekeeper of the criminal justice system."

While psychologists have explored the determinants of *bystanders'* reporting of thefts,[5,6] there has been little corresponding research on the determinants of *victims'* notification of the police. Clearly, there

---
*This research was supported by PHS Research Grant No. MH 27526, NIMH (Center for Studies of Crime and Delinquency). The unpublished manuscripts are available from Martin S. Greenberg, Ph.D., Department of Psychology, University of Pittsburgh, Pittsburgh, Pa. 15260.

is a need for greater understanding of the decision process underlying victims' decision to call or not call the police. This paper describes a program of experimental research designed to illuminate some of the determinants of victim crime reporting. The research focuses on responses to a single category of crime—the crime of petty larceny or theft (i.e. a theft under $50). LEAA/Census Bureau victimization surveys indicate that larceny is the most frequently committed crime and yet the one that victims are least likely to report. Surveys show that only about 25 percent of larcenies are reported to the police.[2]

How does one investigate victim decision making? Decision making by most agents of the criminal justice system takes place at known times and locations and thus can be investigated by naturalistic observation methods. In contrast, decision making by crime victims lacks such predictability, thus making it nearly impossible to observe victims during their decision making and requiring an alternative method of investigation. One reasonable alternative is to question victims afterwards about the basis for their decision to report or not report their victimization. This is, essentially, the rationale underlying use of victimization surveys. However, evidence reviewed by Greenberg, Wilson, and Mills[7] calls into question the utility of unsubstantiated assumptions, namely that (a) victims *know* the reasons for their decisions, (b) they can accurately *recall* these reasons when asked to do so several weeks or months later, and (c) they are willing to *disclose* these reasons to an interviewer. Accurate knowledge about victims' decision making requires methodologies that allow the investigator more direct access to victims' decision making than can be achieved by retrospective self-reports.

AN EXPERIMENTAL APPROACH TO VICTIM DECISION MAKING

Since reliance on naturalistic observation and victim self-reports pose formidable problems for the study of victim decision making, we have chosen an experimental approach in which we create our own victims. This approach looks for an understanding of victim decision making not in victims' introspections but in the systematic manipulation of variables presumed to affect such decision making. The program of research to be described below encompassed four studies and involved nearly 800 persons residing in the greater Pittsburgh, Pennsylvania area. Participants included males and females, blacks and whites, young and old (ranging in age from seventeen to sixty).

Some participants had only a grade-school education, while others had advanced graduate degrees. In addition, a wide variety of occupations were represented, including blue and white collar workers, housewives, students, and retirees. Participants were recruited from ads placed in local daily and weekly newspapers. The ads stated that participants would be paid eight dollars for one and a quarter hours of light work. (An exception occurred in the first study in which they were promised ten dollars for one and a half hours of work). At the time of the initial phone contact, respondents were screened for health problems (e.g. cardiac trouble, hypertension), and those free of such problems were given an appointment time.

The setting for the "theft" was a fictitious research organization ("Industrial Research Associates of Pittsburgh") housed in a set of offices located in a middle-class retail section of the city. The offices were furnished with all the accouterments one would expect to find in an industrial research organization: desks, tables, chairs, file cabinets, as well as such human props as a secretary, supervisor, and other research participants.

The four studies to be described employed essentially the same basic procedure with some minor variations. Shortly after participants arrived for the study they were joined in the waiting room by a second "participant," who was, in reality, a male confederate trained to play the role of "thief." They were told that the organization was conducting research on clerical efficiency for local businesses and that they would be working on several clerical tasks for which they would have an opportunity to earn money in addition to that promised in the ad. At this point they were given the money originally promised them. With the exception of study one, participants worked on an alphabetizing task and subsequently were led to believe that they had done quite well and had earned twelve additional dollars. In the first study they did not "earn" this money, instead it was merely given to them.

After being paid this additional money and signing a receipt for it, they commenced work on a second clerical task (recording numbers on a sheet, adding them, placing the sheet in an envelope, and placing the envelopes in an "outbox.") Participant's outbox containing their completed work was located directly behind them and within easy reach of the thief. Subsequently, they learned that they did very poorly on this task and had lost eleven of their twelve dollars, whereas the thief had done quite well and had earned an additional eleven dollars. They were then told to go to the secretary's office to effect the transfer of the money. In the secretary's office participants were told to give the thief eleven dollars since they had lost eleven dollars and the thief had gained eleven dollars. An assistant then knocked on the door and informed the secretary that there appeared to be a "problem" with the work, whereupon the secretary told the participant and thief to remain seated while she looked into the matter. After the secretary exited, the thief got up and left. A short time later, the secretary returned and inquired where "Mr. Collins" (the thief) had gone. She then proceeded to lay out the evidence of the theft. It consisted of several of the participant's completed sheets that were ostensibly found in the theif's work pile.

In this manner participants were led to believe that they were victims of a small theft. That is, they believed the thief had stolen some of their completed papers from their outbox, which, in effect, caused them to lose eleven dollars. The secretary then explained that her supervisor had left the office and that she did not have the authority to compensate them for their loss. She exited once again to search for her supervisor and returned in a few minutes without being able to locate him. The secretary then employed a series of pre-arranged prods of increasing intensity, which were designed to induce participants to phone the police. A reporting score was given to participants depending on which, if any, prod they yielded to. An assistant concealed behind a one-way mirror coded participants' responses. The experiment was terminated immediately after participants agreed or failed to agree to call the police. For those who agreed to report the theft, no actual report was made since the secretary's phone was not connected.

Participants then received a lengthy debriefing by the supervisor during which all of the deceptions and their rationale were revealed. After participants understood the objectives of the research and the reasons for the deceptions, they were interviewed concerning their perceptions of the events in the experiment, paid a bonus of several dollars, and asked to sign a consent form. Finally, they were asked to complete anonymously a brief questionnaire assessing their reactions to having participated in the study.

OVERVIEW OF THE FINDINGS

In the first investigation[7] this paradigm was used to examine the influence of three variables that previous research had suggested might affect victims' decisions to call the police. The three variables were

(a) the magnitude of the theft ($20 versus $3), (b) race of the thief (black versus white), and (c) proximity of the thief at the time of the report opportunity (thief present versus thief absent). We expected that a theft of twenty dollars would be more likely to be reported than one of only three dollars. We were particularly interested in determining whether the thief's race would affect the likelihood of the crime being reported to the police. Previous work suggested that blacks are more likely to be arrested, be convicted, and receive harsher sentences than whites. We were interested in learning whether victims, as the gatekeepers of the criminal justice system, also take the suspect's race into account in their decision making. We reasoned that the third variable, thief presence or absence, might moderate the influence of the first two variables.

Results yielded no significant differences in reporting between twenty dollar victims and three dollar victims. Nor was a black thief more likely to be reported than a white thief. In contrast to decision making by some agents of the criminal justice system, theft victims apparently do not weigh the thief's race in their decision to call the police. Unexpectedly, the *victim's* race was related to reporting. Black victims were more likely to call the police than were white victims regardless of the thief's race. This difference could not be accounted for by any other demographic characteristics, including socioeconomic class. In addition, there was a significant interaction between magnitude of the theft and thief proximity. When the thief was present, reporting was unaffected by the magnitude of the theft. However, when the thief had left the scene, reporting was greater in the twenty dollar condition than in the three dollar condition. Further, it was found that the proximity of the thief had differential effects on male and female victims. Males were more likely to report when the thief was absent, whereas females were more likely to report when the thief was still present. In addition, victims' attitudes towards the police as measured by six scales did not serve as a useful predictor of their willingness to call the police. The data from the first study indicate, therefore, that victim reporting of a theft is contingent on *situational* factors such as the amount of the theft and the thief's proximity and that victims' reactions can only be predicted from knowledge of these circumstances in *combination* with each other.

The results of the first study raised a number of issues. As we observed most participants' uncertainty while deciding whether or not to call the police, it became obvious that they were amenable to social influence—even from a low status secretary. Conceivably, their decision to report the theft could be influenced by advice received from a bystander. This line of thinking was reinforced by results of a recent survey of crime victims in Kansas City, Missouri[3] showing that most victims consulted with at least one other person prior to calling the police. It was decided, therefore, to conduct a study in which a confederate-bystander would either encourage or discourage "victims" from taking further action. Participants' reactions in the first study suggested an additional function that a bystander could serve. Time after time we noted that participants' emotional state played a decisive role in the decision process. In particular, we noted signs of physical arousal shortly after the secretary presented the evidence of the theft. Various emotional states were evident in our participants. Many became visibly angry, while others presented signs of diffuse arousal. We observed that those who reacted with anger were often most likely to call the police. These observations led us to consider seriously the mediating role of emotional states in victim reporting. Schachter[8] demonstrated that the experience of an emotional state involves two components: an arousal component and an appropriate label for that arousal. Schachter and Singer[9] demonstrated that others in the situation can influence the label that individuals applied to a state of arousal. Thus, all that was required in our paradigm was the presence of a bystander who, in addition to advising participants, would "help" them label their state of arousal.

The second study[10] was similar to the first with the following exceptions. The role of thief was played by a black male. In addition to the thief, a third "participant" was present; she was a white female confederate trained to play the role of "bystander." Further, when participants were encouraged by the secretary to report the theft, the thief in every case had left the scene. Two independent variables were manipulated in this study: the bystander's emotional response to the theft (high anger, low anger, no anger) and the type of bystander advice (advised action, advised no action, no advice). The design thus consisted of a 3 × 3 factional design.

The independent variables were manipulated in the secretary's office after the thief had "fled" the scene, the evidence for the theft had been revealed, and the secretary was trying to find her supervisor. Left alone with the participant-victim, the bystander modeled one of three levels of anger. *High anger:* "He erased your initials and put his own on your papers? I can't believe this. Boy, that really makes me angry. I'm really surprised that something like this happened." *Low anger:* "You know, this really bothers me. It's annoying having something like this happen." *No anger:* The bystander said nothing. She remained seated and responded only if the participant directed a question to her. After displaying one of these three levels of anger, the bystander advised participants to take some action or to take no action or gave no advice. *Advised action:* "I wouldn't let him get away with this. I think you should do something about it." *Advised no action:* "I wouldn't do anything. This probably isn't worth bothering about. He's already gone." *No advice:* The bystander offered no advice. After delivering her lines, the bystander looked at her watch, said she had to keep an appointment, wished the participant luck, and left.

Prior to testing the effectiveness of the independent variables the data were analyzed to see if any of the demographic variables were correlated with reporting. This analysis revealed that the tendency to report the theft was negatively correlated with victims' age and household earnings. In order to control for these two factors, an analysis of covariance was used to test the effects of the independent variables (the covariates being age and household earnings). This analysis yielded a significant advice effect. Those who were advised not to take any action were less likely to call the police than were those who were advised to take some action or were given no advice. No other effects were significant.

A check on the effectiveness of the manipulations revealed that while the level of bystander anger was perceived in line with the manipulations, it did not have the hypothesized effect on participants' self-reported anger. Therefore, in order to test the proposed relationship between level of victim anger and reporting, participants were classified according to their level of *self-reported anger*. An analysis of covariance (using age and household earnings as the covariates) performed on the reconstituted Self-Reported Anger X Bystander Advice matrix yielded a highly significant self-reported anger main effect and a marginally significant bystander advice main effect. Thus, the greater the victim's feeling of anger, the greater the victim's willingness to report the theft. With regard to the advice variable, those who were advised not to do anything about the theft evidenced the lowest report scores. Finally, in comparison with the first study, black victims were no more willing to report the theft than were white victims.

The results of the second study, while demonstrating the importance of the victim's emotional state at the time of the report decision, provide somewhat weaker evidence for the influence of a bystander's advice on victims' decision to notify the police. There are several possible explanations of why the bystander's advice did not have greater impact. First, the bystander's advice was quite diffuse, that is, she merely advised the victim to "do something about it," or not to "do anything." Conceivably, victims intended to heed the bystander's advice "to do something," but this did not involve calling the police. Perhaps if the advice were more specific, such as "*You should call the police.*" the effectiveness of the bystander's advice would have been more visible. Another factor that may have weakened the bystander's influence was the bystander's failure to back up her advice with any supporting argument. Finally, the bystander's influence may have been minimal because after offering her advice, she left the scene. Possibly her absence during the secretary's prodding reduced the salience of her position with regard to calling the police. A stronger test of bystander influence would be for the bystander to be more explicit in her advice, to provide supporting arguments, and to remain present during the victim's decision making process.

These ideas were tested in a third study[11] that involved two types of bystander advice crossed with four types of supporting arguments. As in the previous study, the thief was a black male and the bystander was a white female. The type of advice was manipulated by having the bystander state, "I think you should call the police." or "I don't think you should call the police." The supporting argument stressed one of three themes: (a) *Theft magnitude*—"Eleven dollars is eleven dollars. You can buy a lot with that." or, "It's only eleven dollars. It's really not that much money." (b) *Police effectiveness*—"They can do something about this. I'm sure they could get your money back." or "They can't do anything about this. I'm pretty sure they couldn't get your money back." (c) *Thief punishment*—"I'd like to see him punished. I think it would teach him a lesson." or "I wouldn't like to see him punished. I don't think it would accomplish anything." In addition, there was a *no supporting argument* condition in which the bystander offered no argument in support of her advice to report or not report the theft. Finally, for the purposes of control we included a "baseline" condition in which the bystander gave no advice and no argument, but rather remained silently seated. In all conditions, the bystander remained present during the prodding by the secretary.

Results showed that the bystander's advice to call the police significantly increased reporting above the baseline condition, whereas the advice not to report did not significantly depress the reporting rate below the baseline level. Further, the type of supporting argument had no effect on the reporting rate. As in the first study, black victims were more likely to call the police than were white victims. The results of this study demonstrate that bystanders can influence victim decision making when the advice given is specific and concrete, such as "Call the police." or "Don't call the police."

Was it merely the specificity of the bystander's advice that led participants to accept her influence, or were other factors at work as well? Interviews with participants suggested several promising leads. First, the bystander's presence during the secretary's prodding may have convinced participants that they could count on the bystander's continued support when dealing with the police. Further, although the bystander made no mention of whether or not she witnessed the theft, participants in the advised report condition may have reported because they believed the bystander could provide the police with information that would strengthen their case against the thief.

In order to explore these issues, a fourth study was conducted.[12] As in the previous experiments, the bystander was a white female. However, unlike the previous experiments, the role of thief was played by a white male. Three independent variables were crossed in a 2 × 2 × 2 experimental design. The variables were (a) proximity of the bystander (present versus absent), (b) the bystander's willingness to support the participants in their dealing with the police (support versus no support), and (c) the bystander's firsthand information about the theft (eyewitness versus no eyewitness). In every case the bystander advised participants to call the police. After evidence of the theft was presented, the bystander indicated in half of the cases that she saw the thief take some of the participant's papers but had erroneously believed that the thief had put his papers in the participant's box by mistake and was merely retrieving them (eyewitness condition). In the remaining half of the cases she stated that she "didn't see anything" (no eyewitness condition). In half the instances the bystander indicated her willingness to support participants in their dealing with the police by stating, "I'll back you up. And, if anything happens later on, you can call me at work." She then wrote her phone number on a slip of paper and handed it to the participant. The remaining participants were led to believe that they could not count on the bystander's future support: "But don't use my name, I don't want to get involved." The bystander then either remained present during the secretary's prodding or left after the secretary said she could leave.

An analysis of covariance was used to analyze the data with participant's age serving as the covariate. This analysis yielded a significant interaction between proximity of the bystander and the bystander's willingness to support the participant. When the bystander offered her support, participants were more willing to call the police when the bystander remained present than when she left the scene. In comparison, when the bystander indicated her lack of support for the victim, there was less inclination to report when the bystander was present than when she was absent. The bystander's firsthand knowledge of the theft (eyewitness versus no eyewitness) did not influence reporting. The analysis also yielded a significant sex of participant main effect: Females were more willing to call the police than were males. This sex difference was not obtained in any of the previous studies. Research directed at uncovering the source of this difference is currently underway.

PARTICIPANTS' WELFARE

Every effort was made to ensure the welfare of participants. They were screened for health problems and were given an opportunity to leave with the money promised them prior to completing the study. Moreover, they were paid a bonus of several dollars and received a complete debriefing immediately after their participation, as well as a three-page feedback letter several weeks later. Prior to their departure, they answered an anonymous questionnaire assessing their reactions to having participated in the study. The items consisted of five-point bipolar scales and measured their beliefs about how interesting the research was, the extent to which they were treated with respect, whether they were sorry to have participated, and the extent to which they would recommend to a friend that they participate. Responses were overwhelmingly favorable to each of the items. Many added written remarks indicating that the experience had given them valuable insights about themselves.

SUMMARY AND CONCLUSIONS

The research described here demonstrates the utility of using an experimental paradigm to investigate theft victims' decisions to call the police. The approach afforded us a unique opportunity to observe victims' discovery of their victimization and their subsequent decision making. Our observations suggest that such decision making is influenced by characteristics of the *victim,* the *thief* (and the theft) , and the *bystander.* Characteristics of victims that were related to the reporting decision included victims' age, race, sex, family earnings, and degree of anger. Unrelated to reporting were victims' religion and amount of education. The thief's whereabouts (proximity) at the time of victims' decision making also affected reporting as did the magnitude of the theft. Characteristics of the bystander that affected victims' reporting included the type of bystander's advice, the bystander's willingness to support victims in their subsequent dealings with the police, and the bystander's proximity at the time of the report decision. Neither the bystander's personal observation of the theft nor the nature of the bystander's supporting argument affected victim reporting.

Results of the four studies suggest that victim's decision making can be strongly influenced by features of the social context. In particular, the data provide some understanding of the conditions under which bystanders can exert influence on victim's decision making. Our data suggest that victim reporting can be facilitated if bystanders do the following: (a) provide the victim with specific (e.g. "call the police") as opposed to diffuse advice (e.g. "do something") (b) offer the victim assurances of continued support (c) after offering such assurances, they remain at the victim's side until such time as the report is made.

Additional research is needed to unravel further the bases for victims' decisions to report crimes of theft. The understanding derived from such research can serve to enhance the effectiveness of the criminal justice system since victims constitute the principle gatekeepers of this system. The research program described in this paper represents an effort to increase such understanding.

REFERENCES

1. Black, D.J. and Reiss, A.J., Jr. *Studies of crime and law enforcement in major metropolitan areas: Patterns of behavior in police and citizen transactions,* (Field Surveys III, Vol. 2, The President's Commission on Law Enforcement and Administration of Justice), Washington, D.C., U.S. Government Printing Office, 1967.

2. *Criminal victimization in the United States: A comparison of 1974 and*

1975 findings (A national crime survey report #SD-NCP-N-5), Washington, D.C., LEAA, 1977.
3. Crime victims are slow calling police *LEAA Newsletter, 7, 7,* 1978.
4. Hindelang, M.J. *Criminal victimization in eight American cities: A descriptive analysis of common theft and assault,* Cambridge, Massachusetts, Ballinger, 1976.
5. Bickman, L. Attitude toward an authority and the reporting of a crime, *Sociometry, 39,* 76–82, 1976.
6. Bickman, L. and Rosenbaum, D.P. Crime reporting as a function of bystander encouragement, surveillance, and credibility, *Journal of Personality and Social Psychology, 35,* 577–586, 1977.
7. Greenberg, M.S., Wilson, C.E., and Mills, M.K. An experimental approach to victim decision making, In Konecni, V.J. and Ebbesen, E.B. (Eds.), *Social psychological analysis of legal processes,* San Francisco, W.H. Freeman, in press.
8. Schachter, S. The interaction of cognitive and physiological determinants of emotional state, In Berkowitz, L. (Ed.), *Advances in experimental social psychology,* Vol. I, New York, Academic Press, 1964.
9. Schachter, S. and Singer, J.E. Cognitive, social, and physiological determinants of emotional state, *Psychological Review, 69,* 379–399, 1962.
10. Greenberg, M.S., Wilson, C.E., Ruback, R.B., and Mills, M.K. *Social and emotional determinants of victim crime reporting,* Unpublished manuscript, 1978.
11. Greenberg, M.S., Wilson, C.E., and Ruback, R.B. *Effect of social influence on theft victims' decision to call the police,* Manuscript submitted for publication, 1978.
12. Greenberg, M.S., Ruback, R.B., and Wilson, C.E. *Theft victims' decision to call the police: Some parameters of bystander influence,* Unpublished manuscript, 1978.

SECTION IV

THE FORENSIC PSYCHOLOGIST WORKING WITH POLICE

In recent years as police departments have stressed greater professionalism there have been increased requests for psychologists and other professionals to aid in the selection and training of police officers. Some of the findings and issues are discussed in this section.

Chapter 31

POLICE SELECTION

Allen E. Shealy, Ph.D.

AND

Elizabeth Roberts, B.A.

T HE ORIGINS of police selection in the United States can be traced back as far as the origins of law enforcement itself. Rampant change and growth in the society and therefore in the role of the police officer have caused many methods of selection used prior to the last fifteen years to become outdated and inadequate. Numerous factors associated with the current social and cultural climate have increased the complexity of the job of police work, the variety of skills and strengths required to perform the job, and the focus of public attention on the quality of police performance. Federal agencies and courts have begun to place requirements on law enforcement agencies to upgrade personnel selection procedures and to assure fair hiring practices.[1,2,3] Researchers have responded to these requirements with increased probing into the issues involved in police selection. Whereas fifteen years ago, information regarding police selection was scant in professional literature, recent years have seen a tremendous increase in research and information in this area. Several excellent literature reviews have been published.[4,5,6,7] This chapter will present an overview of the current state of the art and the issues involved in police selection rather than detailed description of the numerous efforts that have been undertaken.

Review of police selection literature indicates that no single method for screening has consistently been found to be predictive of the quality of later job performance. A wide variety of techniques continue to be utilized. Among the most widely used instruments in the screening procedure are various forms of intellectual and ability tests. Intelligence tests have been found to relate to performance in training situations,[8,9] but opinion on the degree to which they relate to later job performance is mixed.[8,10,11,12] Crosby[13] reports a recent study designed to test cognitive abilities by using a three-hour multiple-choice test, the items of the test referring to clusters of tasks reflecting basic dimensions of the police patrol job. This test represents a major effort to demonstrate a predictive link between specific intellectual abilities and police performance.

The premise that the best predictor of future behavior is past behavior underlies the continued use of the background investigation as a screening tool. Biographical and demographic variables from the background investigation and the information available on application blanks have been found to be related to performance. Among these variables are education, family status, former occupation, and religious affiliation.[4,14-19] Heckman et al.[20] point out likely advantages to the approach of statistically weighing items in background information as opposed to clinical predictions made based on the investigation.

Oral interviews, with or without the assistance of the polygraph, are part of most agencies' screening procedure. Results of several studies have cast doubt on the usefulness of the oral board approach as a sole selection technique.[8,9,21-25] Landy[26] has encouraged the use of such interviews, but stresses that the global recommendations usually used are not valid. Identification of specific components in a predictor set is necessary in order to predict measured performance. A variation on the standard oral board interview is put forth by Rhead et al.[27] Use of a group of experienced clinicians is found to increase the effectiveness of the interview for predicting behavior when used in concert with other sources of information. Utilization of clinical skills in conducting the interview, projective questions, and more than one interviewer are seen as important factors in this approach. The clinical interview has also been used in screening in which one experienced psychiatrist or psychologist usually interviews an applicant alone. Anecdotal evidence supports the use of the clinical interview,[27,28] and some data have been reported that support this approach.[29] In such cases, however, the interview is seen as part of the process, which includes other techniques as well.

The use of psychological tests as part of the screening procedure has increased in recent years. In 1971 a survey by the International Association of Chiefs of Police indicated that 30 to 40 percent of law enforcement agencies used some type of psychological screening.[3]

That percentage has no doubt increased since the National Crime Commission directive that psychological screening be incorporated in selection procedures by 1975.[2] By far the most widely used tests are paper and pencil inventories designed to measure personality characteristics, traits, and types. A wealth of studies have resulted, proposing various conceptualizations of the "police personality." While the evidence tends to support the notion that police applicants and officers represent a certain constellation of personality traits,[6,30] the empirical relationship between this "police personality" and outcome measures of job performance remains to be demonstrated. Data also indicate relationships between various measurable traits or characteristics and later job performance.[18,19,27,31–34] In several cases where psychological tests were found not to be strong behavioral predictors, researchers have pointed out that the power of statistical prediction is likely lessened because of the marked degree of homogeneity in the group of applicants tested.[19,35] Henderson[36] has also pointed out that the pressure of the testing situation and related response sets such as social desirability may decrease the relationship of the outcome to later performance measures.

In addition to objectively scored paper and pencil tests, projective techniques calling for clinical evaluation has also been found to yield information regarding an applicant's suitability,[10,27] though caution is urged in overemphasis of their use alone.[29] Measures of attitudes and interests have also been used as predictors of performance. Frequently cited in the literature is the Strong Vocational Interest Blank (SVIB) and its revised form, the Strong-Campbell Interest Inventory (SCII). Scales of the SVIB have been found to correlate with measures of performance.[33,34,37] Other studies report that interest measures do not relate to performance.[9,31] The use of interest tests for placement and career development decisions after employment is being urged by some researchers.[38] Recent years have seen a decline in the use of traditional aptitude tests in police screening. Henderson[36] has suggested that applicants are likely to take aptitude tests more conscientiously under the circumstances of a screening situation than when the tests are administered after hiring. This fact would decrease the predictive power of the tests. Reports of use of aptitude tests in the literature have become less frequent.[9,39,40]

Though motivation for police work has been researched, it has received less attention than other areas.[41–45] High need for job security and social support and low autonomy needs have been reported for successful officers.[29,46–48] Another area in which reports are scant is of values testing. Rush[49] reported that good prospects for highway patrol positions placed low value on aesthetic interests and above average value on religious interests. Sherrid[50] reports on values and the possibility of changing measured values. Rokeach et al.[51] demonstrated a discrepancy between the values of the community and the values of police officers. Hogan's measure of moral judgment discriminates between applicants rated as being a high or low risk of corruption proneness.[19]

An approach to screening as well as training that has received considerable interest recently is that of the situational test or simulation. Based on Henry Murray's use of simulations in World War II with OSS staff, the situational test has several theoretical advantages: It points out strengths of applicants as well as weaknesses; it can more easily be shown to be job-related; it emphasizes action orientation rather than nonaction skills. Although there are reports of studies in which situational tests do not predict performance,[8,52] successful prediction of performance is also found.[53] Mills[53] cites several benefits of this approach: Interpersonal style can be observed; applicants are viewed in stressful situations; and peer ratings and evaluations are utilized. Situational tests are a necessary component of the screening procedures employed in assessment centers. Although the assessment center approach is expensive and time consuming, it is receiving increased endorsement.[54] Requirements in the assessment center approach include use of multiple assessment techniques such as simulation, and the use of multi-disciplinary methods to delineate relevant behaviors to be assessed.[55]

It seems clear from the previous discussion that selection of the most efficient instruments for screening police applicants is a major practical question yet to be answered. Of equal importance is another unresolved issue: How is job performance to be measured? What criteria are to be used in assessing the quality of police performance? Ratings made by supervisors are the criteria most frequently used in selection studies. Performance evaluations are widely used in law enforcement and considerable improvements have been made in the design and use of this technique.

Rating scales are often anchored with behavioral statements. Behaviorally based scales have the potential of greater reliability among raters, are more quantifiable, and are more easily justified a priori than are scales measuring broadly conceptualized traits. Researchers

should be considered by anyone embarking on research in this area or in providing psychological screening services to police organizations:

THE CRITERION PROBLEM: Most available outcome measures, as discussed earlier, define quality of performance from the police perspective, i.e. supervisory ratings, investigation of complaints, employment status, etc. The policed community should have input into the definition of "good" police performance. Commendations from citizens is the only portion of the police personnel records that is clearly input from the citizenry. Other measures are needed. If predictors of the "good police officer" based on the police definition are used in screening, we may be part of the problem rather than part of the solution.

THE SETTING OF THE SCREENING PROCEDURE: If psychological screening is used as part of the selection technique, should the psychologist be an employee of the police department, the Civil Service Board, or an independent consultant? The potential danger of the in-house consultant is his becoming co-opted to the values of the police and thereby losing the independent perspective, while the danger of the outside consultant is that he may not be sensitive to the organizational dynamics of the police department. Our bias is that the advantages of the outside consultant outweigh the disadvantages.

THE USE OF THE RESULTS OF THE PSYCHOLOGICAL EVALUATION: Should the psychological evaluation, if used as a separate part of the screening procedure, result in a pass/fail, hire/no hire decision, or should it be used more tentatively in an advisory capacity? In our own evaluations, no applicant is turned down solely on the basis of the psychological report. A report of questionable psychological suitability alerts the police personnel division to attend carefully to the background investigation and interview. If the psychological findings are not supported, the applicant is hired. We have found that a negative psychological evaluation is usually supported with evidence from the background investigation sufficient to justify the decision to not hire.

METHOD OF REPORTING RESULTS: Whether to issue a narrative report or a series of ratings or probability statements is related to the position one takes on the clinical versus actuarial prediction issue.[72] If the actuarial approach is used, rating scales are more appropriate. It has been our experience that a set of rating scales is more useful than a narrative report, even when clinical prediction is used.

CLINICAL VERSUS ACTUARIAL APPROACH: If the clinical approach is used, the goal will probably be to screen out the unsuitable, either because of the existence of psychopathology or because the personality and characterological attributes of the person render him or her "unsuitable" for police work. The actuarial approach is difficult because of the criterion problems discussed earlier. However, this approach has the clear advantage of enabling probability statements to be made for specific criteria and allows a weighted prediction formula to be developed. This would ultimately result in a cutting score that could be manipulated according to the number of job openings and the number in the applicant pool.

ETHICAL ISSUES: One of the decisions to be made is whether or not to inform the applicant of the findings of the psychological evaluation. If the psychological evaluation is conducted outside of the police department, the client of the psychologist is clearly the police department and not the applicant. Also, the reporting of results to the applicant is potentially damaging. Since we do not make a hire/no hire decision, we have a policy that neither we nor the police department informs the applicant as to the findings of the evaluation. If hire/no hire decisions are made, this cannot be done. Another ethical issue relates to protecting the confidentiality of the psychological files. It is important that the applicant be made aware of the use of the results of the evaluation and the limitations of confidentiality. If the results are to be used only for preemployment screening, agreements should be made with the police department to insure that the psychological report will not be used for post employment personnel decisions such as promotion or dismissal. Reports should not be available to the supervisors of recruits or to anyone other than the personnel division of the department.

While there is always some danger of the psychologist's files being subpoenaed because of legal action against a particular officer and possibly harming the applicant or the police department, at least one legal precedent suggests that this could be prevented because of the research aspect of the data, if research is indeed part of the project.[73] The Law Enforcement Assistance Administration has recently published a manual titled *Confidentiality of Research and Statistical Data*[74] that clarifies the statutory immunity of research data collected in LEAA projects after July 1973.

DEGREE TO WHICH SITUATIONAL VARIABLES CAN BE MEASURED: Ekehammer[75] concluded that the interaction between individual differences and situational differences is more predictive than either person variables or situation variables alone. In police predictive research, little or no effort has been expended in developing ways of categorizing or classifying situations. Research designs that use critical incidents such as complaints, commendations, ratings, etc. typically do not record the situational contexts in which the incident occurs. Measures of situation variables in police research outcome criteria need to be developed including but not limited to the dimensions of shift, beat, and interpersonal context. Perhaps the generally discouraging findings of predictive validation studies in police selection is related to the absence of situation variables in the data base.

REFERENCES

1. Equal Employment Opportunity Commission, Guidelines on Employee Selection Procedures, Federal Register, Vol. 35, No. 149, Washington, D.C., U.S. Government Printing Office, August 1, 1970.
2. President's commission on law enforcement and administration of justice, *Task Force Report: The police,* Washington, D.C., U.S. Government Printing Office, 1973.
3. National Advisory Commission on Criminal Justice Standards and Goals, *Police,* Washington, D.C., U.S. Government Printing Office, 1974.
4. Cohen, B. and Chaiken, J.M. *Police background characteristics and performance,* Lexington, Massachusetts, Lexington Books, 1973.
5. Kent, D.A. and Eisenberg, T. The selection and promotion of police officers, *The Police Chief, 39,* (2), 20–29, 1972.
6. Lefkowitz, J. Industrial-organizational psychology and the police, *American Psychologist, 32,* (5), 346–364, 1977.
7. Smith, D.H. and Scotland, E. A new look at police officer selection, In Snibbe, J.R. and Snibbe, H.M. (Eds.), *The urban policeman in transition,* Springfield, Thomas, 1973.
8. Clopton, W.J. Comparison of ratings and field performance data in validating predictions of patrolman performance: A five-year follow-up study, masters thesis, 1971.
9. Dubois, P.H. and Watson, R.I. The selection of patrolmen, *Journal of Applied Psychology, 34,* 90–95, 1950.
10. Grencik, J., Snibbe, N., and Montgomery, H. *Physiological fitness standards research project,* LEAA Grant No. Hl-70-042, Interim Report, June 1971.
11. Marsh, S.H. Validating the selection of deputy sheriffs, *Public Personnel Review, 23,* 1, 1962.
12. Spencer, G. and Nichols, R. A study of Chicago police recruits, Validation of selection procedures, *The Police Chief, 50*–55, 1971.
13. Crosby, A.C. The multijurisdictional police officer examination, In

Spielberger, C.D. and Spaulding, H.C. (Eds.), *Proceedings of the national working conference on the selection of law enforcement officers*, Florida Police Standards Research Project, University of South Florida, Tampa, March 1977.

14. Cascio, W.F.   Biographical predictors in police performance, In Speilberger, C.D. and Spaulding, H.C. (Eds.), *Proceedings of the national working conference in the selection of law enforcement officers*, Florida police Standards Research Project, University of South Florida, Tampa, March 1977.

15. Cross, A.C. and Hammond, K.R.   Social differences between "successful" and "unsuccessful" state highway patrolmen, *Public Personnel Review, 12,* 159–161, 1951.

16. Levy, R.J.   Predicting police failures, *Journal of Criminal Law, Criminology and Police Science, 58,* 265–275, 1967.

17. McAllister, J.A.   A study of the prediction and measurement of police performance, *Police,* 58–64, March–April 1970.

18. Furcon, J.E., Froemel, E.C., Franzak, R.G., and Baehr, M.E.   *A longitudinal study of psychological test predictors and assessments of patrolman field performance,* Chicago, University of Chicago, Industrial Relations Center, 1971.

19. Shealy, A.E.   *Police integrity: The role of psychological screening of applicants,* Criminal Justice Center Monograph No. 4, John Jay College of Criminal Justice, New York, John Jay Press, 1977.

20. Heckman, R.W., Groner, D.M., Dunnette, M.D., and Johnson, P.D.   *Development of psychiatric standards for police selection,* Washington, D.C., United States Department of Justice, Law Enforcement Assistance Administration, National Institute of Law Enforcement and Criminal Justice, 1972.

21. Blum, M.L. and Naylor, J.C.   *Industrial psychology: Its theoretical and social foundations,* New York, Harper and Row, 1968.

22. Hakel, M.D. and Dunnette, M.D.   *Checklists for describing job applicants, Minneapolis, University of Minnesota, Industrial Relations,* Center, 1970.

23. Mayfield, E.C.   The selection interview — a reevaluation of published research, *Personnel Psychology, 17,* 239–260, 1964.

24. Ulrich, L. and Trumbo, D.   The selection interview since 1949, *Psychological Bulletin, 63,* 110–116, 1965.

25. Webster, E.C.   *Decision making in the employment interview,* Montreal, Eagle, 1964.

26. Landy, F.J.   The validity of the interview in police officer selection, *Journal of Applied Psychology, 61,* 193–198, 1976.

27. Rhead, G., Abrams, A., Trasman, H., and Margolis, P.   The psychological assessment of police candidates, *American Journal of Psychiatry, 11,* 133–138, 1968.

28. Rankin, J.R. Psychiatric screening of police recruits, *Public Personnel Review, 20,* 191–196, 1959.
29. Matarazzo, J.D., Allen, B.V., Saslow, G., and Wiens, A.N. Characteristics of successful policemen and firemen applicants, *Journal of Applied Psychology, 48,* 123–133, 1964.
30. Shealy, A.E. The MMPI and Myers-Briggs Type Indicator in police selection research, In Spielberger, C.D. and Spaulding, H.C. (Eds.), *Proceedings of the national working conference on the selection of law enforcement officers,* Florida Police Standards Research Project, University of South Florida, Tampa, March 1977.
31. Baehr, M.E., Furcon, J.E., and Froemel, E.C. *Psychological assessment of patrolman qualifications in relation to field performance,* Washington, D.C., U.S. Government Printing Office, 1968.
32. Bass, B.M., Karstendick, B., McCullough, G., and Pruitt, K.C. Validity information exchange, (No. 7-024), *Personnel Psychology, 17,* 159–160, 1954.
33. Blum, R.H. (Ed.). *Police selection,* Springfield, Thomas, 1964.
34. Sullivan, E.J. *Psychological testing for police selection, Project report,* (Grant Number 72-2101A), Rhode Island Governor's Justice Commission, 1976.
35. Gottesman, J. *Personality patterns of urban police applicants as measured by the MMPI,* 1969. (No additional reference available.)
36. Henderson, N.D. Criterion related validity: A comparison of validation results under voluntary and actual test conditions, In Spielberger, C.D. and Spaulding, H.C. (Eds.), *National working conference on the selection of law enforcement officers,* Florida Police Standards, Research Project, University of South Florida, Tampa, March 1977.
37. Shealy, A.E. and Roberts, E.P. *The relationship between Strong Vocational Interest Blank scales, age and race in predicting success and satisfaction of police applicants,* Unpublished manuscript, 1976. (Available from Department of Psychiatry, University of Alabama in Birmingham, Birmingham, Alabama.)
38. Flint, R.T. The use of the Strong-Campbell Interest Inventory in selecting police officers, In Spielberger, C.D. and Spaulding, H.C. (Eds.), *Proceedings of the national working conference on the selection of law enforcement officers,* Florida Police Standards Research Project, University of South Florida, Tampa, March 1977.
39. Robinson, D.D. Predicting police effectiveness from self-reports of relative time spent in task performance, *Personnel Psychology, 23,* 327–345, 1970.
40. Eilbert, L.R. *Research on the selection of police recruits,* Washington, D.C., American Institute for Research, 1966.
41. Banton, M. *Police in the community,* New York, Basic Books, 1964.

42. Gorer, G. Modification of national character: The role of the police in England, *Journal of Social Issues, 11,* (2), 24–32, 1955.
43. Mills, R.B. Use of diagnostic small groups in police recruit selection and training, *Journal of Criminal Law, Criminology and Police Science, 60,* 238–141, 1969.
44. Niederhoffer, A. *Behind the shield: The police in urban society,* New York, Anchor, 1967.
45. Reiss, A.J. Career orientations, job satisfaction and the assessment of law enforcement problems by officers, In *Studies in crime and law enforcement in major metropolitan areas,* Vol. II, Washington, D.C., U.S. Government Printing Office, 1967.
46. Cohen, B. Minority recruiting in the New York City Police Department: Part II, The retention of candidates, New York, Rand Institute, 1971.
47. Richard, J.T. A study of the relationship of certain background factors and the choice of police work as a career, *Dissertation Abstracts International, 30,* 1028A–1029A, 1969.
48. Whisenand, P.M. Work values and job satisfaction: Anyone interested? *Public Personnel Review, 32,* 228–230, 1971.
49. Rush, A.C. Better police personnel selection, Lawrence, Kansas, Governmental Research Center, University of Kansas, 1963.
50. Sherrid, S.D. Changes in police values, In Spielberger, C.D., and Spaulding, H.C. (Eds.), *Proceedings of the national working conference on the selection of law enforcement officers,* Florida Police Standards Research Project, University of South Florida, Tampa, March 1977.
51. Rokeach, M., Miller, M.G., and Synder, J.A. The value gap between police and policed, In Tapp, J.L. and Levine, F.J. (Eds.), *Law, justice, and the individual in society,* New York, Holt, Rinehart and Winston, 1977.
52. Mills, R.B. and McDevitt, R.J. Situational tests in metropolitan police recruit selection, *Journal of Criminal Law, Criminology and Police Science, 57,* 99–106, 1966.
53. Mills, R.B. Simulated stress in police recruit selection, *Journal of Police Science and Administration, 4,* (2), 179–186, 1976.
54. Fabricatore, J.M. Performance evaluation at the police academy, In Spielberger, C.D. and Spaulding, H.C. (Eds.), *Proceedings of the national working conference on the selection of law enforcement officers,* Florida Police Standards Research Project, University of South Florida, Tampa, March 1977.
55. Filer, R.J. Assessment centers in police selection, In Spielberger, C.D. and Spaulding, H.C. (Eds.), *Proceedings of the national working conference on the selection of law enforcement officers,* Florida Police Standards Research Project, University of South Florida, Tampa, March 1977.

56. Landy, F.J. and Farr, J.L. *Police performance appraisal*, Unpublished manuscript, Pennsylvania State University, Department of Psychology, 1975.

57. Olson, B.T. *Designing a police performance evaluation form: An experiment in organizational involvement*, (Tech. Bull. B-59), East Lansing, Michigan State University, Institute for Community Development and Services, 1969.

58. Personnel Decisions, Inc. *Police patrolmen test validation study for the suburbs of Minneapolis/St. Paul*, Minneapolis, Minnesota, Personnel Decisions, Inc., 1974.

59. Furcon, J. and Froemel, E.C. *The relationship of selected psychological tests to measures of police officer job performance in the state of Illinois*, Chicago, University of Chicago, Industrial Relations Center, 1973.

60. Eisenberg, T. Performance evaluation: The criterion problem in police selection, In Spielberger, C.D. and Spaulding, H.C. (Eds.), *Proceedings of the national working conference on the selection of law enforcement officers*, Florida Police Standards Research Project, University of South Florida, Tampa, March 1977.

61. Roberts, M.C. Post-employment probationary selection: The San Jose model of field training and evaluation, In Spielberger, C.D. and Spaulding, H.C. (Eds.), *National working conference on the selection of law enforcement officers*, Florida Police Standards Research Project, University of South Florida, Tampa, March 1977.

62. McKinney, T.S. *The criterion related validity of entry level police officer selection procedures*, (TR1-75), Phoenix, Arizona, City of Phoenix, Personnel Department, 1973.

63. Leiren, B.D. Validating the selection of deputy marshals, In Snibbe, J.R. and Snibbe, H.M. (Eds.), *The urban policeman in transition*, Springfield, Thomas, 1973.

64. Van Maanen, J. Police socialization: A longitudinal examination of job attitudes in an urban police department, *Administrative Science Quarterly, 20*, 207–228, 1975.

65. Griggs v. Duke Power Company 401 U.S. 424, 1971.

66. Police training and performance study (Project report submitted to the New York City Police Department and the Law Enforcement Assistance Administration, U.S. Department of Justice), Washington, D.C., U.S. Government Printing Office, December 1969.

67. Johnson, D. and Gregory, R.J. Police-community relations in the United States: A review of recent literature and projects, *Journal of Criminal Law, Criminology and Police Science, 62*, 94–103, 1971.

68. Webster, J.A. Police task and time study, *Journal of Criminal Law, Criminology and Police Science, 61*, 94–100, 1970.

69. Wilson, J.Q. The patrolmans' dilemma, In Huvitt, W.H. and Newman,

C.L. (Eds.), *Police-community relations: An anthology and bibliography*, Mineola, Foundation Press, 1970.

70. McCormick, E.J., Meckan, R.C., and Jeanneret, P.R. *Position Analysis Questionnaire: Form B, 3-74*, West Lafayette, Indiana, Purdue Research Foundation, 1969.

71. Dunnette, M.D. and Motowildo, S.J. *Police selection and career assessment*, (Law Enforcement Assistance Administration, U.S. Department of Justice), Washington, D.C., U.S. Government Printing Office, 1976.

72. Meehl, P. *Clinical v. statistical prediction: A theoretical analysis and review of the evidence*, Minneapolis, University of Minnesota Press, 1954.

73. Culliton, B.J. Confidentiality: Court declares researcher can protect sources, *Science*, August 1976.

74. *Confidentiality of Research and Statistical Data*, Law Enforcement Assistance Administration, U.S. Department of Justice, Washington, D.C., U.S. Government Printing Office, 1978.

75. Ekehammer, B. Interactionism in personality from a historical perspective, *Psychological Bulletin, 81*, 1026–1048, 1974.

Chapter 32

POLICE TRAINING

Anthony M. Pisa, Ph.D.

AND

Wayne A. Mugrauer

THE PAST ten years of development in law enforcement have witnessed a thrust toward community-oriented human service provision. This shift in attitude has fostered an increased recognition among psychologists and other community service professionals of the value of police in providing helping services. One positive ramification of this newly actualized relationship is increased positive contact among police and professionals in the medical, legal, and mental health fields. For these reasons the police are now justifiably viewed as a powerful agency in the network of human service provision.

Concomitantly a growing impetus towards professionalization of the police officer within the law enforcement community has recognized the need for training in a broad spectrum of service areas in addition to traditional law enforcement skills. Contributing factors to this recognition include increased sensitivity to the fact that most of police daily activities are related to providing human services, a need for better police-community rapport, and a recognition of the high degree of judgment and discretion required to perform police activities effectively. These common goals and interests among service professionals have provided the framework for a harmonious working relationship between police and various service-related professionals.

The focus of this chapter will emphasize the various fields in which psychologists have been able to provide police departments with training and expertise that have enabled them to more effectively and efficiently perform their duties. Recent efforts have been made to develop training and consulting programs to improve the police department's image with the general public and target subpopulations within the community. In addition, other specialized programs have been directed at police activities presenting extreme problems such as the provision of specific emergency psychiatric service that police are frequently asked to provide. Programs of this type include family crisis intervention training, specialized training in intervention in psychiatric emergencies, and conflict management techniques. A third area in which psychological expertise is beginning to expand concerns the personal adjustment of the police officer. There is a growing concern and recognition that the stress of police work presents specialized problems for the individual adjustment of the officer and adjustment to both family and society at large.

A review of the relevant training programs in the areas listed above will be followed by a police training model that incorporates many of the strengths of these above programs in addition to emphasizing a specific theoretical orientation to police training. This model capitalizes on the fact that (1) the preponderance of police duties have been documented to fall under the category of service provision rather than law enforcement and (2) the police frequently function as the first line contact for the larger network of available community services. The underlying hypothesis for this model is that the policeman is in fact a service professional and that he should be afforded the status, training, and discretionary privileges afforded to other service professionals.

PUBLIC RELATIONS

In the area of community relations psychological training and consultation have focused on issues that enhance the public image of the police department. The rationale for programs in these areas is to improve the quality of one-to-one encounters between the police and the individual, specifically in volatile or potentially explosive situations. Representative goals of programs with this purpose usually include skills to help police officers become more effective in interpersonal encounters in general, assist the officer in gaining a better understanding of the police role in the community and provide a problem-solving format for community-police interaction.[1] In addition these programs usually have the effect of improving communications and understanding between the police and representative examples of the community while dispelling stereotyping[2] and conflicts based on predetermined role expectations.[3] The tangible benefit to the community is in the improved quality of service the police provide and the image the police present to the media.

Most training in these areas successfully utilizes multimedia presentation methods. Lectures are combined with discussion groups, workshops, and problem solving sessions. In addition to verbal presentation, role play has become a frequently used technique as an aid in refining interpersonal communication skills.[4] The specific areas of psychology that are most applicable to these programs are attitude development, perception, counseling techniques, communication theory, and problem-solving skills. Most police departments have found programs such as these helpful in providing their officers with a better understanding of the sociological and psychological factors that influence their contacts with the public.

FAMILY CRISIS INTERVENTION

Family crisis intervention has been a mutual concern that has provided an arena for the psychologist and the police officer to combine expertise and experience to improve the effectiveness of professionals in both areas. Recent statistics state that 20 percent of police killings are attributed to situations where officers were intervening in family disputes and 40 percent of police injuries were attributed to this type of call for service.[5] This recognition of the intense and volatile nature of family disturbances states a need for a more effective methodology for police in these situations. Concomitantly, professionals in the field of mental health have recognized the need for more effective utilization of treatment personnel indigenous to target population communities. These needs helped to foster the development of family crisis intervention training and programs within the police community. Initial attempts in providing training in this area were made in New York City by Bard and Berkowitz.[6] The need for such programs, and initial program effectiveness of training in this area, produced a proliferation of crisis intervention programs.

Most of these training programs are concerned with providing the officer with information that will help him intervene in a manner that decreases the likelihood of violence in conflict situations. Subject content for these programs considers topics including family dynamics, verbal and nonverbal communication, interviewing skills and techniques, counselling skills, abnormal behavior, and stress and conflict resolution. Methodology for providing the training involves lectures, discussion groups, and simulated interventions, frequently with professional actors in combination with video taping to process interventions. A review of program effectiveness can be found in Liebman and Schwartz, 1973.[7]

OTHER SPECIALIZED INTERVENTION AREAS

The increased effectiveness and consequent positive response received from law enforcement personnel with regards to programs such as these has produced a recognition of the need for psychological and sociological expertise in other service areas in which the police are called to intervene. One area is in the investigation of rape.[8] Handling rape investigations with psychological knowledge can aid the victim's psychological state and reaction while at the same time aiding the police in apprehension and prosecution of a criminal. Information and knowledge about psychological reactions to stress, trauma, and rape can be incorporated into a crisis intervention training program.[9] All the skills related to domestic dispute intervention and learning techniques found in domestic intervention training models can also be used for rape investigation training.

Another specified service area where psychological knowledge and training has aided the police is in the emergency apprehension of mentally disturbed patients. The police are mandated to intervene in emergency situations involving the mentally ill. Legal mandates do not only apply to situations in which the criminal process can be evoked but are also directed by civil law.[10] In these situations the police have no mandated procedures but are required to apply discretionary policies. In addition, recent liberal mental health legislation increases the likelihood of police contact with mentally ill individuals. As a result training in the area of abnormal behavior and mental health legislation has become an increasing concern of police departments. Situations ranging from assisting a severely mentally retarded individual frantically acting out, trying to calm an acutely psychotic individual, or trying to discourage a suicide attempt all require psychological understanding. These techniques insure effective treatment and discourage harm to everyone. Special training and programs have been developed to improve services in these emergency situations. Snibbe discusses a program with the Los Angeles police department that involves training officers on hospital detail.[11] Specialized training includes a familiarization with psychiatric diagnosis and how these psychiatric conditions affect interpersonal contacts.

THE PERSONAL ADJUSTMENT OF THE OFFICER

Programs addressing issues related to the personal adjustment of the police officer have developed out of a recognition of the high degree of stress produced by police work. Stressors have been identified in at least five basic areas: (1) intra-organizational factors, (2) inter-organizational practices, (3) criminal justice practices, (4) public practices, and (5) police work itself.[12] These basic areas cover sources of stress such as role conflict, boredom, shift work, promotion policies, territoriality, hazardous incidents, and court decisions.

These conditions have produced adverse effects for police officers in a variety of areas. Physically, policemen are more prone to psychophysiological disturbance such as hypertension, ulcers, and heart disease.[13] Psychological consequences of job stress in this area have focused on the policeman's tendency to isolate himself from society at large and develop a very restrictive social network that destroys his sense of community.[14,15] This process of progressive isolation and alienation has been outlined by Niederhoffer.[16] The end result of this process, which insidiously extracts the officer from his meaningful interpersonal relationships, results in a condition Niederhoffer describes as anomie.

The end result of both the physiological and psychological manifestations of stress severely affects the individual's personal adjustment and family relationships. Alcoholism is one manifestation of ineffective adjustment to which police are susceptible.[17] Shift work and comaraderie develop around the use of alcohol as a stress release. These two factors tend to reinforce the use of alcohol as a coping mechanism. Another manifestation of job stress on personal adjustment is suicide. The rate of police suicide is significantly higher than that of the general population.[18] In addition to progressive isolation, retirement provides an added sense of alienation for those police officers who have overidentified with their role as an officer.

The area of marital satisfaction is also significantly effected by police work. (Reports of the frequency of divorce among police officers are inconsistent. Studies have shown that the rate of divorce for police range from 4 percent in Salt Lake City to a rate of 33.3 percent in Chicago. More recent studies have shown a tendency for the rate of divorce to substantially increase for field personnel.)[19] Issues related to the fear of danger, shift work, image in the social community, and loss of time with family contribute to the increased adjustment requirements for the police marriage.

Programs have been developed to help officers cope with the manifestations of stress at all levels. At the physiological level, Reiser[13] is presently involved in a three-year research project to help officers control physical responses to stress through biofeedback. Team-building techniques to improve officer's response to stress have utilized physiological outcome criteria such as blood-pressure readings. Progress in this area is oriented toward decreasing the officers' susceptibility to psychophysiological disturbance and their psychological concomitants. Alcoholism programs in police departments have focused on early recognition and appropriate referral for officers with difficulties. Dishlacoff[17] presents a review of an alcoholism program and recommendations for additional program developments in this area. In the area of social isolation and family conflict, police departments have established several types of programs that try to lessen the gap between the officers and their wives and families.

Megerson,[20,21] Webber,[22] and Pisa[23] have developed programs that provide the police wife with a familiarization with police organization, administration, and responsibilities of the officer. Conjoint discussions related to stress is a major focus of these programs. Most of these programs recognize support and recommend use of psychological services for the purposes of early detection and immediate treatment of marital conflict arising from stress of police work.

THEORETICAL FOUNDATIONS OF THE TRAINING MODEL

Police are continually used by the community to intervene in a broad spectrum of emergency service situations. These requests for assistance span the gamut of possible human crises. In consideration of this fact, training should be predicated on the belief that policemen are service professionals with specialized expertise. The police officer is the front line contact for the larger community network of service agencies. As a result of this role, crisis intervention training programs that address the majority of services situations with which the police may be confronted foster an interaction among community agencies.

THE POLICE AS SERVICE PROFESSIONALS

Herman Goldstein notes that police are confronted with recurrent situations in which no guidance is provided. Officers develop informal procedural models for handling matters through a patterned improvisation or employ informal criteria that have developed over a period of years within the agency.[24] This statement recognizes the reality that discretionary power or use of judgment is crucial in defining the officer's duties or course of action in a majority of situations. This use of discretionary judgment in performing human services is one of the cardinal traits of a service professional.

Within the field of police science there has been a hesitancy to publicly recognize the vast use of discretionary power by the individual officer because of the intense scrutiny directed at the police force through public opinion, formalized civil liberties groups, and legislated mandate. As a defensive measure police have been forced to justify their behavior and existence by using criteria reflective of programmed and highly operationalized procedures. The development of such procedures can act as an aid to officers in many situations such as criminal investigations or arrest. However, many other situations including resolution of a family dispute or apprehension of an agitated mental patient, do not lend themselves to mandated unflexible procedure. These occurrences require judgment and discretion based on a body of knowledge and expertise related to the particular situation at hand. The highest sense of professionalism is demanded when discretion and judgment in some way affect the welfare of life in these situations.

Acceptance of this position acknowledges the need for the development of a professional model that embodies the recognition of discretionary powers of a police officer as a service provider. This model cuts across the law and order functions and is most visable in the police role as a service provider. Professionalism requires that the performance of an individual should conform to certain predetermined standards. Such standards recognize that professionals have a specific or particular area of expertise of knowledge in defining the sphere of convenience in which he operates. The professional administers services based on certain ethical constraints and is committed to providing the most responsible service possible. To accomplish this, the professional has a breadth of knowledge enabling perception of a situation objectively while using judgment and discretion based on specialized and general knowledge in the performance of duty. These traits are acquired through an intense mixture of formal education and practical experience.

POLICE COMMUNITY SERVICE AGENCY NETWORK

One of the most important principles of community mental health is an acute sensitivity to the fact that the community functions as a system. The community system is a network of interacting agencies that intimately effect one another. When one arm of the system changes other agencies must adjust. Community provision of service principles, such as utilization of indigenous paraprofessionals, emphasis on prevention, and avoidance of the pathology models, are important but they cannot be implemented or actualized without recognition that programs along these lines must be implemented as part of the community agency network.

McGee strongly emphasizes that services such as crisis programs must belong to the entire community.[25] There is no restriction on the crisis service clientele, thus these service programs must have working and meaningful relationships with most other community service agencies. A list of interdependent community agencies might include fire departments, ambulance and rescue services, Salvation Army, Alcoholics Anonymous, Big Brother, family service clubs, and civic clubs. Examining this list, it is evident that the agency that ultimately has the most intimate contact with a majority of these services is the police. The police have prelegitimized contact with many of these agencies as a function of the breadth of services they themselves provide. This aspect of police activity identifies them as a human link between those in need and referral agencies. At a systematic level the police also have the capability to act as an indigenous integrative link among community service agencies. This integrative function can serve to provide support for police in their attempts to meet the high demand for both law enforcement and service provision while providing a high degree of accessibility for service agencies and providing better services for those in need.

TRAINING MODEL

The most effective training model of those attempted by the authors emphasizes a consulting approach that reinforces the view of the police officer as a service professional. Information is presented and shared with the primary purpose of helping the officer develop the appropriate skills and expertise to increase his discretionary freedom in human emergency service situations. In each of the specific training areas, courses of action are explored from the perspective of short– and long-range consequences of an intervention strategy. This allows the officer an opportunity to integrate strengths in human interactions in developing an approach to a variety of crisis situations.

Secondly, as much as possible an attempt is made to integrate crisis training with appropriate community referral sources. Agencies such as state hospitals, emergency mental health delegates, Women Organized Against Rape, drug treatment facilities, and family counseling resources are included as part of the training program. Whenever possible, consultants are utilized who would ordinarily be in contact with the police trainees. This method of instructional staffing and the development of a personal relationship between the service providers has a carry-over effect causing police to utilize available resources more freely after training completion.[9] This provides a forum where integration of community agencies and the police department can be facilitated. Areas in which we try to incorporate this training philosophy are family crisis intervention, intervention in psychiatric emergency, rape investigations, juvenile delinquency, mental retardation, child abuse, and the personal adjustment of the police officer.

Police departments, faced with new problems in these areas and limited problem-solving strategies and capability, are open to suggestion and assistance believed to be helpful. Frequently outside objective consultants provide a framework for the airing of issues otherwise overlooked and the development of a positive community relations approach. Areas including juvenile delinquency, child abuse, and family crisis intervention all represent great concern and conjure feelings of helplessness and frustration in both law enforcement circles and the community at large. This mutual concern can be the format for discussion, open communications, and joint problem solving. The consultants' role in this process is that of the objective arbitor, bringing involved parties together, focusing concentration, and insuring fairness and discussion relevance. Within the confines of this model logically organized programs informed of the subtleties of community concern offer a unique ability to provide a broadly conceived approach to solving troublesome community issues.

REFERENCES

1. Bielauskas, V.J. and Hellkamp, D.T. Four years of training police in interpersonal relations, In Snibbe, J.R. and Snibbe, H.M. (Eds.), *The urban policeman in transition: A psychological and sociological review*, Springfield, Thomas, 1973.

2. Mann, P.A. *Psychological consultation with a police department*, Springfield, Thomas, 1973.

3. Johnson, T.A. Police-citizen encounters and the importance of role conceptualization for police community relations, *Issues in Criminology*, 7, 103–118, 1972.

4. Danish, S.J. and Ferguson, N. Training police to intervene in human

conflict, In Snibbe, J.R. and Snibbe, H.M. (Eds.), *The urban police-man in transition: A psychological and sociological review*, Spring-field, Thomas, 1973.

5. *Uniform crime reports* FBI, Washington, D.C., Government Printing Office, 1977.

6. Bard, M. and Berkowitz, B.   Training police as specialists in family crisis intervention: A community psychology action program, *Community Mental Health Journal, 3*, 315–317, 1967.

7. Liebman, D.A. and Schwartz, J.A.   Police programs in domestic crisis intervention: A review, In Snibbe, J.R. and Snibbe, H.M. (Eds.), *The urban policeman in transition: A psychological and sociological review*, Springfield, Thomas, 1973.

8. Bard, M. and Ellison, K.   Crisis intervention and the investigation of rape, *The Police Chief*, 166–171, May 1974.

9. Mugrauer, W.A.   *A training program in crisis intervention techniques for Bucks County police officers*, Program sponsored by Bucks County Department of Mental Health and Mental Retardation, 1976.

10. Bittner, E.   Police discretion in emergency apprehension of mentally ill persons, In Niederhoffer, A. and Blumberg, A. (Eds.), *The ambivalent force: Perspectives on the Police*, Waltham, Ginn, 1970.

11. Snibbe, J.R.   The police and the mentally ill: Practices, problems and some solutions, In Snibbe, J.R. and Snibbe, H.M. (Eds.), *The urban policeman in transition: A psychological and sociological review*, Springfield, Thomas, 1973.

12. Eisenberg, T.   Job stress on the police officer: Identifying stress reduction techniques, *Job stress and the police officer*, Washington, D.C., U.S. Department of Health, Education and Welfare, National Institute for Operational Safety and Health, 1975.

13. Reiser, M.   Stress, distress and adaptation in police work, *The Police Chief*, 24–27, January 1976.

14. Hoch, H.H.   Psychological consequences of the police role, In Niederhoffer, A. and Blumberg, A. (Eds.), *The ambivalent force: Perspectives on the police*, Waltham, Ginn, 1970.

15. Skolnick, J.H.   A sketch of the policeman's working personality, In Niederhoffer, A. and Blumberg, A. (Eds.), *The ambivalent force: Perspectives on the police*, Waltham, Ginn, 1970.

16. Neiderhoffer, A.   *Behind the shield*, Garden City, New Jersey, Double-day, 1967.

17. Dishlacoff, L.   The drinking cop, *The Police Chief*, 34–39, January 1976.

18. Heiman, M.   The police suicide, *The Journal of Police Science and Administration, 3*, 267–273, 1975.

19. Durner, J.A., Krocker, M.A., Miller, C.R., and Reynolds, W.R.   Divorce —another occupational hazard, *The Police Chief*, 48–53, November 1975.

20. Megerson, J.S. The officer's lady, *The Police Chief*, 34–38, January 1973.
21. Megerson, J.S. The officer's lady: A follow up, *The Police Chief*, 50–52, January 1976.
22. Webber, B. The police wife, *The Police Chief*, 46–49, January 1976.
23. Pisa, A. Unpublished class curriculum, Montgomery County Community College Police Science Program, Blue Bell, Pennsylvania, 1976.
24. Goldstein, H. Police policy formulation, In Neiderhoffer, A. and Blumberg, A. (Eds.), *The ambivalent force: Perspectives on the police,* Waltham, Ginn, 1970.
25. McGee, R.K. *Crisis intervention in the community,* University Park, Maryland University Park Press, 1974.

LEGAL CASE INDEX

399

SUBJECT INDEX

AUTHOR INDEX

A

Abel, G., 353, 357
Abrams, A., 382
Abramson, D., 344, 347, 356
Adams, S., 248-250, 260
Adorno, I., 160
Albert, M. L., 128
Alexander, J. R., 68
Allen, B. V., 383
Allen, R., 30, 35
Allport, G., 184
Allyon, T., 294, 300
American Civil Liberties Union, 219, 224
American Friends Service Committee, 309
American Law Institute, 224
American Psychiatric Association, 86, 87, 88
American Psychological Association, 72, 86, 87, 88, 242
Amio, M., 344, 356
Anderson, B. J., 202
Asch, S. H., 35, 160
Auerbach, S. K., 240, 243
Aumick, A. L., 203
Averill, J. R., 184
Azrin, H., 294, 300

B

Baehr, M. E., 382, 383
Bailey, R., 302, 309
Bailey, W. C., 249, 250-252, 253, 260
Balcanoff, E. J., 34
Balter, M., 276
Banks, C., 300
Banton, M., 383
Barbash, J. T., 342
Barbre, E. S., 72
Bard, M., 389, 396

Barkley, B. J., 233, 242
Bass, B. M., 383
Bassatt, H. T., 128
Bazelon, D. L., 41
Beck, J., 300, 309
Becker, J., 357
Bedau, H., 224
Bennett, C., 159
Benton. A. L., 128
Benward, J., 277
Beresford, H. R., 112, 119, 127
Berg, K., 160
Berger, M., 59, 60, 71
Berkowitz, B., 389, 396
Bermant, G., 25
Berrigan, D., 161
Bersoff, D. N., 67, 71, 72
Best, B. W., 68
Bickman, L., 369
Bielauskas, V. J., 395
Birdwhistle, R. L., 161, 162
Bittner, E., 396
Black, D. J., 358, 368
Blanchard, E., 357
Blum, M. L., 382
Blum, R. H., 383
Bobbitt, J. M., 36
Bock, J. A., 128
Boehm, V., 160
Bogard, W. J., 35
Bogart, P., 202
BonField, R. J., 34
Boucher, R., 203, 214, 357
Bradwick, J., 277
Bray, H., 277
Brehm, J. W., 300
Brodsky, A. M., 74, 82, 86
Brodsky, S., 32, 34, 36, 129, 232, 242
Brooks, A. D., 87

403